John James Audubon

A BIOGRAPHY

John James Audubon

A BIOGRAPHY

BY

Alexander B. Adams

G. P. PUTNAM'S SONS

NEW YORK

© 1966 by Alexander B. Adams

Library of Congress Catalog

Card Number: 66-15573

To

LUCY D. S. ADAMS

who has made the sun rise for me on the
gloomiest of mornings and the stars shine
for me on the darkest of nights

and to

HESTER F. ADAMS

who has always had faith

Contents

CONTENTS

Illustrations will be found following
pages 128 and 228.

Prologue

U P they came from the south, following the warming days, in a great wave that burst open like a fan and covered the continent—blue geese and snow geese, canvasbacks and mallards, bald eagles and sparrow hawks, passenger pigeons in flocks so immense and tightly packed they barred the sunlight from the earth, huge birds like ospreys, small birds like warblers and sparrows which would disappear inconspicuously in the woods and fields, brilliantly colored birds like the wood ducks, mutely colored birds like mourning doves—all the tremendous variety that composed one of America's miracles. Some flew at night, some in the daytime, some stopped often for food and water, others flew for hundreds of miles without ever pausing. The wave seemed endless and inevitable and infinite, something no man could ever check, no matter how many shots he used, no matter how many arrows he put to his bow, or how many bird traps he set. The supply was inexhaustible. Shooting a hundred birds, or five hundred birds, or a thousand birds, was like taking a cup of water out of the ocean.

What was true of the birds, flying their unmarked but centuries-old routes in the sky, was true also of the land beneath them and the things that grew on it. There were enough trees to replank every ship in the world and not leave the mountainsides bare, enough to house whole cities and keep a nation warm during the winter nights, enough so no one worried about any individual tree or wasted time trying to save it. The best way to get wild honey was to chop the tree down. The best way to dislodge a bear or a raccoon was to chop the tree down. The best way to get sunlight around a cabin was to chop the tree down. The best way to keep the Indians from approaching a lean-to unseen was to chop down the surrounding trees. And the only way to grow corn or barley or rye or potatoes or cotton or jute was to chop down the trees. The axes rang out in a chorus of clanging steel and splintered wood from Mount Desert in

9

northern Maine to the southernmost key on the tip of Florida, from the Atlantic coast to just as far inland as there happened to be men to wield the axes. And if there was not time to cut into the wood, to let the bark and the slivers fly at the touch of the bit, and watch the great trees crash into the nearby brush, their tops snapping off under the force of the enormous impact, they could always be ringed or burned. Starting a fire was one way to get rid of unnecessary, unwanted trees.

Animals? There were enough beavers to put a hat on every dandy in Europe, enough foxes and martens and minks to make a fur coat for every lady. Enough buffaloes to feed a nation and make sleeping robes for them as well. Never before had men known such congregations of animals as the great buffalo herds contained, stretching as far as a hunter could see from horseback, herds grazing quietly on the prairies or, bunched together, stampeding with a force that made the ground shake and tremble beneath their feet.

There was enough water to slake the thirst of millions of people, to turn their mills, to float their boats—first canoes, then boats under sail, then steamboats puffing up the Hudson and the Delaware and the Ohio and the Missouri and the Mississippi and a hundred other rivers—boats that carried first explorers and trappers, then farmers and traders and merchants, and finally people who knew almost nothing about the land, had no link with it, hardly knew an oak from a maple, or a sparrow hawk from a mourning dove, and could not have worried less about not knowing. Yet there was still enough water left after it had turned the mill wheels and carried the boats, still enough pure water left to support the fish—the trout and the bass and the pickerel, the giant muskies, the sturgeon, and the catfish— catfish so large that often a single one would make a meal for an entire family.

As for land, there was enough for everybody. A man did not need to be rich to own land in America. He had only to be strong enough to take it, strong enough to travel to it and grab it from the Indians or the forest, strong enough to cut down the trees and clear it. Sometimes he had to pay for it with money, but if the price was too high in Massachusetts, he could go to New York. If it was too high in New York, he could move to Kentucky or Texas or Arkansas or Indiana or anywhere else, and the only thing that could stop him was the Pacific Ocean. He did not even have to care for the land after he got it. He could plant tobacco in Virginia, cotton in Georgia, onions in Connecticut, until the land was exhausted and lay naked and barren in the sunlight and never bother to fertilize it, for it was not worth fertilizing. He merely loaded his family into wagons and moved westward and took up new land. When that, too, was exhausted, he packed up his family again. Land was cheap. There was enough land for everybody.

So the people came to take the land, first in a trickle, a few lonely adventurers, and then in increasing swarms. Long-bearded Spaniards with swarthy skins. Laughing French *voyageurs*. Hard-drinking Anglo-Saxons, who fought and cursed and scrapped and carried a Bible in their wagons. Poles and Hungarians and Italians and Germans and Scandinavians, each anxious to share some part of the continent's riches. Always in the lead were the explorers, LaSalle, Hudson, Champlain, Croghan, Boone. Then the settlers, the men who were as interested in staying as they were in moving. They cleared the fields and built the farms and sowed the crops and bred the children, driving their roots into the ground and making a living out of it and establishing families that some day would move west again. Then the traders and the merchants and the doctors and the lawyers, the flatboat men who steered the great clumsy arks down the inland waters, the bandits with guns in their hands and prices on their heads, the scientists, the statesmen, the heroes—some moving here in hope of a better life than they had ever known; some, like the black-skinned, sweating slaves, brought here against their will to find one worse than they had ever imagined.

Between them all, riverboat gambler, college professor, New England farmer, Virginia planter, they took their toll. They shot the golden plovers by the thousands. They clubbed the passenger pigeons to death by the millions in Kentucky and Pennsylvania. They stripped the fields of their fertility in Mississippi and Georgia and Vermont. They poured their wastes into the rivers, because it seemed cheaper to get rid of waste that way than any other. They trapped beavers by the thousands, skinned them, and shipped the pelts abroad, while the corpses rotted in the woods or provided food for the wolverines. When they were hungry and wanted meat, they shot a buffalo or a bear or a deer and sometimes they made only one meal from it. Animals were plentiful, and time was short. It required time to dress and cure a whole animal.

Sometimes the men—and their women, too—were harsh and brutal and cruel. They would cheat an Indian or swindle him or lie to him. Although the Indian was here first, his numbers were insufficient to defend his own. They would lash a Negro slave until his back was bloody, shanghai a sailor, or make children work in factories. But, for the most part, they were good people, unthinking perhaps, but good. And they had in common a dim, obscure vision of something they wanted, although they had trouble putting it into words and saying what it really was. Only a few of them could do that, those with a special mastery of language and a special vision. Even fewer could get it down in words about the land and the trees and the prairies and the mountains and the great flights of birds and swarms of animals. It was all too big. They could see, but they had trouble saying what they saw, or writing it, or painting it, and making others understand.

So when the people slaughtered the birds, shooting them down by the thousands, or burned the forests, or left the dead buffaloes rotting and festering in the sun, it was not so much from brutality as from carelessness, not so much from thinking about what they did as from not thinking about what they did. Nobody had told them.

They were pragmatic. They did not believe the buffalo herds could be exhausted, until they had pushed them to the verge of extinction, did not think the flocks of passenger pigeons could be used up, until the last pigeon finally died and the species vanished from the earth altogether. Only when they saw it with their own eyes did they start believing, and often it was then too late. What they needed were men to do their seeing for them, whose vision reached a little further than theirs, who did not have to wait until a bird or an animal or a tree disappeared to know it could disappear. Or not even that. Who could make them, for a fleeting instant, see a bird for what a bird is, make them think of golden plovers as something more than a crop that could be harvested free except for the cost of shot, of beavers as something more than fur for men's hats, of trees as something more than firewood or planks.

There were not many such men.

But there were some. Just enough to check the ravage before, once and forever, it was too late.

Just enough to give the others one last, one irretrievable chance to save what was left.

CHAPTER I

1785 — 1803

ALTHOUGH he sired two illegitimate children by different mistresses while his wife waited at home, and also engaged in the brutal business of trafficking in slaves, Jean Audubon, merchant and sea captain of the town of Les Cayes, was one of the most moral men in San Domingo. In his sins, no matter how evil they may appear, he never fell below the accepted standards of the French colony; in his virtues he rose far above them, indeed far above those of most men in any place or at any time.

Like many Europeans who had come to the island solely to make money—and that included almost the entire white population from the Intendant and the Governor down to the lowliest trader—he had taken a mistress without giving the matter a second thought; and when she had died, he had quickly replaced her with another. This was the social custom in San Domingo, a place where normal sexual morality was practically nonexistent. Of the 7,000 free Negro women listed in the census of 1774, 5,000 were recognized by the government as the mistresses of white men; white mistresses, like those of Jean Audubon, were not officially classified, but were so common that not an eyebrow was raised merely because a man and a woman were living together without having taken vows before a priest.

As for trading in slaves, slaves were not human beings, but a commodity—the essential, although shaky, foundation upon which the whole economy of the rich island was based. Without slaves, the plantations would have lain untilled, the ships unloaded; and instead of providing half the wealth of France's entire colonial empire and enough sugar, coffee, and cotton to supply half the European market, San Domingo would have been a deserted, poverty-ridden island, reverting slowly to the semijungle Columbus had discovered. Slaves were necessary, slaves were indispensable—some half million of them working for the benefit of twenty thousand whites.

Riding through the countryside or walking the streets of the cities, a visitor saw slaves everywhere, harvesting crops, loading ships, serving meals, driving their masters' carriages, digging ditches, repairing roads, performing every conceivable job for which they could be trained. Lack of trust alone limited the type of work forced upon them. The colonists had absolutely no confidence in these black hordes they had brought from Africa, suspecting them of treachery, of waiting only for a propitious moment to drop poison into their master's coffee or to cut him down with a knife while he traveled alone on some mountain road. Out of this constant fear was born horror, a horror to which the flesh of the slaves bore grim evidence. The backs of many, as they appeared in the heat of the San Domingo sun, were crisscrossed by meshes of white scars, each line cut deep into the flesh by an overseer's or planter's whip. Some wore around their necks heavy iron collars with long, protruding studs, collars fastened into place by a blacksmith, because the slave had been suspected of trying to run away. Others were missing an ear or had only a stub where once there had been a finger or even a hand, for French law permitted the owner to mutilate his slaves, either as punishment or as a form of perverted amusement. Only by giving the masters almost absolute power, the government's official policy stated, could the whites hold such vast numbers of Negroes in submission. Such was the state of public opinion toward slavery in San Domingo. To be a slave trader was to engage in a respectable, necessary business, as important to the whites' welfare as being a doctor, a planter, or the Royal Governor himself.

In these matters—mistresses, illegitimate children, slave trading—Jean Audubon abided by the moral standards of the society in which he lived and worked. He was no worse than anyone else, better than many. What distinguished him was the strength of character that permitted him to resist the debilitating effects of the island. With all that cruelty surrounding him, he never became personally cruel. With all that corruption around him, he never became personally corrupt. And nothing, not even San Domingo, could affect his basic sense of loyalty. Never for a moment did he forget his wife, Anne, who was living at Nantes and for whose sake he had come to the island. Even to his mistresses he was loyal. When they were sick he cared for them, paying their doctor's bills and nursing them until they were well. As for his loyalty to his illegitimate children, it was the greatest of all. When it came time to leave the island he did not desert them, as many men would have done. He took them home with him and presented them to his lawful wife. They were his, and he acknowledged his responsibility publicly.

This man, unusual for his own age or any other, was born one of twenty-one children, of which only three reached old age. All his early life, he had been tempered like steel by poverty and hardship. At the age of thirteen he shipped as a cabin boy on his father's boat, loaded with war matériel for the Frenchmen defending the fortress at Louisburg. At fourteen, he was captured by the British and tossed into prison. There he spent part of his boyhood, knowing nothing but stone cells, barred windows, and the harsh treatment he received from his guards. When he emerged, he had developed a violent, lifelong hatred of the British, but otherwise he was unscarred by the experience.

Immediately upon his release, he returned to his birthplace, the small French fishing village of Sables d'Olhonne, and re-entered the merchant marine, making at least four voyages to the cold, fog-shrouded waters of the Grand Banks. After a short hitch in the French Navy he went to Nantes, looking for another seafaring job. Because the shipowners and merchants of Nantes, along with those of Bordeaux and Marseilles, had long monopolized the business of the French half of San Domingo, the part now known as Haiti, to join a Nantes ship meant sooner or later sailing to the island.

On the voyages he subsequently made to the distant colony, Jean Audubon demonstrated his toughness, his shrewdness, and his ability to handle both ships and men and soon rose to having his own command. Then, just as his career seemed firmly established, the hated British interfered. In 1779 they attacked his ship, again made him a captive, and held him as a prisoner-of-war for thirteen months. To his satisfaction, his release quickly brought him an opportunity for revenge. He rejoined the French Navy, and commanded a corvette under Count de Grasse at the Battle of Yorktown. Then he served as captain of several merchant ships traveling between the United States and France, and sank one British privateer.

When he returned home after the war, he longed for a better life than either the merchant marine or the navy could provide and, weary of fighting and the risks of a sailor's life, accepted the offer of Coirond Frères, a Nantes mercantile firm, to act as their agent at the town of Les Cayes in the southern part of San Domingo. For someone in Jean Audubon's position the offer was ideal. San Domingo was the place to make money; perhaps with luck and hard work he could accumulate enough to support himself and his wife, Anne, for the rest of their lives; the job with Coirond Frères would give him a chance to live on the island with financial security, while he looked around for investments he could make on his own behalf with his limited capital.

Kindly but tough after his years at sea, uneducated but naturally intelligent and shrewd, he was the sort of man to take full advantage of the island's opportunities. By April, 1785, some two years after his arrival in Les Cayes, he had reason to congratulate himself on his decision. Not only was he one of the "big whites," a man of property and consequence, but he had just concluded a particularly satisfactory transaction. With a short-term investment of 20,000 livres, made around the first of the year, he had realized a net profit of 15,684 livres—or more than 75 per cent—on the purchase and resale of forty slaves. The operating expenses incurred by him and his partners had been slight: 60 livres for bananas, 24 livres for beef, and, the biggest item of all, 93 livres for medical asssistance to a dying Negro. What made Jean Audubon's profit so enormous, the sort of profit that had lured him to San Domingo, was not so much the cheap, meager diet fed to the slaves as his skill at making his energy and ability serve in place of capital. In this case, he put up only one-third of the total investment and yet received one-half of the profit in exchange for handling the actual purchase and sale of the slaves.

His personal life, however, was not as successful. For almost a year he had been nursing his mistress, a Creole named Mlle. Rabin, through various illnesses, none of which seem to have been serious until April, 1785, when she developed a painful inflammation in her leg. On April 24, the doctor decided to spend the night in Jean Audubon's house, where he would be within easy reach. Mlle. Rabin was not only sick; she was also expecting a child. All night long the watchers waited in her room, but the dark hours passed uneventfully. Perhaps she tossed a little in her sleep, but nothing more. The next night the doctor stayed again, and again the nighttime slipped away, and the sun rose above the little town of Les Cayes, casting its light into the alleyways and streets. Sometime during that day, Mlle. Rabin groaned with the pains of childbirth. The doctor, picking up the small body, slapped its back to start it breathing. Jean Audubon had a son, a son he named after himself, Jean Jacques, or, as he eventually became known, John James.

Who exactly was Mlle. Rabin? No one really knows. She may have been a serving girl who was a fellow passenger with Jean Audubon. She may have been, as the doctor called her when he made out his bill, a Creole, one of those women of European descent who were famous for their beauty, their charm, and also their competence, for they were used to presiding over large households and, if need be, even to running an entire plantation.

Whatever her charms and abilities may have been, Mlle. Rabin played no role in bringing up her son. A few days after his birth, the doctor returned for another night visit because her condition was still serious; and on June 19 he opened an abscess that had been bothering her for a number of weeks. But the results of his cures were only temporary. In August she was sick again, and sometime around the end of 1785 or the beginning of 1786, she died, leaving Jean Audubon alone with his infant child. Loyal to Mlle. Rabin while she was alive, he did not spend long in mourning her when she was dead. Relatively soon afterward, he contracted another liaison, this time with a woman named Catherine Bouffard. She, too, was probably a Creole—Jean Audubon seems to have had no difficulty attracting these beautiful women—and in addition to caring for John James, she also bore a child, a girl born in 1787, whom Jean Audubon named Rosa.

In spite of his love affairs, Jean Audubon never allowed him-self to be diverted from his real purpose in being in San Do-mingo—to earn a respectable fortune, retire, and return to Nantes and his beloved wife, Anne. And if there was ever a time to make money in San Domingo, this was it. Between the end of the American Revolution and 1789, the production of the island doubled. Fresh capital poured in from France; the countinghouses, the plantations, and the sugar mills bustled with activity. In the harbors, the ships came to anchor, their white sails brilliant against the tropical blue skies, unloaded their cargoes of slaves, wines, furniture, machinery—all the es-sentials and luxuries needed for the island's way of life. Then they quickly reloaded with bags of sugar and coffee and bales of cotton, carried on board by sweating, whip-scarred Negroes, until, their hulls low in the water, they raised their sails, cleared the harbors, and set their courses for France.

Yet the planters and the other "big whites" were not entirely happy with their situation. Like Britain, France monopolized its colonies' trade, forcing them to conduct most of their com-merce directly with the mother country. If these restrictions could be removed and San Domingo permitted to bargain with other nations over its imports and sell its exports to the high-est bidder, then, *mon dieu,* the possible profits! In every coffee house, on every plantation, aboard every ship, wherever the "big whites" gathered, sooner or later the conversation turned to the possibility of repealing the export-import laws; and when Louis XVI revived the Estates General, the "big whites" thought they saw their chance.

In April, 1788, when John James Audubon was three years old, they began circulating a secret petition asking for rep-resentation in the Estates General. In this way, they hoped, they could obtain influence over French commercial legisla-tion. What they wanted was an economic benefit; what they re-ceived was a social revolution. By raising the question of repre-sentation, they also raised the question of slavery. Should, or should not, the Negroes be counted, when a delegation from San Domingo was elected? The many liberal elements in France who already favored emancipation now had an opportunity to debate the issue publicly. Jean Audubon was certainly familiar with the island's political thinking, but he did not foresee where it would lead; and when he made a trip to the United States in 1789, he left the major part of his San Domingan funds on the island. In America, however, he purchased a farm outside Philadelphia as an additional investment.

In the next two years, he carried out his plans to return to France, arriving there first by himself and later sending for his two children to join him. And what a homecoming it must have been, as Jean Audubon presented Rosa and John James to his wife; but she, generous woman that she was, swept the children into her arms, loved them for what they were, and cared for them as if they were her own. Blunt and direct, Jean Audubon never attempted to hide from her what had happened. These were his own children, conceived by two different women, not a "niece" and a "nephew" or the "children of a friend." To John James and Rosa, however, he was not so frank, knowing how they would suffer if their own father branded them as illegitimate. Instead of telling them the truth, he spun a wonderful story for them, one with all the touches needed to appeal to the imagination of a child. He went from San Domingo to Louisiana, he said as the children listened wide-eyed, and married a beautiful woman of Spanish extraction, whom he took back to Les Cayes. Then the Negro uprising occurred (here he let an anachronism slip by in the cause of romance); their beautiful, mysterious mother was killed, and he himself was able to flee the island only because several of his loyal slaves helped him. With part of his money, his silver plate, his faithful slaves, and his two children, he eventually reached France, where he met Anne and married her. The story explained everything, and goodhearted Anne gave John James no reason to suspect the truth.

But if Anne and Jean Audubon between them managed to create an atmosphere of normality in their own unusual household, they could do nothing about affairs generally in France. In July, 1789, the Paris mobs, already restless and frenzied by the King's inaction, marched against the Bastille. Its commander, de Launay, swore he would blow up the old fortress rather than surrender it and sat for hours near the powder magazine, a flaming torch held in one hand. But he did not move the flame toward the bags of powder. While he remained motionless, the gates were unlocked, the attackers admitted, the seven prisoners, all that the Bastille held at the time, released. Strategically, the event was inconsequential. But spiritually and intellectually, it rocked the whole structure of France. From touching the King's institutions with rough hands, it was only a step to touching the King himself. The French Revolution had begun.

Jean Audubon tried to stay aloof from the struggle. When further neutrality became impossible, he first joined the National Guard at Nantes, then the Directory of the Department of the Loire, and finally, in June, 1793, the navy, which gave him command of a small coasting vessel. While he was away at sea he was forced to turn over to Anne the major responsibility for bringing up the children, and Anne, although loving and generous, had no taste or talent for discipline. Anything the children wanted to do was all right with her. As John James later admitted, she was "devotedly attached to me, far too much so for my own good, was desirous that I should be brought up to live and die 'like a gentleman,' thinking that fine clothes and filled pockets were the only requisites needful to attain this end. She therefore completely spoiled me, hid my faults, boasted to everyone of my youthful merits and, worse than all, said frequently in my presence that I was the handsomest boy in France. All my wishes and idle notions were at once gratified; she went so far as actually to grant me *carte blanche* at all the confectionery shops in Nantes, and also the village of Couëron, where during the summer we lived, as it were, in the country." With her lack of realism and her misguided love, Anne was surrounding her son with an unreal world and giving him *carte blanche* not only to the confectionery shops, but to illusions about himself. In a short while he became conceited, spoiled, and lazy, not the sort of son Jean Audubon envisioned.

Conflict was inevitable between Anne and Jean when it came to bringing up the children. Where she was weak, he was strong. Where she was lax, he was strict. As John James later described him, looking back at him with a boy's eyes, he was "about five feet ten inches, erect, and with muscles of steel; his manners were those of a most polished gentleman, for those and his natural understanding had been carefully improved both by observation and by self-education. In temper, we much resembled each other ... being warm, irascible, and at times violent; but it was like the blast of a hurricane, dreadful for a time, when calm almost instantly returned." On his infrequent visits home he did what he could, which was not much, to repair the damage wrought by Anne's weaknesses. On one point he was adamant: his son's education. "He believed," John James once wrote, "not in the power of gold coins as efficient means to render a man happy. He spoke of the stores of the mind, and having suffered much himself through the want of education, he ordered that I should be put to school, and have teachers at home. 'Revolutions,' he was wont to say, 'too often take place in the lives of individuals, and they are apt to lose in one day the fortune they before possessed; but talents and knowledge, added to sound mental training, assisted by honest industry, can never fail, nor be taken from anyone once the possessor of such valuable means.' " In the face of Anne's opposition, Jean Audubon enrolled the boy in a nearby school, hired tutors to supplement his regular courses, and set up for him a broad curriculum that included drawing, geography, mathematics, fencing, and music.

Although he could plan carefully for his son's education, he was not home often enough to supervise it. That had to be left to Anne and, with all the goodwill in the world, she went right on spoiling the boy. As John James himself said, "My father being mostly absent on duty, my mother suffered me to do much as I pleased; it was therefore not to be wondered at that, instead of applying closely to my studies, I preferred associating with boys of my own age and disposition, who were more fond of going in search of birds' eggs, fishing, or shooting, than of better studies. Thus almost every day, instead of going to school where I ought to have gone, I usually made for the fields, where I spent the day; my little basket went with me, filled with good eatables, and when I returned home, during either winter or summer, it was replenished with what I called curiosities, such as birds' nests, birds' eggs, curious lichens, flowers of all sorts, and even pebbles gathered along the shore of some rivulet."

When the Audubons moved permanently from Nantes to Couëron, a small town a few miles farther west on the Loire,

John James's temptations became greater and greater until matters finally reached a crisis. On one of his infrequent visits home,
Jean Audubon made his regular trip up to John James's room
and examined the boy's collection of eggs, nests, plants, and
other objects he had picked up in the Couëron countryside.
Being a man of broad interests himself, Jean Audubon was
pleased. He was also suspicious. If so much time went into collecting, how much time went into studies? he asked. John James
did not even try to answer. Instead, he stood silently in front
of his father with a sheepish look on his face.

That evening, when the family was gathered together, Jean
Audubon asked Rosa to play some music for him. When she
had finished, he praised her for the progress she had made since
his last visit and as a reward gave her a book. Then, turning to
John James, he told his son to fetch his violin. The boy went
out and came back, but there was no use even asking him to
play. He had not practiced for several months and, worst of all,
had not bothered to replace several missing strings. Jean Audubon looked at the useless instrument in the hands of his undisciplined son. All right, he had not practiced, he had not
studied, but what about his drawing? Had he completed any
pictures? Once again, the boy trotted upstairs, collected the
few drawings he had made, and brought them sadly to his
father. Not only was the pile small, but the pictures themselves
were badly executed. Jean Audubon examined them. Then he
glanced at Anne, leaned over to kiss his daughter, and, hum-
ming a tune to himself, walked out of the room without another word.

His mind was made up. In spite of Anne's feelings, the boy
had to be taken out of the house and away from his stepmother's supervision. Being a decisive man, Jean Audubon had everything arranged by the following morning. John James's trunk
was packed and a carriage was waiting at the door. The boy
was ordered to get in; his trunk was strapped on to the outside
and his violin case placed under his feet. Kissing his wife and
daughter good-bye, Jean Audubon climbed up the step, thrust
his heavy frame through the door, and sat down in one corner.
The driver cracked his whip; the carriage started forward; and,
without speaking to his son, Jean Audubon pulled a book out

of his pocket and began reading to himself, leaving the boy to his own thoughts.

For several days they traveled together in this fashion, Jean Audubon sitting in the corner, showing no sign of anger but barely talking to his son, as the carriage jolted along the French roads. Finally they reached the French naval base at Rochefort where Jean Audubon was stationed. The carriage pulled up to the door of Jean Audubon's house and halted. The trunks were unstrapped and handed down, the violin case carried inside. Obviously, this was where John James was going to live for a while, away from Anne's influence and right under his father's eye. As they started up the stairs the sentry on duty came to a salute. Jean Audubon raised his hat in reply, then walked toward the man and whispered something to him, pointing at the boy. John James noticed his father was smiling.

Once inside, Jean Audubon sat his son down and talked to him firmly. For a while, he explained, John James would remain in Rochefort, away from his mother's protection, and study. Not only study, but study hard. He could play, but only after his work was done. As a recompense, he offered John James the remainder of the day off and invited him to spend it with him on an inspection tour of the base. John James accepted, and off they went. "I saw much that day," he later wrote, "yet still I perceived that I was like a prisoner-of-war on parole in the city of Rochefort."

Jean Audubon's determination to supervise his son's education may have been increased by the deterioration of his own financial situation. Ever since the planters in San Domingo had opened up the slave question with their ill-considered petition, affairs on the island had been steadily going from bad to worse from the point of view of the "big whites." First, slavery had been abolished. Next, the Negroes had started holding government positions. Finally, Toussaint L'Ouverture, a former slave, had gained control of the island's administration. But San Domingo was no longer proud and prosperous. Its commerce had been disrupted by war with the British and by constant fighting between various elements on the island itself. Although Toussaint L'Ouverture was attempting to restore order and even inviting the French planters to return—many of them had fled

—the island's future was misty and obscure. Knowing that the fortune he had worked so hard to obtain was now endangered, Jean Audubon had decided to stay on in the navy, thus ensuring himself a steady salary; and he also realized that John James must be prepared to make his own living.

Having the boy with him at Rochefort must have been a considerable inconvenience, for the active naval base was no place to raise a child. Yet for all his effort, he could not repair the damage already done by Anne. Even directly under his father's eyes, the boy continued to resist every attempt to educate him. Once, while his father was away on a trip, he was placed under the charge of a man named Gabriel Loyen Dupuy Gaudeau, who served as Jean Audubon's secretary. In open rebellion by this time, John James took the opportunity to cause trouble. When Gaudeau gave him some especially difficult mathematical problems to do, instead of working on them he watched Gaudeau out of the corner of his eye. Sure that the secretary was not paying any attention to him, he slipped quietly over to the window of the room where he was supposed to be studying, leaped out, and escaped into the gardens of the Marine Secretariat. In Couëron, he would then have had a day off from his studies. Nobody, least of all Anne, would have bothered to go after him. But Gaudeau immediately ordered a corporal to catch the young delinquent. Not accustomed to being chased, John James made no effort to hide. He saw the corporal, with whom he had been on friendly terms, coming toward him and, as he said later, "I did not attempt to escape, but," he added ruefully, "our past familiarity was, I found, quite evaporated." The corporal all but arrested him formally and held him in custody until his father's return.

Eventually, however, even Jean Audubon realized that he could not keep up with his duties as an officer and, at the same time, have secretaries trying to pump knowledge into John James's unwilling mind and corporals chasing him around the Marine Secretariat. He took the boy home and placed him in school again, hoping he would concentrate on mathematics so he might become an engineer or a naval officer. But in later years John James's only memory of the school concerned a fight with another student in which the other boy threw a rock, caught him on the temple, and knocked him unconscious. He did, however, start to paint birds on a more systematic basis, trying to make a collection of all those he could find around Couëron, and also undertook one other serious job. Previously, Anne and Jean Audubon, in an act of considerable graciousness on her part, had formally adopted the two children. Now Anne was worried about her son's soul. At her request, he learned his catechism and was baptized. She seems to have been pleased—"all was performed to her liking"—and he was glad of a chance to satisfy her, although otherwise her request left him surprised and indifferent.

Meanwhile, Jean Audubon, for all his physical strength, was beginning to feel the effects of his years. Claiming disability from pulmonary difficulties, he retired from the navy in 1801 and went home for good to Couëron. A few years earlier his regular presence in the household might have offset Anne's destructive influence, but it was now too late. Anne's constant praise, her willingness to overlook each fault, to excuse each mistake, had taken their toll of the boy's character. He was charming when he wanted to be; he was good-looking; but he was lazy, inattentive, and used to having his own way. Even Jean Audubon, with his quarterdeck sternness, could not get him under control.

Making the best of a bad situation, he decided to encourage the boy in his drawing, the one activity that he took at all seriously. From then on, Jean Audubon served as his son's most constructive critic, tempering his sympathy with realism and thus counterbalancing Anne's overly enthusiastic comments. "When, as a little lad," John James later wrote, "I first began my attempts at representing birds on paper, I was far from possessing much knowledge of their nature, and, like hundreds of others, when I had laid the effort aside, I was under the impression that it was a finished picture of a bird because it possessed some sort of a head and tail, and two sticks in lieu of legs; I never troubled myself with the thought that abutments were requisite to prevent it falling either forward or backward, and oh! what bills and claws I did draw, to say nothing of a perfectly straight line for a back, and a tail stuck in anyhow, like an unfinished rudder." As an artist, John James

was not precocious, and those early drawings contained no in-
dication of real talent. What made them unusual was simply
John James's persistence.

In the Audubons' household, the reactions of the adults were,
with the exception of Jean Audubon's, extravagant, but he,
John James wrote, "spoke very differently to me; he constantly
impressed upon me that nothing in the world possessing life
and animation was easy to imitate, and as I grew older he hoped
I would become more and more alive to this." Furthermore, he
believed that the boy should have a teacher better than those
offered by either Nantes or Couëron. He may somehow have
made arrangements for him to have the best: Jacques Louis
David, one of the foremost artists in France and a man of such
political dexterity that he served successfully as a court painter
to both Louis XVI and Napoleon. But even art, if it required
concentrated attention over a protracted period of time, could
not hold John James. If he really, as he later claimed, studied
under David, he drew heads and figures in what must have been
a rather conventional manner, then, quickly bored, threw the
whole business over and returned to Couëron.

By this time, Jean Audubon was in despair. He could not
make John James study at Nantes or Couëron or Rochefort.
When he wanted the boy to learn mathematics and become an
engineer or a naval officer, he got into fights or played truant
and tramped in the woods. When he paid for violin lessons,
the violin remained unstrung for months. He had tried to impress on his son that art requires work, but John James refused
to attend classes regularly. He could shoot; he could fish; but
he could do little else.

Added to this discouragement, Jean Audubon was also wit-
nessing the rapid and apparently conclusive disintegration of
his investments in San Domingo. In the years following the
revolution, Toussaint L'Ouverture and Napoleon had inevitably clashed, partly because Napoleon wanted firmer control
over the island as a base for his projected operations in Louisiana, and partly because he could not tolerate within his government a Negro who, if he did not openly flout the First
Consul's authority, certainly made every effort to sidestep it.
Possibly if Napoleon had used diplomacy, he might have succeeded in regaining control of San Domingo, but he chose an

entirely different course. Having signed the Peace of Amiens, thus gaining a temporary respite from his war with the British, he assembled the largest expeditionary force that had ever sailed from France. He placed in command his brother-in-law, General Leclerc, to whom he gave an explicit, three-phase plan of operations intended to subjugate the Negroes of San Domingo within a matter of weeks. If Leclerc could hold to the schedule set by Napoleon—and Napoleon saw no reason why he could not—the campaign would be ended before the beginning of the rainy season, when the island became pestilent.

The invasion began early in February. Although the campaign moved swiftly in its initial stages, Leclerc quickly realized that Napoleon had underestimated the capabilities of the Negroes. On February 27, he wrote a gloomy report to the Minister of Marine, saying that although he was master of the North, most of it had been burned and the rebels still controlled the South. A month later, although he was still fighting, 5,000 of his original 17,000 troops were dead, 5,000 more were in the hospital, and the rainy season had started.

Then, to the joy of men like Jean Audubon, Leclerc's fortunes took a turn for the better. Christophe, one of Toussaint's most prominent generals, defected; and Toussaint himself agreed to surrender. These outward signs of peace, however, did not mean that the war was over. Among the ruins of the once rich colony, vicious guerrilla warfare continued, and yellow fever, to which the Negro armies were not susceptible, broke out. Then the French committed two serious errors. They enraged the Negroes by arresting Toussaint in violation of the surrender terms, and they reinstituted slavery on the neighboring island of Guadeloupe. When this information reached San Domingo, the war became a war to the finish between the mutilated, whip-lashed Negroes and their former oppressors.

Jean Audubon quickly realized the significance of the news. His West Indian fortune was lost; and instead of being a wealthy colonial merchant, he was now only a retired naval officer. He must also have foreseen that Napoleon's policies were taking France into direct conflict with the British and that years of warfare inevitably lay ahead.

In such circumstances, what should he do with John James? The boy could no longer expect to live on his father's income.

Yet he was unequipped for a professional career and too undisciplined to rise in Napoleon's army or navy. As he pondered the problem Jean Audubon's thoughts turned to the United States, where he still owned the farm he had bought in 1789 and where he still had friends. Perhaps in America John James would gain the self-discipline he needed. At least he would avoid Napolon's draft and be forced to learn English, something he seemed incapable of doing in the classroom.

Not a man to waste words in pointless discussion, Jean Audubon undoubtedly kept his own counsel as he watched the war in San Domingo and the signs of an approaching clash between Great Britain and France. Finally in the year 1803, he thought the time had come.

Unquestionably Anne made a fuss when he announced his decision. To send her boy—she considered John James completely hers—across the ocean. Ridiculous! Impossible! She wept and stormed, but to no avail. Rosa probably did not care much, one way or the other. If anything, she may have been a little weary of sharing the household's attention with her emotional, spoiled older brother.

As for John James himself, what boy would regret leaving home for such a trip? He liked the outdoor life, and there was no better place for it than America. Besides, since his earliest childhood, he had been hearing his father's stories of the sea—tales of maneuvers against the British fleet at Yorktown, fights with privateers, visits to strange tropical harbors in the West Indies and to the ports of France's northern colonies. Even though times had changed since his father's seafaring days, they had not changed much. Most of the compasses were still inaccurate (an official investigation in 1820 revealed that half the compasses of the British Navy were useless); detailed charts were still unavailable for many coasts; the chronometers could not be trusted, making it difficult to determine longitude; and offshore navigational devices were both scarce and crude. Most of the romance and adventure his father had known were still there.

So while Anne wept, Rosa remained indifferent, and Jean Audubon kept his silence, John James himself felt only one emotion. He called it "intense and indescribable pleasure."

CHAPTER II

1803 — 1804

ANNE, with tears in her eyes, might accuse Jean Audubon of irresponsibility, sending such a young boy to America by himself, but in making the arrangements for the trip the old captain was anything but casual. He booked passage for John James on a ship commanded by an old acquaintance, Captain John Smith, and gave him a letter of credit drawn on a banking firm in New York. From New York he was to go direct to Philadelphia, where he would be met by Miers Fisher, a wealthy Quaker, who handled Jean Audubon's business in connection with the farm. Fisher, in turn, was to place the boy in a suitable family. Nothing was left to chance. With the same care he would have used in navigating a ship, Jean Audubon took every precaution to safeguard his son.

As he and John James drove in the carriage from Couëron to Nantes, he undoubtedly repeated every detail and reiterated that this was not a holiday. The trip had a purpose: John James was to learn English. Nothing, however, not even Jean Audubon's admonitions, could repress the boy's holiday spirits as he went on board the ship. Perhaps, for all his excitement, he felt a slight pang of homesickness as he waved good-bye to the old man still standing on the pier; perhaps he felt another as the ship glided past Couëron and the fields where he had played so often; but the homesickness quickly disappeared—there were so many things to do and see. The masts—he had seen many masts before, both at Nantes and Rochefort, but never when he was a passenger bound for America and standing on the planking directly beneath with the white sails stretched by the wind. Captains—he had known many captains, no son of Jean Audubon could fail to, but never before had he seen a captain in actual command of a ship crossing the ocean, speaking to the pilot and giving orders to the mates. He had many times watched men climb into the rigging, racing up the ratlines and out onto the spars, but—except for his brief time at Rochefort—always from the shore, where they had seemed dim and distant as though belonging to another world. Now he was part of that world himself. He could hear the quietly spoken words of the captain, standing aloof and authoritative on the quarterdeck, see the sweat on the men's faces as they heaved on the sheets, and listen to the slap of water against the bow and the sound of ropes running through the blocks.

Suddenly everything changed. Clearing Saint-Nazaire, the ship emerged from the quiet waters of the Loire and entered the Bay of Biscay. Instead of the short, sharp waves which were the worst John James had ever known on the river, he encountered the long, majestic swell of the ocean, surging ribs of foam-flaked water that might well have traveled thousands of miles before reaching him. Compared to the waves of the Loire, through which the ship had moved virtually unaffected, these were irresistible giants making their motion felt the entire length of the vessel. Up went the bow; down went the stern; up went the stern; down went the bow. Up-down-up-down. A slight, twisting motion to port and back to starboard. Then once again, the bow up, down. His nerves caught the rhythmic motion. It seemed to pass through every fiber in his body, his eyes, his legs, his chest, his stomach. Then, like many a landlubber on his first ocean trip, he rushed for the rail, his holiday spirit utterly vanished and his whole being racked with misery.

But even seasickness cannot last forever. As the ship moved westward over the waves, he became accustomed to the rolling and pitching; his appetite returned and so did his intense interest in everything taking place on deck, the man at the wheel holding the vessel steadily on course, the sailors working the sheets at every change in the wind, the quiet pacing of the officers on watch. Day after day, night after night, the ship carried him nearer and nearer to America, until he heard the lookout shout the traditional cry, "Land ahoy!" and soon saw, on the port side, Sandy Hook—a thin, flat spur of tide-washed beaches, barely rising above the surface of the waters that separate it from the New Jersey shore. To early explorers like Verrazano, shoals such as these presaged the danger of venturing into unknown waters where no shipwrights or supplies were available for the repair of a stranded vessel; but in 1803, instead of presenting a menace, Sandy Hook was the site of the principal beacon marking the channel into New York.

There the pilot boat came alongside, the pilot himself climbing up the rope ladder thrown down to him and stepping onto the deck. After the usual exchange of news and cordialities with the captain, he took his bearings and, as John James watched the shoreline with excitement, moved the ship through the Narrows, where the hills of Staten Island almost meet the beaches of Brooklyn, into the Lower Bay and up past Governor's Island. Directly ahead the boy could see the Battery, from which the British gun emplacements had now been removed, turning it into one of the city's finest residential districts. A few degrees off to port he noticed the majestic Hudson, greatest of New York's three rivers, and to the starboard, the East River which, because it was more likely to be ice-free in winter, formed the center of the city's shipping activity. Here stood a jumble of wooden storehouses, built upon wharves that jutted into the river in every direction, their ugliness contrasting dramatically with the handsome ships moored beside them. The pilot turned the bow in their direction, threaded his way through the busy harbor traffic—ships from Boston and Liverpool, Charleston and Bristol, almost every important port on both sides of the Atlantic—then swung his vessel broadside to the river's current and, ordering the hawsers thrown to the men waiting on the pier, warped it in.

Like any teen-age boy, John James was avid for new experiences, and he was now just as anxious to leave the boat and go ashore as he had been earlier to get aboard at Nantes. As soon as he had obtained Captain Smith's permission, he dashed down the gangway and started investigating the city. He walked down Pearl and Water streets, small, narrow lanes that led along the edge of the river, visited the more magnificent thoroughfares like Broadway and Front Street, gazed wide-eyed at the handsome Federal Building where Washington had been inaugurated, and perhaps visited the market where, as a matter of normal business, fifty species of edible birds, all shot in America's wilderness, were daily offered for sale. In addition to his sight-seeing, he also had business to transact, adult business; and with his letter of credit in his pocket, he proudly walked to Jean Audubon's bankers, whose offices were located in the community of Greenwich, some two miles from the tip of the island of Manhattan, received his money, and returned to the ship.

In spite of the good time he was having being his own master, John James's short visit to New York nearly ended in disaster. Back on board the ship, he suddenly felt faint and dizzy. Shortly afterward his temperature soared, and he barely had strength to climb into his bunk, where he lay tossing feverishly. Later, he described his illness as "yellow fever," which in those days was a common seaport disease. Even if this diagnosis was not correct, he was a thoroughly sick young man. Immediately John Smith, who, as a ship's captain, often had to double as a doctor, knew the boy was much too ill to make the trip to Philadelphia alone. The best alternative, he decided, was to find some capable nurses who would be willing to care for him, so bundling him into a carriage, he drove out with him to the country, where he knew two Quaker women who ran a boardinghouse. Yes, they said, they would take the boy in. In spite of all his father's careful planning, there he was within days of his arrival in America, seriously ill and in the hands of strangers.

But Captain Smith had chosen the nurses well. Gradually they brought the boy back to health; and in later years, although he did not mention them by name, he wrote about them in terms of the deepest gratitude. "To their skillful and untiring ministrations," he said, "I may safely say I owe the prolongation of my life." As soon as he was up and about and sufficiently well to travel, the two women sent word to Jean Audubon's agent, Miers Fisher, about his charge's predicament; and the kindly Quaker immediately hitched up his carriage, drove personally to see him, and brought the boy back to his own house on the Trenton Road just outside Philadelphia.

Fisher's instructions from Jean Audubon merely asked him to place John James in a suitable household where he could learn English; but with characteristic generosity Fisher decided the best household for the boy was his own. Why, he asked, didn't John James plan to stay right on with them? The boy agreed, and the arrangement should have been ideal. But placing John James in the quiet, restrained Fisher family was like exploding a bomb in a peaceful countryside.

Almost immediately, the overindulged boy and the self-disciplined man started to clash. Unlike John James, Fisher had gone into business for himself at the age of eighteen, quickly made a fortune, and then added to it by marrying an heiress. Yet he was much more than a successful businessman. He had also been a special confidant of George Washington and, because of his heroism during an epidemic, one of Philadelphia's civic heroes. He knew everybody of consequence in the arts and sciences as well as commerce, men like Gilbert Stuart, for example, and Charles Willson Peale, who, in addition to being a painter, was the proprietor of Peale's Museum, where he displayed birds and a wide variety of animals. These were not merely stuffed specimens in glass cases. Peale, a pioneer in designing modern museum displays, showed his exhibits against painted skies and landscapes. Men such as these, most of whom were noted for assisting younger scientists and artists, could have been immensely helpful to John James, but Miers Fisher, realizing the boy was only concerned with enjoying himself, never introduced him to them.

Later, John James described Fisher as "kindly" and "good and learned," but at the time, angry and resentful over the restrictions of the Quaker's household, he deliberately misinterpreted Fisher's well-meant intentions. When Fisher tried to make him study, John James complained that he "condemned most of my amusements." When Fisher encouraged one of his good-looking daughters to befriend the young foreigner, John James thought he was being pushed into a marriage, as though he were a suitable son-in-law for a man of Fisher's standing. On practically every issue the two differed, until John James, in an effort to escape Fisher's firm hand, haughtily told the older man "that it was his duty to install me on the estate to which my father had sent me." The language was presumptuous, the term "estate" a ridiculous word to apply to Jean Audubon's farm, and Jean Audubon had never suggested such an arrangement. But Fisher was no fool. He had not, under these circumstances, seen John James's charming and gentle side, only the spoiled boy given to tantrums and accustomed to having his own way, so he grabbed the opportunity to rid himself honorably of the responsibility he had impulsively assumed. But instead of letting John James move to Mill Grove, as the farm was called, he first placed him with another family who lived only a few miles away from it. From there John James frequently visited it, and finally Fisher gave way to his incessant pleadings that he be allowed to live permanently with his father's tenant.

As John James later remembered the event, Fisher personally made the arrangements, taking the boy with him. The carriage rolled up the drive, and again John James saw ahead of him the dignified Colonial stone farmhouse, with its cluster of outbuildings to the rear and, as soon as they stepped out of the carriage, the handsome, sloping fields leading down to the Perkiomen Creek which flowed through the valley below. At the door they were greeted by the tenant, William Thomas, who helped carry their luggage inside and quickly made them feel at home. After supper—and Mrs. Thomas was a good cook— John James spent the evening examining the house, with its fine fireplaces and large center hall, and admiring the view from the front porch, while Fisher and Thomas discussed the terms by which he could remain there. In his typically unrealistic fashion, John James later said that he "took possession" of the farm. Actually he was there only as a paying guest in Thomas's household, living on a quarterly allowance that was to be no more "than was considered sufficient for the expenditure of a young gentleman." Once the arrangements were satisfactorily completed between them, Fisher and Thomas went to bed; and the next morning, heaving a sigh of relief, Fisher started back for Philadelphia. For his own part, John James was equally glad to see the older man disappear down the road. "I thought his departure a true deliverance," he wrote later, but added with hindsight, "Yet this was only because our tastes and education were so different, for he was certainly a good and learned man."

If Miers Fisher had quickly given up any attempt to discipline John James, William Thomas never even tried. Under the agreement with Fisher, he had no responsibility whatsoever for the boy except to provide him with a good home—no lessons to teach him, no duties to make him perform. Within reasonable limits and as long as William Thomas, in return for his pay, was willing to keep him on, John James was free to do what he wanted. And he made the utmost of that freedom.

Plunging into his new life with enthusiasm, he immediately set about exploring every inch of the farm. The house itself, although not luxurious, was comfortable and handsome, perched almost at the top of a hill with a wide view over the valley below and off into the distance. Behind the house, where the ground was relatively flat, stood the barns and stables, near enough to be comfortably reached but not where they interfered with the view. The original builder had obviously been a man of good taste, for there was not an unaesthetic object near the house except for the opening of an abandoned lead mine which stood some hundred feet from the main entrance. Used during the Revolution when lead was desperately needed for bullets, it had long since been closed, and time had mellowed the ugly gash in the earth, slowly removing this one eyesore from Mill Grove. Below the house, the fields stretched toward Perkiomen Creek, a tributary of the Schuylkill River. Here a dam of soft-colored stone ran from bank to bank, a distance of perhaps a hundred yards, holding back the water needed to operate the mill; and nearby were the miller's cottage and a sawmill, making a cluster of buildings—almost a small community in itself—at the edge of the stream. On the far side the land had been leveled by the twisting, turning creek, but the bluffs upstream from the farmhouse still rose dramatically from the water's edge. This section of Mill Grove, covered as it was by outcroppings of rock and divided down the center by a deep ravine, was too rugged for cultivation and therefore remained as close to a wilderness as anything John James had ever seen. Shielded from the house by the contour of the land and by screens of hemlocks, it soon became one of his favorite haunts; and hardly a day passed that he failed to visit it.

The time at Mill Grove sped quickly by, with John James completely absorbed in tramping over the countryside, hunting and observing birds, and enjoying to the full every moment of the farm's life. "Hunting, fishing, drawing, and music," he said later, "occupied my every moment; cares I knew not, and cared naught about them. I purchased excellent and beautiful horses, visited all such neighbors as I found congenial spirits, and was as happy as happy could be." This was a better life than he had ever known before, better even than the freedom given him by Anne, for William Thomas never interfered with his plans; and John James was so busy enjoying himself that he did not even have time for the ordinary courtesies of country living. When a new family named Bakewell moved onto the farm they called Flatland Ford, only a half mile away, he refused to take the trouble to call on them formally. In vain Mrs. Thomas, her sensibilities aroused, argued with him, reminding him that, as the older resident, politeness required him to pay the first visit. She even attempted to stir his interest by telling him the neighborhood gossip that William Bakewell had several handsome daughters as well as fine pointer dogs. But John James, too self-centered to care about his neighbor's feelings, refused to budge from the position that he had taken. Besides, he added haughtily, William Bakewell was English, and he "wished to know none of that race."

William Bakewell himself took the first step toward breaking what might otherwise have been a deadlock. Always gracious and friendly, he set aside social custom. If his young neighbor was not going to call on him, he decided, he would call on his neighbor. Unfortunately, when he knocked on the door at Mill Grove, John James was out. So he left his card and an invitation for the boy to come to Flatland Ford. Even this gesture was not enough to break through John James's arrogance and stubbornness. He still refused to make the trip.

By now the days were shorter and colder, the grouse huddled for warmth in the hemlock woods; and John James, always fond of hunting, spent much of his time shooting birds for Mrs. Thomas to cook. On one of these expeditions, when he had risen early in the morning and was striding through the snow, his gun held in the crook of his arm, he noticed in the woods ahead of him another hunter, accompanied by some handsome and well-trained dogs. The two hailed each other and fell into conversation, discussing the merits of their dogs and where the grouse were hiding. To his surprise John James learned that this man, with whom he had so much in common, was his neighbor, William Bakewell; and suddenly his animosity vanished. Swallowing his pride, which was not easy for him, he apologized for his past rudeness and promised to repay Bakewell's visit.

Soon afterward, in a somewhat penitent mood, he made the short trip to Flatland Ford, walked up the steps of the impressive, large house, and knocked on the door. The servant who answered told him Mr. Bakewell was out momentarily but invited him to step into the parlor and wait. John James accepted the invitation and entered the room, where a young woman was seated. She rose, offered him a chair, and sent a servant to call her father. While they waited for William Bakewell, other members of the family came and went, but John James concentrated on the girl in front of him. As he put it, "Other ruddy cheeks and bright eyes made their transient appearance, but, like spirits gay, soon vanished from my sight; and there I sat, my gaze riveted, as it were, on the young girl before me, who, half working, half talking, essayed to make the time pleasant for me." When William Bakewell returned to greet his young guest, John James was already in love with Lucy, the oldest daughter.

Hearty and friendly, William Bakewell immediately made John James feel at home, introduced him to his three other daughters and his two sons, and invited him to stay for lunch. By this time John James had so completely changed his earlier opinion of his new neighbors that he immediately accepted; and Lucy went out to tell the servants to set an extra place at the table.

During that first meeting with the Bakewells, the boy had eyes for no one but Lucy. As she rose from her chair the second time to go to the dining room, he paid special attention to her "form," noting that it "showed both grace and beauty," and, as he said later, "my heart followed every one of her steps." After lunch the dogs and guns were made ready, because John James and William Bakewell were to spend the afternoon hunting together. But even before he left the house that afternoon, John James was convinced that he had made an impression on

Lucy or at least that she "looked upon me with some favor."
He felt, he said, a "certain *je ne sais quoi* which intimated . . .
she was not indifferent to me."

From that time on, he pursued the Bakewell family, first concentrating on William Bakewell, who, contrary to his earlier
snap judgment, he found to be "a most excellent man, a great
shot, and possessed of extraordinary learning—aye, far beyond
my comprehension," and the description was apt. Bakewell had
been brought up in an English village by an uncle who taught
him the excellent marksmanship for which John James so much
admired him. On reaching maturity, he had entered business as
a tea factor in Burton-on-Trent, but when his uncle died moved
back to the family place, which he had inherited. There he led
the life of an intellectual member of the English gentry, supervising his estate, conducting experiments in a chemical laboratory he had built, and enjoying the friendship of such people
as Dr. Joseph Priestley, the scientist and liberal, and Dr. Eras-
mus Darwin, grandfather of Charles Darwin. In association
with such men his own political views became more and more
liberal until, according to the family tradition, he was asked
by the government to resign his position as justice of the peace—
an unpaid office, but one that carried with it a certain dignity.

Whether he was hurt by this request or merely thought life
would be more congenial in America, he came to the United
States in 1798, purchased a brewery at New Haven, Connecticut, in partnership with his brother, Benjamin, and returned
to England nine months later. A year before John James came
to America, he had moved back to New Haven. That same winter the brewery had caught fire and burned to the ground, and
he had then bought Flatland Ford. In spite of his misfortunes,
he was determined to make the farm a good home for his children; and this reveals more of his character than the family
story that when he found his children weeping over a book
called *Simple Susan,* he took the volume from them and threw
it into the fire, saying he would not permit his children to weep
over a mere tale. He may have been opposed to sentimentality
—this would have been compatible with his interest in science—
but, as John James quickly learned, for the problems and people of real life he had only warmth and generosity.

In response to their friendliness, John James showed to the Bakewells only the best he had to offer, all his charm, gaiety, and even consideration for others. When the Perkiomen Creek froze over and the season's skating started, he decided to have the entire family over to Mill Grove. "Being somewhat of a skater myself," he wrote, "I sent a note to the inhabitants of Flatland Ford, inviting them to come and partake of the simple hospitality of Mill Grove farm, and the invitation was kindly received and accepted. My own landlady"—Mrs. Thomas was enjoying the festivity John James brought to the household— "bestirred herself to the utmost in the procuring of as many pheasants and partridges as her group of sons could entrap, and now under my own roof was the whole of the Bakewell family, seated around the table which never ceased to be one of simplicity and hospitality. After dinner we all repaired to the ice on the creek, and there in comfortable sledges, each fair one was propelled by an ardent skater."

The description is encrusted with the vocabulary and sentiment of the time, but the scene comes clear: the flat stretches of the Perkiomen white with ice, the women, particularly the younger ones like Lucy and her sisters, sitting in their sledlike chairs, while the men and boys push them over the surface, their scarves flying in the wind as they try to outdo each other in speed and fancy turns.

Gradually the days grew longer, the ice on Perkiomen Creek melted, the buds started to swell; and one day John James was wandering as usual among the cliffs, jumping from rock to rock in his exuberance, when he noticed an old phoebe's nest fastened to a stone ledge. Going over to examine it more closely, he discovered immediately beneath the ledge the entrance to a light, airy cave, the perfect hideaway for a romantically minded boy. His imagination was fired by the secrecy of the spot and from then on he made it the headquarters for much of his outdoor activity, visiting it almost every day and, whenever the weather permitted, using it as a sort of study. Sometimes, when he went to it, he carried with him a copy of Maria Edgeworth's stories or La Fontaine's *Fables* and, sitting by himself, quietly passed the hours reading; sometimes he came with his pencils and paper and made sketches; often he merely sat there musing, completely secluded from all the activity at the farm or the mill.

One morning, after the winter months had given away to spring and the weather was slowly warming, he went down to the cave as usual. Suddenly he heard a rustling sound overhead and, looking up, saw that the phoebes had returned. Frightened by his appearance, they flew out the entrance and lighted on a nearby tree. The boy, concerned that he might scare them away forever, immediately left and did not go near the cave for the rest of the day. Having given the birds a chance to reestablish themselves, he was up early the next morning and rushed eagerly back. To his pleasure, he found the phoebes flying over the creek in search of insects and gaily entering and re-entering the cave.

In April, when the snow had vanished from the ground and Pennsylvania was turning from the brown of winter to the green of spring, he "decided to spend the greater part of each day in the cave in the enjoyable company of this friendly pair. My presence," he went on, "no longer alarmed them. They brought fresh materials, lined the nest anew, and made it warm by adding a few large soft feathers of the common goose which were strewn along the edge of the creek water. While both birds sat on the edge of the nest, there was a remarkable and curious twittering that is never to be heard on any other occasion. It was, I thought, the soft, tender expression of the pleasure they both appeared to anticipate in the future."

In a short while, he noticed that the female began spending the greater part of her time in her nest, until one afternoon about three o'clock she suddenly rose and flew out of the cave, followed by her mate. Excitedly John James peered into the nest and "saw their first egg, so white and transparent . . . that the sight was more pleasant to me," he wrote, "than if I had seen a diamond of the same size. The knowledge that, in such a frail covering, life already existed, and that before many weeks a weak, a delicate and helpless yet perfect creature would burst the shell and immediately call for the most tender care and attention from anxious parents, filled my mind with the same wonder that I feel when I search the heavens for the meaning of all I see."

Quietly he stood there, hardly moving a muscle, as he looked into the nest. If Miers Fisher could have seen him then, he would not have recognized him as the spoiled, arrogant boy he had known, and William Bakewell would not have believed this was the same inconsiderate neighbor who had rudely refused to return his call. In awe before the miracle, he revealed the side of his character few people had ever seen and even fewer suspected. All his gentleness, all his mysticism, were called forth by the sight of the egg.

Yet his thoughts during those months were not entirely centered on the phoebes' nest. Each time he came or went by the front door of Mill Grove, he had to pass by the abandoned lead mine, and often he stopped to contemplate it, looking at the remains of what had once been a profitable enterprise. Noticing his interest, William Thomas broached a plan. Why not reopen the mine? he asked. Granted the job would be expensive, but the profits might be enormous. After all, everyone knew the mine contained lead. Always a romanticist, John James's imagination was immediately seized by the idea. How exciting it would be, he thought, to make a fortune right there on his father's farm. Since neither he nor Thomas had the authority to start digging, they talked the matter over with a Frenchman named Francis Dacosta, who had come to the United States and replaced Fisher both as Jean Audubon's agent and guardian of John James. Dacosta, who knew nothing about mining either, gave his consent and enthusiastically they started. Soon the grass in the once quiet field was trodden and broken beneath their feet, piles of lumber and machinery covered the roots of what had once been daisies and mounds of dirt began to grow on the hillside.

While the two men and the boy were busy at the mine, the phoebes laid five more eggs. "Day after day passed," John James wrote. "I gave strict orders"—he had now deluded himself into believing that he was the farm's real proprietor, not Thomas—"that no one should go near the cave, much less enter it, or indeed destroy any nest on the plantation." Over at the mill, another pair of phoebes had built their nest in the rafters, while a third pair had taken possession of a shed in the cattle yard. Watching them closely every day, he noticed that each pair staked out its own feeding grounds, that the phoebes nesting in the cave never met the phoebes nesting in the mill, while those in the cattle shed kept themselves strictly to the nearby orchard. Gradually, in a haphazard way, he was becoming a student of bird behavior, coming to conclusions that have been confirmed by modern ornithology.

After thirteen days, all the eggs—except one—were hatched. By this time, John James wrote, "the older birds no longer looked on me as an enemy, and they would often come in close by me as if I were only a post. I now took it upon myself to handle the young frequently."

Until then, he had been merely watching the birds, making notes of their habits and reactions. Now he decided to conduct an active experiment. Finding that he could handle the phoebes freely, he caught them one by one, holding them gently in his strong hands, and attached light threads to their legs so that he could identify them individually. The birds, however, were able to remove the threads either by working at them with their bills or with the assistance of their parents. Patiently, John James kept replacing them day after day. Then, when they were about to leave the nest altogether, he "fixed a light silver thread to the leg of each, loose enough not to hurt the part, yet so fastened that the birds could not remove it." Now he could tell with certainty whether the same birds returned next year.

In the coolness of his cave, the athletic, spoiled boy was, without knowing it, conducting an historic experiment—what may have been the first attempt at banding birds in the United States. Conceivably he might have read about the idea, as sporadic efforts to band European birds had been made in the previous century. But it is far more likely that a combination of circumstances led to his experiment—the proximity of the phoebes' nest, the ease with which he could handle the birds, and, most important of all, his own intense interest in the young, not as types but as individuals. He may not have learned English, he may have irritated Miers Fisher and treated William Bakewell rudely, but as he turned toward the entrance of the cave, opened his hand, and let the last bird fly into the air, he had moved as an ornithologist almost a hundred years ahead of his time.

Although the phoebes occupied much of his attention that

year at Mill Grove—they made such a deep impression on him
that, long afterward, he still referred to them in terms he did
not apply to other species—he continued to observe and draw
many other varieties. If he was not at the mine or sketching
in his room, he was out in the fields and woods of Mill Grove,
walking down the slope toward the creek in the early morning
light when the mists rose from the water and spread through
the valley, or he was striding across the fields when they were
wet with dew and the cobwebs hung from the grass. Sometimes
he was out in the heat of the day, the earth beneath his feet
hard with dryness, or was forced to take shelter under the great
hemlocks when the summer thunderheads gathered and poured
forth torrents of rain. In the cool of the evening, when the life
of Mill Grove was slowing, the miller eating his supper, and
Mrs. Thomas lighting the lamps in the farmhouse, he would
again be roaming the woods and meadows and the banks of the
stream. On some of his trips he left his gun behind, contenting
himself with observing the motions of the birds, how the bald
eagles soared high above the farm, the kingfishers perched like
lookouts on the trees overhanging the creek, or the redwings
shrieked along the marshy edges of the stream. More often, he
carried his gun in his hand, for he loved hunting for its own
sake, rejoicing in the sound of the shot and the sight of the
falling bird.

Because he was an excellent marksman, he had no difficulty
in collecting enough specimens to use as models for his drawings. Racing back with the dead, limp birds in his hand, he
would go to his room in the farmhouse, select one, tie a string
around its leg, and hang it upside down with its wings and tail
spread wide. In this way, he could see and reproduce every detail, but artistically the results were hardly worth the effort.
Not being a good draftsman, he created only mediocre likenesses, and the artificial poses of the birds destroyed any other
value the drawings might have had. Still the untrained amateur
he had been in France, the pictures he completed during this
period he later said might have "made some pretty fair signs
for poulterers."

His affection for the phoebes, however, kept inspiring him
to greater efforts. One day, while he was watching the birds he

had come to love so well, he looked intently at their graceful attitudes and decided that he could never capture their motion by drawing from dead models. Therefore he would try to sketch them while they were still alive. During the succeeding days he drew hundreds of outlines of the phoebes and thought that he had entered a whole new phase of his art. For the first time in his life, he was striving for something above the ordinary and breaking away from the traditional bird drawings of his era.

Like many an artist before him, he soon discovered that his aspirations were far beyond his abilities and his techniques. For weeks he outlined the birds as he watched them in motion, trying to catch their swift movements on paper, but the results were unsuccessful. The constant motion of the live birds made them such poor models that he returned to using dead specimens. In his room in the farmhouse, instead of stringing the lifeless birds up by one leg, he now experimented with laying them on a table and trying to manipulate them into some semblance of their normal positions, but the effects he obtained were always two-dimensional. Next he tried hanging the bodies by strings attached to the wings, the tail, the neck and the head, letting them float suspended in the air; but, as he described the results later, "I had something like life before me; yet much was wanting. When I saw the living birds, I felt my blood rush to my temples, and almost in despair spent about a month without drawing, but in deep thought."

When he wrote about these early experiments at Mill Grove, he undoubtedly permitted himself some poetic license in describing the consistency of his efforts. Yet the fact remained that, for once, he had found a problem capable of holding his attention over a period of time. Finally convinced that hanging the birds by strings was not the answer, he remembered his brief experience with David, when he had been taught to draw from manikins. Could he make a bird manikin? he asked himself. "I labored," he wrote, "with wood, cork, and wires, and formed a grotesque figure, which I cannot describe in any other words than by saying that, when set up, it was a tolerable-looking Dodo. A friend aroused my ire by laughing at it immoderately, and assuring me that if I wished to represent a tame gander it might do. I gave it a kick, broke it to atoms, walked off, and thought again."

With a persistence that would have astounded any of his former teachers, he kept puzzling over the problem until one morning an inspiration struck him. Leaping out of bed, he dashed downstairs and without waiting for breakfast, saddled his horse and rode at a gallop to Norristown, arriving there before sunrise. No stores were open, so he went to the river, took a bath, then returned, purchased some wire in various sizes, and raced back to Mill Grove. Mrs. Thomas offered him breakfast, but John James was too excited to eat. Instead he grabbed his gun, went down to the creek, and shot the first bird he saw, a kingfisher. With the dead body in his hands, he went back to his room to conduct his experiment. After cutting his wire into sections and filing the ends into points, he drove the pieces partway into the kingfisher's body to stiffen it and then mounted it on a board of soft wood. By twisting and bending the wires, he found that he could manipulate the bird into the lifelike position that he wanted and that the stiffness of the wires would hold it in place. The technique was simple but effective, and knowing he had made an important discovery, he started drawing immediately. "I outlined the bird," he explained, "colored it, finished it, without a thought of hunger. . . . This is what I shall call my first drawing actually from nature."

Thus he passed his first months at Mill Grove, hunting, fishing, idling away his time, taking nothing seriously but his pictures. Yet even those he did with no thought of becoming a professional. As for his English, his accent was still atrocious, his writing practically undecipherable. Meanwhile, he and Dacosta and Thomas were spending more and more time at the lead mine, their heads filled with dreams of the money they would make. It was almost as though the poison from the dark metal was rising out of the ground and spilling over the fields and woods in the once placid world of Mill Grove. Thomas was neglecting his responsibilities as a farmer; Dacosta was making the trip from Philadelphia frequently; and John James, so easily given to illusions about himself, was already beginning to fancy himself a man of affairs.

Yet he was not. That summer great changes were taking place

in the United States, but he was indifferent to them. Aaron Burr, brilliant but hate-driven, shot Alexander Hamilton on the heights of Weehawken and fled to Washington. Meriwether Lewis and William Clark were pressing up the Missouri River toward the Columbia in a race against the British; and the country was in an expansionist mood, moving westward into the space made accessible by the recently completed Louisiana Purchase. But these events were of no interest to John James, isolated as he was at Mill Grove. In August he had watched the phoebes lay their next clutch of eggs; and on October 8, when he went to the cave, he found it as empty as when he had first noticed it on that early spring morning. The birds who had entertained him during the summer months had taken off for the south. The trilliums which had carpeted the ground were faded into brown dust, and so were the Dutchman's-breeches, the mayapples, and the many other wild flowers around Mill Grove. By the mill, the cottonwoods started to shed their leaves, and everywhere the green of summer gradually faded into the somber shades of winter, until only the hemlocks growing on the rocky bluffs above the creek gave to Mill Grove a touch of color. The mist rising from the stream became cold and dank. The fields were covered with white frost, disappearing each day in the morning sunlight but presaging the more permanent whiteness of the first of winter's snows. As the sun sank lower and lower in the sky with each passing day, the shadows it cast grew longer and longer. But none were greater than the shadow over the Bakewell household, for Lucy's mother had died that fall, or the shadow that fell from the piles of material and dirt accumulating around the mine opening. It laid a stain of blackness on the happy fields of Mill Grove.

CHAPTER III

1804 – 1805

O N Saturday, November 17, 1804, when the readers of the New York *Herald* unfolded their papers, they saw a favorable announcement of the reopening of the mine at Mill Grove. According to the printed report, the vein had proved to be rich and large, and the editor believed that the mine might turn out to be one of the best in the United States.

So their plan, after all, had been a success. The sweating workmen outside the front door of Mill Grove had already hauled two tons of ore to the surface, creating a great mound at the top of the hill, and had loosened another ton which was lying at the bottom ready to be raised. Dacosta, Thomas, and John James, hanging around the entrance and watching eagerly as the work progressed, could congratulate themselves on their good judgment and, better yet, on having made their fortunes. Soon they would all be wealthy men.

Or would they?

The question suddenly struck them, as they listened to the ropes squeaking over the pulleys, heard the heavy breathing of the men as they lifted and pulled and the dull thuds of picks and shovels at the bottom of the nine-foot pit. Until then, they had assumed they were equal partners with Jean Audubon in the venture and would have a share in the profits. Now, with the rich ore lying on the ground where they could see it, they began to realize they had no legal rights at all. William Thomas was simply the tenant of Mill Grove. He could farm the land and work the mill, but his lease did not cover the exploitation of minerals. Regardless of how much time and thought he contributed to the operation, his compensation would depend not on the profitability of the mine but entirely on the value that

Jean Audubon might care to place on his services. As for Dacosta, he was no better off. So far, he had been acting solely in
his capacity as Jean Audubon's business agent, which meant he
had no personal stake in the venture. Any time Jean Audubon
decided to dismiss him, his connection with the mine would
end. John James, of course, was in a different situation. The authority he exercised—and it amounted to little—came only from
being his father's son and, therefore, from whatever influence
he might have over Jean Audubon. On the other hand, he had
the least to worry about, because supposedly he would be the
eventual beneficiary of his father's wealth.

With the realization that they were only employees, not partners, both Dacosta and Thomas began to eye each other and
John James with suspicion. What if Jean Audubon decided to
have nothing further to do with them, now the two tons of ore
lay on the ground and the mine had been proclaimed a success?
What if John James, as his father's son, notified the captain
that their services were no longer needed? What, thought Dacosta, if Jean Audubon preferred Thomas's services to his own?
What, thought Thomas, if Dacosta, as Jean Audubon's agent,
decided to hold him strictly to his lease and thus split him off
from any connection with the mine? It was not a pleasant situation in which they found themselves. As winter swept its way
across the fields and through the woods of Mill Grove, the coldness on the farm was not merely the coldness of the changing
seasons, it was tinged with the iciness of distrust.

Being the man with the most business experience, Dacosta
was the quickest to evaluate his position and take steps to improve it. As the ice formed on Perkiomen Creek and the grouse
huddled among the hemlock trees, he started a campaign to
protect himself without, of course, saying a word to Thomas
about what he was doing or, for that matter, even to John
James. The person with the final word was Jean Audubon, and
it was to Jean Audubon that Dacosta appealed. In letter after
letter, he insisted that he be permitted to buy a share of the
mine, thus ensuring himself of an owner's claim to part of the
eventual profits. Formerly, Jean Audubon would have turned
to Miers Fisher for advice, but Fisher's opinion was no longer
available to him, and he had to work out the problem for him-

self. Under Dacosta's constant pressure, he finally yielded and sold him a one-half undivided interest in Mill Grove. Worse yet, because Dacosta had no cash, he took as payment in full nothing but a mortgage.

Although this was an ill-advised move and not up to Jean Audubon's old shrewdness, he actually had little other choice. The years were catching up with him; both his mind and his body were working more slowly, and if he lost Dacosta, he had no substitute or any ready means of obtaining one. From all reports, including those he received from his son, the mining operation looked as though it were successful; and to refuse Dacosta meant, in effect, to abandon the venture, at least for the time being.

Meanwhile, Thomas had not been sitting idly by. He had grown suspicious of Dacosta; and when his suspicions were confirmed by learning that Dacosta had become a half owner of the farm, he knew he was completely locked out as far as the mine was concerned. Jean Audubon, having sold one half to Dacosta, was not likely to sell the other to Thomas. For all the work he had done, for all the sacrifices he had made on behalf of the mine, deserting his farming, neglecting his duties, he now saw he would receive no share of the profits, nothing but what Dacosta and Jean Audubon might agree to give him in the way of a salary. Desperately, he began looking for an alternative recompense, however poor. Therefore he asked himself, if the mine near the door contained lead, was it not likely there were other veins on Mill Grove? One section in particular appealed to him as a possibility, and he asked Jean Audubon to sell it to him outright. As soon as Jean Audubon received the letter, his suspicions were aroused. What was the farmer up to? Had he discovered an even richer vein than the one in the mine? Was he, in effect, trying to double-cross the two partners by secretly prospecting around the farm while they concentrated on the one obvious location? His suspicions, of course, were reflected by Dacosta, who wondered along exactly the same lines. The two men closed ranks immediately. Whatever they did, they would sell no land to Thomas. The tenant's worst fears were justified, and further mistrust had been created on the once quiet farm.

To add to the problem, the optimistic report in the New York *Herald* was proving unjustified. Although the mine contained lead, the initial expense of reopening the pit had not yet been recovered. What the operators needed was additional capital to expand the operation in the hope of placing it on a profitable basis. Because Decosta had no money, he was forced to turn to Jean Audubon, but since the defeat of Leclerc's armies in San Domingo, Jean Audubon was no longer wealthy and, on his naval pension, barely able to satisfy his own personal needs. Since supplying additional capital himself was clearly out of the question, he did the next best thing. He talked to his friend, François Rozier, judge of the Commercial Court at Nantes, and persuaded Rozier to put up 16,000 francs. The judge, an experienced businessman, insisted, however, on taking as security a mortgage for one-half the value of the entire farm. Having no alternative, Jean Audubon acquiesced to this demand and, by doing so, plunged over the brink. Dacosta now owned one-half the farm; the other half was mortgaged. In short, Jean Audubon had taken in two other partners, but continued to assume all the risks himself, for unless the mine paid well, he stood a good chance of losing most if not all of his American investment. Yet old age and illness, while they certainly affected his judgment, did not alone account for the dangerous course he took. The mine, it seemed to him, might offer a means of providing financial security for John James. As he constantly reminded Dacosta in his correspondence, if they succeeded, he expected a place in the management of the mine to be held open for John James, so that the boy could make his own living in the future.

During this period, the personal split between John James and Dacosta was also widening. Just as he had earlier clashed with Fisher, John James reacted violently to Dacosta's attempts to regulate his life. So while the Bakewells continued to see the charming, gay side of his personality, Dacosta, in his role of guardian, encountered only the conceited, spoiled boy with the ugly temper. John James resented everything his guardian said or did, and later scornfully remarked that "this fellow was intended to teach me mineralogy and mining engineering; but, in fact, knew nothing of either; besides which he was a covetous wretch, who did all he could to ruin my father, and indeed swindled both of us to a large amount. . . . A greater scoundrel than Dacosta never probably existed."

Their relationship was further complicated by John James's interest in Lucy. In the phoebes' cave, Lucy had given him "the acknowledgement that she was not indifferent to me," and from that point on, impatiently brushing aside all practical considerations, he became determined to marry her as soon as possible. When Dacosta objected to the marriage, the boy grew so angry that years laters he had not recovered sufficiently to give anything but a prejudiced account of what happened. "Mr. Dacosta, my tutor," he said, "took it into his head that my affection . . . was rash and inconsiderate. He spoke triflingly of her [Lucy] and her parents, and one day said to me that for a man of my rank and expectations to marry Lucy Bakewell was out of the question. If I laughed at him or not, I cannot tell you, but of this I am certain, that my answers to his talks on this subject so exasperated him that he immediately afterward curtailed my usual income, made some arrangements to send me to India, and wrote to my father accordingly."

That Dacosta actually threatened to send John James to India is extremely doubtful, but he certainly did oppose the marriage, because he had been instructed to do so by Jean Audubon himself. After all, John James was not yet able to support himself, let alone a wife, and Jean Audubon was unwilling to assume any additional financial responsibilities. In a letter to Dacosta he made his position clear. He wanted Dacosta, first, to find out more about the Bakewells—who they were, and why they had moved to America—and, second, Dacosta was to tell William Bakewell that John James was not wealthy and if he married without his father's consent, would receive no inheritance or help of any kind. Dacosta faithfully carried out his orders; and John James, prevented from doing what he wanted, was furious. In his rage he turned on Dacosta, whom he saw as the cause of his frustration.

Yet in spite of the clouds of suspicion, frustration, and anger slowly gathering over Mill Grove, some days still remained when the farm enjoyed its former tranquillity and John James, apparently without a care or a worry, abandoned himself to his usual pastimes. In these, one of his closest companions was Lucy's brother Thomas, and together that winter they engaged in many boyish pranks and expeditions. Either John James would make the trip to Flatland Ford or Thomas would come to Mill Grove, and then off they would go, sometimes hunting together, sometimes skating, sometimes merely tramping through the snow-filled woods; and, as might be expected, their youthful enthusiasm every so often led them into trouble. One day they had been skating on the creek when, weary of racing each other and competing in fancy turns, Thomas dared John James to skate by him at full speed, gun in hand, and try to shoot down his hat which he would toss into the air. Accepting the challenge, John James moved back some distance from where Thomas stood, dug his skates into the ice, braced himself and, holding his gun firmly in his two hands ready to raise it, started forward, gathering speed as he went. Thomas, waiting until the other boy was almost opposite him, threw his hat in the air as high as he could. Up it went above his head and hung still for a second at the top of its flight, as John James, never slacking his speed, took aim. Crack went the gun; the sound of the report echoed from the banks of the creek, and there on the ice lay Thomas's hat, "as completely perforated as if a sieve."

In spite of William Bakewell's severe displeasure when Thomas brought home his ruined hat, the incident was not nearly as serious as another shooting expedition that almost cost John James his life. One winter morning, after an early breakfast, he and Thomas, along with some other boys their own ages, set off on a duck-hunting expedition up the creek. The stream was frozen hard, so they were able to skate all the way, but as they went they noticed that the smooth surface was marred by numerous air pockets, each one presenting a hazard that had to be avoided. After a good day's hunting and when the light became so poor they could no longer see the sights of their guns, they decided the time had come to return home and, to make the trip more fun, formed a procession with John James acting as their leader. In his usual high spirits, he fastened a white handkerchief to a stick, held it high above his head for the others to see, and started off gaily and quickly, skating toward home in the gathering dusk. As the evening grew darker and darker, he went faster and faster. Racing down the creek, his stick still waving in the air and the other boys following behind, he suddenly saw a large airhole in the ice immediately in front of him. Twisting on the edges of his blades and throwing his whole body into the motion, he tried to stop. The blades ground into the ice, sending slivers of white crystals flying in every direction, but his momentum kept carrying him forward. Over the crumbling, soggy edge of the ice he rushed and plunged into the cold water. Before he could struggle to the surface, the current surged around him and swept him under. The creek, which he had loved so well, was now only a death trap. Even in the darkness, the other boys saw him abruptly disappear and stopped in time, but they were helpless, not knowing where the current had carried him. Luckily for John James, another large air pocket had created a hole some thirty or forty yards downstream, and the stream thrust him toward it. Seeing the opening above him, he somehow managed to check his movement, get his head out of the water, and place his hands on the ice surrounding him. Then he worked his way, slowly and cautiously, back to the hard ice. Soaking wet and chilled by the evening air of winter, he stood there while his friends gathered around him. Swiftly he undressed and borrowed odds and ends of clothing from the other skaters, a shirt from one, a pair of breeches from another, a scarf from still another. Then the strangely dressed group started off again, moving, John James said, "with much more circumspection." As he pointed out, it was "a singular and, in truth, most extraordinary escape from death."

Yet in the midst of all this activity—hunting, skating, working at the mine, going to parties, and courting Lucy—John James still continued to draw birds and study their habits. And who, of all people, encouraged him the most? That "covetous wretch," Dacosta, who, noticing that this was the only subject the boy took seriously, praised his efforts and urged him to keep on. He even went further than that. One day, during one of his frequent visits to Mill Grove, he stood in John James's room watching him draw a great blue heron. As the boy sat there, the heron mounted on wires in front of him, Dacosta turned to the boy and, speaking both solemnly and prophetically, assured him that someday he might become a great American naturalist. The effect on John James, in view of his hatred for Dacosta, was startling. "However curious it may seem to the scientific world that these sayings from the lips of such a man should affect me," he wrote later, "I assure you they had great weight with me, and I felt a certain degree of pride in those words even then."

The only two points on which they seemed able to agree were this and their mutual optimism over the mine. On every other issue, the differences between them were growing greater and greater. What particularly annoyed Dacosta was John James's assumption that because the farm belonged to Jean Audubon, he could regard it as his own. He gave orders to the miller, referred to Thomas as "my tenant" and called Dacosta "my tutor" as though they all were his employees. Under some circumstances, Dacosta might have accepted this as just one more evidence of John James's irritating and overbearing manner, but after he had purchased one-half of the farm from Jean Audubon, he found John James's attitude intolerable. Who did the young whippersnapper think he was? Furthermore, the boy's arrogance was beginning to breed a new suspicion in Dacosta's mind. Was it possible that Jean Audubon was playing a two-faced game, on the one hand giving Dacosta what seemed to be over-all authority and, on the other, encouraging John James to supersede him? Was it possible that in this way Jean Audubon hoped to force Dacosta out of the mining operation, perhaps reneging on the sale he had made or even finding some way to foreclose the mortgage he held? These suspicions grew and grew, until matters finally came to such a pass that Jean Audubon, in addition to the many other burdens that were falling on his weary shoulders, had to write his son a stern letter of rebuke and go to some pains to assure Dacosta he was still in charge.

For Jean Audubon, sitting with Anne in the house at Couëron or walking by himself along the banks of the Loire, events were beginning to assume a nightmarish quality. Everything, in spite of his careful planning, had gone awry. For all practical purposes, he could now write off his San Domingo investments.

They had gone up in the smoke of the revolution that followed on the heels of Leclerc's invasion. His American investment in Mill Grove was now in bad shape, half of it sold to Dacosta, the other half mortgaged to Rozier. All his hopes were pinned now on the mine and that meant on Dacosta, who was the man in charge. Yet, under the prospect of failure, he and Dacosta were beginning to disagree, their disagreement being fanned by the attitude of John James. If only he could go to America, as Dacosta was urging him, and take personal charge of the operation —but, he admitted sadly to himself, he was too old and sick for such a trip.

All in all, at this stage, the reopening of the mine was following the traditional course of such ill-planned ventures. First, the initial excitement and optimism, culminating in the New York *Herald*'s article. Then the need for additional financing, the gradual disappointment, and finally the rising suspicions among the original partners: Jean Audubon, too old to take an active part, too poor to supply more money; François Rozier, who apparently knew when enough was enough and refused to invest more funds; Dacosta, who understood little about mining; Thomas, who felt he had been cheated; and John James, whose only concern was himself.

As if all this were not enough, John James in spite of his healthy way of life, became seriously ill. Whatever the cause— William Bakewell thought it might have resulted from drinking cold water when he was overheated—he was ill enough to require considerable care. As he lay fretfully in his bed, slowly recovering and impatient to be outdoors again, he had plenty of time to review his supposed grievances at the hands of Dacosta: Dacosta's refusal to accept him as master of Mill Grove, Dacosta's efforts to discipline him, and, above all, Dacosta's interference with his plans to marry Lucy. As he went over his grievances one by one and then over them again and again, he became angrier than ever and more convinced that Dacosta was at the bottom of all his trouble. If only he could escape from Dacosta, he mused on his sickbed, life at Mill Grove would be happy again.

Having formed the resolution to flee Dacosta, he wasted no time putting it into effect. His plan was to go to France and talk to his father, but to make the trip he needed money. As soon as he was well, he walked to Philadelphia where Dacosta lived—there was no point in waiting until he came out to the farm—marched into Dacosta's room unexpectedly, and demanded point-blank enough money to pay for his passage back across the Atlantic. The demand, of course, was ridiculous. Jean Audubon had made clear what he wanted done, and Dacosta was doing it. Why put the old sailor to further unnecessary expense? John James, however, kept arguing, determined as usual to have his own way; and Dacosta, by then tired of these tirades and continual complaints, decided to teach him a lesson.

According to John James's later description of the scene, "The cunning wretch, for I cannot call him by any other name, smiled and said: 'Certainly, my dear sir,' and afterward gave me a letter of credit on a Mr. Kauman, a half-agent, half-banker, then residing at New York. I returned to Mill Grove, made all the preparatory plans for my departure, bid a sad adieu to my Lucy and her family," and traveled to New York. There he first went to the house of Mrs. John Palmer, a friend of the Bakewells, and then called on William Bakewell's brother, Benjamin, who was engaged in shipping, importing, and banking, a common business combination in those days. As warmhearted as William and perhaps more capable, Benjamin opened John James's letter of introduction, read it, and insisted the boy spend the night with them, making him welcome with typical Bakewell hospitality.

The boy was up early the next morning—he was always an early riser—and downstairs before the rest of the family, waiting anxiously for breakfast, so that he could be on his way to Kauman's office, collect his money, arrange for his passage, and be off to France. The meal over, he was out the front door and into the street, walking gaily toward the banker's office. This, he congratulated himself, was the end of Dacosta, once and for all. At the office, he gave Kauman what he thought was his letter of credit and sat back full of self-satisfaction, waiting for him to read it. Kauman unfolded the piece of paper, looked at it, and began to smile. Then, turning to the boy and still smiling, he said he had absolutely nothing in the way of money to give him. Indeed, John James later claimed, "Instead of a

letter of credit, Dacosta—that rascal!—had written and advised
him to have me arrested and shipped to Canton!" Whatever
the letter actually said—Kauman could not have had John
James sent to China—it was clear that Dacosta, weary of the
boy's frequent complaints and driven wild by his arrogance,
had played a practical joke by making him travel several hundred miles to no purpose. Perhaps he thought the trip would
bring John James to his senses and that he would then return
to Philadelphia in a more humble and reasonable state of mind,
but he had underestimated John James. Frustrated again, his
face flushed, the boy flew into a rage, later saying that he was
glad he had been unarmed at the time or he would have killed
Kauman on the spot. Leaping from his chair, he dashed out
of the office, slamming the door behind him, and walked, still
storming, back toward Mrs. Palmer's. On the way, as he dodged
between the carriages crowding the busy streets, he plotted his
revenge. As soon as he could leave New York, he would go back
to Philadelphia and kill Dacosta, really settling matters with
that "rascal."

Breathlessly he poured out his plans to Mrs. Palmer, his fists
clenched in anger, while she, good person that she was, listened
to him quietly, letting him have his say and vent his rage.
"Women," he said of the incident later, "always have great
power over me at any time, and perhaps under all circumstances. Mrs. Palmer quieted me, spoke religiously of the cruel
sin I thought of committing, and, at last, persuaded me to
relinquish the direful plan."

Until she was certain he had regained some control over his
feelings, she kept John James with her, gently soothing him.
Then, when she finally let him go, he made his way back to
Benjamin Bakewell's house, not lightheartedly as he had left it
in the morning, but in low spirits. He said nothing to the Bakewells about what had happened, but that night, as he tossed in
his bed, he wondered what to do next. Without money, he
could not go to Europe; without going to Europe, he could not
talk to his father. Money was at the root of his problem, but
he certainly would not return to Mill Grove on bended knees,
place himself at Dacosta's mercy, and beg again for his passage
to France. Almost anything would be better than that.

When he woke up the next morning, he was still so depressed and perplexed that the Bakewells were quickly aware that something had gone seriously wrong. Under their friendly questioning, he broke down and told them the full story. Instead of laughing at his frustration and the comical accent in which he related his experience, they were sympathetic; and Benjamin Bakewell, rather than sending him back to Mill Grove, took the more helpful, but less practical, course of offering to assist him in arranging a loan for his trip and in finding a ship bound for Nantes. If it was not a wise act, at least it was generous.

Together the older man and the angry boy walked down to the docks, wandering among the wooden buildings and jutting piers in search of a ship. The scene along the waterfront had changed little since John James had first arrived, but everywhere seamen, officers, and merchants were now discussing the increasing dangers of an Altantic crossing. England and France were at war again. The Peace of Amiens, as Jean Audubon had foreseen, was nothing but a faded hope on a scrap of paper. As a necessary part of their strategy, the British were beginning to harass American shipping, for American ships were carrying cargoes from the French colonies to France and also providing a refuge for deserting English sailors.

In spite of the hazards of trading with France, William Bakewell and John James located a ship, the brig *Hope,* that was sailing for Nantes and had room for another passenger. When the time came, John James settled himself on board, the captain gave the orders to cast off the hawsers, and the ship moved slowly out into the river's current, swung around, and headed for the Lower Bay. Once more, John James saw the shores of Brooklyn facing the heights of Staten Island at the Narrows and the lighthouse at Sandy Hook reaching toward the sky. But this time the light served as the symbol not of a new hope, but of a dying dream; he was leaving behind him forever the few precious months at Mill Grove where he had been "as happy as happy can be." It was not Sandy Hook that was slowly dropping below the horizon; it was the best part of his youth.

They had not been at sea long when, to his intense annoyance, he discovered the voyage to France was to be neither as

direct nor as short as he had assumed, for on reaching the latitude of New Bedford, Massachusetts, the captain announced
that the ship was leaking. He would, he said, have to put into
port, unload it, repair it, and reload it before putting out again.
John James was furious at this new delay. Everything and everybody were conspiring against him. Then, learning that the captain was newly married and that his bride was living in New
Bedford, he became convinced the captain "had actually caused
several holes to be bored below the water-mark" as an excuse
to go ashore and see his wife. The accusation was absurd, but
typical of his exaggerated reactions when he was thwarted. In
this case, however, there was nothing he could do except stalk
the deck in anger. Whatever the cause, the ship was indeed
taking in water and the sailors were manning the pumps. Instead of the coast of France, John James next saw Pune Island
and Gay Head, past which the captain sailed into New Bedford
Harbor. There—in John James's words—"the apertures were
bunged up," and the *Hope,* after a week's delay, was again
ready for the voyage to France.

Jubilantly John James watched the sails being hoisted, the
lines freed, and the shore gradually recede in the distance as
the ship moved down the channel, headed at last for Europe.
But whereas his first crossing had been uneventful, this time a
violent gale overtook the brig. As the wind tore at the canvas,
the men rushed aloft, standing on the footropes underneath the
massive yards, while the ship tossed and turned beneath them.
One moment the deck was below them, the next, they were
hanging far out over the churning water as the ship heeled to
one side. Then it would swing upright again and the deck
would be underneath once more. Swiftly the men worked as the
ship pitched and tossed, the canvas snapping with retorts as
loud as rifle shots, the ropes wet, yet burning, in their hands;
but finally, despite the fury of the storm, the sails were shortened, and the ship scudded forward through the water, safely
under control but forced to go where the wind carried it. All
night long the violent storm continued, the wind roaring across
the deck and screeching through the rigging, the waves battering the brig. In the darkness, one sailor was lost overboard,
whether dropping from aloft into the ocean with one final

scream of despair, or swept from the deck by a tumbling, whitened mass of water, John James did not say. At last the storm abated, the clouds rolled back, and the blue sky reappeared. Clear days followed; and finally, as he stood on deck, John James could see the distant coast of France, at first little more than a light gray, miragelike line on the horizon, and then growing higher and more distinct as the brig moved toward it. They went past Saint-Nazaire, the outermost port on the Loire, and worked their way up the river to Painboeuf, the lower harbor of Nantes.

Anxious to get home as quickly as he could and knowing that the customs officer in charge of the harbor was a friend of his father's, John James sent word to him that he was on the *Hope;* and the officer, glad to help the son of Jean Audubon, arranged to have him taken to his parents on his own official barge. Late that evening he was in the arms of his parents— parents who were taken completely by surprise at his arrival, for although he had written to say he was coming, he had made the trip faster than his letter.

So here he was home again after more than a year away, sitting in the drawing room of the quiet house at Couëron, talking as fast as he could to his parents and telling them what had happened to him, about Lucy, how charming and delightful she was, about William Bakewell and his dogs, about Thomas Bakewell, the farm, the mine, and, of course, Dacosta's injustices. It all came out in a jumbled heap of excited words; but as he talked, weary Jean Audubon must have questioned whether the whole undertaking had been worth it. From what the boy said, he gathered he had only played at this and at that. Certainly, he had drawn some pictures of birds, but they were not especially good. He had skated, hunted, fished, and become engaged to a girl whom he could not support. Yet he had not learned to write coherent English, his accent was atrocious, he had made the trip to France at his father's expense but without his father's permission. What a difference, Jean Audubon must have thought, between this first homecoming and his own. When he, at about John James's age, had returned to Sables d'Olhonne, he too had been to the New World and back, but not as a passenger. He had known what it was to climb the rigging on a stormy night when the ship was shaking as each wave struck it. He had known what it was to be a prisoner-of-war in a rough, crude prison among rough, crude men. And when he came back home, he had a trade—the sea—and a toughness and resiliency that seemed to be entirely lacking in this boy for whom he had tried to do so much. Nevertheless, there was no touch of bitterness or reproach in his greeting as he took John James into his arms.

"Most welcome . . . I was," said John James in later years; "I found my father hale and hearty, and *chère maman* as fair and good as ever."

In his heart, though, the old, grizzled sea captain must have wondered what would become of this son of his; and as he wondered, spring crept across the face of France from the blue Mediterranean to the coast of Normandy; and in the United States it slowly unlocked the frozen waters of Perkiomen Creek. The alders and the cottonwoods shot forth their buds, the mayapples unfurled their giant leaves, and on the rafters of the mill and the ledge above the cave where John James had spent so many happy hours, the phoebes came back to build their nests.

And of those that returned to Mill Grove that spring, several wore around their legs worn and discolored rings of white thread.

CHAPTER IV

1805 – 1807

I FOUND my father hale and hearty."
So wrote John James, describing his return to France, but actually Jean Audubon was neither. Still bothered by the pulmonary ailment that had forced him to resign from the navy, he was also deeply worried about the lead mine. On top of all this, he now had his son to contend with.

John James later claimed to have had two objectives when he put his father to the expense of the trip. He wanted, first to dispose of Dacosta and, second, to obtain permission to marry Lucy Bakewell. His hatred of his father's agent was so great that he listed them in that order. By "disposing" of Dacosta, he did not mean finding a new agent to help his father; he simply meant escaping from Dacosta's guardianship, and that objective was accomplished the moment Benjamin Bakewell offered to lend him the money for his passage. His second, permission to marry Lucy, he also achieved, but only in a manner of speaking. To the satisfaction of both parents, a correspondence developed between William Bakewell and Jean Audubon, who agreed their children could marry at some future date, but only when they were older and when John James was capable of supporting himself. This agreement, however, had hardly necessitated the long, costly trip to France.

Meanwhile, here was John James at Couëron with nothing to do, except one unimportant piece of business to conduct for William Bakewell. In the spring of 1805, he sat down and reported on it to his future father-in-law, using the best English he could command. "I am here in the snears of the eagle," he wrote. "he will pluck Me a little and then I Shall [an illegible word appears] on a Sheep [probably a ship] have good wind all the way and as Soon a land under My My feet My Compagnon of fortune Shall Carry Me Very Swiftly Toward you...." Even William Bakewell, who was thoroughly familiar with John James's spoken English, was puzzled by the note when he received it. Sending it on to a cousin in England, he commented: "I enclose you a short letter I lately recd. from Mr. Audubon who is at his Father's near Nantes. You must make it out as you can for I cannot exactly understand it.... His 'companion of fortune' is an ass of the Spanish kind which I desired him to procure for me for breeding mules. I do not understand his snares of the eagle but suppose it is that the government are wishing to put him in requisition for the army...."

Yet John James, for all the affection he expressed in his letter for the Bakewells, did not seem to be in the least hurry to return to Mill Grove and took what, in effect, was a long vacation at his father's expense. "In the very lap of comfort," he wrote later, "my time was happily spent; I went out shooting and hunting, drew every bird I procured, as well as many other objects of natural history and zoology." The drawings, some two hundred of them, he said "were very bad to be sure, but still they were of some assistance to me."

All the time John James was fishing, shooting and enjoying himself at Couëron, Lucy Bakewell was wrestling with the problems of running the household at Flatland Ford. The summer there was hot, dusty, and altogether unpleasant, and the tragedy of her mother's death hung over the family. William Bakewell, however cheerful he might seem to his neighbors, was still mourning his wife's death and passed the summer months selecting appropriate lines to be inscribed on her tombstone, a rather macabre activity considering that she had been dead for months. Elizabeth, Lucy's younger sister, had made a trip to New York to visit the Benjamin Bakewells, but no such relief was possible for Lucy. Too young to marry, she was not too young to assume many of the duties of a married woman; and since her mother's death she had not once left Flatland Ford, simply because she could not be spared. On her fell a grown woman's burden and, like women everywhere, she was having difficulty obtaining adequate help. "You wished to know how our servants went on," she wrote to a cousin in England. "The

Hollander is improved, but the Swiss whom we thought the best is become worse. I have much ado to make her milk the cows clean and I am often obliged to go with her. How people forget their former situations! When they came here they were thankful for linsey gowns and now though my Papa bought each of them a printed cotton, yet nothing would do but a white dimity and they have each, out of some money given them bought one." She was cheered, however, by the thought that John James would be back in the fall. He had promised her he would, and she had no reason to suspect he might not.

In Perkiomen Creek, as the summer wore on, the water flowed more slowly. At the cave, the phoebes raised a new brood. August faded into the haze of September; and in October the forerunners of the winter's winds blew through the valley. Meanwhile, the chances that John James could avoid conscription became less and less. On the coast of Spain, the navies of France and its allies were locked in the harbor of Cadiz, seeking some means of escape; and outside, the British fleet— with Nelson newly arrived to take command—hovered ready for battle. On October 21, in the light airs blowing off Cape Trafalgar, the ships engaged in action, and by the end of the day the naval power of France was broken. Less than two months later, the French armies under Napoleon faced the combined forces of Austria and Russia near the small town of Austerlitz. Believing Napoleon was attempting to retreat from his position, the opposing armies attacked, following a completely inadequate plan, and by the end of the day were utterly defeated. Either of these two battles by itself might have made peace possible. The combination, however, left France with a broken navy but a triumphant army, neither strong enough to force a peace nor weak enough to sue for one. In the effort to build up his forces, Napoleon began to rely more and more heavily on conscription, and it looked as though John James would inevitably be drafted. This, of course, was the last thing Jean Audubon wanted, so he began to develop a strategy to meet the crisis. At the time, it looked as though he were moving in opposite directions at once, trying to enlist his son in the armed forces of France on the one hand and, on the other, making plans for him to leave France forever. But in spite of the ap-

parent contradiction in his actions, the old captain knew precisely what he was doing.

His first step was to discuss matters with his friend François
Rozier. Rozier's son, Ferdinand, had returned that spring to
France after serving three years in the French Navy, and Rozier
too was anxious to get his boy out of the country. Jean Audubon suggested that the two fathers combine their interests.
Rozier had money and commercial connections which would
be useful; Jean Audubon had Mill Grove and also a sea captain's knowledge of passports and harbor officials. This could be
useful in helping the boys escape.

Agreed, said Rozier, so the next step was to bind the two
boys together in a sort of partnership. This was accomplished
by a document, signed on March 23, 1806, which was not so
much an agreement between equals as an effort by two fathers
to settle their sons' affairs. Some of the provisions were specific.
John James and Ferdinand were to go to Mill Grove on their
fathers' behalf, examine Dacosta's books, and decide if Dacosta's
plans for the future should be followed. In doing this, of course,
they represented only a one-half interest, the other half still
remaining with Dacosta. To help support the boys, the two fathers turned over to them any income or profits from Mill
Grove, which they were to divide equally. The other provisions
of the agreement were less specific. They were to share their
living expenses, look for business connections for François Rozier, and remain in the United States for at least six months.
Other than that, they could engage in any business they desired.
Less of a partnership than an effort by Jean Audubon and François Rozier to bind their two boys together, the agreement was
to hold for nine years.

This document was reinforced by a power of attorney, dated
April 4, 1806, which gave the boys full authority to deal with
Dacosta on behalf of their fathers, but it contained one important restriction: On every matter of consequence they were to
consult Miers Fisher, who was described as a mutual friend and
good adviser. Jean Audubon, with his usual thoroughness, was
trying to safeguard the boys from any mishaps.

Jean Audubon's next step was to protect John James from
Napoleon's army draft while he completed the rest of the neces-

sary arrangements, such as booking the boys' passage and obtaining their passports, none of it easy to do in war-torn France.
Paradoxically, he decided the safest place for John James was
in the French navy. There, the army recruiters could not touch
him, and yet Jean Audubon still exercised enough influence in
naval circles to secure his release when he wanted it. So back
to Rochefort went John James, took what he later described as
"a mockery of an examination," was enrolled as a midshipman,
and after a short cruise was discharged and permitted to return
to Couëron, where Jean Audubon had everything ready. He
had obtained passage for two on the American brig *Polly* and
excellent papers for John James. Somehow he had been able to
buy a Dutch passport for Ferdinand Rozier, even though the
boy "did not speak a word in that language"; and he had gathered a collection of gold coins, most of them probably supplied
by François Rozier, so John James and Ferdinand would have
a little ready cash in addition to the dubious profits they might
receive from Mill Grove.

The passengers on board the *Polly*, Captain Samis commanding, were in a holiday mood when the ship left Nantes on April
12, 1806. Most of them, like two members of the nobility and
a pair of fleeing monks whom Captain Samis had hidden below, were refugees; and if they could pass the final inspection at
Saint-Nazaire, farther down the river, they would have cleared
the last obstacle between themselves and freedom.

Jean Audubon must have gone down to the harbor to see
his son off, but as he stood among the milling crowd, his mood
contrasted strangely with the prevailing gaiety. He had bound
John James to the son of an able merchant for a period of nine
years, given him all the profits from Mill Grove, and turned
over to him the last gold coins he could spare. But he knew this
was the end; he had nothing more to give if this plan, like the
others, failed to work out. All his life he had done what he
could for his family, but his best had never seemed enough.
Now he stood at the water's edge, waved his farewell, turned toward the shore where the carriage was waiting, and rode back
down the lonely road to Couëron.

On board the *Polly*, neither John James nor Rozier gave
much thought to the old sea captain who had made this trip

possible for them. Instead, like the other passengers, they were waiting in suspense for the final check at Saint-Nazaire. When the *Polly* reached the port, hove to, and the official in charge climbed aboard, hardly anyone except an American Congressman who was on the ship could help wondering if this was the place at which their flight would be stopped. While they all stood by, the official, with French formality, checked the ship's papers given to him by Captain Samis. Everything was in order. He looked at the papers of the Congressman. No difficulty there, of course. He looked at the papers of the other passengers. Everything in order. He came to Ferdinand Rozier with his Dutch passport, obtained by Jean Audubon from heaven knows where. Everything in order. Then he looked at John James's papers and broke out with feeling. "My dear Mr. Audubon," he said, "I wish you joy; and would to God I had such papers; how thankful I should be to leave unhappy France under this same passport." Jean Audubon knew how to do things well.

As soon as the official had left and the *Polly* had reached the open sea, the passengers began behaving as though they were on a vacation cruise. The ship was well provided with pigs, sheep, coffee, wines, and other luxurious foods. Down in the hold, well hidden under the ballast, Captain Samis had an even more valuable cargo: a load of gold being shipped to America. Someone had thought to bring musical instruments aboard, and there was dancing. And for those who did not like dancing, there was gambling or, of course, shipboard romances.

Soon everyone was watching two other young Frenchmen pursuing a pretty girl from Virginia, each trying to find some opportunity for outdoing the other. As the ship was moving quickly under fair winds one day, a loose rope end struck the girl's bonnet and knocked it overboard. Ah! said one of the Frenchmen to himself, here is a chance to prove my love, and over the side he jumped. Ordering the helm thrown over hard, Captain Samis brought the brig into the wind, launched the ship's yawl, and rescued the young Frenchman, who reappeared on deck, dripping wet and clutching the bonnet. Stepping up to the girl, he bowed and handed it to her, while her rival glowered.

Early the next morning, before the passengers were up, shots were heard. Thinking they were being attacked by pirates, the crew and passengers tumbled out of their bunks and rushed up to the deck. There they found the young Frenchman who had jumped overboard lying dead, killed in a duel by his rival.

Except for this tragedy, the voyage went well until about a fortnight after leaving France, when the *Polly*, running before the wind under full sail, noticed another ship overtaking it to windward. When it came within about a half mile, it fired a shot across the *Polly*'s bow, but Captain Samis held his course. The stranger fired another shot and another, all the while closing in until it was in position to let go with a broadside. At this point, even Captain Samis realized he was caught. He ordered the helm over; and the *Polly*, its sails fluttering uselessly, hove into the wind. Immediately the stranger lowered a boat and sent out a boarding party of two officers and about a dozen seamen, while John James, dashing to his cabin, grabbed up the gold coins belonging to him and Rozier, wrapped them in some clothing and hid them under a cable in the bow. In a matter of minutes, the boarding party were climbing over the side, identified their ship as the British privateer *Rattlesnake*, and demanded to see Captain Samis's papers. These being in order, none of the passengers were molested, but the seamen were lined up in the usual manner and two of them were selected for impressment, while the Congressman futilely objected.

Then the boarding party quickly transferred the pigs, wines, and other fancy provisions from the *Polly* to the *Rattlesnake* and started to search for the treasure Captain Samis had hidden in the hold. Apparently they knew it was on board, for they searched for a whole night and day, even shifting the ballast, but failed to find it. Finally, in disgust, they gave up and returned to the *Rattlesnake*, which, under full sail, took off to look for another victim. John James waited until it was some distance off and certain not to return. Then he rushed forward and pushed aside the coils of cable hiding his cache of gold coins. Fortunately they were still there.

About thirty miles off Sandy Hook, a fishing boat hailed the *Polly* and warned Captain Samis that two British frigates were lying at the entrance to New York Harbor and stopping American ships. After his experience with the *Rattlesnake*, Captain

Samis was taking no more chances. Turning up the coast of Long Island, he entered the sound. Suddenly a gale struck. Once more John James felt the fury of an ocean storm and saw the men trying to shorten sail as they frantically grabbed at the ripping canvas. While they were working, the wind drove the *Polly* onto a sandbar. With a dull scraping sound, the hull scratched along the bottom; the forward motion of the ship stopped; it rested motionless, tipping slightly to one side. Fortunately the storm soon died, so the *Polly* was not broken up by the waves crashing against it. Then the tide rose and, as Captain Samis patiently waited, the water carried the boat free, its hull undamaged, so that they were able to continue on to New York, which they reached in the first week of May, 1806. "Mr. Audubon (Lucy's Beau)," Benjamin Bakewell wrote to a cousin, "arrived from France a few days ago to the great satisfaction of his and her friends, as from the difficulty of leaving France which all young men now find we were apprehensive he would be detained. He is a very agreeable young man, but volatile as almost all Frenchmen are."

From New York, the two partners hurried to Mill Grove, which John James had last seen when the ground was covered with snow and the Perkiomen Creek was locked with ice. He came back to it when the leaves of the cottonwoods shone green in the sun and the mayapples again covered the ground. In many respects, though, it was almost as though he never had been away. There was William Bakewell, as cheery and generous-minded as ever, with his new wife, Rebecca Smith, whom he had married in John James's absence. There was Lucy, still in love; Mrs. Thomas, still churning butter for the Philadelphia market; and William Thomas, doing his chores on the farm. Down near the river, the phoebes, some of them wearing white threads around their legs, were back at their nests. The lead mine was still there, too, and still not making money. And there, also, was Francis Dacosta.

Writing at a later date, John James greatly oversimplified the events that took place on his return to Mill Grove. "Mr. Dacosta," he said, "was at once dismissed from his charge." Actually nothing could have been further from the truth. As long as Dacosta owned one half of Mill Grove, the two partners might be able to buy him out, but they could not dismiss him. Their fathers knew this, so they merely instructed the boys to examine Dacosta's accounts, evaluate his plans for the future, and then decide whether they should go along with what he had in mind or try to sell their interest. The responsibility for doing this fell largely on Rozier, since he had by far the better business sense, and he quickly reduced the problem to its fundamentals. Either they had to form a company and sell shares to obtain more capital or take in another partner with greater financial resources than their own. Even then, as Rozier put it, the mine was nothing more than a lottery; it might make its owners' fortunes, or it might cost them their entire investment.

While they were studying the mine, Rozier and John James lived at Mill Grove, and John James quickly resumed his old mode of living, visiting the Bakewells, hunting, fishing, and wandering over the countryside. Yet all the while, he never forgot the birds. One of Lucy's younger brothers, William, was invited up to John James's room one day and said that on entering it, "I was astonished and delighted to find that it was turned into a museum. The walls were festooned with all sorts of birds' eggs, carefully blown out and strung on a thread. The chimneypiece was covered with stuffed squirrels, raccoons, and opossums; and the shelves around were likewise crowded with specimens, among which were fishes, frogs, snakes, lizards, and other reptiles. Besides these stuffed varieties, many paintings were arrayed upon the walls, chiefly of birds. He had great skill in stuffing and preserving animals of all sorts. He also had a trick of training dogs with great perfection, of which art his famous dog Zephyr was a wonderful example."

He then went on to describe his future brother-in-law in more personal terms. "He was an admirable marksman, an expert swimmer, a clever rider, possessed great activity, prodigious strength, and was notable for the elegance of his figure and the beauty of his features, and he aided nature by a careful attendance to his dress. Besides other accomplishments, he was musical, a good fencer, danced well, had some acquaintance with legerdemain tricks, worked in hair, and could plait willow-baskets." In short, he was the kind of man who would appeal to a younger brother and capture the heart of a girl like Lucy, living a comparatively secluded life in the Pennsylvania countryside. But not the kind of man to deal with Dacosta and the confused state of the mining operation. That had to be left up to Rozier.

As soon as Rozier had decided that Dacosta would never agree to forming a company, he suggested the businesslike alternative: to find a way of dissolving their relationship completely. The first step was to divide the property at Mill Grove into two separate parcels. This removed the complication of having Dacosta and Audubon each hold a one-half undivided interest. By terms of an agreement reached on September 5, Dacosta took one area of 113½ acres, which contained the buildings and the mine. Jean Audubon was to have another area of 171 acres. In addition, because of the difference in the values of the two properties, Dacosta was to owe Jean Audubon $800 with interest, payable in three years, and another $4,000, payable out of the products of the lead mine. It was not the best of arrangements, particularly the provision that the $4,000 was to be paid from the products of the mine; but, given the circumstances, it was certainly not a bad settlement.

Other details also remained to be settled, and Rozier plunged into these, too. He went over Dacosta's accounts, decided which items were chargeable to Jean Audubon and which were not, and chose arbitrators to settle any differences between the two men. He kept in touch with Benjamin Bakewell, too, and arranged to have him send several shipments of goods to François Rozier for sale in France.

He also began laying out plans for the future. Having secured the opinion of several farmers, he decided that the part of Mill Grove belonging to Jean Audubon should not be sold for less than $8,000. This meant renting the property until they could get their price. He and John James, meanwhile, would find jobs to augment their income so they could start trading on their own account. Reporting all this to François Rozier, he told his father not to worry about them. They were not being rash and were using the good advice offered them by people like Fisher and William Bakewell. When Jean Audubon heard the news, he must have sighed with relief. His choice of a partner for John James had been good.

During this period, John James reached an important personal decision. A few days after Rozier sent his report back to Nantes, John James appeared before the District Court at Philadelphia and filed a statement declaring his intention to become a naturalized citizen of the United States. From then on, he considered himself an American and no longer a Frenchman.

The next step was for the two partners to find the paying positions they needed. Rozier, who was even less fluent in English than John James, decided to stay in Philadelphia and work for a French importing firm. As for John James, in his characteristically naïve but appealing turn of phrase, he said, "Too young and too useless to be married . . . William Bakewell advised me to study the mercantile business; my father approved, and to insure this training under the best auspices I went to New York, where I entered as a clerk . . . for Benjamin Bakewell." So, in the fall of 1806, he said good-bye to Mill Grove and headed for the city—a young businessman in his own imagination, but far from it in fact.

He was now nearly twenty-one, in an era when twenty-one-year-olds often commanded ships or held other responsible positions, and without any preparation was about to enter the highly speculative business of importing and exporting at one of the riskiest of times. The British-French struggle was worsening. No sooner had he begun visiting the warehouses and piers on errands for Benjamin Bakewell than he must have heard the merchants and the sea captains discussing such topics as the *Essex* decision, whereby the British Admiralty Court prohibited the American practice of carrying French colonial goods to France; Fox's blockade, which closed the coast of Europe to neutral shipping; the Berlin Decree, by which Napoleon declared a blockade of the British Isles—all those measures and countermeasures which the two warring powers took in their effort to strangle each other.

Into this confused world of commerce and speculation John James plunged with all his enthusiasm and in January, 1807, sent one of his first business reports to François Rozier. Gravely, he thanked Rozier for a shipment of linen, which had arrived on consignment, for Rozier was obviously trying to help the two young partners by letting them have merchandise for sale on credit. Then he asked for a shipment of what he called "fashionable articles," saying these were in great demand in the United States, but without bothering to specify what they might be.

As he worked away at Benjamin Bakewell's office, trying to learn the fundamentals of this life into which he had plunged himself, winter closed in on New York. Ice formed on the Hudson River, and the winds, whistling through the ramshackle wharves along the East River, turned into a gale farther south and drove the French fleet into Chesapeake Bay, where they were blockaded by the British. In early spring, a boat's crew deserted from one of the British ships; and one of the seamen, a man named Jenkin Ratford, enlisted on the U.S.S. *Constitution,* an American frigate, thus laying the basis for an international crisis.

Seemingly unaware of what was happening in the world at large and the effects it might have on his business, John James continued to represent the partnership in New York and by April could report at least one favorable venture. In a letter to François Rozier, he acknowledged receipt of a cargo of wines and said that Ferdinand had already disposed of sixty cases in Philadelphia at a good profit. On the less optimistic side, he expressed concern about a shipment of indigo made on his behalf by Benjamin Bakewell. He was afraid, he said, that he and Ferdinand had paid too much for it. Looking back on those days later, he wrote that "the mercantile business did not suit me. The very first venture which I undertook was in indigo; it cost me several hundred pounds, the whole of which was lost." In spite of the profitable transaction in wine, the partnership was not doing well, for Ferdinand, too, was having problems; he had sent a shipment of hams to the West Indies and had lost four-fifths of his investment.

Such misfortunes did not result entirely from youthful mismanagement. Even without the hazards of the English-French conflict, international trade in those days was risky, for a firm doing business abroad had no way of establishing prices or demand in a foreign port with any degree of accuracy. When it made a shipment it had to rely entirely on its general knowledge of market conditions—these, of course, could change abruptly—on the trading skill of the captain carrying the cargo, and on the acumen and honesty of the firm with which it was doing business. For those who had the right touch, fortunes were to be made and made quickly, but the same conditions rendered it possible to lose money just as fast.

In spite of their difficulties, however, John James wrote François Rozier that they were seriously considering expanding their business and hoped to act on his suggestion that they set up a retail store of their own. As usual, John James looked forward to entering a new enterprise with pleasure, optimism, and over-simplification. "Goods that have been well selected, bought at reasonable prices, and shipped carefully are always sure of a good market," he commented ingenuously.

In the same letter he enclosed a note, written in English, to his father; and Jean Audubon, who knew the language well, must have shaken his head as he read such sentences as this: "Mr. L. Huron deed few days ago Received some wines on a/c of Mr. Rozier and his they prove goods and will bring a good profit!" Yet for all its misspellings, lack of punctuation and poor grammar, the note was filled with affection. John James was sending his father several packages of seeds and birds as well as enough turtle meat to make a soup for the household at Couëron. As for his own wants, he would like a lock of his father's hair and a miniature of his father dressed in his naval uniform.

Also included in the letter was this statement: "I am allways in Mr. Benjamin Bakewell's store where I work as much as I can and passes my days." But this was not the complete truth, because he was doing some part-time work, probably on an unpaid basis, for Dr. Samuel Latham Mitchill, one of the leading naturalists in New York. Dr. Mitchill, who had studied at the University of Edinburgh and traveled widely in Europe, was an outstanding physician, but his interests were far from being limited to medicine. He was an active politician, serving in the New York State Legislature and both Houses of Congress; a strong supporter of Robert Fulton's steamship; an adviser to President Jefferson on the Lewis and Clark expedition; and an outstanding scholar in botany, zoology, and geology.

Some people found him irritating because his knowledge was so overwhelming (Jefferson called him the "Congressional Dictionary" and John Randolph of Roanoke, "the stalking library"), but he was no snob. He was well liked by the fishermen of New York who called at his house regularly, carrying with them any unusual specimens they happened to find among their catches, and by the whaling captains who brought him odd discoveries they had stumbled upon during their long cruises.

The work John James did for Dr. Mitchill consisted mostly of mounting specimens and preparing skins, employment that led him into trouble with his neighbors, for the odor in his room became so bad they called in the constable. In spite of involving him with the law, this apprenticeship under Dr. Mitchill should have been an ideal experience, because few people in the United States were better equipped to help a young ornithologist. Dr. Mitchill knew every American of consequence in the field of science and, what was equally important to a young man just beginning his studies, knew the particular types of work that most urgently needed doing.

But the acquaintanceship between him and John James remained casual, in spite of their common interests. Undoubtedly several factors were at play. One was John James's own character. Benjamin Bakewell had described him as "volatile"; William Bakewell had doubted his capacity to make a good husband; Miers Fisher had failed to be impressed by his scientific interests and had practically washed his hands of him in all other respects as well. No one, with the exception of Lucy, took him seriously during this period of his life; and Dr. Mitchill probably felt as the others did, that this was not a young man who inspired confidence. Another possible factor was John James's obsession with his new career. He was convinced he was a businessman, and although he continued to draw birds while he was in New York, his real goal was becoming a merchant.

As he wrote François Rozier on May 6, what he most wanted was to open the retail store, and he had already worked out the necessary inventory, including music boxes that played lively tunes, wafers of sealing wax, and sixty dozen powder flasks, a rather miscellaneous assortment. A few weeks later he wrote François Rozier again. Buried among the routine items he mentioned appeared two ominous portents for the future. The partners had not yet been able to sell their share of Mill Grove and were therefore so short of cash that they could not start their business on the scale they would have desired. Pressing this point further, John James went so far as to acknowledge the partners' complete dependence on the credit extended to them by François Rozier, without which the partnership, for all practical purposes, would cease to exist. This situation, of course, imposed severe limitations on them, for they could neither buy for cash, which restricted their sources of goods, nor carry themselves over a period when prices dropped. The other danger signal contained in the letter was Audubon's reference to a shipment of Martinique coffee and sugar he had forwarded to Nantes. Apparently the partners were being lured into the high-profit, but exceedingly hazardous, business of transshipping between France and its colonies. This was no business for two inexperienced and undercapitalized partners to enter, particularly in view of the deteriorating relations between England and the United States.

Still angry over the desertion of his seamen, the commander of the British fleet in America issued orders that any naval vessel meeting the *Chesapeake* should stop the frigate and conduct a search. On June 21, 1807, the *Leopard,* bearing his orders, dropped anchor in the harbor at Lynnhaven, Virginia, at the mouth of Chesapeake Bay, the very day the *Chesapeake* moved down from Portsmouth to Hampton Roads, ready to leave on its cruise. The next day when the *Chesapeake* set sail, the *Leopard* drew alongside, fired one of its guns, and asked the *Chesapeake* to heave to and receive some dispatches. The boarding party, however, instead of carrying dispatches, brought with them descriptions of four deserters thought to be on the *Chesapeake.* Rightfully, the *Chesapeake's* captain refused to let the British search his ship, but he had made one vital mistake. Contrary to standing orders, he had failed to call his men to quarters on the approach of another ship. Therefore he was unprepared to fight, while the *Leopard* had its guns manned and ready. Three broadsides were fired by the *Leopard,* to which the *Chesapeake* was able to return only a single shot, fired by a desperate officer who dashed to the galley, picked up a live coal, and used it to set off the gun. Then the *Chesapeake* hauled down its flag, and the brief fight was over. Unfortunately, the boarding party discovered Jenkin Ratford and therefore could justify the search.

In the wake of the *Leopard's* attack, for which the British refused to apologize, American opinion reached a new pitch. Jefferson's attempts to settle the differences between the two countries by diplomacy came to nothing; and since he had no navy with which he could enforce American rights on the high seas, he turned to his only alternative—economic warfare. On July 2, he issued a proclamation which forbade English ships to enter American ports, cut off all communications between the vessels of both countries, prohibited Americans from supplying ships flying the British flag, and, at the same time, called a special session of Congress. In New York, Robert Fulton dropped work on his steamboat to concentrate on experiments with torpedoes and, to convince the navy his new weapon would be useful against the British, blew up a brig he had anchored in New York Harbor as a target.

In spite of these signs of forthcoming trouble, John James went right ahead with his plans to open a retail store. In a report to François Rozier on July 19, he explained that the partners intended making a trip down the Ohio River, for they had decided to locate in Kentucky, not in New York where they would have had the help of men like Benjamin Bakewell. On their trip, he said, they would do some trading and decide which town to settle in permanently. For such an undertaking they could not have chosen a more inauspicious time, with the *Leopard's* cannon shots still echoing. Furthermore, their scheme forced them to go into debt, for on August 4, in order to obtain the additional capital they needed, they gave Benjamin Bakewell their note for $3,647.29, payable within eight months.

A few days later, Robert Fulton took his steamboat out into the Hudson River. Its paddle wheels were not yet finished, but still it reached a speed of three miles an hour. In a letter Fulton told what had happened and gave his own plans for the future. He had beaten all the sloops that were sailing against the tide and could have gone even faster if he had raised his own sails. But he was not so interested in the success of steamboats on the Hudson. What he had proved to his own satisfaction was that they could operate on the Mississippi, where he thought they would be extremely profitable. Yes, the frontier was the place to make a fortune, not New York, not Philadelphia, not Boston, not any of the older cities along the seaboard. So thought Robert Fulton. So thought the thousands of emigrants, some rich, some poor, but all hopeful, who annually crossed the Alleghenies. And so, like everyone else, thought John James and Rozier.

Before leaving, they decided to pay one short, last visit to Mill Grove. Except for the mine at the front door, everything there looked unchanged since John James had first seen it that day he arrived with Miers Fisher—the farmhouse, the fields, the mill dam, the hemlock groves, the cave down by Perkiomen Creek; but for John James, it could never be the same. Vanished forever were the happy days when he could wander without a care through the woods or skate on the frozen surface of the stream. In part, they had been destroyed by the ruinous idea of reopening the mine, that venture he and Thomas had discussed so hopefully around the dinner table at night. But more responsible than the mine was the mere process of growing up. John James was a man now, with a man's love and a man's responsibilities, and could no longer take refuge in the illusionary world he had once created for himself on the farm.

So at the end of August, he said good-bye to Mill Grove and the Bakewells and went with Rozier to Philadelphia to catch the stage west. He was going to try to find in Kentucky what he had not found at the farm or at New York or at Couëron—the means of at last supporting Lucy.

CHAPTER V

1807 — 1808

T HE countryside slumbered in the dusty peace of late August as John James and Rozier rode along the Lancaster Pike toward the West and what they hoped would be their fortune. Hardly a bird could be seen from the fast-moving coach except for the crows, whose black silhouettes rose from the wheat fields. The other birds were hidden in the shadowy depths of the woods, resting and gathering strength for their fall migration. As the stage crossed a bridge, Rozier and John James would hear the rattle of hooves and wheels on the loose wooden planking and, looking out, see the stream drifting lazily among the rocks and shrunken pools, its springtime liveliness long since vanished in the August heat.

Swept away by enthusiasm over this new adventure, John James talked faster and faster with Rozier in French. Then, switching to English, he would chatter to the other passengers, who listened incredulously to his strange accent and misused words. What a fast trip they were making, he told them. The Lancaster Pike was certainly a marvel of engineering, one of the best roads in the country. Yes, he and his friend were partners in the firm of Audubon & Rozier. Yes, they were in the mercantile business. No, they had no office or store yet; they were going west to establish one. Yes, somewhere in Kentucky, probably on the Ohio River, for that was the place for enterprising young men like themselves. No, they had never been to Kentucky before, but everybody knew about Kentucky. In Kentucky, a man could make a fortune.

As he talked on about his plans, the coach raced through the Pennsylvania countryside, stopping every so often to pay the toll, or drawing up before a tavern where the passengers would

leap down, dash to the taproom, drink a quick glass of grog—
brandy, rum, or whiskey, mixed with a little water—rush out,
and climb back into the coach or take a seat on top. With a
crack of the driver's whip, the team would lurch forward and
off they would go, tearing down the road in what was then
considered a miracle of speed.

By four o'clock in the afternoon, they reached Lancaster, one
of the largest inland cities in the United States, had dinner,
and pressed on nine miles more to Big Chickers. There, weary
and stiff from their long ride, they stopped at a tavern recommended by the stagecoach company. After a light supper they
went upstairs to their room, which they shared with several
other guests—private rooms were almost unknown. Climbing
between the dirty sheets left by previous travelers, they lay for
a minute or two thinking of their day's experience, and fell
sound asleep.

The next morning they were up and impatiently waiting
when the stage drew up to the door at eight o'clock. As their
luggage was being strapped on, they resumed their seats. With
a rumbling of the wheels the coach started forward. Yesterday
Rozier had been in a good mood; today he was not. Eight
o'clock in the morning and no breakfast after a night in filthy
beds. As Rozier was rapidly learning, most American taverns
outside the major cities were disreputable places and grew
worse the farther west the traveler went. Then, as now, their
profits came largely from liquor, but the landlords operated
with less restraint. Drinks were served at all hours, and drunkenness encouraged; meals were offered only if the landlord was
not busy. When the stage was leaving, for example, he had too
much else to do to make breakfast for the passengers. If they
were hungry, they could purchase a meal farther down the road;
and what miserable meals they were, hardly worth eating unless a man was hungry. Generally, breakfast consisted of bad
tea or worse coffee and some small slices of fried ham. When
the landlord was especially hospitable, he might add some eggs
and a boiled fowl. Dinner was not much better, usually salt
beef and roast fowl. As for clean sheets, they were known only
on laundry day, whenever that occurred—once a week, once
every two weeks, or maybe once a month.

None of this was to Rozier's liking, and his temper was not improved by the condition of the road, which, compared to the Lancaster Pike, was rough and filled with potholes. After nine miles of bouncing, they stopped to add two more horses to the team in order to get up the steep grades that lay ahead. All this time Rozier's spirits were getting lower, but John James enjoyed every minute of it, his enormous physical exuberance and enthusiasm carrying him through every discomfort.

Soon the roads improved; and by the time they reached Harrisburg, Rozier had recovered his good humor and was able to enjoy the ferry ride across the Susquehanna. He felt even better when they arrived at Walnut Bottoms and stopped for the night at a tavern he considered excellent.

The next morning they paused for a brief rest at Chambersburg, where they purchased tickets for the remainder of the trip to Pittsburgh. At this point, they had reached the end of the regular stage line and were starting to follow the old military trace over which the British had marched and remarched so often during their attempts to hold the West from the French and Indians. Now the country changed character abruptly. The soil was poor, and the land was divided by the steep, thin ridges of the Alleghenies, which cut the communities off from each other. A town located in one valley might be only twenty miles away from a town located in another, but the distance between them could not be measured in miles on a map. They might as well have been a hundred or two hundred miles apart. Industry was nonexistent; and even farming was difficult, as help was almost impossible to hire. A man with several hundred acres often had to be content with cultivating merely six or seven, just enough for his own subsistence. If John James and Rozier had not known that farther west the land again became level and useful, they might have turned back. But everyone had heard about the mountains. And beyond the mountains lay the promised land of Kentucky.

As they approached the first ridge, the roads became so rough and steep that John James and Rozier decided it would be pleasanter to walk than to ride. Up they went, the coach behind them, circling around boulders, bouncing across ditches cut by the rains, skidding in sandy places, or miring down in the mud. For three and a half hours the horses pulled and strained, the passengers also pushing when the driver ordered them to, until they finally reached the top. In those three and a half hours they had gone only three miles. At the summit they paused for a short rest at another mountain tavern and then started down the other side. With relief, the two partners climbed back into the coach, glad of a chance to rest. As the coach struck one boulder, sheered past it and struck another, plunged through a ditch, spun through a mudhole and then hit another boulder, the bouncing and jostling inside the coach became so severe they decided it was again preferable to walk. All day long they traveled on the terrible road. That night they had covered only forty miles, and both partners, in spite of their youth, were exhausted.

For two more days the nerve-racking, bone-bruising journey went on, until they finally reached Bedford, Pennsylvania, where they could congratulate themselves the worst of the trip was over. Having made the trip over the Alleghenies, John James and Rozier were not surprised to learn that the people of Bedford found it more advantageous to send their flour to New Orleans and from there to the Antilles than to ship it back over the ridges they had just crossed to Philadelphia or Baltimore. With their backs to the mountains, the people of Bedford looked westward; and although they continued to trade with the East, their real interest was in the great region that had been opened up, once and for all, by the Louisiana Purchase.

The two partners were not yet at the edge of the wilderness, however. The countryside through which they rode after leaving Bedford seemed tamer and more cultivated than anything they had seen in the mountains, for the land was flatter and more accessible, farms and small towns more common, and the roads better. That night John James and Rozier stopped at Somerset, rose at four o'clock the next morning, and reached Greensburg by nightfall. The next day they arrived at Pittsburgh.

Like most travelers, John James and Rozier were at first somewhat offended by the city's dark and heavy appearance. Pittsburgh, even then, burned soft coal in enormous amounts. The hills were filled with it, and coal, delivered at a housewife's door, cost only six cents a bushel, whereas firewood cost two dollars a cord. But Rozier was quick to appreciate the commercial significance of the city's location. From the north came the Allegheny River, rising near Lake Erie and winding down from New York State. From the south flowed the Monongahela, which found its sources in Virginia. At Pittsburgh the two rivers joined to become the Ohio. The city stood at the juncture of three important transportation routes—the Allegheny and Monongahela rivers and the old military trace to the west— and at the beginning of a fourth: the waterway which led through the United States to the Gulf of Mexico in the south, the Rockies in the west, and the pine woods near the Canadian border on the north. Anyone from the northeast who moved westward found, like John James and Rozier, that the normal means of communication brought him to Pittsburgh, and from there he could go by water almost anywhere he wished.

Pittsburgh dominated the east-west trade, and for the two partners it was an important stopping point. They spent several days visiting the city's businessmen, principally the representatives of the commercial houses in Philadelphia and other eastern cities. The general practice of these mercantile firms was to purchase goods in the East, take them down the rivers, selling and trading as they went. At New Orleans they would dispose of the remainder of their original stock and the goods they had taken in barter, receiving in exchange either ready money or an equal value in cotton, indigo, or clayed sugar, which they sent by sea back to Philadelphia or Baltimore.

Because of this trade, shipbuilding had become an important industry in Pittsburgh and its environs. As John James and Rozier walked along the waterfront, either on the Monongahela or Allegheny River, they saw boats drawn up against the shore by the hundreds, strange-looking, clumsy crafts, operated by some of the hardest, toughest men the American frontier had ever produced. In order to proceed down the river, the two partners had to select the type of boat on which they would like to travel. As they soon discovered, the choice was wide.

Sometimes what might be classed as a boat was nothing more than a raft of lumber, loaded with shingles and lathes and often covering an acre of water. A family moving westward would buy such a raft, float on it to their destination, and then sell the lumber to cover the costs of their trip. At the other extreme were large sailing ships, destined eventually for ocean use. In 1803, for example, a 170-ton brig was built on the Allegheny, moved down the river, picked up a load of cotton and, after leaving New Orleans, sailed to Liverpool.

Of greatest interest to John James and Rozier were the flatboats and keelboats, for these were the ones most commonly used for commerce on the rivers. The keelboats, pointed at each end and generally forty to eighty feet long, were manned by a crew of four to twelve tough frontiersmen, many of them former trappers and Indian fighters, under the command of a captain who was often called a "patroon." To obtain a better view of the water ahead, he either stood on the roof of the cabin or took up his position on an upended log placed at the stern. From there he called out his orders and worked the long steering oar.

Sometimes the keelboat merely drifted with the current. Sometimes the men rowed or hoisted their single sail and let the wind push them along. Sometimes when they were advancing upstream, they walked along the shore, dragging the boat behind them with ropes, or used winches which they attached to trees. As there were no towpaths, the men had to force their way through the underbrush lining the banks. Occasionally they would have to walk at the top of a cliff while they pulled on the lines attached to the boat in the valley far below. Usually they stayed on board and, if they could not row, pushed the boat with long poles. It was hard, backbreaking work that attracted only the rough-and-tumble members of the frontier society.

Even more common than the keelboats were the flatboats. These ranged from twenty to a hundred feet in length and twelve to twenty feet in width. Although the bow was raked, they were square at both ends and designed for downstream traffic only. Once they reached their destination, they were either broken up and sold for their lumber or left to rot along the shore. They, too, were operated and steered by oars; and it was on a boat of this type that Rozier and John James took passage.

After placing their luggage in the cramped cabin they stood
on deck as the flatboat, loaded with passengers as well as supplies for the river communities, slipped past the point of Pittsburgh between the two sandbars created by the Allegheny and
Monongahela rivers, and into the Ohio running between the
high hills rising from either side of the riverbed. Soon the boat
approached Hamilton's Island, keeping close to the right-hand
shore to miss one bar and swinging quickly in the opposite
direction to miss another. Avoiding the rocks that gave the
town of McKee's Rocks its name, it moved on toward Irwin's
Island, twisted to one side to miss the long sandbar that led
from one end of the island toward the right-hand shore, then
swerved quickly to miss another rock, and turned back toward
the island to avoid the ripples—rough water caused by the river's breaking over a bar. Mile after weary mile, day after weary
day, in this tortuous manner, the flatboat continued down the
river.

The country through which it passed was in every respect
magnificent, the river flowing through the deep cuts in the
surrounding hills and the shores covered with heavy forests,
stands of trees unbroken except where some settler had made a
clearing or a small town had sprung up. Yet neither John James
nor Rozier found the trip enjoyable. Having been unable to
obtain space in the cabin, they slept at night huddled in their
coats on bare pine boards on deck. Frequently the flatboat
grounded on a sandbar. Then everyone, including the paying
passengers, was ordered into the water to push and heave in an
effort to free it. If this technique was not effective, the crew
and passengers would try to lever the boat off the sandbar or
dig a channel down which it could be floated to deeper water.
When all else failed, someone would go in search of a nearby
farmer and employ him to use his team of horses to get the
boat off the sand.

But this was not the worst of their problems, for the river
was filled with many hazards far more dangerous than the bars.
Uncharted rocks lay across its channel in clusters. Often, when
the river undercut some bank, tons of dirt and trees would be
flung into the water. These sometimes collected in a large
mass, forming an impassable obstacle. (One on the Red River

grew to 153 miles in length and became so firm a man could cross it on horseback.) At other times a single tree would become embedded root down in the riverbed with the sharp, broken point of the trunk aimed directly at the hull of any approaching boat. A boat, driven against such snags by the force of the current or by the oarsmen, could be pierced and sunk.

The strain of the journey on John James and Rozier was increased by their lack of confidence in the captain, who, they thought, managed the boat incompetently and was also disagreeable and ungentlemanly. What they did not realize at the time was that the captains and other boatmen were for the most part the roughest products of a rough frontier. They drank heavily; when the work was hard, they were entitled to one drink every hour. Their favorite sport was "blackguarding," which consisted simply of swearing at the crews of other boats and also at people on the shore, although sometimes the straight cursing was punctuated with flashes of true wit and humor. They fought frequently and fiercely, sometimes with guns and knives, sometimes with "devil's claws"—metal hooks attached to their hands and used to disfigure their opponents' faces— and sometimes in one of the two styles they called "fair," by which they meant a fistfight, or "rough and tumble," in which they kicked, gouged or bit. Often these fights were not the result of a quarrel but merely an exhibition of strength, a friendly test to prove which of the two men was the better. But in spite of the many crudities and dangers of flatboat life, it was not all bleak. The same boisterous spirits that drove the boatmen into senseless fights also gave them the capacity to enjoy themselves. Card games, storytelling and singing were favorite amusements; and many times the passengers went hunting without leaving their boats. Ducks and geese were found on the river, turkeys and partridges along the shores, and bears and deer at the water's edge or swimming from bank to bank. Certainly, John James did not miss the opportunity to exhibit his marksmanship to men who placed a high value on this skill.

Day after day slipped by. In stretches of clear water the passengers and crew relaxed, for only an occasional sweep of the oars was necessary to straighten the boat on its course and keep it in the channel. At other times they pulled hard as they veered

suddenly to avoid a snag, swung the boat around to miss a
sandbar, or heard a dull thud as the hull struck a shoal. Around
them the woods were taking on the sharp, bright colors of fall,
and overhead the birds were flying southward, vast numbers of
them fleeing before the encroaching cold.

Past places with names like Big Sandy Creek and Letart's
Rapids the flatboat made its way, past Vanceville, Stout's Run,
Massey's Island, and the village of Manchester, until it came to
Maysville, sometimes called Limestone, Kentucky. Here John
James and Rozier, probably with feelings of relief, disembarked,
for they had reached the general area where they intended to
set up their business. Traveling overland, they visited Lexington, Frankfort, Paris, and Danville, and came at last to Louisville, where they went immediately to the Indian Queen, one
of the most famous inns on the river.

The morning after their arrival they were up when the first
breakfast bell rang at seven-thirty, washed with the rest of the
male boarders in the courtyard at the back of the hotel and
went into the dining room at eight, when the second bell
sounded. At the Indian Queen, the serving of meals was simple. As soon as the last boarder appeared, the doors were locked;
a boy walked from table to table and took down the names of
the guests while they helped themselves, so a charge for the
meal could be added to their bills. After breakfast, they walked
into the lounge and the taproom, where the informality was
carried a step further. Here stood an open bottle of whiskey.
Anyone who wanted a drink simply stepped up, filled his glass
for ten cents and, if he cared to, picked up the dipper hanging
nearby and added a little water from the open barrel standing
in the room. Since the price was the same regardless of the
quantity, most of the guests took generous amounts, and many
of them spent the entire day drinking while they sat in the
lounge and exchanged news with each other. The Indian Queen
was their club, their newspaper, and, for some, their office.

After the usual pleasantries with the other guests, John James
and Rozier set out to explore the town. Situated on a high
bluff overlooking the river, Louisville was famous for its fine
site. The view from the city extended across the river to the
hills of Silver Creek some five miles away and, two miles below,

to Clarksville. Downriver from the town lay the Falls of the
Ohio, where for a distance of two miles the water boiled in
a series of rapids as it ran across the limestone ledge that extended from one side to the other. When the river was at
flood, flatboats and keelboats could descend without difficulty,
although sometimes rushing forward at speeds up to thirteen
miles an hour. In low water, wise captains took on one of the
licensed pilots from Louisville, who were adept at maneuvering
the boats through the three possible channels. Because the falls
formed a natural break in the navigation of the river, Louisville was a center of considerable commercial importance.

Louisville's advantages were apparent to Rozier, and he and
John James decided this was the right location for their business. Next they had to find a suitable building, fill it with their
slender stock, and wait for the first customers to appear. To be
successful, they needed to carry a wide variety of goods. As one
contemporary writer, describing the typical frontier store, said,
"These storekeepers are obliged to keep every article which it
is possible the farmer and manufacturer may want. Each of
their shops exhibits a complete medley; a magazine where are
to be had both a needle and an anchor, a tin pot and a large
copper boiler, a child's whistle and a pianoforte, a ring dial and
a clock, a skein of thread and trimmings of lace, a check frock
and a muslin gown, a frieze coat and a superfine cloth, a glass
of whiskey and a barrel of brandy, a gill of vinegar and hogs-
head of Madeira wine."

The transactions were often complicated. As the storekeeper's customers grew more prosperous, their products became
greater in value than their purchases. This left them with a
credit balance at the store, since they had no other market.
Sometimes they used up this credit, particularly if it was small,
in unnecessary purchases. Otherwise, they usually asked for and
received either land or cash. "Thus," the same writer said, "the
great landowners ultimately absorb all the hard money; and as
they principally reside in the large towns in the Atlantic States,
the money finds its way back to those, and leaves many places
here without a single dollar. This is productive of distressing
incidents to small farmers who supply the markets with provisions; for whatever they have to sell, whether trivial or im-

portant, they receive in return nothing but an order on a store for the value in goods; and as the wants of such persons are few, they seldom know what articles to take. The storekeepers turn this circumstance to advantage, and frequently force on the customer a thing for which he has no use; or, what is worse, when the order is trifling, tell him to sit down at the door and drink the amount if he chooses. As this is often complied with, a market day is mostly a scene of drunkenness and contention, fraud, cunning, and duplicity."

This was the business John James and Rozier intended to enter. The profits were high—sometimes the markup was 300 percent—but the dangers and risks were also great. A merchant required capital, not only to stock his store with the wide variety of goods demanded by his customers, but also to carry him over the long periods before he could turn his receipts into cash by selling them downriver. He also needed an extraordinary amount of shrewdness to survive in this barter economy and make the best of the bargains offered him. Above all, he had to have an instinct for long-range speculation. This was something John James did not possess; and even Rozier, for all his commercial leanings, was not yet sufficiently experienced to meet the financial crisis toward which Jefferson's international policy was leading the United States.

Jefferson had begun to press the British hard in his negotiations over the *Chesapeake* affair, so hard in fact that, by insisting they abandon impressment, he threatened their national security and destroyed the conciliatory attitude they had at first adopted. Meanwhile the French, in an effort to retaliate against the British blockade, began to take more aggressive measures against American ships dealing with the English, hoping to cut Great Britain off from this source of supplies.

When all Jefferson's diplomatic efforts failed, he intensified his strategy of economic warfare. On December 18, 1807, the Senate heard a presidential message, which had been approved by the Cabinet, requesting the passage of a law prohibiting American merchant vessels from setting sail for any foreign port and permitting foreign vessels to leave the United States only in ballast. On December 22, Jefferson's Embargo Act was signed and became effective.

Within weeks its effects were felt, not by the warring powers
but by the United States itself. The shipbuilding industry was
ruined. So were many of the men who owned and sailed the
ships, the merchants who engaged in international trade, and
the manufacturers who made articles for export. Kindly Benjamin Bakewell, who had so readily befriended John James,
was one of those who found himself in serious trouble. For
some while, largely through his connection with François Rozier, he had been engaged in the highly profitable French trade.
At the time of the passage of the Embargo Act, he had just received on his ship the *Clyde* a cargo of French wines which he
had intended to resell in the French West Indies, whose ports
were now closed to him. After an unsuccessful attempt to dispose of the wines in New York—they did not suit New York's
taste—he decided to ship them to New Orleans, sending the
Clyde south with Lucy's brother Thomas on board as his agent.
In New Orleans Thomas, in a businesslike way, set about un-
loading the cargo, rented a store, and established himself as a
wine merchant on his uncle's behalf. But this was not Benjamin
Bakewell's only poor investment, and in New York his creditors
began to close in on him. One of them, learning about the
presence of the *Clyde* and its cargo in New Orleans, brought
legal action, and the sheriff attached both the ship and the
wines. "The situation," Thomas Bakewell wrote later, "was
very embarrassing to an inexperienced young man of scarce
twenty years of age." For the Bakewell family, who had never
known poverty, the change was startling. Never before had they
considered the possibility that their belongings might be seized
like any common debtor's or that the man whom John James
had described as a "wealthy merchant" could be reduced to
bankruptcy. Fortunately, Benjamin Bakewell had always had a
capacity for making friends, and one of them, a merchant
named William Kenner, came to the rescue. Taking Thomas in
charge, he helped him file a countersuit and thus regain control
of the *Clyde* and its cargo. In this way the ship was saved, but
its value was not enough to cover Benjamin Bakewell's other
liabilities. The debt due him from Audubon & Rozier was
therefore no longer a family matter; it was the asset of a bank-

rupt. Regardless of Benjamin Bakewell's personal desires, its eventual collection was a responsibility he owed his creditors.

Paying no heed to the financial crisis that was developing around him, John James started back to Flatland Ford. He could hardly argue he was well established in his new business or that he was in a position to support a young wife. But he was determined this time to press his suit, not with Lucy, who needed no urging, but with her family.

So in the spring of 1808, he was at Flatland Ford again, charming and gay as he always was with people he liked, enjoying Lucy's company, making up to Lucy's stepmother, Rebecca, who was not in the least impressed by this volatile young man with the terrible accent, hunting and fishing with Lucy's brothers, but concentrating most of his effort on William Bakewell.

It had been a long while since the boy and the older man had met in the woods on that winter's day when they were both hunting for grouse; and during that time William Bakewell had come to like, even if he may not have respected, John James. Certainly he saw there was no hope of ever changing Lucy's wishes. Since the moment she had pledged herself in the phoebes' cave, her affection had never altered. William Bakewell bowed to the inevitable and gave his consent.

On April 5, 1808, in the parlor of Flatland Ford where he had seen her first, "snugly seated at her work by the fire," John James—just three weeks before his twenty-third birthday—stood beside Lucy Bakewell, repeating after the minister the centuries-old oath of eternal fidelity. At the conclusion of the short ceremony, the family remained for a brief moment in silence. John James and Lucy looked at each other; their dream, after all these years, had come true. The younger brothers and sisters, impressed by the solemnity, were quiet. Rebecca Bakewell, still somewhat disapproving, nevertheless smiled. William Bakewell smiled, too, but said nothing. Of all the people in the room, including John James, he knew the most about the affairs of Audubon & Rozier.

"For better for worse, for richer for poorer." So ran the words. Which, he asked himself, would it be?

CHAPTER VI

1808 — 1810

Aт four o'clock in the morning, while the city slept in darkness and the buildings were mere shadows against the sky, the westbound stage departed from Philadelphia, Lucy and John James started down the Lancaster Pike on the long journey to Kentucky. As dawn approached, the countryside began to take form again through the windows of the stage, and they could see the fields and woods and carefully tended farms emerging from the blackness. Stopping only to pay tolls, change horses, and permit the passengers to alight briefly at the many taverns, the stage dashed through eastern Pennsylvania and past Lancaster, putting a greater and greater distance between Lucy and her family. At seven o'clock that evening, Lucy and John James finally stopped for the night, probably, since the choice was not wide, at the same dirty tavern where he and Rozier had stayed before. For a girl of Lucy's upbringing, it was not an ideal honeymoon.

Every day, stormy weather or clear, the newly wed couple spent fifteen hours in travel, bouncing on the stagecoach seat, but never, after leaving the Lancaster Pike, making more than thirty or forty miles. On the third day they reached the mountains, those sharp-faced ridges that every traveler disliked, where both the country and the people were wilder than anything Lucy had ever seen before. "The great stones beneath the wheels make the stage rock about most dreadfully," she said, but since it rained almost the entire time, she could not get out and walk when the riding became unbearable. Once the skidding, lurching coach tipped over with a crash, the frightened horses dragging it on its side until the driver quieted them. Then he and the passengers who were walking at the time opened the

doors and helped the other passengers, including Lucy, to climb
out. Pushing and pulling and heaving, they finally righted the
heavy stage. Then they untangled the harness, hitched up the
horses again and were on their way. After days of this sort of
travel, Lucy and John James, weary and tired, finally reached
Pittsburgh.

Although the couple stayed in the city for twelve days, Lucy's
eyes were closed to the magnificence of its situation between the
Monongahela and the Allegheny. Her only impression of the
city was disagreeable. "High mountains on all sides environ
Pittsburgh," she wrote to a cousin, "and a thick fog is almost
constantly over the town, which is rendered still more disagreeable by the dust from a dirty sort of coal that is universally
burnt. Coal is found at the surface of the earth in the neighborhood of this place, which is really the blackest-looking place I
ever saw."

At Pittsburgh, Audubon found passage for his bride and
himself on a flatboat, which Lucy described in the same letter
as a "large square or rather oblong boat; but perfectly flat on
all sides; and just high enough to admit a person walking upright. There are no sails made use of owing to the many turns
in the river which brings the wind from every quarter in the
course of an hour or two," and she noted, with her housewife's
interest in such matters, that "beer, bread and hams were bought
at Pittsburgh, but poultry, eggs, and milk can always be had
from the farm houses on the banks."

Although once the wind blew so hard and the water became
so rough that some of the passengers were seasick, the journey
on the whole went smoothly. Most of the time the weather was
clear, so, instead of tying up at night, they were able to keep
going and make the trip much shorter. To Lucy's disappointment, John James had failed to bring his drawing materials
along with him, so he could not sketch some of the scenes they
passed. On the other hand, she did not think either the river
or the surrounding countryside particularly beautiful. "There
are not," she wrote, "many extensive prospects on the river, as
the shores are in general bound by high rocks covered with
wood." Altogether, Lucy's first impressions of the West were not
favorable.

Down the river they drifted toward their new life, Lucy somewhat discouraged by the wildness of the country, John James enthusiastically pointing out each sight as they passed by. There was Maysville, where he and Rozier had landed on their first trip. There was the pleasant town of Augusta, Crawfish and Deer creeks, the Licking River and Cincinnati, the Great Miami River and Lawrenceburgh, Big Bone Lick, one of the most important fossil deposits in the United States, Port Williams and Westport. Finally, after what must have seemed ages to Lucy, there was her new home, Louisville.

Taking her by the hand, John James helped her ashore, and together they walked to the Indian Queen, where he introduced her proudly to the proprietor and to the guests gathered in the lounge. Yes, this was Mrs. Audubon, the bride he had gone east to fetch; and the boarders, embarrassed by having a woman in their midst, because women were almost unknown at the tavern, bowed sheepishly and wished their boots were cleaner and that somebody had thought to close the door to the taproom so the whiskey bottle would not be so obvious.

As John James had not found a house for them—houses were difficult to find in the frontier towns—the proprietor of the Indian Queen offered them accommodations where, as Lucy said, she and John James could be as "private as we please." On the whole, she thought the town "a very pleasantly situated place," but went on to add that, contrary to the general impression, she thought "the country round is rather flat."

Audubon, on the other hand, with his usual enthusiasm, was enraptured by the town. "The prospect from the town is such that it would please even the eye of a Swiss," he wrote later. "It extends along the river for seven or eight miles, and is bounded on the opposite side by a fine range of low mountains, known by the name of Silver Hills. The rumbling sound of the waters as they tumble over the rock-paved bed of the rapids is at all times soothing to the ear. Fish and game are abundant. But, above all, the generous hospitality of the inhabitants, and the urbanity of their manners, had induced me to fix upon it as a place of residence."

Describing their arrival in glowing terms, he went on, "No sooner had we landed, and made known our intention of re-

maining, than we were introduced to the principal inhabitants
of the place, and its vicinity . . . and could not but see, from
their unremitting kindness, that the Virginian spirit of hospitality displayed itself in all the words and actions of our
newly formed friends. . . . The matrons acted like mothers to
my wife, the daughters proved agreeable associates, and the
husbands and sons were friends and companions to me." That
was not quite how Lucy saw it. After three weeks of living in
Louisville and still with no home of her own, she wrote a relative, "I am sorry there is no library here or book store of any
kind; for I have very few of my own, and as Mr. Audubon is
constantly at the store I should enjoy a book very much whilst
alone."

Whatever John James may have told her, Rozier could have
explained that her husband's absences were not occasioned by
his work. Even with his own business and a wife to support, he
was finding it as difficult to concentrate on a job as he had at
Mill Grove. Instead of standing behind the counter, he was
more likely to be off visiting his new friends—Nicholas Berthoud, or the Tascarons, who operated a shipbuilding business
at Shippingport, just below the Falls of the Ohio, or Dr. W. C.
Galt, who was not only a physician but also a capable botanist,
or the venerable Indian fighter, General George Rogers Clark.
An able military commander during the warfare of 1778 and
1779, when the British incited the Indians to attack the Ohio
settlements, Clark was now little more than a discredited drunk-
ard, lazy and shiftless. Around Louisville where he was well
known, people accepted him for what he had done in the past
although they did not respect what he was in the present. Yet
John James, always impressed by adventure or even the shadow
of adventure, soon became one of his closest friends and often
visited Clark's holdings across the river from Louisville, where
he watched the ospreys nesting in the tops of the trees that
overhung the river.

Later he wrote about those birds but never with the enthusiasm with which he described his social life at Louisville.
No matter what the occasion, he was there, happy and gay, led
the dances, played his fiddle, flirted with the ladies, and was
popular with the men. On Independence Day, when all Louis-

ville gathered at Beargrass Creek, which formed the town's harbor, he was there, too. Independence was not something that had been handed down to the people of those times; they had won it for themselves. Many men remembered serving under General Washington, and many women remembered watching them march off to serve. Therefore they celebrated the day with particular festivity. At Beargrass Creek the underbrush had been cut down, and soon the wagons drew up with their loads of food. While some of the men set out the provisions, others loaded the wooden cannon bound with iron hoops, cramming it with homemade powder. When everything was ready, they shot the cannon, and its echoes reverberated along the banks of the Ohio. Then the orator chosen for the day delivered his speech, the fifes and drums played *Yankee Doodle,* and the audience cheered.

After that, they sat down to lunch, during which one man after another rose to propose a toast to his native land. Rozier may have sat quietly to one side, but John James certainly did not. With his new patriotism—he was going to be a citizen, wasn't he?—he undoubtedly called for silence as often as anyone and, in his thick French accent, poured out his sentiments about Kentucky and America.

Lunch over, the women withdrew, and the men settled down to a little serious drinking. This took only a short time, for the men of Kentucky knew how to drink fast. Then the dancing started, and John James always liked dancing. Certainly he had love only for Lucy, but he was not above flirting with the others. As he had said, women always held great power over him, and here they were, the finest-looking women in Louisville and therefore, many men would have claimed, the finest-looking women in the United States. One after another, John James led them out and charmed them with his good looks and his gay manner. Yes, he told Lucy, as he took her home to the Indian Queen that evening, it had been a good occasion, very gay; but Lucy must have wondered whether she had left the comfort of Flatland Ford just for this. Married life with John James was not quite what she had expected it to be.

Nor did John James take time off merely for holidays or visits to his friends. He was an expert marksman—Thomas could attest to that after picking up his hat from the ice of Perkiomen Creek—and John James liked to participate in the many shooting contests that were held. Often he would assemble with his friends "to drive a nail." They would set up a target and in the center place a nail, which they would hammer in to about two-thirds of its length. Stepping back forty paces, they would then attempt to hit the nail on the head. Sometimes they missed it completely, sometimes merely bent it, but at least one time out of three they hit it squarely and drove it into the wood.

On other occasions, they would try to snuff a candle with a rifle ball. Going out at night, they would place a candle on a stump and, at a distance of fifty yards, attempt to snuff it without either putting it out or damaging the candle itself. At least once, John James saw a rifleman accomplish this feat three times in seven shots.

When he was not shooting at targets, he might leave Lucy to spend the night alone at the Indian Queen, while he stayed at some lonely cabin whose owner had proposed they go raccoon hunting. Describing one such hunt, John James told how they set off right after dark, accompanied by the farmer's sons and his laborer, Toby, with a pack of dogs running ahead of them. One or two members of the party carried torches whose light flickered against the trunks of the enormous beech trees of the surrounding forest. In his impetuous haste to catch up with the dogs, John James stumbled and somehow jammed his foot between the roots of two trees, while at the same time he tangled his neck in the limb of a sapling. Wrenching both his ankle and his back, he came to an abrupt halt; and, as he said, "There I stood perfectly shackled." Amid great laughter—and he was the first to see the joke—the farmer and Toby came to his rescue, eventually cutting him free with an ax.

By then, the boys had caught up with the dogs, which had cornered the coon in a small pool of water. Audubon and the farmer quickly joined them and stood there, holding the glaring torch and watching as the dogs closed in. "One seized him by the rump," Audubon wrote, "but was soon forced to let go; another stuck to his side, but was soon taking a better directed bite of his muzzle than another dog had done of his tail, Coon made him yelp; and pitiful were the cries of the

luckless Tyke. The raccoon would not let go, but in the meantime the other dogs seized him fast, and worried him to death,
yet to the last he held by his antagonist's snout. Knocked on
the head by an axe, he lay gasping his last breath, and the
heaving of his chest was painful to see. The hunters stood gazing at him in the pool, while all around was by the flare of the
torch rendered trebly dark and dismal. It was a good scene for
a skillful painter.

"We now had two coons, whose furs were worth two quarters
of a dollar, and whose bodies which I must not forget, as Toby
informed me, were worth two more. 'What now?' I asked. 'What
now?' quoth the father; 'why, go after more, to be sure.'" So
they did, the dogs ahead, the hunters behind. All night long
they hunted, the moon rising and casting weird shadows among
the trees, the lights from the torches wavering against the trunks,
the dogs baying. Once they chopped down a tree to capture a
whole family of coons, shooting one and killing the others with
axes and clubs, because, as John James said, "a shot in those
days was too valuable to be spent when it could be saved." This
was the life, vigorous and gay, better than Couëron or New
York, better even than Mill Grove at its best. And while John
James hunted and fished, Lucy lamented the lack of a home
and Benjamin Bakewell set about the long and difficult task of
rebuilding his fortune.

In spite of Benjamin Bakewell's financial troubles, so many
people still respected him that two of his creditors, Thomas and
Arthur Kinder, set themselves up as his friends and counselors.
They gave Thomas Bakewell a job, thus taking the young clerk
off his uncle's hands, and began looking for a company that
Benjamin Bakewell might run. Their search brought them to
Pittsburgh, where they purchased a small flint glass company
for Benjamin Bakewell to operate. The firm quickly prospered
under his capable management, and he was soon a relatively
wealthy man again.

All this while, John James continued his gay life in Louisville. The cold came and went; the spring sent new floods of
water down the Ohio, making navigation on the river easier
for the boatmen. "We had by this time," John James wrote,
"formed the acquaintance of many persons in and about Louis-

ville; the country was settled by planters and farmers of the most benevolent and hospitable nature; and my young wife, who possessed talents far above par, was regarded as a gem, and received by them all with the greatest pleasure. All the sportsmen and hunters were fond of me, and I became their companion; my fondness for fine horses was kept up, and I had as good as the country—and the country was Kentucky—could afford. . . . The simplicity of those days I cannot describe; man was man, and each, one to another, a brother."

There was considerable excitement around the Indian Queen that spring, for all the men, boarders and transients, knew Lucy was expecting a child. How could she keep it from them when she appeared for meals or walked around the grounds? Yet with the delicacy that often seems to be a trait of rough frontiersmen, they never, of course, mentioned it to her, merely saying an anxious word now and then to John James, drawing him aside as he passed through the lounge and quietly asking him how things were coming. Finally, on June 12, 1809, the suspense ended. A boy was born to the Audubons, and John James announced to the visitors in the lounge that his name was Victor Gifford. Undoubtedly the bottle was emptied often that day and the proprietor collected many dimes.

For the next month John James was content to stay in Louisville to be near his wife and new baby, and then in the middle of July started preparations for one of his many business trips east. Every so often one of the partners had to go to Philadelphia and Pittsburgh to talk with the firms supplying them with goods, and John James, because he liked the trips, was the one who usually went. On this journey, instead of going by keelboat as he had before, he rode a horse which Rozier had chosen for him and once was able to make fifty-two miles in one day, and almost always forty to forty-five. He stopped at Pittsburgh, dealt with some of the business firms there, saw Benjamin Bakewell, and then pressed on to Flatland Ford, which he reached in six days. There he discussed business with William Bakewell, who had taken it upon himself to act as agent for Audubon & Rozier, hoping to build up connections for the firm in the East. His work finished, John James set out for the West again. Although the purpose of such trips was to advance the

firm's interest, he often was careless with the property belonging to him and Rozier, and later admitted, "Were I to tell you
that once, when traveling, and driving with several horses before laden with goods and dollars, I lost sight of the pack-saddles,
and the cash they bore, to watch the motions of a warbler, I
should only repeat occurrences that happened a hundred times
and more in those days." Yet for all his cavalier attitude toward
his firm, John James was seriously interested in making money.
He had no ambition to become either an ornithologist or an
artist. What he wanted to be was a successful merchant, a man
of wealth. Yet he would not work at it.

Even the arrival of his young son, Victor, did not cause him
to change his ways. Always charming to those he liked, always
loving to Lucy, always sincere in everything he did, he still
failed to face reality. At Mill Grove, which he had never owned,
he had fancied himself the young, but wealthy, master of the
estate. At Louisville, without working hard, he saw himself
as the young, but successful, businessman. Nothing, not even
Lucy's occasional remonstrances and complaints, seemed able to
penetrate the illusions with which he had surrounded himself.

Yet he did not entirely neglect the store. At the insistence
of Rozier, who was weary of trying to manage the firm by himself, John James took his place from time to time behind the
counter, and he was there in the middle of March, 1810, when
the door opened and a strange man entered. "How well do I
remember him," John James wrote, "as he walked up to me!
His long, rather hooked nose, the keenness of his eyes, and his
prominent cheek bones, stamped his countenance with a peculiar character. His dress, too, was of a kind not usually seen in
that part of the country,—a short coat, trousers, and a waistcoat
of gray cloth. His stature was not above middle size. He had
two volumes under his arm, and as he approached the table at
which I was working, I thought I discovered something like astonishment in his countenance." On coming closer, the stranger,
instead of ordering goods like an ordinary customer, placed his
two volumes on the counter, and introduced himself as Alexander Wilson, author of the newly published *American Ornithology*. He had arrived by skiff only the night before, and he
had already heard Mr. Audubon spoken of locally as a man in-

terested in birds. Perhaps Mr. Audubon would enjoy looking at his book; he might even be interested in becoming a subscriber. Only the first two volumes were off the press, but they would indicate to Mr. Audubon the quality of the volumes to follow. No need, of course, to pay in advance. The price of each book was due only when the subscriber received his volume.

Of course John James was interested, and Wilson opened his two books and began turning their pages. To John James's surprise, the birds of America were before him, each one portrayed in a colored plate and described in a detailed text which told about its appearance and habits. As Wilson explained, the work was not yet completed. So far he had concentrated almost entirely on the birds of the East and part of the South, but subsequent volumes would cover those of other areas. Indeed, his reason for being in Louisville was not only to sell subscriptions; he was also collecting specimens, and after leaving Louisville intended to go down the Ohio to the Mississippi and on to New Orleans. This trip, he thought, would provide the basis for at least one volume in addition to those he had already prepared for the press.

As he turned the pages, John James was struck with amazement. Never had he seen anything like this before, never even imagined such a book might exist. Of course, he would be delighted to subscribe regardless of the expense, and he took up his pen and was about to sign his name in Wilson's subscription book when Rozier, who had been looking over his shoulder, spoke to him in French. As John James remembered it later, Rozier told him it was foolish to spend money on someone else's bird pictures, when his own were so much better. In any case, John James put the pen aside and reaching back above the counter, took down a portfolio containing some of his own drawings.

"His surprise appeared great," John James said later about Wilson, "as he told me he never had the most distant idea that any individual than himself had been engaged in forming such a collection. He asked me if it was my intention to publish, and when I answered in the negative, his surprise seemed to increase. . . . Mr. Wilson now examined my drawings with care, asked me if I should have any objections to lending him a few during his stay, to which I replied I had none; he then bade me good-morning, not, however, until I had made an arrangement to explore the woods in the vicinity with him, and had promised to procure for him some birds of which I had drawings in my collection, but which he had never seen."

Because Wilson was also staying at the Indian Queen, the two men saw much of each other during Wilson's visit, which lasted almost two weeks. John James introduced him to Lucy, took him around to meet the other roomers in the lounge, went hunting with him, and showed him most, if not all, of his pictures. As they talked together, he must have learned something about Wilson's life.

Wilson had begun work as a weaver in Paisley, Scotland, but, hating the trade, he had become a peddler, making long, lonely trips with his pack on his back. His real interest, however, was in writing poetry. At that time, Robert Burns's popularity made many obscure Scotsmen believe they could open the doors to fame and fortune simply by writing down in rhyme their native stories in their own dialect. All over Scotland new poets made their appearance, most of them being little more than poor imitators of Burns. Wilson, who had somewhat more talent than the rest, soon joined this group and, having collected enough poetry to fill a small volume, decided to go into debt and produce a book. He was both courageous and foolish, for although the volume was modestly successful, the effort to pay for it placed an enormous burden on him.

While engaged in making a career for himself as a poet, he also became involved in the liberal movement sweeping England and Scotland and stood firmly beside some of the dissident weavers of Paisley in their attacks on the loom owners. In the course of this activity, Wilson wrote a poem accusing one of Paisley's prominent businessmen of cheating his workmen by using false measures to determine how much cloth they had woven. When the authorship of the poem became known, Wilson faced the possibility of being charged with several serious offenses, including libel, blackmail, and sedition. During the legal action that followed, he was arrested and released several times and, in the end, was fined, assessed costs, and ordered to pay damages to the businessman—all expenses well beyond his means. Worst of all, he was required to put up a bond for his future good behavior; since he did not have the money himself, he had to ask help of a friend who would have been ruined if the court had ever declared the bond forfeit. To escape from this untenable position, Wilson came to the United States in the spring of 1794.

Unlike Audubon, he arrived in America penniless, with no friends and nowhere to go. But also unlike Audubon, he was accustomed to supporting himself and had a trade. For a short time he worked as a weaver for a man who owned the property adjoining Miers Fisher's farm outside Philadelphia and, either then or later, struck up an acquaintance with Audubon's former guardian. As weaving had never appealed to him, he turned with considerable success to schoolteaching and finally conceived the idea of writing and illustrating a book on birds. For even the most experienced person, the undertaking would have been considerable, as nothing like it had ever been attempted before, and Wilson, of course, had had no formal training in either art or natural history. Nevertheless, with his usual tenacity, he set out to learn both subjects. He employed his students to help him collect specimens; he spent long nights trying to learn how to draw and even went so far as to experiment with making his own engravings in order to gain a better understanding of the process.

Meanwhile, in spite of the solitary life he lived, he gradually built up a small circle of friends: Charles Willson Peale, the Philadelphia artist and proprietor of Peale's Museum; William Bartram, the owner of the botanical gardens; and a number of other prominent people in Philadelphia who expressed interest in his ideas—all the men John James might have met, but had not.

In 1804, while Audubon was living at Mill Grove, Wilson was teaching school at Gray's Ferry, a small community on the Schuylkill only a short distance from Philadelphia. On May 12, Wilson sat down and wrote an engraver he knew—Alexander Lawson, who lived in Philadelphia—and stated his definite intentions of writing, illustrating, and publishing a book on the birds of America. Lawson was brutally frank in his reply. Even if Wilson were equipped to write such a book, its production would be prohibitively expensive. Each engraving, and there would have to be hundreds of them, would cost between $50 and $80; and the engravings, of course, would only be black and white. Once the pictures had been printed, they would have to be colored by hand at twenty-five cents a sheet. Two hundred plates, therefore, would cost not less than $10,000; and the expense of hand-coloring every page would raise the total enormously. In Lawson's opinion, no one would pay the necessary price for the book. But Wilson was not discouraged. He was determined to produce it and, although he had no publisher, began to work on it.

Two years later, when Audubon and Rozier were landing in New York and paying their respects to Benjamin Bakewell, Wilson was working at a new job he had taken in Philadelphia, serving as an editor in the publishing house of William Bradford. His primary responsibility was preparing a new edition of Rees's twenty-two-volume *Cyclopedia*. In addition, he had secured Bradford's agreement to publish *The American Ornithology*. Bradford was sufficiently enthusiastic to underwrite the cost of the first volume—the book was to come out, one volume a year, over a five-year period—provided Wilson could obtain two hundred subscribers. From that time on, Wilson had only one cause in life: the completion and sale of his publication.

Although Wilson and Bradford had been to some trouble in estimating the expense of producing the book, they had been overly optimistic. As the labor progressed it became more and more evident that there would be little, if any, profit for Wilson. Another difficulty was the reluctance of the public to subscribe. Even though they were to pay for each volume only as they received it, many people thought the charge of $120 for the set was far too much. One of the exceptions was Miers Fisher. While he was handling the affairs of the Audubon family and trying to untangle Jean Audubon's investment in Mill Grove, he and his family offered to take five sets of Wilson's book, thus giving Wilson their financial support and also the prestige of their patronage, an important factor in gaining more sales.

Wilson's visit to Louisville was part of the longest collecting and selling trip he had yet taken. Although he had obtained many new specimens and added copiously to his notes on American birds, he could not persuade a single person in Louisville to subscribe. From Audubon's point of view, however, the visit was of extreme importance. It was the first time he had ever seen what he regarded as a hobby transformed into professional work. When Wilson opened his books on Audubon's counter and displayed his pictures, he was opening up a new world to the young merchant. Heretofore Audubon's drawing had been haphazard. He had drawn birds when, and if, he found them and they happened to attract his attention, not on a systematic basis. Now he saw before him the results of concentrated, organized work. The pictures themselves, if judged for their artistry alone, were not up to the work that Audubon would do later, but they were similar in their approach. Wilson, too, was trying to represent birds in their natural surroundings. His text, unlike many of the scientific texts of the day, was informal and based on his own observations of the birds around him, making a complete break with much of the scientific work of the past. "In speaking of the *American Ornithology*," said one critic a few years later, "it is quite out of the question, to attempt to give any account of its contents. So much is made to meet the eye, that description, however excellent, falls infinitely short of the figured and coloured delineations. Natural history is a study . . . entrenched with so many scientific terms, in dead or foreign language, that to gain a thorough knowledge of these requires a severe and laborious discipline. When subjected to experiment, the student must pass through so long a train of blood and slaughter, of torture and dissection, that the heart revolts at the threshold. . . . In the classification of birds, for instance, it is necessary first, to attend to a minute description of feet, toes, talons, and bills. . . . Mr. Wilson, when he put down the birds in their orders and classes . . . presented them to the view in the simple and beautifully isolated state, in which they are formed, and left by the hand of nature. . . . He has chosen the most elegant and animated attitudes for representing the forms and manners of these lovely and interesting animals. Here is one slowly trailing along the ground; another sliding rapidly through the air; a third, with keen and piercing eye, in quest of its prey; while a fourth, distinguished for its voice, is in the very attitude of uttering those sounds which make the woods ring with melody." Wilson was creating a new attitude toward the natural sciences and was pioneering in the direction that Audubon would follow.

During those days they spent together, John James never heard a word of Wilson's financial difficulties—his book had made him practically a pauper—for Wilson was a proud man, too proud to talk about his desperate need for money. All John James saw was the respected, successful scientist, a man to admire. In the margin of his own drawing of a yellow warbler, one he had made in 1808 near the Falls of the Ohio, he carefully wrote: "This bird was copied by Mr. Wilson at Louisville." After all, it was a matter of some consequence to have given information to a man of Wilson's standing, really the highest recognition he had ever received.

He did not, however, change his mind about subscribing. If, as he later claimed, he was about to yield to impulse to do so when Rozier spoke to him, the words that checked him were probably not words of praise for his own drawings but a severe reminder that the firm was running short of funds. Although John James had always been free with other people's money, taking every cent given him by Jean Audubon, borrowing liberally from Benjamin Bakewell, and using the credit of François Rozier, the firm was still struggling, and business conditions throughout the country were growing worse. All this should have pushed him into making a greater effort, but, as he explained, "I seldom passed a day without drawing a bird, or noting something respecting its habits, Rozier meantime attending the counter. I could relate many curious anecdotes about him, but never mind them; he made out to grow rich, and what more could he wish for?" John James's contribution to the business was to appeal to William Bakewell for help in selling the part of Mill Grove that still belonged to him, not to provide Lucy with a house or the comforts she was accustomed to, but to sustain the business he was neglecting, while he went hunting and could afford, or thought he could afford, the finest riding horses in the country.

William Bakewell obviously knew the firm was having difficulties. He was a country gentleman, however, and unlike his
brother Benjamin, had had little business experience. It was
therefore difficult for him to temper his love for his daughter
and son-in-law with the proper amount of financial caution. He
simply could not bring himself to do it and, hoping for the
best, finally acquiesced to their request. In the spring of the
year, he sold the hundred and seventy acres of Mill Grove—all
that was left of Jean Audubon's original investment in America—for some eight thousand dollars. The whole business, he
wearily explained, had caused him much trouble and anxiety—
it was a difficult time to sell property, what with a depression
sweeping the country—and he had been forced to make several
trips to Norristown and Philadelphia. The balance, after he had
deducted his expenses and a small commission, was deposited
with the Kinders' firm to the account of Audubon & Rozier. To
make the title to the property good, would Lucy sign papers
renouncing any future claim of dower; in other words, a widow's right to a share of her husband's possessions? Although this
was a routine request, it emphasized Lucy's situation. Everything the Audubons owned, including their one important asset, was being poured into the business.

Without seeming to realize that he had stripped Lucy of her
last resource in the event of the firm's failure and relieved that
he was momentarily out of his financial difficulties, John James
continued to spend most of his time fishing and shooting; and
one night, to his great pleasure, found himself staying in the
same house with Daniel Boone. By then Boone was an old man,
living in Missouri, but he had come back to Kentucky on a trip
to see his brother, Squire. He and John James struck it off
immediately, and he offered to show Audubon how to bark
squirrels. They walked out together and followed the banks of
the Kentucky River until they found a flat stretch of land covered with black walnuts, oaks, and hickories. Because the nuts
were plentiful that year, there were squirrels in almost every
tree. "Boone," Audubon wrote, "pointed to one of these animals which had observed us, and was crouched on a branch
about fifty paces distant, and bade me mark well the spot where
the ball should hit. He raised his piece gradually, until the *bead*

(that being the name given by the Kentuckians to the *sight*) of the barrel was brought to a line with the spot he intended to hit. The whip-like report resounded through the woods and along the hills, in repeated echoes. Judge of my surprise when I perceived that the ball had hit the piece of the bark immediately beneath the squirrel, and shivered it into splinters, the concussion produced by which had killed the animal, and sent it whirling through the air, as if it had been blown up by the explosion of a powder magazine. Boone kept up his firing, and before many hours had elapsed, we had procured as many squirrels as we wished; for you must know ... that to load a rifle requires only a moment, and that if it is wiped once after each shot, it will do duty for hours."

At the end of their hunt, John James and Boone walked back to the house. To Audubon, these hours spent in the company of the famous frontiersman were a precious experience, and his artist's eye noted Boone's physical features so closely that later he did a portrait from memory. After supper they went to the bedroom they were to share for the night. Audubon undressed; Boone merely took off his hunting shirt. Folding the blankets and placing them on the floor, he lay down, remarking that he preferred to sleep on the floor than on the softest bed. All day long, John James had hoped Boone would talk about his early adventures in Kentucky and at last, just before they dropped off, he began reminiscing. Once, he said, while camping in southern Kentucky, he had been captured by a band of Indians who, creeping up to his campsite, pinioned him before he could move. Without complaining or struggling, he let them carry him off, knowing that he could gain their respect only by showing no fear. Two squaws searched his clothing and, with delight, took away his flask of whiskey and started drinking. The braves soon joined in, and the bottle passed from mouth to dirty mouth, while Boone kept wishing it contained more. Suddenly the report of a gun was heard in the distance. The braves went off to investigate, while the squaws, now thoroughly drunk, fell asleep. Quietly, Boone rolled over closer and closer to the fire until he came near enough to char the ropes which bound him. Once free, he thought briefly of killing the squaws as they lay in their stupor, but thinking it evil to slaughter people who were so utterly helpless, he left them and vanished in the woods.

As he told the story in the quiet of their room, the scene became vivid and real. The drunken Indians cavorting around the fire, the flames licking at the logs and casting their light into the surrounding forest, and the frontiersman, his hands tied, waiting for the first moment he might attempt an escape. This, to John James, was the real life, far better than managing a store.

The next morning he and John James separated, never to see each other again. But the casual meeting made a profound impression on Audubon, and years later he could clearly recall the sound of the rifle reports ringing in the forest, the sight of the squirrels spinning in the air as they fell dead to the ground, and the stories told in the evening after the day's hunting.

Such adventures, however, did nothing to add to the profitability of his business. For all of Rozier's efforts and hard work, and in spite of selling the land at Mill Grove, the firm did not flourish. Louisville, with its strategic position at the falls, was becoming an increasingly important commercial center, but Audubon & Rozier could not meet the competition.

Finally, the two partners made a decision. They would leave Louisville and move to the smaller town of Henderson, Kentucky, some 125 miles down the river. There, they thought, competition would be less severe and they might do better. Lucy gathered together her belongings at the Indian Queen and, with Victor in her arms, set off on a visit to Flatland Ford, while the partners established themselves in their new location. Everyone at the Indian Queen wished her good-bye and a fine trip and were sorry to see her go. She had many friends in Louisville.

But for all the time she had spent in the town John James liked so well, she had little else to regret leaving.

CHAPTER VII

1810 — 1811

ACH time before, in his vague search for something better
than what he already had, John James had been guided
by some semblance of logic, but reason deserted him when he
decided to move to Henderson, Kentucky. Today, Henderson
is a pleasant county seat lying in a sharp bend of the Ohio
River; but in 1810 what pretensions it possessed existed only on
paper. Laid out on part of the 200,000 acres granted to the
Transylvania Company, its promoters intended it to be a magnificent river town, with streets a hundred feet wide, and the
entire riverfront, two and a quarter miles of it, reserved as mu-
nicipal property for parks and docks. That was the dream; the
reality was considerably less. One traveler, passing down the
river a few years before John James, described Henderson as a
town "of about twenty houses, and inhabited by a people whose
doom is fixed." His opinion was exaggerated, but in the next
twenty years, while Louisville jumped to a population of more
than 11,000, Henderson crept forward to a total of only 485.

Nor was the community's reputation enhanced by having
served for six years as the headquarters of Samuel Mason, one of
Kentucky's most notorious outlaws. Mason had preyed on the
flatboatmen walking home upriver along the Natchez Trace; he
had attacked boats tied up at night along the banks, leaping on
board with his armed gang and stripping away everything valuable like a horde of locusts; he had even stooped to having
his men impersonate legitimate river pilots. Once on board and
at the helm, they would deliberately wreck the craft where
Mason lay in ambush.

Driven from Henderson in 1796, he had moved to an island
fifteen miles down the river and then to Cave-in-the-Rock, a

gigantic cave, some 180 feet deep, overlooking the Ohio. Here, it was rumored, the bandits established an inn, providing liquor, meals, overnight accommodations, and even women, to anyone hardy enough to enter the torchlit vault. Mason eventually disappeared, but at the time Audubon moved to Henderson his memory was still fresh in southwestern Kentucky. Hanging on poles along the Natchez Trace, where they had been placed as a warning to other river pirates, the skulls of two of his henchmen were still bleaching in the sun; and just outside Henderson, Audubon could have found the skull of another bandit, Macijah Harpe, also hanging from a pole. Macijah had been known to blindfold a man, tie him to a horse, and whip the horse over a cliff, not as revenge or punishment, but as a joke, just as he had once pushed two lovers off a cliff for the sheer pleasure of watching them fall and hearing them scream.

This was the town selected by Audubon for his next venture at storekeeping—a forlorn little river community with a few log buildings and an unenviable reputation for recent banditry. Even he, despite his supreme self-confidence, seems to have had misgivings, because he first took Lucy and their son, Victor, back to Flatland Ford, leaving them there for a prolonged visit while he and Rozier set up the shop in Henderson. Almost immediately they recognized their mistake. "We took there," Audubon wrote later, "the remainder of our stock on hand, but found the country so very new, and so thinly populated that the commonest goods only were called for." Most men would have found this discouraging, but not Audubon. He at last had a practical excuse for his hunting and fishing. "I may say our guns and fishing lines," he commented proudly, "were the principal means of our support, as regards food." Then he added, casting light on Rozier's position, "John Pope, our clerk, who was a Kentuckian, was a good shot and an excellent fisherman, and he and I attended to the procuring of game and fish, while Rozier again stood behind the counter."

Oh, this was the good life, out in the woods all day, while Rozier waited patiently for the customers who never came. What if Rozier complained? What if Rozier worried about the future? What if Rozier charged that Audubon was failing to do his share of the work? They had enough to eat and could always get more, just as long as he and Pope had powder and bullets and fishing lines and hooks and the freedom and time to use them. Indeed, in Pope, rather than in his partner, Audubon had found the perfect companion, a man who was "a good woodsman, hunter, and angler, and like me, thought chiefly of procuring supplies of fish and food. To that task accordingly we directed all our energies."

One of their projects was the construction of an enormous trotline for the purpose of catching catfish. Selecting a piece of stout line about two hundred yards long, they attached to it a hundred smaller lines, each about five feet in length, to which they tied hooks baited with toads. All the effort and expense involved were clearly out of proportion to their needs, but Audubon and Pope were swept away by their enthusiasm. Nothing would satisfy them but the largest trotline ever seen in Henderson. Of course they caught fish with it; they could not have failed. They caught enough to supply themselves and their neighbors, and Audubon undoubtedly enjoyed delivering the fish to his friends and receiving their thanks. Rozier, too, was certainly grateful for the free meals—they helped reduce the firm's expenses—but they were not the answer to the problems of Audubon & Rozier. Those could be solved only by more hard work than Audubon was doing.

Nor did Audubon, during those early days at Henderson, neglect his hobby of collecting birds. After his hunting and fishing was done, even if he did not have time to help Rozier, he had hours left to look for new species. That first spring, for example, he shot and killed a blue-headed vireo, which he called a "solitary flycatcher," the second time he had collected one of those small, warblerlike birds. So while he ignored the store, the sketches and notes grew in number, although still without definite purpose, the trotlines snagged catfish, and the turkeys, ducks, and deer fell before his gun. In this happy fashion, the spring and early summer of 1810 slipped away as quietly as the waters flowing down the Ohio, until the time came to break the interlude and bring Lucy back from Flatland Ford.

In the fall of the year, he went to fetch both her and Victor. Leaving Philadelphia together, they again crossed the flat eastern section of Pennsylvania, followed the tortuous roads over the mountains, bumping and skidding all the way, and spending their nights in the miserable taverns. In Pittsburgh they broke their journey with a short visit with Benjamin Bakewell, whose glass business was still prospering. Then they moved on to Louisville, stayed there a few days to see their friends, and went on to Shippingport, downstream from the falls. Because the water was low and travel by flatboat was difficult, Audubon purchased a skiff for the trip between Shippingport and Henderson.

"It was in the month of October. The autumnal tints already decorated the shores of that queen of the rivers, the Ohio. Every tree was hung with long and flowering festoons of different species of vines, many loaded with clustered fruits of various brilliancy, their rich bronzed carmine mingling beautifully with the yellow foliage, which now predominated over the yet green leaves, reflecting more lively tints from the clear stream than ever landscape painter portrayed, or poet imagined," he later wrote.

"The days were yet warm. The sun had assumed the rich and glowing hue which at that season produces the singular phenomenon called there the 'Indian Summer.' The moon had rather passed the meridian of her grandeur. We glided down the river, meeting no other ripple of the water than that formed by the propulsion of our boat. Leisurely we moved along, gazing all day on the grandeur and beauty of the wild scenery around us."

At least for these few days, Lucy had her husband to herself, away from their friends, the store, the scowls of Rozier, and the distraction of the hunting and fishing trips. All Audubon's restlessness, his constant desire to be somewhere else, were subdued, as they quietly drifted with the current, alone except for the oarsmen. "As night came," Audubon wrote in recollection, "sinking in darkness the broader portions of the river, our minds became affected by strong emotions, and wandered far beyond the present moments. The tinkling of bells told us that the cattle which bore them were gently roving from valley to valley in search of food, or returning to their distant homes. The hooting of the great owl, or the muffled noise of its wings, as it sailed smoothly over the stream, were matters of interest to us; so was the sound of the boatman's horn, as it came winding more and more softly from afar. When daylight returned, many songsters burst forth with echoing notes, more and more mellow to the listening ear. Here and there the lonely cabin of a squatter struck the eye, giving note of commencing civilization. The crossing of the stream by a deer foretold how soon the hills would be covered with snow."

Looking back on the journey, John James said of his days on the river with Lucy, "Purer pleasures I have never felt," and she must have thought the same. Yet the idyll could not last forever. After more than a hundred miles of travel, they reached Henderson, where Lucy came face-to-face with the crudities of keeping house in a frontier village. Although there were relatively few buildings in Henderson, Audubon had obtained a log cabin in which they could live. Afterward, he was careful to explain that it was a "log *cabin,* not a log *house;* but as better could not be had, we were pleased. Well, then, we were located. The country around was thinly populated, and all purchasable provisions rather scarce; but our neighbors were friendly, and we had brought with us flour and bacon-hams. Our pleasures were those of young people not long married, and full of life and merriment; a single smile from our infant was, I assure you, more valued by us than all the treasure of a modern Croesus would have been. The woods were amply stocked with game, the river with fish; and now and then the hoarded sweets of the industrious bees were brought from some hollow tree to our little table. Our child's cradle was our richest piece of furniture, our guns and fishing lines our most serviceable implements, for although we began to cultivate a garden, the rankness of the soil kept the seeds we planted far beneath the tall weeds that sprang up the first year."

His picture of their domestic happiness exudes masculinity, a man's pleasure at living on the edge of the wilderness and spending his days and nights hunting and fishing to provide his wife and child with food. Lucy, on the other hand, could hardly have found life at Henderson much of an improvement over what she had known at Louisville. True, she at last had her own house instead of living in the Indian Queen, but it was not much of a house. As for family life, her husband was still away much of the time, hunting in the forests or fishing in the river; and regardless of his enthusiasm, at least in retrospect, for catfish, it is improbable she took much pleasure in dropping one of those weird creatures into the pot as the first step in preparing dinner. By any standard, the Audubons' existence was crude; and Lucy, coming as she did from a family with comparative wealth and high cultural interests, must have found her first days at Henderson lonely and discouraging. Except for Dr. Adam Rankin, who had a farm about three miles out from the village, she had almost no cultivated, educated person to whom she could talk.

But the worst was yet to come. No sooner had she arrived in Henderson and settled down in the cabin than Audubon began to express doubts about staying on. The profits on each sale, as he expressed it, were "enormous"—in frontier stores, the markup was often several hundred percent—but the volume was insufficient. Henderson was just too small to support them.

If Audubon & Rozier were to grow, nothing remained except to find a new location. Rozier suggested that they try one of the river towns on the Mississippi above the mouth of the Ohio, perhaps Ste. Genevieve, in what was then Upper Louisiana and is now part of Missouri. It was one of the oldest towns in that section of the country and had a population of more than a thousand inhabitants and a diverse economy, based on river commerce, farming and mining. Furthermore, it retained much of its original French character, which especially appealed to Rozier, who was still having difficulty with his English.

All in all, it seemed a more promising location for the store as well as a better place in which to live, and Audubon and Rozier agreed to pack up their small stock of merchandise and transfer it to Ste. Genevieve without further delay, even though this meant making the trip during the winter months. Lucy, of course, was to be left behind again, as there was no possibility of taking her and Victor along on such a journey. Before setting out, however, Audubon talked to Dr. Rankin and made arrangements for her to leave the log cabin and move out to the Rankins' farm. This was more practical than spending the lonely winter by herself, but she had to surrender the only home of her own she had ever had.

With Lucy settled, Audubon, Rozier, and Nat Pope, their clerk, began loading the keelboat they had purchased for the trip. On board went their entire stock: sundry drygoods, a supply of gunpowder, and three hundred barrels of whiskey for which they had paid twenty-five cents a gallon. Their cargo safely stowed away, the men spent one last night on shore saying good-bye to their small circle of friends. On rising the next morning, they found the skies heavy and gray, the wind cold, and the air filled with snow. Gone was the peaceful Ohio down which Audubon and Lucy had drifted only a few weeks before. Its place had been taken by a a dark, ominous band of water, ruffled by gusts of winds and obscured by snow squalls. In these dismal conditions, the crew untied the mooring lines and took their places at the four oars; the patroon—the captain employed by John James and Rozier—picked up the steering oar; and the bulky craft swung out into the current, headed downriver, and disappeared from Lucy's sight in a flurry of snowflakes.

After three days of bitter weather, they entered the mouth of Cash Creek, a small stream about eight miles from the Mississippi and the last good harbor on the Ohio. Another boat was moored there, and from its patroon Audubon learned that the Mississippi was covered with floating ice which made it impossible to ascend the river. The only course was to remain at Cash Creek until conditions improved, causing a delay that brought into sharp conflict the contrasting personalities of Audubon and Rozier. On the one hand, John James welcomed the unexpected excuse to spend more time in the woods. On the other, Rozier, alarmed by the additional expense, chafed with impatience. Nor was his mood helped by the rather superior attitude assumed by Audubon. "He brooded in silence," Audubon wrote later, "over a mishap which had given me great cause for rejoicing."

To add to Audubon's enjoyment, fifty families of Shawnee Indians were camped nearby, having been attracted to the spot by the mast of the forest, which in turn had brought together many deer, bears, and raccoons. On the dawn of the second morning, while Rozier still lay huddled in his buffalo robes,

Audubon "heard a movement in the Indian camp and discovered that a canoe, with half a dozen squaws and as many hunters, was about leaving. I had heard that there was a large lake opposite to us, where immense flocks of swans resorted every morning, and asking permission to join them, I seated myself on my haunches in the canoe, well provided with ammunition and a bottle of whiskey, and in a few minutes the paddles were at work, swiftly propelling us to the opposite shore. I was not much surprised to see the boat paddled by the squaws, but I was quite so to see the hunters stretch themselves out and go to sleep. On landing, the squaws took charge of the canoe, secured it, and went in search of nuts, while we gentlemen hunters made the best of our way through thick and thin to the lake. Its muddy shores were overgrown with a close growth of cotton trees, too large to be pushed aside, and too thick to pass through except by squeezing yourself at every few steps; and to add to the difficulty, every few rods we came to small nasty lagoons, which one must jump, leap, or swim, and this not without peril of broken limbs or drowning.

"But when the lake burst on our view there were the swans by hundreds, and white as rich cream, either dipping their black bills in the water, or stretching out one leg on its surface, or gently floating along. According to the Indian mode of hunting, we had divided, and approached the lagoon from different sides. The moment our vedette was seen, it seemed as if thousands of large, fat, and heavy swans were startled, and as they made away from him they drew towards the ambush of death; for the trees had hunters behind them, whose touch of the trigger would carry destruction among them. As the first party fired, the game rose and flew within easy distance of the party on the opposite side, when they again fired, and I saw the water covered with birds, floating with their backs downwards, and their heads sunk in the water, and their legs kicking in the air.

"When the sport was over we counted more than fifty of these beautiful birds, whose skins were intended for the ladies of Europe. There were plenty of ducks and geese, but no one condescended to give them a shot. A conch was sounded, and after a while the squaws came dragging the canoe, and collecting the dead game, which was taken to the river's edge, fastened to the canoe, and before dusk we were again landed at our camping ground. I had heard of sportsmen in England who walked a whole day, and after firing a pound of powder returned in great glee, bringing one partridge; and I could not help wondering what they would think of the spoil we were bearing from Swan Lake."

During their enforced stay at Cash Creek, while Rozier grumbled, Audubon spent as much time as he could with the Indians and was invited by three hunters to go after a particularly large bear that they knew was nearby. About half a mile from camp, although Audubon could see nothing, one of the Indians said he could observe the animal's tracks, which they followed through the canebrake until they came to an immense, decayed log. The Indian was certain the bear was hiding in the log and, throwing off his blanket and drawing his knife, told Audubon to climb a small sapling. Bears, he explained, can go up a large tree easily, but not one too small to support their weight. The other two Indians sat down at one end of the log to prevent the bear's escape, and the first Indian dropped to his hands and knees and crawled into the hollow trunk. Audubon could hear no sound, but within a few minutes the Indian reappeared and said the bear was dead. By tying vines to its body, they were able to pull it out of the log. Then they skinned it, hung the meat in quarters on some branches, and went on with their hunting, while Audubon and one Indian returned to the camp to tell the squaws to collect the meat.

After the Indians had gathered most of the nuts near Cash Creek, the game grew scarce and the hunters spent most of their hours around their fire. One day they made up their packs, broke their camp and, putting all their possessions into their canoes, paddled off toward the Mississippi with plans to go downstream to the Arkansas. Their obvious assurance that the Mississippi was again navigable aroused Rozier's impatience, and he urged Audubon to scout ahead on foot and see for himself whether the river could be ascended. Taking two members of the crew with him, Audubon set out across the snow toward the Mississippi. Instead of following the bank of the Ohio which, with its turns and bends, made the distance eight miles,

he took the direct route overland. Walking westward past the
present site of Cairo, Illinois, he soon reached the shore of the
Mississippi. There at his feet ran the great river which, fed by
the waters of thirty-one states, twists and winds its way for more
than two thousand miles through the heartland of America.
When Audubon saw it on that December day in 1810 under the
gray winter sky, the ice had almost disappeared, and it had
once again become passable. Instead of returning immediately
to Cash Creek to report this information, Audubon decided to
make an exploring trip upstream first. Coming to a point opposite the small town of Cape Giradeau, Missouri, located on a
high bluff overlooking the river, he saw several of the town's
three hundred inhabitants gathered at the landing at the river's
edge. In response to Audubon's hail, one of them quickly
launched a canoe and paddled across. On learning of Audubon's desire to move the boat to Ste. Genevieve, he offered his
own services as pilot as well as agreeing to provide six additional men to bring the total crew to ten. He and Audubon
settled on terms, hid the canoe in the woods, blazed some trees
to mark the spot against their return, and started out with the
enlarged force for the return trip to Cash Creek.

Once they got back to the snug harbor and the moored boat,
they wasted no time in making their preparations. "The night,"
Audubon wrote, "was spent in making tugs of hides and shav-
ing oars, and at daylight we left the creek, glad to be afloat once
more in broader water. Going down the stream to the mouth of
the Ohio was fine sport; indeed my partner considered the
worst of the journey over, but, alas! when we turned the point,
and met the mighty rush of the Mississippi, running three miles
an hour, and bringing shoals of ice to further impede our progress, he looked on despairingly. The patroon ordered the lines
ashore, and it became the duty of every man 'to haul the cordella,' which was a rope fastened to the bow of the boat; one
man being left on board to steer, the others, laying the rope
over their shoulders, slowly warped the heavy boat and cargo
against the current."

This was weary, brutal work. The bulky boat was not designed to slip easily through the water and bucked and jerked
at the end of the line. Occasionally it caught on a snag, the

broken tree stump poking at the hull and stopping it as effectively as though someone had jammed on a powerful set of brakes. Then the men had to release the line, let the boat drift backward, thus losing some of their hard-gained distance, and warp the craft around the obstacle. They were often waist-deep in the cold water or, because there were no towpaths to follow, they had to fight their way through the heavy brush and undergrowth that lined the river. It was a case of men using the brute strength of mules to perform a task that mules were not sufficiently agile to do. Muscle and weight and brawn were pitted against the steady current of the Mississippi for mile after mile, while the cold wind blew around them, freezing their faces and hands, and the remaining hunks of ice, drifting southward, bumped against the sides of the boat and created an additional hazard. At the end of the day they had gone only seven miles up the Mississippi, a small fraction of the total distance that lay between them and Ste. Genevieve. That night they camped on the shore and, after supper, posting a sentinel to warn them against river pirates, fell sound asleep.

The next morning they were up two hours before sunrise and again heaving on the long line, splashing through the water and beating a pathway through the brush, while the boat tugged steadily backward against their straining backs. Fighting the current at every step of the way, they made approximately one mile an hour. Although they carried a sail, as many boats did, it was useless in the face of a head wind, so they continued tugging and hauling and at the end of the day had moved upstream only ten miles farther. They kept up their labors for two more days. Then the weather suddenly turned worse and the patroon, refusing to go on, insisted on mooring in the bend of a river at Tawapatee Bottoms, still a number of miles below Cape Giradeau.

For the next two days, the party was busy making a camp in which they could live during the worst of the winter weather. First they moored the boat close to shore, where they could get to it easily, if they needed to. Then they scraped away the snow from an area thirty yards square, piling it in a wall around the perimeter to protect them from the wind. This done, the men began to hunt, bringing in turkeys, deer, raccoons and opossums, while others bored holes in the ice and went fishing in order to augment their supplies.

By now, as the boat's captain had feared, the weather had turned worse and worse, and the river became almost entirely frozen over. Out on the ice, large flocks of swans gathered, and these in turn attracted wolves. "It was curious," Audubon wrote describing the scene, "to see the snow-white birds lying all flat on the ice, but keenly intent on watching the motions of their insidious enemies, until the latter advanced within the distance of a few hundred yards, when the swans, sounding their trumpet-notes of alarm, would all rise, spread out their broad wings, and after running some yards and battering the ice until the noise echoed like thunder through the woods, rose exultingly into the air, leaving their pursuers to devise other schemes for gratifying their craving appetites."

But the beauty of the swans did not impress Rozier or divert him from his troubles. For him, this enforced encampment was the final blow, and all he could see ahead were long winter weeks spent in the wilderness, while the slender capital of the partnership dwindled further. He became even more morose and gloomy, passed the hours wrapped in his blanket, and seldom appeared except at mealtime. Nor was his mood improved by Audubon's obvious delight over what was happening.

There was not a white man's cabin within twenty miles, Audubon recalled later with enjoyment and probably some exaggeration. So they cut down some trees and made a winter camp, while Audubon rambled through the deep forests on the Indian trails and explored the neighboring lakes. Occasionally he met Indians in the woods, and gradually, as they learned of the white men's encampment, they began to collect around the boat. Most of them were Osages and Shawnees. The Osages in particular appealed to Audubon as being a superior tribe, and he often visited them and made sketches of them in red chalk which both astonished and delighted them.

The bones they threw around the camp attracted many wolves, which Audubon enjoyed shooting, and at the end of each day he contentedly lay down to sleep next to the camp-fire. This was composed of four or five ash trees, three feet in diameter and sixty feet long, which the men cut and threw into a pile some ten feet high. Then a fire was kindled at the top with brush and dry leaves, and the men rolled up in their blankets under the smoke.

After two weeks of this life, their bread gave out. They tried using the breasts of wild turkeys as a substitute with bear's grease in place of butter. But this combination and their continual diet of opossum and bear meat became so revolting to them that, although they were in no danger of starvation, they decided to send Audubon and Pope to the nearest settlement, Cape Giradeau, to purchase some Indian meal. The men, both experienced woodsmen, went overland toward the Mississippi, thus avoiding two sides of a triangle. As they walked through the snow, they came upon several deer, followed them, shot one, and hung its carcass to a tree. Then they marked the spot carefully, so they could pick up the body on their return trip. To save time, they moved ahead instead of retracing their tracks to the point where they had first seen the herd. By dusk they were completely lost and still searching for the Mississippi.

In the fading light, they came across an Indian trail, which Audubon thought might lead them to the river. Instead, it brought them directly to the camp they had left early in the morning. To the boatmen the mistake was a wonderful joke on Audubon and Pope, and even the Indians, seeing the two hunters' amazement at finding themselves back, joined in the laughter. Audubon and Pope also thought their mistake was funny. After all, the best woodsmen sometimes wander in circles. But Rozier, not knowing this, ascribed the blunder to outright carelessness. His temper was badly frayed by years of doing Audubon's work, and he was seriously upset by the delays on the trip. Bursting into a rage, he called both Audubon and Pope "boobies." From his point of view, Audubon had already demonstrated his incompetence in the business world; now he had just shown himself a fool in the woods. Under the strain of the journey, the enforced intimacy of the camp, and the lonely winter, the last shreds that held the partnership together were rapidly disintegrating.

Audubon, however, was not in the least discouraged and had no doubts about his ability to reach Cape Giradeau and complete his errand. The next day they tried again. This time they went directly across the bend and did not allow themselves to be diverted by the game they saw. An hour before sunset, they reached the bank opposite Cape Giradeau. Chunks of ice were floating down the river, making it dangerous for a small boat to put out, so no one responded to their hails. That night they slept in an abandoned log cabin, and the next morning, which dawned fair and clear, they saw a canoe picking its way toward them through the ice. Their visitor listened to their needs, went back to Cape Giradeau, and brought them a barrel of flour, several bags of Indian meal, and a few loaves of bread. By then it was almost sundown, so Audubon and his friends rolled the barrel into a safe hiding place, hung the bags on trees, and carried the bread back to camp by thrusting their gun barrels through the loaves and then slinging them over their shoulders. The next day four men went out with axes, made a sledge, and returned with the remainder of the supplies.

All this time, the river had been slowly rising, creeping upward against its banks. Now it suddenly started to fall. With the help of the Indians, the men quickly unloaded the cargo, carried it into the woods, and covered it with the sails to keep it dry. Within a short time the boat was lying stranded, careened on one side, and the ice, with no water to support its weight, had shattered into heaps which lined the banks. Should the river rise again before the weather turned warm and melted the heaps, the chunks of ice would float free and crash against the boat's hull. The men, therefore, felled large trees and, fastening the ends to the shore, constructed heavy booms to protect the boat. "We were now indeed in winter quarters," Audubon wrote, "and we made the best of it. The Indians made baskets of cane, Mr. Pope played on the violin, I accompanied on the flute, the men danced to the tunes, and the squaws looked on and laughed, and the hunters smoked their pipes with such serenity as only Indians can, and I never regretted one day spent there." Rozier alone remained gloomy. A solitary figure, with nothing to do, he permitted the wrongs and injustices of the past years to fester in his mind.

Four nights after Audubon had gone to Cape Giradeau in search of bread, the party as usual threw their buffalo robes around themselves and went to sleep. The flames from the campfire, which was kept burning, lighted the branches of the surrounding trees and cast shadows on the snow wall encircling the camp. All was quiet except for the occasional hoot of an owl in the distance, the howling of a wolf, or the weird sound of two branches rubbing against each other in the wind. Every once in a while, one of the sleeping men turned in his robe, or the flames of the fire licked at a fresh log and made it crackle. It was like every other night at Tawapatee Bottoms.

The boat's captain, however, had refused to fall asleep with the others and was pacing the camp restlessly. Suddenly through the silent night, he heard a sharp noise like the snapping of a whip. The first crack had appeared in the ice. Then came another and another. As Audubon described it, ". . . startling catastrophe threatened us without warning. The ice began to break, and our boat was in instant danger of being cut to pieces by the ice-floes, or swamped by their pressure. Roused from our sleep, we rushed pell-mell to the bank, as if attacked by savages, and discovered the ice was breaking up rapidly. It split with reports like those of heavy artillery; and as the water had suddenly risen from an overflow of the Ohio, the two streams seemed to rush against each other with violence, in consequence of which the congealed mass was broken into large fragments, some of which rose nearly erect here and there, and again fell with a thundering crash, as the wounded whale, when in the agonies of death, springs up with furious force, and again plunges into the foaming waters. To our surprise, the weather which in the evening had been calm and frosty, had become wet and blowy. The water gushed from the fissures made in the ice, and the prospect was extremely dismal. When day dawned, a spectacle strange and fearful presented itself; the whole mass of water was violently agitated; its covering was broken into small fragments, and although not a foot of space was without ice, not a step could the most daring have ventured to make upon it. Our boat was in imminent danger, for the trees which had been placed to guard it from the ice were cut or broken into pieces and were thrust against her. It was impossible to move her; but our pilot ordered every man to bring down great bunches of cane, which were lashed along her sides: and before these were destroyed by the ice, she was afloat, and riding above it. While we were gazing on the scene, a tremendous crash was heard, which seemed to have taken place about a mile below, when suddenly the great dam of ice gave way. The current of the Mississippi had forced its way against that of the Ohio; and in less than four hours we witnessed the complete breaking up of the ice."

The boat was afloat again, the river open to navigation, and the travelers could proceed on their way. But this time the captain abandoned the use of the cordella—the heavy towing rope —and instead resorted to the poles. Every crew member, except the captain who stood in the stern gripping the long steering oar, took up his pole. Walking in turn to the front of the boat, he drove the end of the pole into the ice or, if the ice had melted at that spot, into the bottom. Then, dropping down onto his hands and knees, he placed the other end of the pole against his shoulder and crawled toward the stern over the wet, slippery decks. Once there, he picked up his pole and ran forward again to repeat the performance, so that, on either side of the boat, two lines of men were working, some making their painful way aft on all fours, others running up to take their places. In this crude, nearly inhuman fashion, they moved slowly against the current toward Cape Giradeau.

The world around them had many of the fantastic qualities of a nightmare but also contained aspects of unbelievable beauty. On either bank, the melting snow clung to the branches, pressing them down toward the earth as though winter were determined to make its last burden the heaviest. On the river itself, the ice, having formed while the water was high, now hung from the banks in great flat platforms, sometimes considerably above the heads of the men and completely unsupported from below. Underneath these platforms were dark caverns where the river swirled and foamed. As they passed through this strange landscape, Audubon pondered on the dangers of a quick thaw, for then the ice would lose its hold on the banks and, buckling under its own weight, come crashing down into the river, perhaps onto the boat. Fortunately the cold weather held, and they reached Cape Giradeau in safety.

Here the partners stopped for a short while, thinking they might sell some of their merchandise and perhaps even settle permanently. But the town, like Henderson, was too small to support a store, and there was no demand even for the small stock they had brought with them. Consequently, they decided to press on together to Ste. Genevieve, where they moored their boat in the harbor at the mouth of the Gabourie River. The town itself lay a mile farther back between two branches of the Gabourie and replaced an older settlement, damaged in the floods of 1784. Behind the town the land rose slightly, while in front of it, starting at the mouth of the Gabourie, a rich section of bottom soil, particularly adapted to growing wheat, stretched for some eight or nine miles. Nearby were several remarkable springs, one of them pouring into a pool fifteen or twenty feet square and almost as deep, and producing enough water to turn a mill a short distance away. Farther from the town were three of Missouri's principal lead mines, which produced some 350,-000 pounds of metal a year. Between the mines, the farms, and the river commerce handled by the town, the settlement had grown wealthy, its usual purchases, according to one contemporary traveler, amounting to the considerable sum of $150,000 a year. For Audubon and Rozier, the prospects offered by the community were good, certainly much better than they had been at Henderson. Almost immediately they were able to dispose of the greater part of their cargo and found to their pleasure that their twenty-five-cent whiskey went quickly at two dollars a gallon, giving them a good profit on this one commodity alone.

But the two partners looked at Ste. Genevieve from different points of view. Rozier soon made friends with some of the French-speaking families and recognized the settlement as a great improvement over Henderson. He wanted to stay. Audubon, on the other hand, took an immediate dislike to the town. "I found at once," he wrote, revealing his capacity for snap judgments, "that it was not the place for me; its population was then composed of low French Canadians, uneducated and uncouth, and the everlong wish to be with my beloved wife and children [he had only one child at the time] drew my thoughts to Henderson, to which I decided to return almost immediately. Scarcely any communication existed between the two places, and I felt cut from all dearest to me. Rozier, on

Bust of Audubon by Joy Buba. This bust of Audubon stands in the lobby of the National Audubon Society at 1130 Fifth Avenue, New York City. The society is one of the national conservation agencies working to preserve the wildlife and countryside whose beauty Audubon showed in his pictures.

New York in 1803. When Audubon first arrived in America, he landed at New York City and almost at once became seriously ill. The captain of the ship that had brought him from France made arrangements for him to receive nursing care. Shortly after his recovery, Audubon moved to his father's farm, Mill Grove, in Pennsylvania.

Mill Grove as seen from Perkiomen Creek. At his first home in America, Audubon, in his own words, was "happy as happy can be," until he speculated with his father's money in reopening a deserted lead mine on the property. This proved disastrous financially, and Audubon left the farm to seek his fortune in the West.

A whippoorwill by Audubon, 1806. Although his interest in both birds and art commenced at an early age, Audubon was not precocious, as this picture, made at Mill Grove, shows. It took him years of practice and study to achieve the mastery that eventually made him world famous.

A crayon portrait by Audubon, 1819. After his bankruptcy and before the publication of *The Birds of America,* Audubon relied heavily on his abilities as a portraitist to earn a living. Because he did not know how to use oils, he was sometimes handicapped in obtaining customers. This picture is an example of some of his better work during this period.

A wild turkey by Audubon. This is the first plate in *The Birds of America* and was engraved in Edinburgh by Lizars. With this and four other pictures as examples of his work, Audubon set out to sell enough subscriptions to make the completion of his book possible.

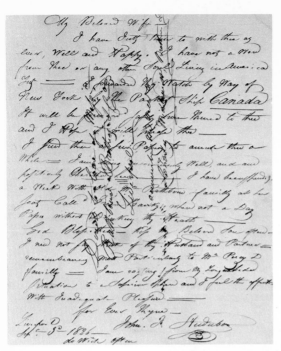

A letter from Audubon to Lucy, Liverpool, 1826. To save postage, Audubon often wrote twice on the same sheet of paper. Here he has added only a few words, but sometimes he filled whole pages with one set of lines written at right angles over the other.

Courtesy of the Princeton University Library

Portfolio used by Audubon. With this heavy portfolio, large enough to contain his collection of life-sized bird pictures, Audubon traveled from city to city in the United States and Europe, showing his plates and soliciting subscriptions to *The Birds of America*.

Courtesy of the American Museum of Natural History

An uncolored impression of a "sea-side finch" (seaside sparrow) for *The Birds of America.* The picture shows the detailed work done by the engraver. The black and white prints then had to be colored by hand. This meant that each individual plate had to be carefully inspected before it was delivered to a subscriber.

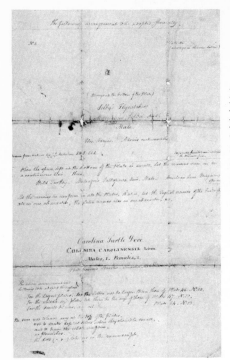

Instructions from Audubon to Havell, 1831. Although Havell proved himself one of the finest engravers in England, Audubon supervised his work closely, taking final responsibility for each plate wholly upon himself. In these notes, he told Havell to re-engrave the legends on the first forty-four plates to make them conform with each other in style.

Courtesy of the
Princeton University Library

Title page of the *Ornithological Biography*. This book was the text to accompany *The Birds of America*. In it, Audubon included all the information he had obtained about birds and added several chapters dealing with his life and travels in the United States.

Courtesy of the
Princeton University Library

ORNITHOLOGICAL BIOGRAPHY,

OR AN ACCOUNT OF THE HABITS OF THE

BIRDS OF THE UNITED STATES OF AMERICA;

ACCOMPANIED BY DESCRIPTIONS OF THE OBJECTS REPRESENTED
IN THE WORK ENTITLED

THE BIRDS OF AMERICA,

AND INTERSPERSED WITH DELINEATIONS OF AMERICAN
SCENERY AND MANNERS.

BY JOHN JAMES AUDUBON, F. R. SS. L. & E.

FELLOW OF THE LINNEAN AND ZOOLOGICAL SOCIETIES OF LONDON ; MEMBER OF THE LYCEUM
AND LINNEAN SOCIETY OF NEW YORK, OF THE NATURAL HISTORY SOCIETY OF PARIS, THE
WERNERIAN NATURAL HISTORY SOCIETY OF EDINBURGH ; HONORARY MEMBER OF THE
SOCIETY OF NATURAL HISTORY OF MANCHESTER, AND OF THE SCOTTISH ACADEMY OF
PAINTING, ARCHITECTURE, AND SCULPTURE, &c.

EDINBURGH:

ADAM BLACK, 55. NORTH BRIDGE, EDINBURGH;

R. HAVELL JUN., ENGRAVER, 77. OXFORD STREET, AND LONGMAN, REES,
BROWN, & GREEN, LONDON ; GEORGE SMITH, TITHEBARR STREET,
LIVERPOOL ; T. SOWLER, MANCHESTER ; MRS ROBINSON, LEEDS ;
E. CHARNLEY, NEWCASTLE ; POOL & BOOTH, CHESTER ; AND REILBY,
KNOTT, & BEILBY, BIRMINGHAM.

MDCCCXXXI.

Mockingbirds by Audubon. This dramatic picture, showing a rattlesnake attacking the birds' nest, proved to be one of the most controversial done by Audubon. His enemies claimed that rattlesnakes could not climb trees and that the picture was therefore a fake. Subsequent research has demonstrated that Audubon was correct.

the contrary, liked it; he found plenty of French with whom
to converse. I proposed selling out to him, a bargain was made,
he paid me a certain amount in cash, and gave me bills for
the residue."

When he was trying to justify himself, Audubon, like almost
anyone else, shaded facts to suit his purpose, and none of the
reasons he gave for returning to Henderson stands the test of
examination. Ste. Genevieve was not composed of "uneducated
and uncouth" citizens. Most contemporary travelers spoke of
it highly, far more highly than they did of Henderson. Furthermore, he was not obliged to leave Lucy in Kentucky while he
worked in Ste. Genevieve. She had lived at the Indian Queen
in Louisville and in the log cabin at Henderson; there was no
reason she could not have lived equally well, or even better, at
Ste. Genevieve.

The truth behind the breakup of the partnership lies in the
disparate temperaments of the two men. They had always been
an ill-sorted pair: Rozier, the businessman doing the work;
Audubon, the dilettante doing the playing. What is remarkable
is that the partnership lasted as long as it did. Its endurance
was a tribute to their respect for their fathers' wishes and to
Rozier's forbearance and patience. Because he was not the
type of man who writes memoirs, his side of the story does
not come down to us; but clearly the trip from Henderson
to Ste. Genevieve had thrown the two men into a close, day-
to-day relationship which had sharpened the differences between them. Throughout the journey Audubon had rejoiced in
every dangerous moment, welcomed every unexpected chance
to explore the woods or watch the Indians, completely unconcerned about the future of the partnership. Rozier, on the contrary, had worried at every step about the financial effect of
such a trip on the firm; and all the while he had borne the
brunt of the unkind remarks the woodsman traditionally makes
about the tenderfoot.

Now at Ste. Genevieve, Rozier decided to assert himself, and
it is not difficult to imagine the unpleasant scenes that must
have taken place, with Rozier demanding that Audubon at last
assume his share of the responsibility for the business, and
Audubon flashing back at him with the type of derisive com-

ment he later used when he wrote about his partner. The outcome, of course, was inevitable. Rozier stayed and prospered,
while Audubon, faced with a realistic appraisal of his own short-
comings, ran away just as he had run from his tutor at Rochefort and Miers Fisher at Philadelphia. This time his flight
snapped the ties formed by his father five years ago in France
in the hope of steadying him, ties that were supposed to last
for four more years.

It was the premature end of Jean Audubon's final effort to
provide a future for his son; it was for John James the beginning of still another era of irresponsibility.

CHAPTER VIII

1811 – 1812

WHEN Audubon said good-bye to Rozier at Ste. Genevieve, it never occurred to him that he was cutting himself off from the one person who had provided stability to the former firm and that from now on, when he went hunting, no one would remain behind to tend the store or manage any other business he might have. Setting off gaily in the spring of the year for the return trip to Henderson, he decided to take the direct overland route rather than go by water. "The weather was fine," he wrote, describing his trip, "all around me was as fresh and blooming as if it had just issued from the bosom of nature. My knapsack, my gun, and my dog were all that I had for baggage and company. But, although well moccasined, I moved slowly along, attracted by the brilliancy of the flowers, and the gambols of the fawns around their dams, to all appearances as thoughtless to danger as I felt myself."

Yet danger was never far distant on the frontier. A traveler, when he came to a cabin, usually received a warm welcome, but he might also find himself among thieves or murderers; and since the law was nonexistent except in a few courthouse towns, he had to provide his own defense, sometimes against people who were utterly depraved. In that rough society, even the leading citizens might stoop to brutality, cutting off the head of a bandit and placing it on a pole, castrating a man suspected of rape, or putting a thief in a barrel lined with spikes and rolling him down a hill. Several of Louisville's citizens had once killed a squaw by ripping her up the abdomen and then hacking at her quivering body with their knives, and another time had dug up some long-buried Indians, scalped the rotting corpses, and claimed bounties for each scalp they took. If the best men

could behave in such a fashion—often in the name of justice—
nothing was too evil for the worst.

Nevertheless, as night came and Audubon saw firelight in
the distance, he had no hesitation in approaching it. "I moved
towards it," he wrote, "full of confidence that it proceeded
from the camp of some wandering Indians. I was mistaken; I
discovered by its glare that it was from the hearth of a small
log cabin, and that a tall figure passed and repassed between
it and me, as if busily engaged in household arrangements.

"I reached the spot, and presenting myself at the door, asked
the tall figure, which proved to be a woman, if I might take
shelter under her roof for the night. Her voice was gruff, and
her attire negligently thrown about her. She answered in the
affirmative. I walked in, took a wooden stool, and quietly seated
myself by the fire. The next object that attracted my notice was
a finely formed young Indian, resting his head between his
hands, with his elbows on his knees. A long bow rested against
the log wall near him, while a quantity of arrows and two or
three raccoon skins lay at his feet. He moved not; he apparently
breathed not.

"Accustomed to the habits of Indians, and knowing that they
pay little attention to the approach of civilized strangers (a
circumstance which in some countries is considered as evincing
the apathy of their character), I addressed him in French, a
language not infrequently partially known to the people in that
neighborhood. He raised his head, pointed to one of his eyes
with his finger, and gave me a significant glance with the other.
His face was covered with blood. The fact was that an hour
before this, as he was in the act of discharging an arrow at a
raccoon in the top of a tree, the arrow had split upon the cord,
and sprung back with such violence into his right eye as to
destroy it forever."

Audubon asked for something to eat. The woman told him
to help himself; there was bread under the ashes and plenty of
venison and jerked buffalo meat. When he was ready for bed,
she added, he could sleep on one of the bear or buffalo hides
piled in the corner. Before starting his meal he took out his
watch; and the moment the woman saw it, her eyes began to
glitter. Audubon handed it to her to look at more closely. "She

was," he wrote, "all ecstasy, spoke of its beauty, asked me its value, and put the chain around her brawny neck, saying how happy the possession of such a watch would make her."

Audubon thought no more of the matter until, after supper, the Indian began behaving curiously. He rose from his seat and paced the floor as though he were in extreme pain. As he passed Audubon, he reached out his hand and pinched him so hard that Audubon was about to shout at him in anger. Before he did so, however, he caught the Indian's eye. His look was foreboding, and Audubon remained silent. The Indian then sat down again, drew his knife from its greasy scabbard, examined its edge, replaced it, took out his tomahawk, and filled the pipe with tobacco. All the while, he glanced at Audubon in such a way that he appeared to be trying to warn him of danger.

But how many people were in the woman's family? Where were they? When would they return? To what lengths would she go to keep the watch? These were the questions that raced through Audubon's mind. Knowing flight was useless—the woman was familiar with the area; he was not—he did the next best thing. He pretended to be unaware of his danger. He asked the woman for his watch, wound it up, and under the pretense of wishing to see how the weather might be turning, took up his gun and walked out of the cabin. Once outside, he slipped a ball into each barrel, scraped the edges of his flints, renewed the primings, and returned to the hut. There he lay down on some bearskins, his gun close to his body, and in a few minutes was, to all appearances, sound asleep.

A short time had elapsed when he heard some voices and, out of the corner of his eye, saw two young men enter, carrying a stag on a pole. They placed their load on the floor and asking for whiskey, helped themselves to it freely. Observing Audubon and the Indian, they asked who the two visitors were. The woman told them to speak less loudly, mentioned Audubon's watch, and took them to one corner of the room, where they whispered to each other.

"The lads had eaten and drunk themselves into such a condition that I already looked upon them as *hors de combat*," Audubon later wrote, "and the frequent visits of the whiskey bottle to the ugly mouth of their dam, I hoped would soon reduce her to a like state. Judge of my astonishment when I saw this incarnate fiend take a large carving-knife, and go to the grindstone to whet its edge; I saw her pour the water on the turning machine, and watched her working away with the dangerous instrument, until the cold sweat covered every part of my body, in despite of my determination to defend myself to the last. Her task finished, she walked to her reeling sons, and said, 'There, that'll soon settle him! Boys, kill yon ——— ———, and then for the watch.' "

Unless the Indian, in spite of his wounded condition, were willing to take sides, it would be three against one, and Audubon's gun with its long barrel would have been difficult to use effectively in the small cabin. Nevertheless, he quietly cocked both barrels and was on the point of shooting the woman when the door suddenly opened and two more travelers entered. Audubon immediately leapt to his feet, explained the situation, and the new arrivals helped him disarm and tie up the woman and the two young men. Most of that night they sat up talking, and the next morning were ready to punish their captives. "We marched them into the woods off the road," Audubon said, "and having used them as Regulators were wont to use such delinquents [the name "Regulators" was given to informal posses] we set fire to the cabin, gave all the skins and implements to the young Indian warrior, and proceeded, well pleased, towards the settlements."

What Audubon lacked was not physical courage; it was patience and self-discipline in the face of the ordinary. Lost in the woods on the way to Cape Giradeau, he could laugh at himself; forced to spend six weeks in a winter encampment on the Mississippi, he could joke about it. But behind the counter of the store, his mastery of himself vanished and he became restless and distraught. He could lie awake with a loaded rifle in his hand waiting for a woman to attack him with a knife, but he could not wait in the store for a customer to appear. He would walk miles to get bread for Rozier, but did not hesitate for one moment to leave the day-to-day work to him. Until he felt a sense of drama, he could not act. But there was no drama in his return to Henderson in early March, and he quickly slipped back into his old way of life, busying himself with the inconsequential. Even in May, when he shot two small birds of a kind he had never collected before and named them "carbonated warblers," the accomplishment amounted to nothing in the end. No one has ever seen such birds since, and it is probable that he did not take pains to draw them accurately.

During that lazy interval in Henderson—the vacation of a man who had not earned one—one of the few events that stood out in his mind was the purchase of a horse named Barro that became one of his particular favorites. The horse belonged to a Henderson resident who had bought it on a trip to the headquarters of the Arkansas River.

The moment Audubon saw the horse, he wanted it; and, with a skill he rarely showed in his business affairs, he began bargaining. Finally the owner agreed to let him try the animal. Audubon jumped the horse several times, then rode him through a muddy swamp to test his strength, took him to the river, swam him upstream and down, and shot a turkey cock from his back to see if he would shy from either the sound of the shot or the sight of the dead bird. Barro passed each trial perfectly, and Audubon "sent word to the owner of the horse that I should be glad to see him. When he came, I asked him what price he would take; he said, fifty dollars in silver was the lowest. So I paid the money, took a bill of sale, and became master of the horse. The doctor [his old friend Dr. Rankin], who was an excellent judge, said smiling to me, 'Mr. Audubon, when you are tired of him, I will refund you the fifty dollars, for depend upon it he is a capital horse.' The mane was trimmed, but the tail left untouched; the doctor had him shod 'all around,' and for several weeks he was ridden by my wife, who was highly pleased with him."

It was fortunate that she was, because the purchase of Barro used up a large part of Audubon's total earnings for the year. Since the preceding May when he had moved to Henderson, he had engaged in scarcely a single profitable activity except for the trip to Ste. Genevieve. His profits on the whiskey, which had been the firm's most lucrative item, amounted to $267.50. Against this amount and the money the two partners had made on their gunpowder and drygoods, they had had to charge the cost of the trip. The flatboat crew were probably paid somewhere between $150 and $240 for the trip, and the patroon undoubtedly received another hundred dollars. This, in addition to the cost of the food, would have reduced Audubon's share of the profit on the whiskey to not much more than a hundred or a hundred and ten dollars. Viewed in this light, Audubon's purchase of Barro was pure self-indulgence, and Lucy might have been pardoned if she had been less enthusiastic than Audubon made her appear.

In the fall, however, occurred an event that must have brightened her life. Her brother Thomas, she learned, was going to New Orleans to set up an office, because Thomas and Arthur Kinder, the partners who had befriended Benjamin Bakewell, had worked out an arrangement whereby he could act as an agent for a mercantile firm in Liverpool. On his way south, he wanted to meet Lucy and Audubon either in Louisville or Henderson. They had been planning another trip east to Flatland Ford, but on hearing that Thomas might be arriving, they decided to postpone their departure and wait for him at Louisville. What a pleasure it was to see him! Not only was he Lucy's brother, but he and Audubon had been close friends ever since those happy days when they had gone skating and hunting together at Mill Grove. By day he and Audubon undoubtedly explored the Kentucky countryside together, once more engaging in all the sports they had shared together. By night they talked about each other's business prospects. Here was Thomas Bakewell, ready to open an office in New Orleans with a connection already formed for him in England. Here was Audubon with no job or other commitments and a knowledge of French that would be useful in Louisiana. Why not get together and establish their own firm? Having ridded himself of Rozier, Audubon was ready to form a new connection but with a younger partner over whom he could exercise more influence. The idea was another youthful and impractical dream that took no account of the international situation.

On May 1 of the same year, the British frigate *Guerrière* had appeared off the entrance to New York's harbor at Sandy Hook and had impressed an American citizen from the American brig *Spitfire*. On May 4 the *Guerrière* halted an American sloop and impressed another sailor. This time, Madison, who was now

President, ordered the frigate, the *President,* to proceed immediately from Annapolis to Sandy Hook. Arriving at its new station, the *President* spotted another ship and, thinking it was the *Guerrière,* headed toward it, but failed to overtake it until after sundown. The other boat turned away; the *President* went in pursuit. As the two vessels ranged alongside on the rolling water, a shot was fired in the darkness by the stranger. The *President* responded with broadside after broadside, and within fifteen minutes the stranger was lying helpless and defeated. When the sun rose above the Atlantic, the officers of the *President* were able to identify their enemy. It was not the *Guerrière* at all, but a much smaller British sloop of war, the *Little Belt.* At the court of inquiry held afterward, it was established that indeed the *Little Belt* had fired the first shot of the engagement, and the matter was considered closed. The engagement, however, had a curious effect on Anglo-American relations. By then the British had decided to make some concessions in regard to the *Chesapeake* affair, but the American people, flushed by their victory over the *Little Belt,* were no longer interested in the *Chesapeake.* The British concessions did nothing, therefore, to relieve the tension between the two countries.

Anti-British sentiment was further enflamed by the suspicion that Great Britain was surreptitiously supporting two Indian chiefs, the Prophet and his brother Tecumseh, in their attempt to invalidate the land treaties between the United States and the Indians. According to the two chiefs, all the land belonged to each Indian and could not be sold without the consent of every warrior. This philosophy eventually led to the battle of Tippecanoe, in which General Harrison drove the Indians from the field and burned their village.

These two victories, one over the *Little Belt,* the other over a tribe of Indians, gave the United States a new sense of strength in dealing with England; and nowhere was the rising war spirit greater than in Kentucky, which elected Henry Clay to the House of Representatives for the express purpose of giving him a forum from which he could make his strong anti-British opinions heard.

Thomas Bakewell, coming from the East where anti-British sentiment was not so strong, might easily have underrated the public's desire for war, but Audubon was living in the heart of the warmongers' country. Yet he never seems to have drawn a connection between their stated policies and the fate of Audubon & Bakewell, whose sole business asset was its tie with a firm in Liverpool. If Henry Clay and men of his thinking had their way, that asset would be valueless. Unworried by what was happening, the two new partners continued with their plans. Thomas Bakewell was to go on to New Orleans; Audubon and Lucy would return to Flatland Ford for their visit, stopping at a number of towns on the way to conduct business. Then they would join Thomas early in the following year.

Because of his pride in owning Barro, Audubon was determined to make the trip on horseback and later wrote an exultant account of the journey, how he traveled at the rate of four miles an hour, never made less than forty miles in a day, and often, because of his business, deviated from the main roads. Only in a single sentence did he admit that he was not alone. "My wife," he wrote, "rode on a single horse from Henderson to Philadelphia at the same rate."

Lucy, too, gave an account of their trip, but she did not share Audubon's enthusiasm for the fast pace. "We were on horseback and Victor rode before his Papa all the way," she wrote to a cousin. "Now the difficulties and fatigues are over, I can scarcely realize that I have rode on horseback nearly eight hundred miles. The country from Louisville to Pittsburgh is flat, rich woodlands. There are some cultivated farms which diversify the scene a little, but the chief part of the road is through thick woods, where the sun scarcely ever penetrates. We crossed a number of rivers and creeks. The rivers are all navigable and have their banks lined with a variety of trees and shrubs." They spent four days with Benjamin Bakewell, who greatly pleased Lucy by telling her that Victor looked much as she had at his age. Then they continued across the mountains, which have "really most dreadful roads at all seasons of the year," except at "the top of the last mountain there is a most beautiful view of a level well cultivated country, and from having travelled so far through woods where the eye can scarcely see fifty yards, the scene is particularly pleasing."

Much of Lucy's attitude toward the West comes through her

simple words: the depression caused by the deep, dark forests, which can indeed be disheartening to someone who loves the sunlight, and her relief at seeing before her the well-cultivated farms of eastern Pennsylvania. She was back in civilization at last. "You will easily conceive," she continued in her letter, "I must have suffered from cold and fatigue considerably at that season, but the prospect before me of seeing my family and friends ... buoyed up my spirits, and enabled me to endure more than in any common cause I perhaps should have done."

Unfortunately, she found bad news awaiting her on her arrival at Flatland Ford. Her sisters Sarah and Anne were both well, although they had grown so much she could hardly recognize them, but her sister Eliza was being treated for a growing blindness that affected one eye. "We have felt much alarm about her," Lucy wrote, "but I trust she will recover the use of it entirely, as it is even now better." Aside from Eliza's illness, the visit was a happy one.

When Audubon and Rozier had dissolved their partnership, they had not been able to reach a final settlement of their joint accounts. Being short of cash, neither partner could buy out the other, so they continued to have a mutual interest in the assets and liabilities of the former firm. During his first week at Flatland Ford, Audubon occupied himself with some of the business remaining between himself and his earlier partner. In Pittsburgh, he reported to Rozier, he had paid twenty dollars to Benjamin Bakewell against the money the former firm still owed him. (Fifty dollars for his horse, Barro; twenty dollars against a legitimate business debt: that was typical of Audubon's general thinking in respect to finances.) At Flatland Ford, he had been surprised to learn that Dacosta had abandoned the lead mine and sold Mill Grove. After two unsuccessful attempts to see Dacosta, he had concluded that Audubon & Rozier might as well write off the money Dacosta still owed them. In a sketchy fashion, he tried to give Rozier a picture of business conditions in the East. Merchandise, he wrote, was very scarce and consequently costly, and at the end of his letter he stated rather obviously that "the times are not brilliant for business, particularly ours."

After remaining about a month at Flatland Ford he saddled

up Barro and set out for Kentucky again, leaving Lucy behind to enjoy a longer visit. He planned to stay at Henderson until Lucy rejoined him. Then they would move permanently to New Orleans, the headquarters of Audubon & Bakewell.

At one of the crossings of the Juniata River, he fell into conversation with another traveler who was mounted on a superb horse, for which he had paid three hundred dollars, and who was accompanied by a servant on horseback leading another as a change. Audubon approached the stranger, complimented him on his horse, and fell into conversation with him. They were both going to Bedford and, according to Audubon, decided to race to the inn. The first to arrive was to order trout for the other, and Audubon later claimed that he was the winner.

Over the trout, the stranger introduced himself as Vincent Nolte, a European merchant who was traveling to New Orleans to set up a firm of his own. Unlike Audubon, he was well known and was starting his venture with capital amounting to 6,000 pounds and a line of credit of 10,000 pounds against which he could draw. But, like Audubon, he had failed to foresee the impending clash with the British, although he had a better excuse. His principal business connections were with Englishmen, and because British intelligence agents had failed to go west, most Englishmen were convinced that war with America was a practical impossibility.

When Nolte wrote his version of their meeting, he omitted any mention of the race to the inn. Perhaps he forgot it; perhaps he wished to forget it; or perhaps Audubon only imagined the contest. In any case, Nolte only said, "Early one morning, I rode in great loneliness over the summit of the Alleghenies, called Laurel Hill, and arrived about ten o'clock at a small inn near the falls of the Juniata River. Here I ordered a heavy breakfast. The landlady showed me into a room and asked if I would mind eating at the same table with a strange gentleman who was already seated there. 'He is quite a stranger,' she said to me. As I entered, I found this man, who immediately struck me as being what is commonly called an odd duck. He was sitting at a table before the fire with a Madras handkerchief wrapped around his head in the manner of a French sailor or dockworker. I went up and greeted him politely with the words, 'I hope I don't incommode you by coming to take my breakfast with you.' 'Oh, no, sir,' he answered with a strong French accent that made the words sound like 'No, sare.' 'Ah,' I said, 'you are a Frenchman, sir?' 'No, sare,' was the answer, 'hi em en Henglishmen.' 'Why,' I asked, 'how do you make that out? You look like a Frenchman, and you speak like one.' 'Hi em en Henglishmen, because hi got a Henglish wife,' he answered. Without going into the subject further, we decided during breakfast to stay together and ride until we got to Pittsburgh. He proved to be more and more of an original and finally admitted that he was born a Frenchman, came from La Rochelle and, as a child, had moved to Louisiana. He had gone to sea, he said, and had gradually become a real American. 'Well,' I answered, 'how does that reconcile itself with your being an Englishman?' Upon this, he made himself more comfortable by lapsing into French. 'When all is said and done,' he replied, 'I am somewhat cosmopolitan; I belong to all countries.' This man, who since then won so great a name in natural history, particularly in ornithology, was Audubon. At that time, he had no thought of making a career of the study of natural history. He wanted to be a merchant."

Both Nolte and Audubon had people to see on reaching Pittsburgh and remained there for several days. Again Audubon wrote to Rozier, this time about the money he believed Rozier still owed him after selling some of the remaining assets of Audubon & Rozier. Audubon had taken a note in payment for his share and wanted to invest the proceeds in his new business.

Before arriving at Pittsburgh, Nolte had sent an employee ahead to purchase two flatboats for him, one for himself and one to carry his horses—an elegance to which most riverboat passengers were unaccustomed. They usually took their horses, smell and all, on the same boat with themselves. The employee was also to buy four hundred barrels of flour. When this was sold in New Orleans, according to Nolte's calculations, it would cover all the expenses of the trip; Nolte, in spite of his high style of living, was not one to waste money.

By this time, he had become extremely fond of Audubon, although he laughed at Audubon's pretensions as a businessman. "As he was a good and pleasant person and, besides which, a lovely draftsman, I offered him a free berth in our cabin. He took advantage of the offer; and we left Pittsburgh in very cold weather, with the two rivers, the Monongahela and the Ohio, filled with drifting ice, on the first day of January, 1812. I did not know anything about his traveling plans until we reached Limestone. . . . Here we both took our horses ashore, and I decided to go by land with him to visit the capital at Lexington and from there to Louisville. . . . We had scarcely finished our breakfast at Limestone when Audubon, all at once, jumped up and cried out in French, 'Now I am going to lay the basis for my business firm.' Thereupon he took a small packet of visiting cards and a hammer from his coat pocket, and also some nails from his vest, and began to nail one of the cards to the door of the inn where we were eating. The card read as follows: 'Audubon & Bakewell, Commissions Merchants (Pork, lard, & flour), New Orleans.' So, I thought to myself, you have got competition before you get to the city yourself. But it did not bother me much, because they could not boast of the names of Hope or Baring [the two important firms that were backing Nolte], and pork and lard, moreover, were not attractive to me. I was very glad to console myself by thinking that competition of this nature could not amount to much."

After staying at Lexington for eight days, Audubon pushed on to Louisville, hoping to find a letter from Rozier waiting there for him. No word had come, so Audubon sat down and penned a rather stiff note to his former partner. "I wish to know," he asked sternly, "if you will pay at New Orleans the bill of 1,000 dollars which I have on you, or if I shall have to go to Ste. Genevieve to get them, and, at any rate, what has become of you? We promised each other mutual correspondence and I am afraid that it is all on my side." As for his future plans, he told Rozier he expected to stay in Kentucky for about thirty or forty days before going on to New Orleans.

Although so hard pressed for funds, he still kept Barro and was riding him one day when the horse began to behave strangely, so strangely indeed that, for a moment or two, Audubon thought the animal might be dying. A short time before, he had observed a sudden darkness rising in the sky but believed it was nothing but an approaching thunderstorm. After he had gone about a mile farther, he heard a distant rumbling that sounded like a tornado and gave the spurs to Barro. But instead of galloping forward, the horse moved slowly and cautiously as though he were walking over a smooth sheet of ice. Suddenly he stopped altogether and stood still, with his four feet spread apart as if to keep from falling. Audubon was on the point of dismounting, when the trees and shrubs began to move at their roots, the ground rose and fell in furrows like ripples on a lake, and Audubon realized that he was in the midst of an earthquake. For several moments he remained sitting on Barro, the ground rocking beneath him, and in terror that the earth would split apart. Then the shaking ceased, Barro pulled his feet together into their normal position and set off at a gallop.

What Audubon had experienced was one of a series of earthquakes, centered around New Madrid, Missouri, which during the winter of 1811–1812 shook the western frontier for miles and miles around. Altogether during a three-month period approximately 2,000 tremors occurred, and three of them are believed to have been of an intensity greater than the 1964 earthquake in Alaska. In the rivers whole islands suddenly disappeared. (The loss of one of them was considered beneficial, as it had served as headquarters for a gang of river pirates. Nature had accomplished what the "Regulators" and other law enforcement groups had been unable to.) So great was the force of these quakes that one of them blocked an entire river, resulting in the formation of present-day Reelfoot Lake in Tennessee, and another so twisted the ground that for a few minutes even the mighty Mississippi ran back uphill, as the earth rose beneath it.

Although the first sensations were terrifying, everyone soon became accustomed to the tremors; and a few, like Audubon, began to see a humorous side to the convulsions. "Shock succeeded shock almost every day or night for several weeks," he wrote, "diminishing, however, so gradually as to dwindle away into mere vibrations of the earth. Strange to say, I for one became so accustomed to the feeling as rather to enjoy the fears manifested by others. I can never forget the effects of one of the slighter shocks which took place when I was at a friend's house, where I had gone to watch the merriment that, in our western country, attends a wedding. The ceremony being performed, supper over, and the fiddles tuned, dancing became the order of the moment. This was merrily followed up to a late hour, when the party retired to rest. We were in what is called, with great propriety, a *log-house,* one of large dimensions, and solidly constructed. The owner was a physician, and in one corner were not only his lancets, tourniquets, amputating knives, and other sanguinary apparatus, but all the drugs which he employed for the relief of his patients, arranged in jars and phials of different sizes. . . .

"As I have said, we had all retired to rest, some to dream of sighs or smiles, some to sink into oblivion. Morning was fast approaching, when the rumbling noise that precedes the earthquake, began so loudly as to waken and alarm the whole party, and drive them out of bed in the greatest consternation. The scene which ensued it is impossible for me to describe, and it would require the humorous pencil of Cruikshank to do justice to it. Fear knows no restraint. Every person, young or old, filled with alarm at the creaking of the log-house, and apprehending instant destruction, rushed wildly out to the grass enclosure fronting the building. The full moon was slowly descending from her throne, covered at times by clouds that rolled heavily along, as if to conceal from her view the scenes of terror which prevailed on the earth below. On the grass-plat we all met, in such condition as rendered it next to impossible to discriminate any of the party, all huddled together in a state of great deshabille. The earth waved like a field of corn before the breeze; the birds left their perches, and flew about, not knowing whither; and the doctor, recollecting the danger of his gallipots, ran to his shop room, to prevent their dancing off the shelves to the floor. Never for a moment did he think of closing the doors, but, spreading his arms, jumped about the front of the cases, pushing back here and there the falling jars; with so little success, however, that before the shock was over he had lost nearly all he possessed.

"The shock at length ceased, and the frightened women, now sensible of their undress, fled to their several apartments." The men, of course, followed them back to the house, the doctor ruefully examined his shattered bottles of supplies, and the rising sun found the household returning to normal.

And so, laughing at earthquakes, still unwilling to work seriously, his partnership with Rozier dissolved and a new one formed with Thomas Bakewell, Audubon entered the year 1812, unconcerned by the present, hopeful of the future.

CHAPTER IX

1812 — 1814

O N his return to Henderson in the winter of 1812, Audubon seemed suddenly determined to put his business affairs in order. One of his first acts was to sell Barro, for whom
he received $125. (Lucy must have been pleased when she heard
about this profit on a purchase she could only have regarded as
an extravagance.) Next, he gave up the idea of moving to New
Orleans, finally realizing that war between the United States
and England would make it impossible for Audubon & Bakewell to act as agent for a British firm. Instead, he made a trip
to Ste. Genevieve to talk to Rozier and settle their differences
in person.

After this brief flurry of activity, he dropped back into his
old state of lethargy. Thomas Bakewell had not yet returned
from New Orleans to discuss alternate plans, and, until then,
Audubon apparently thought he could do nothing but wait.
Having no better use for his time, therefore, he decided to go
back to Flatland Ford that spring for another visit.

On this journey, he made no pretense of conducting any
business and enjoyed to the full all the amusements Flatland
Ford offered, shooting, fishing, and tramping through the woods
and fields. One day, when he was out hunting with Lucy's
brother William, he noticed in the distance a nest that puzzled
him; he could not tell whether it belonged to a crow or a hawk.
Coming closer, he saw that the parent bird was sitting on it, but
in the bad light he was still unable to distinguish its species.
In order to identify it, he asked William to climb the tree and
get one of the eggs. On reaching the nest, William called back
that, for some curious reason, the bird refused to move. Au-

dubon told William to cover the bird with his handkerchief and bring it down.

What they captured was a broad-winged hawk, a small, chunky hawk about the size of a crow, with broad white and black bands on the underside of its tail. "I put the bird on a stick made fast to my table," Audubon said, in an unusually detailed description of his method of drawing. "It merely moved its feet to grasp the stick, and stood erect, but raised its feathers and drew its neck in upon its shoulders. I passed my hand over to smooth the feathers by gentle pressure. It moved not. The plumage remained as I wished it. Its eye, directed towards mine, appeared truly sorrowful. I measured its bill with the compass, began my outlines, continued measuring part after part as I went on, and finished the drawing without the bird ever once moving. My wife sat at my side, reading to me at intervals, but our conversation had frequent reference to the singularity of the incident.

"The drawing being finished, I raised the window, laid hold of the poor bird, and launched it into the air, where it sailed off out of my sight, without uttering a single cry or deviating from its course."

At Flatland Ford, life was as quiet as it had always been; and the capture of a new bird was one of the spring's exciting events. In the outside world, however, matters were taking a serious turn. Four days after Audubon had completed his picture of the broad-winged hawk, President Madison delivered a stinging message to Congress. British cruisers, Madison charged, had been violating the American flag on the high seas, seizing persons sailing under it, and had been harassing American commerce. He complained also of their lawless proceedings in American harbors and their attacks within the jurisdiction of the United States. Furthermore, he accused the British of inciting the Indians to warfare. It was a summation of American grievances expressed in strong and bitter terms, one that would lead in three weeks to a declaration of war.

Two days afterward, Audubon went from Flatland Ford to Philadelphia and appeared in the United States District Court before Judge Peters. Accompanied by a lawyer, Stephen Du Ponceau, and a merchant, William Taylor, Jr., who attested

to his good character and to his residence in Pennsylvania,
Audubon swore "that I will support the Constitution of the
United States, and that I do absolutely and entirely renounce
and abjure all allegiance and fidelity to every foreign Prince,
Potentate, State or Sovereignty whatever and particularly Napoleon the first Emperor of the French of whom I was heretofore a subject."

With this important business accomplished, he took Lucy
back to Henderson, up over the mountains and down the long
stretches of the river. This time they traveled again by stagecoach and boat, not by horseback, but even with this comparative luxury, the trip could not have been easy for Lucy.
She was more than three months pregnant.

Back in Kentucky, Audubon went through another period
of indecision. Having made up his mind to wait at Henderson
for Thomas Bakewell, he now reversed himself. In August, long
after war had been declared, he wrote Rozier that he was planning to go to New Orleans that fall. While Audubon was still
vacillating, Thomas was on his way north to join him at Henderson. Later he briefly described what happened. "Defeated
in the brilliant prospects at New Orleans by the war," he said,
"I continued the business connection with Audubon on a small
scale of storekeeping at Henderson."

Storekeeping at Henderson?

Yes, storekeeping at Henderson.

Incredible as it may seem after his first disastrous experience,
Audubon had no suggestion to offer his partner other than to
open another store at Henderson. The town was a little larger,
the surrounding area slightly more prosperous, a few more
flatboats stopped on their way down the river, but the community was still small and its commerce negligible. Nevertheless, with a few hundred dollars in his pocket, some of them
Thomas's, some of them his own, Audubon went up to Louisville, purchased a small amount of stock, half on credit and
half for cash, and was back at storekeeping again, this time with
Thomas to stand behind the counter while he went hunting. And on November 30, 1812, Lucy gave birth to another
son, John Woodhouse Audubon. He now had two children to
support.

His new business and his children did not interfere, however, with his continued observations of birds, and he kept on
taking time off from his work whenever he wanted to. On one
of his many business trips to Louisville, he stopped to revisit
an old sycamore tree where, five years before, he had watched
the chimney swifts gather. With interest, he noted that the
birds were still there in large numbers.

During the autumn of the same year, he took an opportunity
to observe closely the flights of passenger pigeons. Although
now extinct (the last one on earth died at exactly 1:00 P.M. on
September 1, 1914, at the Cincinnati Zoo), throughout Audubon's lifetime these pigeons comprised a large part of all the
individual birds flying across the skies of America. Audubon
was again traveling from Henderson to Louisville, he wrote,
when "a few miles beyond Hardinsburg, I observed the passenger pigeons flying from northeast to southwest in greater numbers than I had ever seen them before, it seemed to me. Feeling
an inclination to count the flocks that might pass within the
reach of my eye in one hour, I dismounted, seated myself on
an eminence, and began to mark a dot with my pencil for
every flock that passed. In a short time, finding this task im-
practicable because the birds were pouring by in countless mul-
titudes, I arose. But before I travelled on, I counted the dots
that I had put down and found that one hundred and sixty
flocks had been recorded in twenty-one minutes. I met still
more, further on. The air was literally filled with pigeons, and
the noon-day light was obscured as by an eclipse. The dung
fell in spots not unlike melting flakes of snow; and the con-
tinuous buzz of wings tended to lull my senses.

"While waiting for dinner at Young's Inn at the confluence
of the Salt River with the Ohio, I saw, at my leisure, immense
legions still going by. Their front reached far beyond the Ohio
on the west, and the beechwood forests directly east of me.
... Before sunset I reached Louisville, fifty-five miles from
Hardinsburg. The pigeons were still passing in undiminished
numbers."

Today, the scene seems almost incredible, but it became even
more so when the birds finally landed. "As soon as the pigeons
discover a sufficiency of food to entice them to alight," Audu-

bon went on, "they fly around in circles, reviewing the countryside below. . . . On alighting they industriously throw aside the
withered leaves in quest of the fallen mast. The rear ranks continually rise, passing over the main body and alighting in front,
and in such rapid succession that the whole flock still seems on
the wing. The quantity of ground swept in this way is astonishing. So completely has it been cleared that the gleaner who
might follow in the rear of the flock would find his labor
completely lost."

As soon as the pigeons appeared in an area, the pigeon hunters gathered at the roosting grounds and made preparations for
the slaughter. It was not hunting as we think of it today; it was
more like driving a combine through a field with the determination to cut and harvest every blade. "Let us inspect their
place of nightly rendezvous," Audubon continued. "One of
these curious roosting places on the banks of the Green River
in Kentucky I repeatedly visited. As always, it was in a part
of the forest where the trees were huge and where there was
little underbrush. I rode through it for more than forty miles,
and on crossing it in different parts I found it rather more
than three miles wide on the average. My first view of it was
at nearly two hours before sunset, about two weeks before the
coming of the pigeons. Few of these birds were then to be seen,
but a great gathering of persons with horses and wagons, guns
and ammunition had pitched camp on the edge of the forest.

"Two farmers from the vicinity of Russellville, more than a
hundred miles distant, had driven more than three hundred
hogs to be fattened on the pigeons they hoped to slaughter.
Here and there, people were busy plucking and salting birds
already killed, and they sat amid large piles of them. The dung
lay several inches deep, covering the whole roosting place. I
noticed that many trees two feet in diameter were broken off
at no great distance from the ground; and the branches of many
of the largest and tallest had given away, proving to me that
the number of birds must be immense beyond conception.

"As the time of the arrival of the passenger pigeons approached, their foes anxiously prepared to receive them. Some
persons were ready with iron pots containing sulphur, others
with torches of pine knots; many had poles, and the rest, guns.

... Everything was ready, and all eyes were fixed on the clear sky which could be glimpsed amid the tall tree-tops."

Evening had fallen, when "suddenly a general cry burst forth, 'Here they come!' The noise they made, even though still distant, reminded me of a hard gale at sea, passing through the rigging of a close-reefed vessel. As the birds arrived and passed over me, I felt a current of air that surprised me. Thousands of the pigeons were soon knocked down by the pole-men, while more continued to pour in. The fires were lighted, then a magnificent, wonderful, and almost terrifying sight presented itself. The pigeons, arriving by the thousands, alighted everywhere, one above another, until solid masses were formed on the branches all around. Here and there the perches gave way with a crash under the weight, and fell to the ground, destroying hundreds of birds beneath, and forcing down the dense groups of them with which every stick was loaded. The scene was one of uproar and confusion. I found it quite useless to speak or even to shout, to those persons nearest to me. Even the gun reports were seldom heard, and I was made aware of the firing only by seeing the shooters reloading.

"No one dared venture nearer the devastation. Meanwhile, the hogs had been penned up. The picking up of the dead and wounded birds was put off till morning. The pigeons were constantly coming, and it was past midnight before I noticed any decrease in the number of those arriving. The uproar continued the whole night. I was anxious to know how far the sound could be heard, so I sent off a man used to roaming the forest, who returned in two hours with the information that he had heard it distinctly three miles from the roosting place.

"Towards the approach of day, the noise somewhat subsided. Long before I could distinguish them plainly, the pigeons began to move off in a direction quite different from the one in which they flew when they arrived in the evening before. By sunrise all that were able to fly had disappeared. The howling of the wolves now reached our ears, and the foxes, the lynxes, cougars, bears, raccoons, opossums and polecats were sneaking off. Eagles and hawks, accompanied by a crowd of vultures, took their place and enjoyed their share of the spoils.

"Then the authors of all this devastation began to move

among the dead, the dying, and the mangled, picking up the pigeons and piling them in heaps. When each man had as many as he could possibly dispose of, the hogs were let loose to feed on the remainder."

In Audubon's times, the Carolina parrakeets, small blue-bodied parrots, also arrived in enormous numbers. Landing in a wheat field, they would cover it, he said, "like a brilliantly colored carpet" and destroy much of the farmer's grain. Or, if they lighted in an orchard of pear or apple trees, they would leave the branches completely stripped of fruit. "These outrages," he wrote, "meet with severe retaliation from the farmers, who destroy the parrakeets in vast numbers while they are plucking fruit or tearing the grain from the stack. The husbandmen then approach them with perfect ease and commit great slaughter among them. All the survivors rise, shriek, fly around about for a few minutes, and again alight on the very place of most imminent danger. The gun is kept busy, with eight, ten, or even twenty being killed at each discharge. As if conscious of the death of their companions, the living birds sweep over the bodies, screaming as loudly as ever. Yet they return to the stack to be shot at until so few remain alive that the farmer does not consider it worth his while to spend more of his ammunition. I have seen several hundred destroyed in this manner in a few hours, and have procured a basketful with a few shots in order to make a choice of good specimens for drawing the figures." A basketful for one drawing seems a poor exchange even for a picture as magnificent as those Audubon painted.

Yet Audubon, like other people living on the frontier, had difficulty in believing that the endless swarms of birds could be diminished by the slaughter. Writing about the passenger pigeons, he said that "persons unacquainted with these birds might naturally conclude that such dreadful havoc would soon put an end to the species." But he was not completely blind to the possibility of their eventual extinction, because he added this significant remark, "I have satisfied myself by long observation that nothing but the gradual diminution of our forests can accomplish their decrease." Hunting, of course, was an important factor in the disappearance of many birds and animals, but

Audubon was ahead of his time in recognizing the disastrous effect of a changing environment. On the continent of Europe, where the changes wrought by man came sufficiently gradually for the birds to adjust to them, no bird has become extinct in modern times. In America, where the settlers moved swiftly in hordes across the countryside, the impact was too sudden. Today many of the birds that Audubon knew are gone, passenger pigeons, parrakeets, ivory-billed woodpeckers, heath hens, Labrador ducks. Many others have been greatly diminished like vireos and redheaded woodpeckers. On the other hand, some birds have benefited from the changes. Chestnut-sided warblers were a rarity in Audubon's day; today they are relatively common; and other birds like indigo buntings, orioles, goldfinches, and towhees have also increased. Not every change has been for the worse.

This period, when Audubon watched the passenger pigeons and the parrakeets, took long trips across the prairie, and lived with the Indians, was one of the happiest times in his life. "The pleasures," he later wrote, "which I felt at Henderson . . . can never be effaced from my heart until after death." With Thomas Bakewell as a junior partner and no one to supervise or scold him, life was going so smoothly for Audubon that he decided to become a permanent resident of Henderson and, on December 22, 1813, purchased two one-acre lots.

Nevertheless, he realized he could not confine all his efforts to the store or even to Henderson, if he were to make the fortune he so much wanted. February, 1814, found him, therefore, on a boat working his way against the current of the Mississippi, making another trading trip into the region above the mouth of the Ohio. The weather was cold, so cold that even Audubon had lost interest in his surroundings after they had passed Cape Giradeau. Eight or nine miles above the town, they approached the Great Tower, a fragment of rock fifty feet high rising from the river bed. Audubon, wrapped in his blankets, was lying on the deck when his patroon, a Canadian and former fur trapper, suddenly shouted. There, flying above them, was a dark-colored eagle which the patroon said he had only seen a few times before and then never anywhere except at the Great Lakes.

Instantly he was on his feet and, having observed it as closely as he could under the circumstances, was unable to identify it. Convinced that the bird was unknown to other ornithologists, he wanted to find out more about it. This was the constant challenge, to discover in that relatively unexplored country a new species. In this case, however, he saw no more of these birds until later, when he happened to be collecting crayfish near the junction of the Green River and the Ohio. He had noticed a nest on one of the high cliffs bordering the river, and because none of his companions could identify it, he decided to watch it himself. Seating himself about a hundred yards from the foot of the rock, he waited patiently for two hours until one of the old birds made its appearance. The second arrived soon after with some fish for the young but, noticing Audubon, began to scream with alarm, and both birds soon disappeared. The next day was rainy and stormy, and so was the next. On the third, he went back, but the birds were gone, perhaps frightened away. After all this time, time he should have spent at the store, he still was unable to identify the mysterious birds, although the frontiersmen who had accompanied him during his watch jokingly told him they were nothing but immature bald eagles.

He had better luck with two American avocets—long-billed, long-legged shorebirds—which he discovered that June on a business trip from Henderson to Vincennes, Indiana. They were hovering at the edge of a pond, and although it was late and he was tired and hungry, he stopped to watch them.

From the cries made by the four birds, he felt confident that they had nests and that their mates were either sitting or tending their young. The pond, which was about two hundred yards long and half as wide, was surrounded by tall bulrushes along its margin. Near the center were several small islands, eight or ten yards in length and arranged in a line. Walking through mud up to his knees, Audubon waded out to the islands, discovered three nests, and then, back on shore and covered with slime, mounted his horse and went on to Vincennes.

He finished his business there as quickly as he could and the next morning at sunrise was back and concealed himself in a spot that gave him a clear view of the whole pond. For hours he lay among the rushes, watching the avocets look for food. Then, because he wanted to see one of the birds sitting on its nest, he left his hiding place and crawled to the nearest island on all fours through the muddy water. Soon he was within three feet of the nesting bird, peering at her through the tall grasses. Then she observed him and scrambled off, running, tumbling, and finally rising in the air with clucking noises. Having learned all that he could that day, he shot down five specimens. Among them, he said, he unfortunately found three females.

So he passed much of the year 1814, leaving Lucy and the two boys for long periods to trade at Ste. Genevieve, Cape Giradeau and Vincennes, all the while searching for birds, shooting them, observing them, and adding to his already considerable knowledge. Sometimes his journeys were uneventful, sometimes they were exciting and filled with danger. One time he was returning from the town of Shawnee, which lay farther down the river, and, as he later said, was for once concentrating on business matters. The weather was pleasant, and he had just forded a river and entered a tract of bottomland when he noticed that the skies had suddenly changed. For a while he expected another earthquake, but his horse showed none of the usual signs. Coming to a brook, Audubon dismounted and was just starting to drink when he heard an extraordinary murmuring sound in the distance. He then noticed in the southwest a yellowish oval spot, and at the same moment a strong breeze began to shake the limbs of the tallest trees. As the wind increased in intensity, small twigs and branches fell to the ground.

"Turning instinctively towards the direction from which the wind blew," Audubon said, "I saw to my great astonishment that the noblest trees of the forest bent their lofty heads for a while, and, unable to stand against the blast, were falling into pieces. First the branches were broken off with a crackling noise; then went the upper parts of the massy trunks; and in many places whole trees of gigantic size were falling entire to the ground." The winds had risen to at least sixty miles an hour, but "so rapid was the progress of the storm that before I could think of taking measures to ensure my safety the hurricane was passing opposite the place where I stood. Never can I forget the scene which at that moment presented itself. The tops of the trees were seen moving in the strangest manner. . . . The masses of branches, twigs, and foliage, and dust that moved through the air were whirled onwards like a cloud of feathers, and on passing disclosed a wide space filled with fallen trees, naked stumps, and heaps of shapeless ruins which marked the path of the tempest. . . . The horrible noise . . . was impossible to describe. The principal force was now over, although millions of twigs and small branches that had been brought from a great distance were seen following the blast, as if drawn onwards by some mysterious power. They even floated in the air for some hours after, as if supported by the thick mass of dust that rose above the ground. The sky now had a greenish lurid hue, and an extremely sulphurous odor was diffused in the air."

Audubon had had a close escape. He had been standing within a few hundred yards of the track of a tornado—not a hurricane, as he called it. Yet during those horrible moments, when the forest directly in front of him was being torn by winds that may have reached several hundred miles an hour, he coolly observed every aspect of the storm and reported it with remarkable accuracy. The noise, the strange smells, the actions of the trees, these have all have been substantiated by other observers. Once the storm had passed, he led his horse forward through the maze of broken treetops and branches, at times becoming almost desperate in his effort to get through them.

Finally reaching Henderson, he told Lucy about his experience. To his astonishment, she replied that there had been little wind around the town. One of the characteristics of a tornado, which Audubon did not realize, is the narrowness and sharp delineation of its path. It can, for example, move down one side of a village street, tossing giant trees as though they were matchsticks and leave the trees on the other side virtually untouched. In fact, many curious stories have been told about the capricious behavior of these storms, how they have snatched the mattress from under a sleeping child but never harmed the child itself, picked up a cow and carried it for a mile and then set it down alive and well, or driven hay straws into hard wood.

Audubon had some stories of his own to relate. "Many wondrous accounts of the devastating effects of this hurricane were circulating in the country after its occurrence," he wrote. "Some

log houses, we were told, had been overturned and their in-
mates destroyed. One person informed me that a wire sifter
had been conveyed by the gust to a distance of many miles. Another had found a cow lodged in the fork of a large half-broken
tree."

To Lucy, however, such matters were not of great concern.
Audubon had escaped the tornado; that was enough for her.
And meanwhile the year brought her sad news and good news.
The sad news came from Flatland Ford, so many miles away.
During the year, her father suffered a stroke from which he
never fully recovered. Alone so much of the time and living in
a country that she never found congenial, she must have felt
a deeper than ordinary sense of sadness, for gradually the ties
of her former life were being loosened one by one. Her mother
was dead, the children were gradually moving away, and now
her father was seriously ill.

On the other hand, in September, Audubon took a step that
must have made her rejoice. He purchased two more lots in
Henderson, thus reaffirming his decision to remain in the community permanently. Although Henderson was not everything
Lucy might have wished, it was the closest to a home she had
known since leaving Flatland Ford. She must have taken pleasure, too, in realizing that her husband was a respected member
of the little community, part owner of the store, a landholder,
and, for all his trips into the wilderness, a man of business by
Henderson's standards.

He was well liked, too. Around the town he was recognized
as one of the best riders, best marksmen, best judges of dogs,
and, above all, a person with a sense of humor, ready to play
a joke or be the victim of one. All Henderson was laughing over
the story about the skunk and the foreigner he called "D. T."
As Audubon himself told it, he was coming back from Louisville with D. T., when they saw a skunk. D. T., being unfamiliar with American animals, mistook it for a species of squirrel.
Seizing the opportunity for a practical joke, Audubon assured
him that it was not only a squirrel, but a variety that could
easily be captured by hand. Whereupon D. T. picked up a stick
and advanced toward the skunk, while Audubon roared with
laughter at the inevitable result. "I could not suffer his ap-

proach," Audubon wrote later, "nor could my horse; it was with difficulty he mounted his own; and we were forced to continue our journey far asunder, and he much to the leeward." That night they stopped at a strange cabin to take shelter from a snowstorm; and, Audubon continued, still laughing, "When we had stood the few stares to which strangers must accustom themselves, no matter where, even in a drawing-room, we approached the fire. What a shock for the whole party! The scent of the pole-cat, that had been almost stifled on my companion's vestments by the cold of the evening air, now recovered its primitive strength. The cloak was put out of the house, but its owner could not well be used in the same way. The company, however, took to their heels, and there only remained a single black servant, who waited on us until supper was served."

Skunks were not the only wild animals that provided Audubon with amusement during those days at Henderson. Wolves were still common, and he had an opportunity to participate in the vicious, bloody sport of wolf-baiting. He was traveling between Henderson and Vincennes, and he happened to stop for the night with a farmer who showed him the three wolf pits he maintained about a mile and a half from his house. Each pit was eight feet deep and somewhat broader at the bottom than the top, so that a wolf which fell in would have difficulty climbing back out. Covering each pit was a platform composed of light twigs on which the farmer placed several pieces of putrid venison as bait.

The next morning, when Audubon and the farmer returned, they found the bait had been taken from the first pit, but the wolf had been able to dig its way free. In the second pit, however, they discovered three wolves, two black and one brindled. When Audubon asked how they were going to get the animals out of the trap, the farmer explained that he intended to hamstring them.

Ordinarily, to hamstring wolves a man leaned over the edge of the pit and caught the rear legs of a wolf in a large hook. Jerking it upward, he could hold the animal helpless long enough to slit its tendons. Audubon's acquaintance, however, preferred a more direct method, for he climbed straight into the pit, "taking with him his axe and knife, and leaving his

rifle to my care. I was not a little surprised to see the cowardice
of the wolves. He pulled out successively their hind legs, and
with a side stroke of the knife cut the principal tendon above
the joint, exhibiting as little fear as if he had been marking
lambs." The wolves were now crippled. Unable to use their
bleeding hind legs, they could only crouch on their haunches
and drag themselves forward by desperately working their front
feet.

The next stage of the sport was to lift the wolves from
the pit one by one and turn the dogs on them. Although the
wolves could not run away, they could snap and bite with their
tremendous jaws. The farmer asked Audubon to raise the covering platform while he threw a noose over the neck of one of
the wolves, which they hauled up, its disabled legs swinging to
and fro, its jaws hanging wide open, and the gurgle in its throat
alone indicating that it was still alive. With a stick, the farmer
loosened the rope and left the wolf to the dogs, which soon
worried it to death. The second was disposed of in the same
manner, but the third showed more fight. This wolf, Audubon
said, "scuffled along on its fore-legs at a surprising rate, giving
a snap every now and then to the nearest dog, which went off
howling dismally, with a mouthful of skin torn from its side.
And so well did the furious beast defend itself, that apprehensive of its escape, the farmer levelled his rifle at it, and shot it
through the heart, on which the curs rushed upon it, and sati-
ated their vengeance on the destroyer of their master's flock."

Bloody, cruel, and useless, wolf-baiting was nevertheless a
popular sport on the frontier; hunters said it was necessary for
training their dogs. Bearbaiting was another common game. A
captured bear would be turned loose in the middle of a pack
of dogs, while the spectators formed a ring around the fighting
animals. Not only was the bear killed, several dogs were usually
maimed or destroyed; and the greater the flow of blood, the
greater the pleasure of the audience. Still another sport was
gander-pulling. The participants would grease the neck of a
live gander, then hang it by its legs from the limb of a tree
just low enough to be within reach of a horseman. Taking
turns, they would gallop underneath and try to wrench the
bird's head off. Because of the grease and the toughness of the

neck, this required considerable strength and dexterity; and the suffering bird would be subjected to one attempt after another until it finally died. The real trick was to snap the head off so quickly that the onlookers could hear the bird's breath still rushing through its headless windpipe. That feat always brought applause.

Such sports were brutal, but these men were no more considerate of their own bodies than they were of the animals'. They fought freely and for the joy of it. In the game of snick-a-snack, which they played for fun, they sat down around a table; and at a given signal, each man whipped out his clasp knife and began slashing at the others' hands and heads. The frontier was friendly and warmhearted; it was also rough and cruel and slowly gave Audubon some of the toughening he needed. But it could not teach him patience, the patience to attend to the humdrum routine of his business. In that respect, he had not changed much since his carefree days at Mill Grove.

CHAPTER X

1815 – 1818

I N 1815, Audubon was like a traveler who follows an unfamiliar trail which is clearly marked by a patch of sunlight. On one side, however, is a deep precipice, which is
obscured by the rising morning mists. To the traveler, the land
looks flat and safe in every direction, but his security is only an
illusion. One misstep, and he will plunge over the edge.

At Henderson, Audubon seemed to have everything he
wanted: a wife he adored, two sons, a junior partner who left
him alone, country in which to shoot and fish, and a respected
place in the community. His gay humor, his good looks, his
willingness to enter any sport, all these made him, as Vincent
Nolte had said, a "companionable" man; and he was also a
person of some consequence and influence in Henderson. Moreover, the times were good; everything along the frontier was
booming.

Although the War of 1812 had not settled a single basic difference between the United States and Great Britain, it had
given the United States a new sense of national unity. The western country now considered itself definitely part of the larger
nation and no longer had room for men who, like General
Wilkinson, believed the frontier could profit from an alliance
with Spain or France. Congress began voting appropriations for
internal improvements such as the development of the Cum-
berland Road; steamboats were puffing and smoking their way
up and down the rivers; and the great western migration had
started. By the thousands, new settlers were pouring across the
mountains and down the rivers; land values were skyrocketing;
and on the surface everything looked wonderful. Even a slen-

derly financed firm like Audubon & Bakewell could survive, and not only survive, prosper.

Under the surface, however, currents were running that alarmed the more wary. In 1811, Congress had refused to re-charter the Bank of the United States; and by 1815 the mon-etary situation had become so serious that the Secretary of the Treasury said publicly that such a state of affairs could not con-tinue. But if Congress delayed until 1816 to charter a new national bank, everyone else with capital was trying to enter the banking business, thinking it a quick way to get rich. In 1813, for example, the governor of Pennsylvania vetoed a bill establishing twenty-five new banks in the commonwealth only to be faced at the next session of the legislature with a bill that passed over his veto, establishing forty-two. Kentucky also joined in the bank craze. Thinly populated as it was, it soon had forty-six banks of its own. Most of these new banks were undercapitalized and badly managed. Yet they had the right to issue their own currency, which they circulated freely.

It was a time when fortunes could be made quickly by those astute enough to play on the speculative fever of others and yet sufficiently self-disciplined to control their own optimism. But in many respects it was the worst possible time for someone like Audubon with his boundless enthusiasm and his unbridled energy. More than ever, he needed the restraining hand of Rozier; but as the firm of Audubon & Bakewell now had no wiser partner than himself, he immediately began enlarging its operations.

Thomas Pears, whom he and Thomas Bakewell had both known when they worked together as clerks for Benjamin Bake-well in New York, had come west and was looking for a perma-nent connection. He had $3,000 or $4,000 he was willing to in-vest in the business, and so they took him in. Later Audubon held Pears at arm's length even in memory. Thomas Bakewell, he wrote, persuaded "me to join to our partnership an English-man by the name of Thomas Pears, now dead." At the time, however, he was the senior partner and could easily have kept Pears out.

Because the store and their various trading trips down the river no longer offered sufficient scope for their energy, they decided to construct and operate a steam mill. To assist them with this project, they employed a full-time engineer, David Prentice. Prentice had come to the United States from Scotland some years before and had erected a threshing mill for William Bakewell at Flatland Ford. Bakewell was so impressed by his accomplishments that he helped him establish a milling business in Philadelphia. At Thomas Bakewell's invitation, he agreed to move to Henderson and become their engineer.

Almost anyone except Audubon could have seen the direction in which they were heading. From two partners, they had grown to a firm with three partners and a full-time employee, not a clerk like Nat Pope who had worked for Audubon & Rozier, but a man who was really a member of the firm's management. Yet they had no intention of moving to Louisville or some other larger community which might have supported this increased activity. They planned to stay right there in Henderson.

The four were a thoroughly ill-assorted lot: Audubon, who retained his position as the senior partner but continued to spend as much time as possible hunting and fishing; Thomas Bakewell, who had moved from one failure to another, first with Benjamin Bakewell during his one ill-starred period, then with his own venture in New Orleans; Thomas Pears, who, at this stage of his life at least, was an inexperienced nonentity; and David Prentice, whom Thomas later described as having "an excellent head, but no hands," an apt description of an engineer who was long on theory but short on practical application. In a large company, Prentice might have been useful. But Audubon & Bakewell needed an engineer not only to handle the designing but also to supervise the construction and do much of the work himself.

Although their biggest and most important project was the steam mill, they allowed themselves to be distracted by a new plan. In 1811, *The New Orleans,* the first steamboat on the western waters, had passed the Falls of the Ohio. Ever since, it had been plying a busy trade between Natchez and New Orleans and, according to contemporary estimates, had made a net profit of $24,000 in the first year alone. Such financial success touched off a wave of steamboat building. Everyone with a little capital wanted to build a steamboat, and Audubon was among them. After all, why not? They had money and a full-time engineer who knew all about steam power. The firm of Audubon & Bakewell, therefore, decided to use David Prentice's skills to enter this new and booming business.

Together, they purchased a keelboat, ripped up the deck, inserted a steam engine, built paddle wheels, and rechristened the awkward craft *The Pike.* After a series of experiments at Henderson, with most of the town watching from the river-bank, they managed to make their creation work; and off it went to Louisville, puffing and chugging all the way and arousing concern among the bystanders who watched it pass. After it arrived safely in Louisville, the partners decided to press their luck further. Loading their boat with a cargo and keeping "Captain" Prentice in command, they sent it upriver to Pittsburgh. For some distance, the trip went well, the engine steaming and turning, *The Pike* forging its way against the current; but several miles below Pittsburgh the voyage came to an abrupt halt. Ahead were a series of ripples, stretches where the river poured over a bar. Whether the water was too shallow for the paddle wheels or the current too strong for the engine, none of the partners said. But there was *The Pike,* powerless to continue on its way.

Whenever anyone who knew Benjamin Bakewell was in trouble and needed help, the first thing they did was to send for him, if he happened to be nearby. And that is what David Prentice did. If he himself could not get *The Pike* over the ripples, perhaps Benjamin Bakewell could. When word of the boat's predicament reached him at Pittsburgh, Bakewell, with his customary good nature but also perhaps with a sigh, put aside his own business and went to Prentice's rescue. Somehow, under his direction, *The Pike* ascended the ripples, arrived in Pittsburgh, and then made the trip safely back to Louisville. There the partners received an offer to sell the boat. In one of their few wise moves, they accepted it.

The steam mill was quite a different matter. Who first had the idea that Henderson needed a steam mill is not at all clear. Audubon, writing at a later date, placed the blame squarely on Thomas Bakewell, although he himself was the senior partner. Thomas, he said flatly, persuaded him into the venture. In any

case, "Up went the steam-mill at enormous expense, in a country then as unfit for such a thing as it would be for me to
attempt to settle in the moon." But Audubon wrote these words
with the benefit of hindsight. At the time, he was just as enthusiastic as the others, studying the plans, ordering materials,
hiring workmen, helping supervise the construction, and playing his role of enterprising businessman.

And what a mill it was! It was really more than a mill; it
was a monument to Audubon & Bakewell. The joists were
rough logs, many of them a foot in diameter. The foundations
were built of rock, laid stone on stone to a thickness of four
and a half feet. The millstones were the finest; the engine the
largest the partners thought possible. No expense, no effort, was
spared. The steam mill was meant to last. Indeed, it was not
just one mill; it was two, because it could saw wood as well as
grind grain.

Although he was investing most of his remaining capital
in this giant structure, Audubon's interest in birds remained
strong; and he was delighted one day when, on his way to Dr.
Rankin's house, he saw again the same kind of eagle the patroon
had shown him as their boat pushed up the Mississippi, and
whose nest he had watched with the frontiersmen at the Green
River. This time, when the bird rose from a small enclosure a
hundred yards away and lighted on the branch of a nearby tree,
Audubon was certain of his ability to shoot it. Moving forward
slowly and cautiously, he came closer, raised his gun, and fired.
The bird fell from the limb on which it was perched.

As he looked at the lifeless body he held in his hands,
stretched the limp wings to measure their spread, and admired
the fierce curve of its beak and its large, sharp talons, Audubon was struck by its beauty and by the thrill of having made a
major discovery. This was no ordinary bird, and it deserved a
special designation. In a flush of patriotism, he wrote, "The
name which I have chosen for this new species of eagle, the
'Bird of Washington,' may be considered by some as preposter-
ous and unfit. But as it is indisputably the noblest bird of its
genus that has yet been discovered in the United States, I trust
I shall be allowed to honor it with the name of one yet nobler,
who was the saviour of his country, and whose name will ever

be dear to it. To those who may be curious to know my reasons, I can only say that as the New World gave me birth and liberty, the great man who insured its independence is next to my heart."

For all Audubon's excitement, for all the lurid, nineteenth-century prose of his dedication, the name Washington Sea-Eagle does not appear in any contemporary list of American birds. It has vanished, although the bird is not extinct. Just as the frontiersmen had tried to tell him when they watched the nest, it was in truth merely an immature bald eagle, which sometimes mates before it grows its white head feathers.

If Audubon was unfortunate that year in deluding himself that he had made an important ornithological discovery, he was even more unlucky in his business. As the fall of 1816 approached, Thomas Bakewell wrote to his father and stepmother at Flatland Ford, reporting to them on the affairs of Audubon & Bakewell. First, however, he discussed his parents' own problems. William Bakewell, as a result of his stroke, was now old in spirit as well as body, only a shadow of the hearty man Audubon had met in the snowy woods so many years before. For some time he had been trying to sell Flatland Ford and rid himself of all its responsibilities, but he could find no buyers. He also wanted to visit his children in Henderson. This last plan disturbed Thomas, who, faithful son that he was, thought his parents should not try to make the trip alone. Why not, he asked, wait until spring? Then either he or Audubon would go east and bring them back. If that was not agreeable, perhaps they could take the stagecoach to Pittsburgh and stay there with Benjamin Bakewell. As soon as possible, he would go up the river, meet them, and bring them back himself to Henderson. Under no circumstances, he insisted, should they try to make the trip by themselves. Then he went on to discuss the affairs of Audubon & Bakewell. "Business is with us, as with everybody in every place just now, extremely dull," he wrote. William Bakewell's heart must have sunk. He himself could not sell Flatland Ford; Thomas had borrowed from him more than $5,000 to invest in Audubon & Bakewell; now, to top it all, the firm's business was bad.

That was in September. In December, the news was even

worse. As the partners added up their bills, they realized the mill had cost them at least $5,000 more than they had expected. In part, according to Thomas, this was "owing to going through so many hands, and so many different plans begun and not finished, together with the inexperience of the parties in that business." For one thing, he said, "the trials of getting water otherwise than the way we now get it (i.e. from the river) has cost us $1,000 for no purpose but to the account of experience," and they had paid $2,000 for millstones, when ones costing $200 would have served equally well. Much of the difficulty, he thought, had been caused by Prentice. "We have a very good engine," he wrote, "put up in a very slovenly fashion which we are remedying by degrees ourselves." As for Prentice, Thomas said, "he is a capital man to prescribe, but not to administer— his *advice and opinion* in matters of his profession are invaluable but his execution worthless."

To make matters worse, the store was also in difficulty. Not only were their sales negligible, but when they did sell something, they could not collect the money. Business was now so bad that Thomas and Audubon decided to dissolve their partnership. How deeply in debt they were is revealed by the terms of their settlement. Audubon was to assume all the assets and liabilities of the firm, giving Thomas a note for $5,500, which was to be paid when the firm collected its own debts. In addition, Thomas was to write off $5,000 of his original investment. Even then he was not free to leave, although he was anxious to move to Pittsburgh. "As we are both liable for the debts due by A. & B.," he wrote his parents, "I have agreed to remain here and give my assistance to Mr. A. till 1st July next and to let the business be carried on in the name of the firm as usual. Times are so hard and money so extremely scarce, it will require both our efforts to get along."

Thomas Pears had also become disillusioned with both the firm and Henderson, and he too wanted to move to Pittsburgh, where Benjamin Bakewell had offered him a job. By this time he had invested his $3,000 or $4,000 and wanted his money back. The firm bought him out, but this act further reduced its cash.

Audubon was now in serious trouble. Rozier, the best business partner he had ever had, was gone. So was Thomas Pears, along with his capital. Thomas Bakewell was trying to withdraw what money he could and only planned to stay on a few more months because he felt he had to. No more money was forthcoming from Jean Audubon, and he had absolutely no hope of any further credit from Benjamin or William Bakewell. The older members of the family were weary of investing their funds in Audubon's ventures. He still had the mill, the store, and what bills he could collect. But he had also assumed all the liabilities of Audubon & Bakewell.

At least one matter of business, however, had a happy ending and even a humorous side. Among his many ventures, Audubon decided to buy and sell raccoon skins and contracted with a hunter in Indiana to supply him with a hundred pelts. When the man failed to meet the terms of the contract, Audubon hailed him into court. The defendant's argument on his own behalf was simple. He had had absolutely every intention of fulfilling his contract, he assured the court, but he had had an accident. Before he got around to going hunting, he cut down a tree with his dog as usual standing nearby. He himself jumped clear, but the dog did not and was killed by the falling trunk. Now, he asked the judge, how can a man hunt coons without a dog?

Not having a dog of his own anymore, he did the next best thing; he asked Audubon to lend him one, but Audubon refused. Contract or no contract, law or no law, the hunter argued, it was impossible to shoot coons without a coon dog. The judge, who was as much a coon hunter as he was a lawyer, listened to this argument and liked its lucidity. The hunter was absolutely right; to hunt coons a man needed a dog. Bringing down his gavel, he ordered the case continued for three months, during which time Audubon was to lend the hunter a dog, and the hunter was to procure one hundred pelts for Audubon. At the end of the period, the defendant and the plaintiff again appeared before the judge, who, on learning that both sides had complied with his order, dismissed the case without costs. The constable purchased a bottle of whiskey from a trading boat anchored nearby, and they all celebrated the happy ending.

Another venture ended less happily. In spite of his straitened circumstances, Audubon had purchased from the government 1,200 acres of timberland to supply cordwood for the mill's steam engine, but he had trouble finding men to do the cutting. When a flatboat arrived in Henderson with ten or twelve men and their families, looking for work cutting wood, Audubon hired them although he knew they were Yankees. On the southern frontier Yankees were known as sharp traders, not above selling nutmegs and cucumber seeds fashioned out of wood. In fact, Daniel Boone had once said he would trust an Indian further than any Yankee.

Mooring their boat to the shore, the men set up camp, the women cooked the game they shot, and the trees began to fall. Audubon and his miller paid several visits to the camp and were well satisfied with the arrangement. The men and their families kept a neat camp and delivered the daily and weekly quotas of cordwood right on schedule. To help the men perform their work even better, Audubon began to lend them equipment, a team of oxen and various tools and utensils. One day, on approaching the camp, Audubon found everything still and quiet; not a sound of a voice or the crashing of a felled tree broke the silence. Coming closer, he discovered the entire area was deserted. No men; no women; no boat. What was worse, no oxen or other equipment either. The men had decamped, taking Audubon's supplies with them. Although he and the miller pursued the woodcutters, they were not able to catch them.

Yet such mishaps did not discourage him. His capital was dwindling, his two businesses—the store and the mill—were both doing badly, but he was still a man of consequence in Henderson; and although he was beginning to worry about his finances, the woods of Kentucky still contained plenty of game. He could always shoot enough to feed his family. A deer or two, for example, would fill their plates for several weeks.

All the while, whether he was hunting deer or merely wandering through the countryside, his mill was puffing and steaming away whenever there was work for it to do. In the evenings when the day's tasks were ended, he would sometimes walk down to the river to watch the muskrats emerge from the stone foundations, each carrying a rat in its mouth and holding it high above the ground. Once he took Lucy with him to see the sight, and years later she had not forgotten it.

Nor could she or Audubon ever forget the visit of Constantine Samuel Rafinesque, whose career was almost as bizarre as his name. " 'What an odd-looking fellow!' I said to myself," Audubon later wrote, "as, walking by the river, I observed a man landing from a boat, with what I thought a bundle of dried clover on his back; 'how the boatmen stare at him! sure he must be an original!' He ascended with a rapid step, and approaching asked me if I could point out the house in which Mr. Audubon resided. 'Why, I am that man,' said I, 'and will gladly lead you to my dwelling.'

"The traveller rubbed his hands together with delight, and drawing a letter from his pocket handed it to me without any remark. I broke the seal and read as follows: 'My dear Audubon, I send you an odd fish, which you may prove to be undescribed, and hope you will do so in your next letter. . . .' With all the simplicity of a woodsman I asked the bearer where the odd fish was, when M. de T. [Audubon, out of kindness, disguised Rafinesque's name] . . . smiled, rubbed his hands, and with the greatest good-humor said, 'I am that odd fish I presume, Mr. Audubon.' I felt confounded and blushed, but contrived to stammer an apology.

"We soon reached the house," Audubon continued, "where I presented my learned guest to my family, and was ordering a servant to go to the boat for M. de T.'s luggage, when he told me he had none but what he brought on his back. He then loosened the pack of weeds which had first drawn my attention. The ladies were a little surprised, but I checked their critical glances for the moment. The naturalist pulled off his shoes, and while engaged in drawing his stockings, not up, but down, in order to cover the holes about the heels, told us in the gayest mood imaginable that he had walked a great distance, and had only taken passage on board the ark [a common name for a flatboat], to be put on this shore, and that he was sorry his apparel had suffered so much from his late journey."

During supper, Audubon had a chance to study his guest more closely. "His agreeable conversation," he said, "made us all forget his singular appearance; and, indeed, it was only as we strolled together in the garden that his attire struck me as exceedingly remarkable. A long loose coat of yellow nankeen, much the worse for the many rubs it had got in its time, and stained all over with the juice of plants, hung loosely about him like a sack. A waistcoat of the same, with enormous pockets, and buttoned up to his chin, reached below over a pair of pantaloons, the lower parts of which were buttoned down to the ankles. His beard was as long as I have known my own to be during some of my peregrinations, and his lank black hair hung loosely over his shoulders. His forehead was so broad and prominent that any tyro in phrenology would instantly have pronounced it the residence of a mind of strong powers. His words impressed an assurance of rigid truth, and as he directed the conversation to the study of the natural sciences, I listened to him with as much delight as Telemachus could have listened to Mentor."

Aside from Dr. Mitchill and Alexander Wilson, Rafinesque was one of the few professional biologists Audubon had ever met. Two years older than Audubon, Rafinesque had emigrated from Europe to Philadelphia shortly before Audubon with the idea of becoming a naturalist. While Audubon was living at Mill Grove, he had already attained sufficient stature to consider himself a nominee for the post of botanist with the Lewis and Clark expedition. Failing to obtain the appointment, he returned to Europe for a few years and then came back to the United States to continue his work. However ridiculous he may have appeared to Audubon, he himself was deadly serious. Never once, in spite of many discouragements, did he abandon his effort to contribute to the world's scientific knowledge. He was respected among his contemporaries; Dr. Mitchill thought enough of him to become his patron; and Transylvania University in Kentucky made him a professor, a position he held for nine years; his ninety-page book *Ichthyologia Ohienses* was a pioneering attempt to describe the fish of the Ohio River and its tributaries and was highly regarded by his peers. There is also little question that he foresaw the principles of evolution as Darwin later described them.

On the other hand, as a person, he was erratic, self-centered, contentious, and stubborn. At Transylvania University he made numerous enemies through his tactlessness and his insistence on fighting every issue to the finish. For these faults he paid to the full in the later years of his life, being dismissed from the university and dying a pauper. As a scientist, he had also a serious failing, one that detracted from his many real accomplishments: He was far too interested in discovering new species and often announced them without adequate investigation.

Although not yet a professor, he was making the trip down the Ohio in the hope of finding new plants and fishes that would help to increase his reputation; and he had stopped at Henderson, according to Audubon, "expressly for the purpose of seeing my drawings, having been told that my representations of birds were accompanied with those of shrubs and plants, and he was desirous of knowing whether I might chance to have in my collection any with which he was unacquainted. I observed some degree of impatience in his request to be allowed at once to see what I had. We returned to the house, when I opened my portfolios and laid them before him.

"He chanced to turn over the drawing of a plant quite new to him. After inspecting it closely, he shook his head, and told me no such plant existed in nature. . . . I told my guest that the plant was common in the immediate neighborhood, and that I should show it to him on the morrow. 'And why tomorrow, Mr. Audubon? Let us go now.' We did so, and on reaching the bank of the river I pointed to the plant. M. de T., I thought, had gone mad. He plucked the plants one after another, danced, hugged me in his arms, and exultingly told me that he had got not merely a new species, but a new genus. When we returned home, the naturalist opened the bundle which he had brought on his back, and took out a journal rendered water-proof by means of a leather case, together with a small parcel of linen, examined the new plant, and wrote its description. The examination of my drawings then went on. . . .

"When it waxed late," Audubon continued, "I showed him to the apartment intended for him during his stay, and endeavored to render him comfortable, leaving him writing materials in abundance. I was indeed heartily glad to have a naturalist under my roof. We had all retired to rest. Every person I imagined was in deep slumber save myself, when of a sudden I heard a great uproar in the naturalist's room. I got up, reached the place in a few moments, and opened the door, when to my astonishment, I saw my guest running about the room naked, holding the handle of my favorite violin, the body of which he had battered to pieces against the walls in attempting to kill the bats which had entered by the open window. probably attracted by the insects flying about his candle. I stood amazed, but he continued jumping and running round and round, until he was fairly exhausted, when he begged me to procure one of the animals for him, as he felt convinced they belonged to 'a new species.' Although I was convinced of the contrary, I took up the bow of my demolished Cremona, and administering a smart tap to each of the bats as it came up, soon got specimens enough. The war ended, I again bade him good-night, but could not help observing the state of the room. It was strewed with plants, which it would seem he had arranged into groups, but which were now scattered about in confusion. 'Never mind, Mr. Audubon,' quoth the eccentric naturalist, 'never mind, I'll soon arrange them again. I have the bats, and that's enough.' "

He had his bats, but he was also in trouble. Audubon was the man who had lured the unsuspecting traveler into catching the skunk and who had laughed heartily when, during the earthquake, the women had gathered on the lawn in their nightgowns. In Rafinesque, gullible and eager, he quickly recognized the perfect victim. During the weeks that followed, Audubon helped his guest look for birds and shells and plants. But he also drew a picture of an imaginary fish that looked somewhat like a sturgeon, except that it had no ventral fins. Placing it among his other pictures, he waited for Rafinesque to come across it. Rafinesque, of course, was excited when he finally discovered it. No one, he said correctly, had ever seen a fish like that before. But Audubon assured him they were quite common in the Ohio River. He had caught them often himself. Impressed, Rafinesque took out his journal and made careful notes.

Unable to resist further temptation, Audubon drew a picture of a fish whose head was equal to one fourth of its length and whose nose had a truncated appearance. Again Rafinesque found the picture and asked where the fish had been discovered. In the Ohio River, Audubon told him. Out came the journal and once more Rafinesque took down a careful description. From Audubon's point of view, this was too good to be true. While he continued to help Rafinesque collect real specimens, he also continued to draw a picture now and then of some imaginary fish, laughing to himself each time Rafinesque whipped out his journal.

Rafinesque also wanted to explore a canebrake, and Audubon gladly volunteered to guide him. The cane, which reached a height of thirty feet and a diameter of one or two inches, grew in heavy thickets at intervals along the riverbanks. "If you picture to yourself," Audubon wrote, "one of these canebrakes growing beneath the gigantic trees that form our western forests, interspersed with vines of many species, and numberless plants of every description, you may conceive how difficult it is for one to make his way through it, especially after a heavy shower of rain or a fall of sleet, when the traveller, in forcing his way through, shakes down upon himself such quantities of water as soon reduce him to a state of the utmost discomfort. The hunters often cut little paths through the thickets with their knives, but the usual mode of passing through them is by pushing one's self backward and wedging a way between the stems."

This, according to Audubon's plans, was to be no ordinary trip through a canebrake. Instead of approaching it directly from the river, he took Rafinesque across the Ohio, walked inland with him, and then, circling around, came at it from behind. By taking this devious route, he thoroughly confused Rafinesque's sense of direction before they entered the thicket which he himself knew so well. Leading his visitor on, he carefully cut down the canes that were most likely to bother him, until he had brought him to the very center of the brake. Then slowly he closed his trap. As he himself said, "The difficulties gradually increased, so that presently we were obliged to turn our backs to the foe, and push ourselves on the best way we could. My companion stopped here and there to pick up a plant and examine it. After a while we chanced to come upon the top of a fallen tree, which so obstructed our passage that we were on the eve of going round, instead of thrusting ourselves through amongst the branches, when, from its bed in the centre of the tangled mass, forth rushed a bear, with such force, and snuffing the air in so frightful a manner, that M. de T. became suddenly terror-struck, and, in his haste to escape, made a desperate attempt to run, but fell amongst the canes in such a way that he looked as if pinioned."

For Audubon, the expedition was working out even better than he had hoped, and "perceiving him jammed in between the stalks, and thoroughly frightened, I could not refrain from laughing at the ridiculous exhibition he made. My gaiety, how- ever, was not very pleasing to the *savant*, who called out for aid, which was at once administered. Gladly he would have retraced his steps, but I was desirous that he should be able to describe a cane-brake, and enticed him to follow me by telling him that our worst difficulties were nearly over. . . ."

Instead, "the way became more and more tangled," as Au- dubon deliberately picked out the worst areas. "I saw with de- light that a heavy cloud, portentous of a thunder gust, was approaching. In the meantime, I kept my companion in such constant difficulties that he now panted, perspired, and seemed almost overcome by fatigue. The thunder began to rumble, and soon after a dash of heavy rain drenched us in a few minutes. The withered particles of leaves and bark attached to the canes stuck to our clothes. We received many scratches from briers, and now and then a switch from a nettle. M. de T. seriously inquired if we should ever get alive out of the horrible situation in which we were. I spoke of courage and patience, and told him I hoped we should soon get to the margin of the brake, which, however, I knew to be two miles distant. I made him rest, and gave him a mouthful of brandy from my flask; after which, we proceeded on our slow and painful march. He threw away all his plants, emptied his pockets of the fungi, lichens, and mosses which he had thrust into them, and finding himself much lightened, went on for thirty or forty yards with a better grace. . . . I led the naturalist first one way, then an- other, until I nearly lost myself in the brake, although I was well acquainted with it, kept him tumbling and crawling on his hands and knees until long after mid-day, when we at length reached the edge of the river." There, at last, Audubon considered the joke played out. With the wet and ragged Rafinesque standing beside him, he blew his horn to signal the boat to come and carry them back across the Ohio.

For three weeks Rafinesque remained at Henderson, collecting new specimens and taking notes of Audubon's spurious drawings. Then, according to Audubon, "one evening when tea was prepared, and we expected him to join the family, he was nowhere to be found. His grasses and other valuables were all removed from his room. The night was spent in searching for him in the neighborhood. No eccentric naturalist could be discovered. Whether he had perished in a swamp, or had been devoured by a bear or a gar-fish, or had taken to his heels, were matters of conjecture; nor was it until some weeks after that a letter from him, thanking us for our attention, assured me of his safety."

Thus Rafinesque vanished from the Audubons' house, going down the sad, dim path that led eventually to his death from cancer, so friendless and poor that his landlord tried to sell his corpse to pay for the back rent. Yet Rafinesque, simple as he was, had his revenge on Audubon; but his revenge was unpremeditated. It came solely from his generosity. In his book *Ichthyologia Ohienses,* he listed the sturgeonlike fish with no ventral fins; and underneath he carefully wrote: "This genus rests altogether upon the authority of Mr. Audubon, who presented me with a drawing of the only species belonging to it."

Ten times in his book he put down fish described from Audubon's fake drawings; ten times he gave Audubon full credit for the new discoveries.

IN 1818, the weak and fragile banking system that had been supporting the American emonomy collapsed. One after another, the small, undercapitalized banks closed their doors, unable to pay their depositors or reedeem their currency. The calamity was nationwide, but the western states, including Kentucky, were hit particularly hard.

Later on, when Audubon told his children about this period of his life, he said, "It was now our misfortune to add other partners and petty agents to our concern; suffice it for me to tell you, nay, to assure you, that I was gulled by all these men. The new-born Kentucky banks nearly all broke in quick succession; and we again started with a new set of partners; these were your present uncle N. Berthoud [the Audubons' friend at Shippingport who had married Lucy's sister] and Benjamin Page of Pittsburgh. Matters, however, grew worse every day; the times were what men called 'bad,' but I am fully persuaded the great fault was ours, and the building of that accursed steam-mill was, of all the follies of men, one of the greatest, and to your uncle [Thomas Bakewell] and me the worst of all our pecuniary misfortunes. How I labored at that infernal mill! from dawn to dark, nay, at times all night. But it is over now; I am old and try to forget as fast as possible all the different trials of those sad days."

Nor were his misfortunes limited to his business life. At home, he watched with worry while Lucy nursed their newest child, a girl named Rosa, through one sickness after another. No matter what Lucy did, no matter what medicines Dr. Rankin prescribed, Rosa was never truly well. Then came the sad news of Jean Audubon's death in France on February 19, 1818.

Although they had been far apart for years, Audubon had always retained a deep affection for the old sea captain and slave trader who had tried so hard to provide for his family. In spite of all Jean Audubon's work and planning, however, by the time of his death his fortune had almost entirely vanished. His former holdings in San Domingo were, of course, worthless; Mill Grove was gone; and John James's share of the estate had evaporated in senseless speculations. What little remained Jean Audubon left to his wife Anne for her use during her lifetime. For the present at least, his children could expect nothing; and only the slightest possibility existed that they would ever receive anything.

After all John James's years of carelessness and negligence, his world was beginning to collapse around him. The mercantile business was practically ruined; the steam mill was absorbing the last of his funds; his father was dead; his brother-in-law, Thomas Bakewell, was disgusted with him; his father-in-law was sick and old; and even his uncle-in-law, Benjamin Bakewell, refused to put any more money into Audubon schemes.

As matters went rapidly from bad to worse and he tried to stave off financial disaster, one of his few remaining consolations were the Canada geese he kept in the pond in the backyard. On his trips to the Green River in Kentucky, he had, for three years in succession, noticed one goose in particular that seemed larger than the others. Whenever he visited the nest, the bird would fly directly toward him as though to attack him and drive him off. Indeed, it twice struck Audubon such a blow with its wing that he thought his arm might be broken. Audubon was so impressed by the courage and beauty of the goose that he made a trap, baited it with corn, and finally caught the bird. Then he captured the female and her young and brought the whole family back to his pond at Henderson.

Another Canada goose he obtained in a much more unusual manner. On a hunting expedition he had shot and killed a female bird which he brought home to be cooked. When the bird was being dressed, the cook discovered it contained an egg. Audubon was immediately intrigued with an idea for an experiment. Placing the egg under a common hen, he successfully hatched it. The bird grew up and in turn mated and produced a brood. Because she had spent all her life with humans, she was especially gentle and permitted anyone to come close and pat her.

So as the year 1818 drew to its conclusion, Audubon still found pleasure in watching his tame geese in the pond behind his house, observing the muskrats clamber from under the mill, or making trips into the woods that he loved so well. But aside from these diversions, he had little else for which to be thankful. The mill was steaming and puffing away, eating into the last of his capital, and the clouds of smoke it sent up might just as well have been fueled with dollar bills as with wood. In every respect, Audubon was repeating, step by step, his experience with the lead mine at Mill Grove: first, the boundless, but economically unjustified, enthusiasm; second, the gradual realization that the preliminary optimism had been falsely based; and finally, the determination to hang on at all costs, wildly throwing good money after bad.

By March, 1819, Thomas Bakewell, who had withdrawn from all connection with the business and was operating a foundry at Louisville, expressed concern about his own new company. Writing to his parents at Flatland Ford, he said, "It is true we have on paper been doing a very good business, but we can make no certain calculations these times till we have the money in our pockets. If we had the amounts overdue to us on contracts for machinery we should be very easy, but as it is we are, like all our neighbors, pretty tight run."

As for the prospects of the former firm of Audubon & Bakewell, he was even gloomier. The $5,000 he had borrowed from his father in order to enter the partnership was still in Audubon's hands and "was likely to be for some time longer." Not one cent of the money owed him on the dissolution of the firm had been paid and, in addition, he had been compelled to make further advances, totaling somewhere around $3,000, to help the firm pay off its debts. Nor was this a burden that his father could pick up and carry for him. Weary and sick, William Bakewell himself was feeling the effects of the financial crisis. Flatland Ford was still unsold; and instead of advancing more money to his son, he was anxious to receive an accounting of the amounts due him from Audubon & Bakewell and, hopefully, their repayment.

Audubon, however, refused to abandon the hope of salvaging his fortunes; but instead of concentrating his energies on the mill, making one last effort either to put it in a profitable basis or get rid of it altogether, he began casting about for additional investments; and his attention was again drawn by the steamboat business. Characteristically, he rushed into a new venture without thinking twice; and, also characteristically, he attracted a new set of investors. One of them was George Keats, brother of the English poet, John.

In 1819 disaster was overwhelming John Keats. His brother Tom had died of consumption; unfavorable reviews had threatened his poetic career; he was heavily in debt and having great difficulty collecting the funds owed him by the executor of his mother's estate; he was unsuccessfully attempting to publish another book of poetry; and his last play remained unproduced. In the gray world in which he then existed, he had only one ray of brightness: his love for Fanny Brawne, who brought him a type of comfort he had never found before. His plans to marry her, however, were frustrated by his lack of money. His hope lay with his brother George. George and his wife, Georgianna, had moved to the United States, planning to take up farming in the West and by this means recoup the family's fortune. With him had gone every penny John Keats could spare. But instead of farming, George, after the trip down the Ohio River, had stopped at Henderson, met Audubon, and became deeply involved in the new steamboat venture, investing in it practically all his available funds. Thus, at a critical juncture in his own career, John Keats found his life tied with Audubon's and his own future dependent on Audubon's business judgment.

Using what was left of his own money and what he could raise from others, including George Keats's, Audubon purchased a boat and resold it to another group of men at what he thought was a good profit. With his usual carelessness, he accepted their notes without checking their credit. The notes proved to be worthless, and the papers were apparently drawn up improperly. For once, he could take direct physical action to solve a business difficulty. With a skiff and two Negroes as rowers, he

chased the boat all the way to New Orleans, where he tried to
have it attached. His efforts to regain his money proved fruitless, however, and he returned to Henderson, walking part of
the way and traveling by steamer the remainder. On arriving
home, he learned that one of the purchasers—"Mr. B—" as Audubon called him—had reached the town ahead of him and had
sworn to kill him for having taken legal action.

Lucy was naturally terrified and insisted that her husband
wear a dagger. With his short temper—he was still the man who
had once threatened to kill Dacosta—and with his great physical courage, he was not one to be bullied easily. According to
his own account, "Mr. B— walked about the streets and before
my house as if watching for me, and the continued reports of
our neighbors prepared me for an encounter with this man,
whose violent and ungovernable temper was only too well
known. As I was walking towards the steam-mill one morning,
I heard myself hailed from behind; on turning, I observed Mr.
B— marching towards me with a heavy club in his hand. I stood
still, and he soon reached me. He complained of my conduct to
him at New Orleans, and suddenly raising his bludgeon laid it
about me. Though white with wrath, I neither spoke nor
moved till he had given me twelve severe blows, then, drawing
my dagger with my left hand (unfortunately my right was disabled and in a sling, having been caught and much injured in
the wheels of the steam engine), I stabbed him and he instantly
fell."

Such violent scenes were common in the river towns, and
the populace of Henderson knew exactly what to do. Audubon's friends gathered on the spot, loaded the wounded Mr.
B— on a plank, and carried him off. Mr. B—'s friends, on the
other hand, took up their guns and began patrolling the streets
of Henderson, particularly in the vicinity of Audubon's house.
This, of course, was the signal for Audubon's supporters to
arm themselves also and form a bodyguard for him. With this
escort he marched to the court, which was then sitting, and
surrendered himself. The judge, however, with the usual frontier sense of justice, refused to take the matter seriously. He
did not have Audubon arrested and held for trial; he scolded

him for not having killed Mr. B— instead of merely wounding him.

But the matter was not yet closed. The purchasers, still angry over Audubon's attempt to attach the boat in New Orleans, brought suit against him, charging him with malicious action. He was held in $10,000 bond, for which a friend went security, and was ordered to be tried. Fearful that Mr. B—'s friends were too powerful in Henderson and that he might not receive a fair trial there, he asked for a change of venue, which was granted. When the case came up in court, the plaintiffs requested and received a continuance. The second time it came up, they failed to appear, and the action was dismissed.

Exactly what happened is difficult to determine. Mr. B—, if he had been completely wrong, would not have returned to Audubon's home town and threatened him openly, nor would Audubon have asked for a change of venue. On the other hand, if all the right was on his side, why did he not press his suit? Clearly, something was wrong with the whole transaction, although it is unlikely, as George Keats once thought, that the steamboat was at the bottom of the river when Audubon asked him to put money into it. Whatever the details, two facts remained: Audubon was a heavy loser; and he had once more persuaded others to make a bad investment.

The effect on John Keats was disastrous. Already desperate, when he received the news from George he wrote in bitter and heartrending fashion: "Your present situation I will not suffer myself to dwell upon—when misfortunes are so real we are glad enough to escape them, and the thought of them. I cannot help thinking Mr. Audubon a dishonest man. Why did he make you believe he was a Man of Property? How is it his circumstances have altered so suddenly? In truth I do not believe you fit to deal with the world, or at least the American world. But good God—who can avoid these chances—You have done your best—Take matters as coolly as you can, and expecting help from England, act as if no help was nigh." And in the same letter he returned to the subject again: "I cannot help thinking Mr. Audubon has deceived you. I shall not like the sight of him."

When John Keats asked his brother those questions, "Why did he make you believe he was a Man of Property?" and "How

is it his circumstances have altered so suddenly?" he was echoing the opinion of Henderson. Audubon, as owner of the mill
and proprietor of the store, presented an imposing face to the
small world in which he lived even though he was going broke.
He always talked convincingly; he always put up a good front,
not because he was dishonest, but because he did not understand what was happening. Never having been realistic with
himself, how could he possibly be realistic with others?

Ever since his arrival in America, he had moved from one
business venture to another, actually from one failure to another, with supreme self-confidence. Whether he was dealing
with the lead mine, the steam mill, or offering advice to his
father, he does not seem to have suffered any doubts. If he had
had any business acumen, this self-confidence might have carried him far. If he had been truly dishonest, he would have
made the best of confidence men, for he had an innate ability
to persuade others to his own way of thinking. But actually, as
he racked up his long list of victims, starting with his own
father and ending with Thomas Bakewell, George Keats, and
the others whom he knew at Henderson, he could count as
the greatest victim of all—aside from Lucy—his own self.

But the steamboat affair spelled the end. George Keats was
not the only person who had thought him a man of property
and had discovered that the appearance he presented hid nothing but an empty financial shell. Bitter and angry at their disillusionment, his former friends began to demand the immediate repayment of their debts in full.

From the beginning Audubon's financial collapse had been
inevitable. Now it came swiftly. "From this date," Audubon
wrote for his children's benefit, "my pecuniary difficulties daily
increased; I had heavy bills to pay which I could not meet or
take up. The moment this became known to the world around
me, that moment I was assailed with thousands of invectives;
the once wealthy man was now nothing. I parted with every
particle of property I held to my creditors, keeping only the
clothes I wore on that day, my original drawings, and my gun."

What he did not tell his children was that he could not satisfy his creditors' demands. All his remaining resources were
insufficient to meet his debts, and it was impossible for him, on

the basis of any prospects he had, to obtain additional credit. He was arrested and brought to the jail at Louisville. There, in front of the judge and witnesses, he took the oath of insolvency—in other words, declared himself bankrupt.

His humiliation, however, was not over. When Benjamin Bakewell was in financial trouble, he continued to command so much respect that his creditors helped set him up in business again. Not so with Audubon. No one wanted him as a partner. No one wanted him as an employee. Many people, because of his earlier carelessness, now decided he was nothing but a fraud. Certainly John Keats did. Writing to his sister-in-law at the beginning of 1820, he again gave vent to his bitterness. "Give my compliments to Mrs. Audubon," he wrote, "and tell her I cannot think her either goodlooking or honest—Tell Mr. Audubon he's a fool." John Keats, of course, had reason for his bitterness. The steamboat investment ended his last hope of ever marrying Fanny Brawne. Not long afterward, he noticed blood in the phlegm of his cough for the first time, and it was only a few months more before he was dead.

As a member of the family and as a man who was already becoming successful, Thomas Bakewell had less reason for disliking Audubon; but in 1821, at the time of his father's death, he wrote to his stepmother: "I, and I doubt not but Lucy will also, relinquish all pretensions to any claim on the estate, at any rate until the debts due by the late firm of A. & B. be fully discharged—this debt has given me much uneasiness. . . . My individual loss by Mr. Audubon *exclusive* of the debt due to my Father is about $14000—so that you see I have had my full share of bad luck in worldly matters." Not counting Lucy's money, Audubon had cost the Bakewells at least $19,000.

The people of Henderson also turned against Audubon. The men who had gone hunting and fishing with him, who had laughed at his practical jokes, had no further use for him. The women with whom he had flirted and who had been amused by his gay remarks and his violin playing no longer invited him to dinner. He was, in his own town, an outcast, the victim of a complete reversal in public opinion. To make his loneliness even greater, the Audubons' daughter Rosa had died just before the bankruptcy proceedings. They had buried her on the grounds of their house near the pond where the pinioned geese swam.

But now they no longer owned either the grounds or the pond. They owned nothing.

Audubon did not even have a trade.

Only one thing was certain. He could not remain in Henderson. There, as he said, he was surrounded by "the surly looks and cold receptions of those who so shortly before were pleased to call me their friend." Not knowing what to do next, he decided to go to Louisville. Perhaps in the larger town he could find some means of making a living. Lucy, however, had to remain in Henderson. For one reason, he had no idea what he would do after he reached Louisville. For another, she was again pregnant. But she at least had friends who were willing to take her in, even though they had no use for her husband.

Packing his few remaining belongings, such as his gun and his art materials, Audubon made the trip from Henderson to Louisville, the trip that he had made so often in happier days. This time there was no singing in his heart; the old gay manner was vanished. Yet he had not given up hope. He had many friends in Louisville: the proprietor of the Indian Queen, where he and Lucy had stayed so long; the Tascarons, who were in the shipping business just below the falls; the Berthouds, one of whom had married a sister of Lucy; all the men with whom he had hunted and fished; all the women with whom he had danced during that happy Fourth of July celebration at Beargrass Creek. Surely, among these people he could find employment.

But he could not.

No one wanted him at Louisville. Not a single friend offered to advance him a cent of capital; not a single friend had a job he could fill. Every error he had committed in the past rose to haunt him: each time he had been arrogant over some transaction, each time he had been careless in handling someone else's money. As long as he had seemed rich, these faults were overlooked. Now they were not. Yet he was better off in Louisville than he had been at Henderson; at least, he was not the object of so much personal animosity. He also had one friend, James Berthoud. During the last frantic days at the steam mill, the Berthouds had tried to help him stave off disaster. Having failed in their effort, they were unwilling to join Audubon in another commercial venture; but James Berthoud was not ready to let his old associate flounder without offering him a helping hand. If Audubon would paint his portrait, he said, he would pay for it.

Never before had Audubon received a professional commission to do a picture of any sort, but he was in no position to hesitate. He needed money, any amount, however small, and he accepted. The portrait was not good—this was not Audubon's field—but it was not bad. James Berthoud showed it to other people. Benjamin Page, who was living at Shippingport and whose family were partners of Benjamin Bakewell, said he would like one; and soon Audubon was launched on a new career. He became a local portrait painter. As he said later, "To be a good draughtsman in those days was to me a blessing; to any other man, be it a thousand years hence, it will be a blessing also. I at once undertook to take portraits of the human 'head divine,' in black chalk, and, thanks to my master, David, succeeded admirably. I commenced at exceedingly low prices, but raised those prices as I became more known in this capacity. . . . In the course of a few weeks I had as much work to do as I would possibly wish, so much that I was able to rent a house in a retired part of Louisville."

A friend offered to pay Lucy's expenses from Henderson, and taking advantage of this assistance, she came by carriage to rejoin her husband. Shortly after her arrival, the Audubons had another daughter, whom they named Lucy. This gave them at least one cause for rejoicing, for they both took great pleasure in their new baby.

Although he was able to support his family with his black chalk drawings, Audubon's work during this period was not significant artistically. His position in the community was that of a journeyman craftsman who made likenesses for the family's personal enjoyment. Often the family waited until the last minute, or sometimes even beyond the last minute, before ordering a picture. As Audubon later told his children, "I was sent for as far as four miles in the country, to take likenesses of persons on their death-beds, and so high did my reputation suddenly rise, as the best delineator of heads in that vicinity, that a clergyman residing at Louisville (I would give much now to recall and write down his name) had his dead child disinterred, to procure a facsimile of his face, which, by the way, I gave to the parents as if still alive, to their intense satisfaction."

Although he was in this fashion able to obtain some income, his life was far from satisfying. What prestige he had enjoyed was gone and the future was nothing but a gray blank. Later he rarely mentioned these times, but once for his two sons he briefly drew aside the veil and revealed the depth of his despair. "After our dismal removal from Henderson to Louisville, one morning, while all of us were sadly desponding, I took you both, Victor and John, from Shippingport to Louisville," he wrote. "I had purchased a loaf of bread and some apples; before we reached Louisville you were all hungry, and by the river side we sat down and ate our scanty meal. On that day the world was with me as a blank, and my heart was sorely heavy, for scarcely had I enough to keep my dear ones alive." Then, in either a more philosophical mood or perhaps reaping the advantages of hindsight, he continued, "Yet through these dark ways I was being led to the development of the talents I loved, and which have brought so much enjoyment to us *all.*"

He continued his interest in birds, or at least that is the way he remembered it. "One of the most extraordinary things among all these adverse circumstances," he went on, "was that I never for a day gave up listening to the songs of our birds, or watching their peculiar habits, or delineating them in the best way I could; nay, during my deepest troubles I frequently would wrench myself from the persons around me, and retire to some secluded part of our noble forests; and many a time, at the sound of the wood-thrush's melodies, have I fallen on my knees, and prayed there earnestly to our God."

But even the birds could not compensate for the next tragedy. When she was seven months old, the Audubons' new daughter Lucy died at Louisville. Disaster after disaster was overtaking them; and if ever a man paid in full for his past follies, Audubon did so in the years 1818 to 1820. Nothing he did was right, and even events over which he had no control conspired against him.

Then came the realization that portrait painting was nothing but a temporary expedient. As he walked through the streets of Louisville, calling on friends and strangers alike, he found commissions more and more difficult to obtain. He traveled to Shippingport, he visited the outlying districts, but each time with less success. More often than not, when he returned to the house in the evening he had nothing to report to Lucy except another day without any accomplishment. After all, no matter how well he drew—and he did not draw portraits particularly well—Louisville and its environs was not large enough to support a full-time artist. There were just so many people who wanted pictures of their relatives, and he had now reached them all.

At the end of a few months he was back, therefore, where he started, once more looking for permanent employment—but now at the age of thirty-four. Yet few avenues were open to him. Without funds or credit, he could not go into business for himself, and no one, on the basis of his past record, was likely to offer him a responsible position. As for his bird pictures, they were valueless. There was no market for them individually, and the collection was neither large enough nor good enough to appeal to a library or a university. As a naturalist, he was without professional standing. All he possessed was a portfolio of amateurish pictures and a collection of miscellaneous notes. Nevertheless, one of his friends suggested that he apply for a job with the Western Museum, which had just been founded at Cincinnati.

The person to see was Dr. Daniel Drake, an energetic physician who spent much of his life bringing culture to the frontier. Drake's education had started when, as a boy in Kentucky, he had read and reread the four books owned by his parents: an almanac, a collection of hymns, a speller, and a romantic novel about the days of chivalry. When he was twelve, his father gave him a book on surveying which he had purchased from a neighbor; it was the only book he could find for sale. At fifteen, Drake went to Cincinnati to become an apprentice in medicine, later attending the medical school at the

University of Pennsylvania. On returning to Cincinnati, he established a successful medical practice and also participated in the founding of an extraordinary number of public institutions: the Lancaster Seminary, which later became the University of Cincinnati, a library society, a medical school, and a hospital. In 1818 he had founded the Western Museum. As he told the public, "I have drawn up the constitution in such a manner as to make the institution a complete school for natural history, and I hope to see concentrated, in this place, the choicest natural and artificial curiosities in the western country."

If Audubon has been serious about his ornithological studies, he could have met Drake much earlier, for Drake had been a student in Philadelphia when Audubon was living at Mill Grove and had attended the many scientific meetings in which Audubon had shown no interest. Furthermore, he was an acquaintance of Dr. Mitchill, who wrote him in 1817 asking for specimens for his own museum in New York. As it was, Audubon had to go to him as a stranger, but Drake did offer him a job as a taxidermist to stuff fish for the museum. (Fortunately, Rafinesque's book had not yet been published. Otherwise, Drake might have had a second thought.) The salary was to be $125 a month, good pay in those days. Audubon, of course, was delighted and moved to Cincinnati immediately, leaving Lucy in Louisville until he found a place for them to live.

At the museum Audubon's immediate supervisor was the curator, a young Englishman named Robert Best. Something of the nature of their work is revealed by the list of possessions that the museum published only a few years after Audubon had left. It then owned some hundred mammoth bones, 50 giant sloth bones, 33 stuffed quadrupeds, 500 stuffed birds, 200 fish specimens, thousands of invertebrates, as well as specimens of plants and minerals. Nor was this all. It also had in its collection 150 Egyptian antiquities, some pictures of American scenery and buildings, and an "elegant" organ, to say nothing of the tattooed head of a New Zealand chief. The fish were Audubon's first concern and then the birds, for Best had many other matters to attend to. Not only was he in charge of the entire collection, including the tattooed head, but he had numerous other duties. As Dr. Drake optimistically announced to the public, "Among the variety of objects which it is designed to embrace in the museum, are several kinds of philosophical instruments, calculated to illustrate the principles of magnetism, electricity, galvanism, mechanics, hydrostats, optics, and the mechanism of the solar system. The whole of these can be fabricated by our ingenious Curator, Mr. Best." With Dr. Drake as secretary of the museum, there would always be plenty to keep the staff busy.

As soon as he could, Audubon sent to Louisville for Lucy and they settled down to life in their new home. Cincinnati, they found, was a pleasant place to live. Compared to Henderson, it was both large and cosmopolitan, with a population of almost ten thousand inhabitants; and although the number of taverns outweighed the number of churches, seventeen to ten, it also had a dozen doctors and four book and stationery stores, which must have been particularly pleasing to Lucy. Even if she could not afford to buy books herself, in a town like Cincinnati she could at least borrow them from friends. What was perhaps even more important, the Audubons found homekeeping inexpensive. "Our living here," Audubon wrote, "is extremely moderate; the markets are well supplied and cheap, beef only two and a half cents a pound, and I am able to provide a good deal myself; partridges are frequently in the streets, and I can shoot wild turkeys within a mile or so; squirrels and woodcock are very abundant in the season, and fish always easily caught." Nevertheless, Audubon decided to augment his museum salary by establishing an art school, giving classes three times a week at what he considered "good prices."

Although he was busy with the routine work of the museum and teaching his students, Audubon found time to do his own independent research. In fact, his association with the museum gave him additional opportunities to study birds, because the people around Cincinnati brought in information and new specimens. One day, for example, a woman arrived with a least bittern—a long-necked shore bird—carrying it in her apron. She said it had fallen down her chimney the night before and that when she awoke at daybreak it was the first thing she saw, perched on her bedpost. He placed the bird on the table in front of him and made a careful drawing. Then he took two books and arranged them so as to leave a passage of an inch and a half for the bittern. It walked through with ease. Then he reduced the passage to an inch. Again the bird made its way between without moving either book. Although it measured two inches and a quarter in width, he found it could contract its breadth greatly. Experiments such as these, although not important scientifically, were adding greatly to his knowledge of birds and their behavior. More and more, he was becoming not only a collector and artist, but also an interpreter.

At Cincinnati he also had a chance to go on with his observations of cliff swallows. Four years before, at Henderson, he had seen a few of these birds for the first time, but most of them had been killed by the cold weather. He had written a description of them, but for some years had despaired of seeing any more. Then one day at the museum, Best remarked that a strange species of birds was reported nearby.

Audubon immediately crossed to Newport, Kentucky, and obtained permission from the commander of the army garrison there to examine the walls where the birds were building their nests. He found that about fifty nests were finished. A few days later another flight arrived and built thirty more. All summer Audubon watched them and, in addition to his own observations, questioned the commander about their previous arrivals and departures.

What led him into making such careful studies was his interest in investigating what he called "the long-debated question respecting the migration or supposed torpidity of swallows." In classical times the belief had become firmly established that swallows, instead of moving south in the winter, buried themselves in the mud and went into a state of hibernation. In various forms, the legend persisted through the centuries; and even that accurate observer, Gilbert White, whose *Natural History of Selbourne* remains an English classic, had been inclined to agree. In trying to prove or disprove the theory, Audubon showed the influence that the Western Museum had on his attitude. For the first time, he was taking a specific problem and examining it systematically.

Yet his appointment at the Western Museum did not answer Audubon's needs. For all Doctor Drake's enthusiasm and his many connections in the city, he was unable to make the museum a financial success. In 1818 he had set it up as a stock company, with each member taking up $500 worth of stock, which was transferrable; and when he made his first public announcement of his enterprise, he already had in hand $4,000, a rather considerable amount in those days. Furthermore, he had avoided the pitfall into which many nonprofit organizations drop by refusing to erect a separate building and, instead, made use of rooms that were already constructed. Nevertheless, Audubon said, "I found, sadly too late, that the members of the college museum were splendid promisers but poor paymasters." According to his memory afterward, he was owed $1,200 which was never paid him, although Lucy later received $400. As a consequence, he had to develop other means of supporting himself and so, in addition to his art classes, turned again to painting portraits. Financially he was not much better off than he had been at Louisville.

The problem was what to do next. Nothing had happened to improve his chances of re-entering business. No one had changed his mind about lending Audubon capital; no one was willing to offer him a job. Working for the Western Museum had seemed like an excellent idea, but if Dr. Drake could not raise money to pay for the staff's salaries, there was little point trying to hang on. As he discussed the question with Lucy, a seventy-five-foot stern-wheeler named the *Western Engineer* arrived at the Cincinnati riverbank. Painted on the boat was a large serpent whose mouth belched clouds of smoke from the boilers, a sight calculated to strike fear in the hearts of the western Indians. On board were a distinguished group: Major Stephen H. Long, an army officer and leader of the group's expedition toward the Rocky Mountains; Thomas Say, a Philadelphian about Audubon's age, who was already a distinguished zoologist; and Titian Peale, the Philadelphia artist. The latter two were men Audubon might easily have come to know when he was living at Mill Grove; but he was a stranger to them when they stopped to visit Dr. Drake and look at the collection of the Western Museum. While they were there, someone, probably Dr. Drake himself, persuaded them to glance at Audubon's portfolio. In their lives it was a minor event; in his, one of major consequence. Years later, he remembered it. "The expedition of Major Long passed through the city," he wrote, ". . . and well do I recollect how he, Messrs. T. Peale, Thomas Say, and others stared at my drawings of birds at that time." Wilson and Rafinesque had, of course, looked at his pictures, but these latest visitors were on an expedition sponsored by the government. They were important people, so important the government paid their expenses and supplied them with a steamboat. Even if the Western Museum could not meet its payroll, perhaps there was money in science after all. What Audubon needed was more pictures, he thought. Lucy agreed with him.

The two of them also talked about Alexander Wilson. Everybody connected with the Western Museum knew about Alexander Wilson and referred to him whenever the subject of birds came up. He was a distinguished authority, a famous man. His book must have sold well; it was so widely known. Looking at the copies available to him in Cincinnati, Audubon kept wondering if he could not produce a bird book also. Wilson had a rather long text about birds; Audubon had his notes and the results of the observations he had made for years. Wilson had pictures; Audubon had pictures—some of Audubon's pictures were even better than Wilson's. At least, he and Lucy thought they were. He did not have as many pictures as Wilson, but— and this was extremely important—he had some pictures of birds that Wilson did not have. Dr. Drake had pointed that out. Wilson's book, therefore, was not complete. Possibly it could be replaced with a better book.

Dr. Drake had practically said so in a speech he made on June 10, 1820, in the chapel of the Cincinnati College. Audubon was probably there, accompanied by Lucy and surrounded by the leading citizens of Cincinnati; and even if he was not, he had ample opportunity to read what Dr. Drake said. In the quiet of the summer evening, Dr. Drake stood before his audience and began his report on the museum he had created. "We have this evening assembled," he began, "to commemorate the establishment of the Western Museum Society," which was now prepared to open its doors to the public. The doctor was not a brief speaker. On and on he went, using the elaborate language of a nineteenth-century orator; and some of his listeners, even in those days when long speeches and sermons were commonplace, must have dropped off to sleep in the hot summer air. But after his long preamble and a discussion of the museum's animal collection, the doctor came to the subject of ornithology. This is what the Audubons wanted to hear, and Dr. Drake did not disappoint them.

"It would be an act of injustice," he said, "to speak of our ornithology, without connecting with it the name of Alexander Wilson. To this self-taught, indefatigable and ingenious man we are indebted for most of what we know concerning the natural history of our birds. His labors may have nearly completed the ornithology of the middle Atlantic states, but must necessarily have left that of the western imperfect." Audubon and Lucy probably nodded to each other; Wilson's book was not complete.

"When we advert to the fact," Dr. Drake continued, "that most birds are migratory, and that in their migrations they are not generally disposed to cross high mountains, but to follow the courses of rivers; when we contemplate the great basin of the Mississippi, quite open to the north and south, but bounded on the east and west by ranges of lofty mountains, while the river itself stretches through twenty degrees of latitude, connecting Lake Superior and the Gulf of Mexico, it is reasonable to conjecture, that many birds annually migrate over this country which do not visit the Atlantic states, and might, therefore, have escaped the notice of their greatest ornithologist in the single excursion he made to the Ohio." Dr. Drake, in this statement, recognized the existence of the separate flyways over which the birds of America migrate north and south—and he also pointed out that Alexander Wilson had concentrated on the Atlantic flyway.

The doctor went on, and while many of his audience may have missed the import of what he was saying, Audubon did not, because he was mentioned by name. "As a proof of this supposition," Dr. Drake continued, "it may be stated that Mr. Audubon, one of the artists attached to the museum, who has

drawn, from nature, in colored crayons, several hundred species
of American birds, has, in his portfolio, a large number that
are not figured in Mr. Wilson's work, and which do not seem
to have been recognized by any naturalist." The doctor then
reported on other departments of the museum—"the obscure
and imperfect animals that swim in our lakes and rivers," "the
problems offered by our fossil zoology," "our cabinet of geological specimens," the Indian artifacts in the collection—and ended
with a peroration on military matters. "If not equal to Europe,"
he said, "in the application of science to works of national defense, we have obviously passed the weakness of childhood; and
might repel, almost without bloodshed, an invasion, to which
our fathers could only oppose their dauntless and patriotic
bosoms."

The audience must have cheered those noble words and even
the drowsiest nodded their heads. But Audubon and Lucy
were still thinking of those earlier words, ". . . . has in his portfolio, a large number that are not figured in Mr. Wilson's
work." As lucidly as possible, Dr. Drake had said that America
needed another ornithologist to complement the work done by
Wilson and that the new ornithologist should concentrate his
efforts on the Mississippi flyway. But how would he go about
doing it? By making a trip down the rivers, of course, observing
and sketching as he went. For a man like Audubon, the task
should not be difficult. He already had, as Dr. Drake pointed
out, a number of birds that Wilson did not. With just a few
more, he could illustrate his own book; and the book would
make him famous and, if not rich, at least well off.

Six weeks after Dr. Drake's speech to the members of the
Western Museum Society, Audubon wrote a letter to Henry
Clay, Representative from Kentucky. "After having spent the
greater part of fifteen years in procuring and drawing the birds
of the United States with a view of publishing them, I find
myself possessed of a large number of such specimens that usually resort to the Middle States only. Having a desire to complete the collection before I present it to my country in perfect
order, I intend to explore the territories southwest of the
Mississippi.

"I shall leave this place about the middle of September for

the purpose of visiting the Red River, Arkansas, and the countries adjacent. Well aware of the good reception that a few lines from one on whom our country looks with respectful admiration, I have taken the liberty of requesting such introductory aid, as you may deem necessary to a naturalist, while at the frontier forts and agencies of the United States."

No, it was not quite the truth. He had not been working for fifteen years collecting bird drawings in order to publish a book. He had not even thought about a book until recently, but he had to make his career sound impressive. He could not confess to Henry Clay that he was a bankrupt whom no one would trust in business. As for the expedition he planned to make, it was certainly casual. Visiting the Red River and the adjacent country might be all that was necessary. He could also go to New Orleans, if he had to. Certainly one or both of those places would give him all the additional pictures he needed. Anyway it would be better than remaining at Cincinnati, drawing no money from the Western Museum and barely eking out a living by painting portraits and giving drawing lessons to young ladies.

In any case, it would not take long. At the most seven or eight months.

CHAPTER XII

1820

O N the afternoon of October 12, 1820, Audubon stood on
the banks of the Ohio River at Cincinnati, ready to
board a flatboat and embark on his great adventure—an adventure that he hoped would bring him fame and a means of
livelihood. Everything was the usual bustle. Men were carrying
the last of the cargo aboard; the crew were assembling; a few
well-wishers lined the shore waiting to see the boat off.

Audubon had made the best preparations he could for the
trip. From Captain Jacob Aumack, the patroon of the flatboat,
he had apparently procured his passage at a reduced rate. To
assist him he had an eighteen-year-old pupil, Joseph Mason, to
whom he was to teach art in return for help in collecting specimens. Already on board were the few possessions he needed:
some clothing, his art materials, and his gun, as well as the letters of introduction he had been soliciting for several weeks.
One was from General William Harrison, the hero of the Battle of Tippecanoe, recommending him to the army general
commanding the post at the fork of the Arkansas. Elijah Slack,
a member of the board of managers of the Western Museum,
had written to some friends down the river, as had Dr. Drake
and other acquaintances of Audubon. Henry Clay had also
answered his request by giving him a general letter that said,
"I have the satisfaction of a personal acquaintance with Mr.
John J. Audubon; and I have learned from others who have
known him longer and better, that his character and conduct
have been uniformly good." With these opening remarks, he
suggested that the officers and agents of the United States government might, whenever practical, assist him with his work.

In addition, Clay had taken the time to write Audubon per-

197

sonally. He was unfamiliar with the particular places Audubon intended to visit, he said. Therefore he thought a general letter of introduction would serve. In closing, he wrote one short paragraph that struck at the root of Audubon's inadequate planning. "Will it not be well for you," Clay suggested, "before you commit yourself to any great expense in the preparation and publication of your contemplated work to ascertain the success which attended a similar undertaking of Mr. Wilson?" Clay, the practical man-of-the-world, was offering advice that Audubon had no thought of heeding. He probably showed the letter to Lucy, but how could they find out about Wilson, who had died seven years before in Philadelphia? And for what purpose? Wilson was famous; he must have made money from his book.

So there stood Audubon at the edge of the river on a fall afternoon, prepared to leave his wife and two children for many months with no real idea whether he could, or could not, provide for them by his effort. He had, however, made a resolve which to some extent reflects his naïveté, but to a greater extent his courage. "Without any money," he wrote in his journal, "my talents are to be my support and my enthusiasm, my guide in my difficulties, the whole of which I am ready to exert. . . ."

As the crew carried the last of the cargo and the passengers' luggage on board and stowed it away in the hold or in the cabin, Audubon looked at the men with whom he would be traveling. Captain Jacob Aumack was a strong young man, brave, generous, and accustomed to hardship, although Audubon thought him inclined to be timorous on the river. Also on board were a Mr. Loveless, good-natured, ready to work, fond of women and of making money; a Bostonian, Mr. Shaw, who owned most of the cargo and was, according to Audubon, interested only in his own welfare and "would live well if at anyone else's expense"; and a crew of five. One of these, Ned Kelly—heavily built and always in good spirits—came from Baltimore. Two others, Anthony P. Bodley and Henry Sesler, both carpenters by trade, were from Pennsylvania. Luke, a shoemaker from Cincinnati, had been hired as cook. The fifth member was a good-for-nothing named Joseph Seeg, lazy, fond of grog, and a man who slept so soundly by the fire that his clothes could catch aflame without awakening him. A close friend of Audubon was also a passenger, Captain Samuel Cummings of Cincinnati. As a private venture, he planned a make a record of the channels of the Ohio and Mississippi rivers.

Another boat was to make the trip with them—each could help the other on the difficult stretches of the river; and at four o'clock, when both craft were ready, the captains picked up the long, cumbersome steering oars, and the crews rowed their boats out into the current. There they swung down river and began the long journey south. All that night they drifted, the dark shadows of the banks rising on either side, the night silent except for the occasional swish of the steering oar, the hoot of an owl, or the sound of a man snoring in the cramped, stuffy cabin. Because the water was low and the current feeble, they covered only fourteen miles before the new day broke.

As soon as they could, Mason, Cummings, and Audubon went ashore. They could easily keep up with the flatboat by walking and at the same time do some hunting. The abundance of the game they found is indicated by the record of their first day of shooting: thirty partridges, one woodcock, twenty-seven gray squirrels, a barn owl, and a young turkey buzzard—a rather indiscriminate bag that indicates they were as interested in testing their marksmanship as in providing the flatboat with food. Audubon, however, had not forgotten the principal purpose for his expedition, for he also shot a bay-breasted warbler and mentally quarreled with Wilson's contention that it was a separate species, not merely the young of one already known. (He had to prove that he was better informed than Wilson, did he not? His success as an ornithologist depended on it.) Carefully, he sketched the bird for his records and then dissected it, finding in its stomach the remains of "small winged insects" and the seeds of some berries.

This was the sort of trip Audubon had made so many times before, as a young man coming west with Rozier to seek his fortune, as a bridegroom with Lucy, as a young merchant with Nolte. Always his hopes had been high; always he had been searching for something new. This time, too, he was searching, but not as confidently as before. In the ruins of his life at

Henderson, he had left much of his self-assurance; and although he was still capable of presenting a brave face to the world at large, grave misgivings had begun to gnaw at him.

For three days the trip went smoothly, but at ten o'clock on the 15th, while the crew and the passengers were asleep and only the helmsman was on duty, the two boats ran on some rocks. As usual, everybody was ordered on deck and into the water to start the heavy work of heaving and pulling. Finally the boats were freed, but the next morning, another cold day, Audubon was taken ill. That evening the two boats struck a sandbar and lodged fast. Once more the crew and passengers leaped in the water, finally freeing Aumack's boat, but the other stayed fast on the bar all night. When he had been traveling up the Mississippi with Rozier in midwinter, Audubon had plunged into the icy water without a complaint for himself or a thought for the others. But now he noted in his journal that "the hands suffered much from the cold."

By the 18th of October he still was not feeling well, but he was in relatively good spirits, going ashore to hunt—he killed two turkeys with a single shot—and watching the chimney swifts flying overhead in a southerly direction. When Joseph Mason shot his first wild turkey and received three cheers from the crew, he joined in the shouting, but by November 1, when the weather turned bad and it started to drizzle, he was thoroughly depressed and wrote in his journal, "Extremely tired of my indolent way of living, not having procured anything to draw since Louisville."

What was bothering him, however, was neither the weather nor his recent failure to collect specimens; it was simply that the boat was approaching Henderson. With every mile it covered, the scenes along the banks were becoming more and more familiar. Just off that sandbar he had gone fishing with John Pope, his former clerk. Under that clump of brush he had shot a deer. In that canebrake he had once hunted a bear. There was the road down which he had once ridden on his horse, Barro. Every tree, every small rise in the ground, every bend in the river, brought back memories, but they were no longer happy. Each was colored by the disgrace he had felt on leaving Henderson, each revived that disgrace, made him live through it again and again. In his mind, he was not now shooting with Pope; he was watching the bitter looks on his neighbors' faces. That voice he heard echoing was not the laughing voice of a fellow hunter; it was George Keats cursing him. That hand he felt on his shoulder was not Lucy's as she stepped from their skiff; it was the rough hand of a creditor just before they arrested him and took him to Louisville. This was the country where he had once been so respected, so gay, so popular. Now he had only one tie with it, one single possession he could claim. That was a female hunting dog named Dash.

But he did not dare to go ashore to fetch her. He did not have the courage to face the memories, to look in the blank faces that had once belonged to friends.

Captain Cummings understood his dilemma. Audubon wanted the dog; he had so few possessions left that one hunting dog made a difference. But he did not want the dog as much as he wanted to avoid Henderson, to obliterate it from his memory, to erase from his mind this stretch of the river and all it had meant. Cummings therefore said he and Joseph Mason would take the skiff, row ahead to Henderson, pick up Dash, and bring her back.

The wind was blowing hard when they climbed into the small boat. Audubon stood on deck and watched them disappear in the gray mist. He did not hunt; he did not draw. He simply sat and waited and thought. At one o'clock in the morning, they returned with Dash, emerging out of the black like ghosts. Both men were exhausted by rowing against the wind, which was still whistling across the deck and forming small whitecaps on the river. They did not say much to Audubon; they were tired and there was not much to say. The dog was not glad to see him; the dog hardly knew him. He tied her up and tried to sleep.

At five o'clock in the morning, Aumack decided to start moving again. The wind, the incessant wind with its gray skies, was still blowing. It whipped the gusts of rain across the deck. It blew through the chinks in the cabin walls. It chopped the surface of the river. To escape the wind, Aumack steered the boat toward the Indiana shore, trying to get under the lee of the bank. But the bank did not offer sufficient protection, so he tied up again two miles above Henderson.

There was no help for it; the boat could not move ahead, although Audubon desperately wanted to pass Henderson and leave it behind. All day he stayed on the boat. No one came out to see him, although they knew he was there; Cummings had told them. Not a single soul, not even a child, came to the opposite bank and waved to him. He tried drawing the scene around him, but the wind tore at his paper and he could make only the roughest sketch. Then he wrote in his journal, "I can scarcely conceive that I stayed there eight years and passed them comfortably, for it is undoubtedly one of the poorest spots in the western country, according to my present opinion."

On board the flatboat, the crew and passengers huddled in the small, smoky cabin. Skeeg complained as usual; Luke, the cook, decided he would go no farther. "A poor sickly devil," Audubon called him. No one regretted his departure, although they would have to take turns from there on cooking their own meals. During the night the wind finally dropped, the storm was over, and at daybreak they untied the mooring lines, manned the oars, and moved out into the main current again. Just as the sun broke over the horizon, they came to Henderson. There was the town where he and Lucy had once been so happy, bathed in the fresh morning light that follows a storm. There were the streets he had walked, the doors that had once opened to him, but Henderson paid no attention to his passing. He was nobody as far as Henderson was concerned, just another one of the thousands of travelers descending the river. From the deck he saw the mill, its chunky bulk rising from the edge of the water. It was in other hands now. It, of all the places he had seen, aroused the bitterest memories. "I looked on the mill," he wrote in his journal, "perhaps for the last time and, with thoughts that made my blood almost cold, bid it an eternal farewell."

Standing on deck, Audubon watched Henderson disappear around the bend. Indian summer was now in full sway. The trees along the banks cast brilliant reflections on the water, the air was cool and crisp. Overhead, the sky was obscured by the smoke of a distant fire. Ever since they had left Cincinnati they had noticed this smoke, which at times was dense enough to irritate their eyes. At first they thought the Indians might be burning the prairies to the west; but when the easterly winds failed to roll the smoke back, they decided it was caused by forest fires, for the river was low and the ground dry.

That night they anchored at Diamond Island, where the outlaw Mason had first fled after he was driven from Henderson. Now it was quiet and peaceful, but at nine o'clock in the evening, the wind began to blow again. All night, as it roared around them, the men lay wrapped in their buffalo robes, while the flatboat rode safely in the lee of the island. The next morning, however, it was impossible to go on. Restless and depressed, Audubon went shooting. At least, he would have a chance to try out Dash and see whether she was a good hunting dog; but the day was unsuccessful. He killed a large buck, which died somewhere in a heavy growth of cane where he was unable to reach it; he shot a winter wren which was too damaged to use as a model for sketching; to crown his misfortunes, he found that Dash was useless as a hunting dog and "good for nothing."

On the following day the weather improved greatly. Although the temperature dropped below freezing, the sun rose clear and bright. The frost was thick on the decks and glittered crystal white when the light fell on it. To Audubon it was beautiful beyond expression, and his spirits were raised by the easy progress of the boat. At this point the channel was narrowed by sandbars, and the river flowed more quickly. To add to the gaiety, the flatboat was overtaken by several pleasant young men, traveling to New Orleans in a skiff.

Two days later, the temperature reached fifty, but the weather turned rainy and disagreeable. At Shawnee, which Audubon had visited so many times and where he once had had many friends, the crew and passengers went ashore, but he again preferred to remain on board. He even asked some one else to mail the letter he had written to Lucy. He was, however, delighted when Aumack shot a rusty blackbird and brought it to him. That evening Ned Kelly, the genial crew member, and Seeg, the lazy one, provided them all with amusement. Sitting in the cabin and drinking, both men reached for the bottle more frequently than usual, and as the evening wore on,

instead of becoming gayer, they turned surly and started arguing. The first sharp words were followed by others. Soon there
was nothing left but to settle the argument in frontier fashion
by a fight. Everybody stepped out on the deck, a space was
cleared, and Kelly and Seeg dove for each other, grabbing,
hitting, and clawing. Audubon, like the others, favored Kelly
over the unpleasant Seeg and was delighted to see him send
Seeg to the deck with his eyes and nose battered and bleeding.

During the next ten days, Audubon's state of mind was better. With interest he watched some crows bedeviling a barred
owl, chasing it from a tree where it had found a daytime perch,
and he especially enjoyed the stop at Cave-in-the-Rock, making
careful sketches of the cave where the pirates had operated their
inn. A day or so later, he shot a loon which proved to be an
excellent specimen and chased two others in the skiff, incredu-
lous at the speed with which they could dive on hearing the
sound of his gun. The weather turned better, some of the more
difficult stretches of the river were behind them, and Audubon
was taking greater pleasure in what he saw. Captain Cummings
caught a possum, brought it back on board, and gave it to Dash
to play with. The dog, which had proved disappointing on an
actual hunt, attacked the animal so viciously that Audubon
thought every bone must be broken and threw the body into
the water. Whereupon, in true possum fashion, it came to life
and swam toward the boat. They pulled it back on board and
finally had to kill it with an ax.

In this fashion the days followed one another. Audubon
found enough to do to keep himself busy, collecting specimens
and adding to his portfolio of drawings. On November 16 they
were a few miles above the Mississippi and near Cash Creek,
where he and Rozier had made the first of their two winter
camps. He went hunting with Cummings and Mason but, having no luck, returned to the boat, only to find Aumack in bad
humor. What happened next, Audubon never said, but his own
sensitivity probably magnified the insult. In his journal he
merely stated that he had "received a humorous lesson that
I shall never forget." Apparently Aumack made some jibe
about the state of his finances and his inability to pay the usual
fare, for the next lines in his journal, addressed to his two sons,

say, "My dear children, if ever you read these trifling remarks pay your attention to what follows—

"Never be under what is called obligations to men not aware of the value or the meanness of their *conduct*.

"Never take a passage in any stage or vessel without a well understood agreement between you and the owners or clerks, and of all things, never go for nothing, if you wish to save mental troubles and bodily vicissitudes.

"Well aware that I shall never forget this night as long as I live, I close."

That night was bad; the next day was worse. The bitterness and despair he had thrown off since passing Henderson came rushing back. In the morning, instead of riding with the others on the flatboat, he took the skiff and rowed by himself to the Mississippi, recalling the trip he had made with Rozier to Ste. Genevieve "in a large keelboat loaded with sundries, to a large amount *our* property," and he underscored the word "our" in his journal. Now, he said, writing of the Mississippi, "I enter it poor, in fact destitute of all things and relying only on that providential hope, the comforter of this wearied mind—in a flatboat, a passenger." As the full flood of his despair broke over him he added, "I bid farewell to the Ohio at two o'clock P.M. and felt a fear gathering involuntarily. Every moment draws me from all that is dear to me, my beloved wife and my children." His state of mind was so poor that he envied two Indians he saw passing in a canoe. They had bear traps with them, a few venison hams, and a gun, and "looked so independent, free and unconcerned with the world," he wrote, "that I gazed on them, admired their spirits, and wished for their condition."

At the Mississippi, the captains of the two boats decided to separate, now the worst stretches of the river were safely passed. Audubon and the other travelers felt better for this—apparently there had been differences of opinion on the way down—and he hoped that everyone, himself included, would become more cheerful. For a day or two longer he stayed in better humor. Then, in a high wind, they stopped at New Madrid, the town which had been the center of the earthquake through which he had ridden years before. There he noted that "this almost deserted village is one of the poorest that is seen on this river having a name. The back country was represented to us as being good, but the looks of the inhabitants contradicted strongly their assertions. They are clad in buckskin pantaloons and a sort of shirt of the same material. This is seldom put aside, unless so ragged or so blooded and greased, that it will become disagreeable even to the poor wrecks that have it on.

"The Indian is more decent, better off, and a thousand times more happy. Here family dissensions are at their zenith, and to kill a neighbor is but little more than to kill a deer or a raccoon."

Going ashore, he called on a woman he had known at Ste. Genevieve. She recognized Audubon immediately and was glad to see him, but the visit was unsuccessful; it reminded Audubon too strongly of what he had been and might have become. He wrote in his journal, "Felt dull this evening, for every object that brings *forward* the *background* of my life's picture shows too often with poignancy the difference in my situation—" These reminders of the past were proving almost unbearable, whether he was floating by Henderson, recalling his trip with Rozier, or merely meeting a woman he had known slightly at Ste. Genevieve.

When they left New Madrid, he took the skiff, as he often did, and, with Joseph rowing, went ahead of the flatboat looking for birds. That day was uneventful, except that Dash, the dog, went after a possum, making such a fuss about it that everyone thought she must have cornered a bear. The next day, however, brought better luck. After their usual breakfast of fried bacon and biscuits, Joseph and Audubon again climbed in the skiff to range ahead of the flatboat. This time a bald eagle, a handsome, white-headed bird, flew in sight about a hundred and fifty yards away. With one shot Audubon brought it down, and he was pleased not only with the specimen he had procured but with his marksmanship. Immediately he returned to the boat and started making a drawing without waiting to look for more birds. As he studied his eagle he became more and more convinced that the bird shown him by the flatboat captain near Cape Giradeau and the bird he had before him were entirely different species, clinging to his mistaken belief that his Washington Sea-Eagle was an important discovery.

The next day, again in high winds, he woke up early and went hunting at daybreak. Seeing a deer crossing a river below where the boat was tied, he went in pursuit and finally shot it. Although it was a miserable deformed creature, he brought it back to the boat and cleaned it. Almost all the rest of the day, he either worked on his pictures or watched some crows and turkey buzzards hovering near the spot where the deer's body hung in the woods.

Anchored just below the flatboat was a skiff carrying a dissolute family of three—two men and a woman. They were too lazy, Audubon observed, to make any provision for themselves and, instead of building a bed, lay down on the damp earth near the river. For food, they ate raccoons and drank the muddy river water to help the meat down. They had no future nor any way of finding one and were, he thought, "moving to a worse part of the worst." Although the weather turned warm, the wind kept blowing hard, so they remained anchored all the following day, November 25, and Audubon continued to draw his bald eagle. One of the crew visited the family in the skiff and persuaded the woman to come on board the flatboat and do their laundry. At sunset the wind shifted, great clouds rolled over the sky, and it was apparent that the weather was at last about to change. When they woke up in the morning, the temperature had dropped below freezing; and they invited the family in the skiff to come to the flatboat and warm themselves in the cabin.

Formerly Audubon would have paid little attention to this poverty-stricken group beyond talking to them casually and perhaps giving them a little money. Now as he watched them in the cabin, destitute, forlorn, dressed in rags, he felt close to them. They did not belong to a separate world; they were more like him than the other passengers on the flatboat. "Look on these people," he wrote in his journal, "and consider coolly their condition; then compare it to mine; they certainly are more miserable to common eyes—but, it is all a mistaken idea, for poverty and independence are the only friends that will travel together through this world." He had begun almost to envy the completely poor, those with no ties, no responsibilities, no positions, and, above all, no appearances to keep up.

By the following day, he was sick again. The deformed deer
he had shot and eaten proved to be diseased. Everyone who
touched the meat was ill, but the effect on Audubon was more
serious because it deepened his depression. Moving away from
the others to be by himself, he took out the picture of Lucy he
had drawn and brought with him. He kept looking at it and
looking at it, and so morbid had his state of mind become that
he thought the picture changed before his very eyes. The face
he had drawn was altering; its expression was becoming sorrowful. This was not the picture he had composed. As he watched
it, he had "an immediate sensation of dread of her being in
want."

He was verging on the brink of insanity.

Somehow he managed to fall asleep that night. When he
awoke, it was raining so hard that hunting was an impossibility.
Huddled in the cabin of the flatboat, he took out his journal
and began writing a brief account of his life which he hoped
his sons would someday read. Like many people in times of discouragement, he turned to the past for happiness—the further
back, the better. He thought of his mother as being beautiful,
his father as nobly generous, and only when he dealt with
events closer to him in time did he write harshly about what
had happened. During the day, Aumack moved the boat to the
other side of the river to shelter it from the wind. The visibility
was so poor, only twenty or thirty yards, that he did not dare
go downstream. Consequently Audubon did not have the relief of continuing the journey or collecting new birds. Instead,
when he finished his autobiographical sketch he played on the
flute he had brought with him, studied his drawings, and tried
to read, "yet found the day very long and heavy."

Nor did matters improve much in the succeeding days. Most
of the time the weather was bad, cloudy, cold, and often raining. Mason was out of sorts because Aumack insisted that he
substitute for the cook who had left them at Henderson. Even
hunting, which had served as an outlet for Audubon's energy,
became more difficult. He could not walk along the banks of
the Mississippi and keep up with the flatboat as he had done
on the Ohio. The only way he could hunt now was to take the
skiff and go ahead of the flatboat. When he saw game he would

lie down in the bow and drift toward it until he was within shooting distance. Although this was awkward, he continued to take a large number of birds, some of which he used as models, some as food for the passengers and crew.

All this while, he fought back the waves of emotion that threatened to engulf him, trying to find pleasure in the activity around him. On December 3, he saw a flight of mallards winging their way southward against the setting sun, while a rainbow arched across the sky and the clouds piled up in magnificent heaps. His spirits rose temporarily at the sight, but that afternoon was followed by another windy, restless night. The boat was moored near a sandbar and rubbed against it, creating a noise that kept him from sleeping. As the wind grew stronger, Aumack roused the crew; they stumbled out of their bunks in the darkness, took up their oars, and moved the flatboat to a more sheltered location. Yet even this maneuver did not make it quiet; the boat still rocked and shook in the wind.

The next day, however, Audubon caught a catfish—he often dropped a line over the boat's stern—and found it weighed 64½ pounds. Even more important to his state of mind, he became absorbed in comparing it to those he had caught at Henderson and wondered if it might be a different species. That evening Aumack inadvertently provided him with further amusement. They had covered thirty miles, when they decided to tie up for the night. Suddenly everything went wrong. In attempting to approach the shore, Aumack drove the boat on a mudbank. For half an hour the crew sweated and strained to get it off, pushing with their poles and battling against the current. In the middle of the struggle, the sweep oar—the long oar used for steering—snapped in two; and from then on, Aumack had a lively time of it, shouting out orders and, in between, swearing as hard and loudly as he could. Audubon, still filled with resentment at Aumack's earlier jibes, enjoyed every minute of the captain's discomfiture. At the end, he felt as though he had been repaid in full and the score was even. From then on, relations between the two men improved.

At the mouth of the St. Francis River, Audubon was excited to learn that flocks of pelicans had moved southward only a few days before. Perhaps the flatboat would catch up with them,

and this possibility added zest to the trip. Then Aumack, shooting at a bald eagle, only winged it and was able to capture it
alive. In order to keep it for observation, Audubon tied a string
around one leg and attached the other end to a pole weighing
about fifteen pounds. That, he thought, would hold the eagle on
board. Much to his surprise, the bird, although it could not fly,
was able to drag the pole by walking. In a matter of seconds, it
dove over the edge into the water and began to swim toward
shore. Mason, seeing what was happening, leaped into the skiff
and took after it. Fortunately he recaptured the bird before it
reached the land. With the live specimen before him, Audubon
took out the drawing he had made earlier and compared it
closely with the bird before him. He found, to his pleasure,
that the picture stood the comparison well. Then, putting some
fish on the end of a stick, he set about feeding his captive. At
first it refused the food, but within an hour Audubon had encouraged it into eating. Pleased with this success, he became
overconfident and moved too close. The bird shot forth its
talon and stabbed him painfully in the right thumb.

Meanwhile the boat had been drawing closer to Arkansas
Post, where Audubon thought he might stay for a while, using
some of the letters of introduction that he had brought with
him and perhaps persuading the governor to help him. Near
the mouth of the White River, Aumack suggested they walk
to Arkansas Post, going up the river partway by skiff and then
overland to the settlement. At ten o'clock in the morning he,
Audubon, Mason, and one crew member left the flatboat, taking with them a few biscuits and a small bottle of whiskey.
Turning into the White River, they found the water high and
the current running violently. Unable to row any longer, they
cut the vines of wild grapes and made a towrope with which
they could pull the boat. For seven miles they tugged and
jerked the skiff against the current, seven miles that Audubon
said felt like at least ten, until they came to a cutoff leading
into the Arkansas River.

Here they left the skiff and went on by land but soon became
so tangled in briers that they had to give up and take a longer
route which led through cypress swamps, past ponds and deep
into thickets of cane until they finally reached a house belong-

ing to a Frenchman. Although he was about to get into bed,
the Frenchman put on his clothing and guided them for seven
miles through mud and water until they reached the only tavern in the area.

This was a pleasant place, run by a woman who made them
welcome and served them a meal which they ate as though
they were wolves tearing at a carcass. She then took them to a
large building which contained three beds in which five men
were already sleeping. Everything was arranged in a few minutes. Aumack and the crew member climbed into one bed;
Joseph and Audubon into another. Then came the usual conversation with the other men as they introduced themselves to each
other. There were not enough blankets, but Audubon soon
found a snug place in the turkey-feather mattress. As the voices
droned on, he fell asleep and slept as he had not slept for weeks.

The physical exercise during the day and the escape from
the flatboat had been what he most needed. The next day when
he awoke and heard the cardinals and meadowlarks singing outside the building, he commented that mirth was all about him.
It was the first time he had been his former self since leaving
Cincinnati.

At Arkansas Post, he almost at once came across a man whose
acquaintance he had made earlier on a steamboat. Not knowing anything about Audubon's recent past, this man did not
snub him as he had been so often snubbed in the past months,
but instead introduced him to others. One of them was a man
he had known previously in Pittsburgh; another had traveled
through the surrounding country with the English naturalist
Thomas Nuttall, a former journeyman printer who had emigrated to the United States in 1808, the year Audubon moved
west. In 1818 Nuttall had published a two-volume book on
American plants, which he followed with numerous other publications as he broadened his interests to include ornithology.

The men Audubon met at Arkansas Post gave him the companionship he sorely needed, but he was disappointed to find
that the officials to whom he carried letters of introduction had
gone on a mission some 150 miles inland. Yet even this did not
discourage him much. His hope that they might help him in
his work had been only a wild speculation, one of several pos-

sibilities, and since they were absent, he might just as well continue down the river. For his purposes, one place was almost as good as another.

He was still on board Aumack's flatboat, therefore, when the crew untied the moorings on December 14 and rowed the boat out from the shore. A fog lay over the river, cloaking it in mystery; the air was warm; off in the distance came the frequent rumbling of thunder. Soon the fog lifted and it began to rain, and by two o'clock they decided to tie up. Although the weather remained cold and wet during the next two days, Audubon did not became depressed again. Both Aumack's struggle landing the boat and the stopover at Arkansas Post had done him good, and he was able to hold his emotions under control.

Then he saw the pelicans. He was standing on the bow one evening when he spotted them—a hundred or more—resting on a sandbar downriver from the boat. Jumping hurriedly into the skiff, he and Mason rowed toward them. As they approached, the pelicans woke from their sleep and, one at a time, shook their wings as though testing them for flight. When the skiff came within some hundred yards of them, they rose quietly into the air and flew off. Audubon tried to shoot one, but at that distance his shot went wide of his mark.

For three more days, the rain continued. On the third night they were sitting in the cabin drinking, while the water streamed across the decks. This time it was Aumack who reached for the bottle more frequently than usual. The more he drank, the more he thought about pelicans; and the more he thought about pelicans, the more convinced he became that the time had arrived for a pelican hunt. If no one else was interested, well, then, he would go by himself. At ten o'clock in the evening, with the rain still pouring down and the night outside pitch-black, Aumack rose unsteadily to his feet, took up his gun, slammed the cabin door behind him and went out into the storm to shoot a pelican. They listened as he clumped across the deck, clambered over the side, and disappeared in the darkness, thrashing through the brush, stumbling over stones, and making a commotion that could be heard yards away. After a while he came back, pelicanless but somewhat sobered by the wet and cold. Without a word, he entered the cabin, put away his gun, and went to bed to sleep it off.

In spite of Aumack's efforts to help, Audubon saw no more pelicans until the 23rd of December. This time he was out in the skiff with Mason and, landing below the birds, crawled toward them on his stomach for about three hundred yards until he was within forty-five yards of his target. Then, raising his gun carefully, he fired at three which were perched together on a stick some seven feet above the water. As his shot rang out, all three birds dropped like stones from their perch, but to his astonishment they, as well as twenty others nearby, immediately dove and began swimming underwater. After going about fifty yards, they rose to the surface and flew off with the exception of one which was wounded. Audubon and Joseph Mason rowed after it, the bird swimming and diving ahead of them. For more than a mile up the Yazoo River they went on their mad chase, Audubon refusing to give up because he noticed the bird was becoming more and more weary and unable to dive as frequently. Finally the skiff came close enough for Joseph Mason to shoot the bird through the head. It keeled over and, rowing alongside the floating body, Audubon lifted it into the skiff with a feeling of triumph.

On Christmas Day, Captain Aumack shot a duck hawk, which pleased Audubon tremendously. For fifteen years he had been watching these birds, particularly in Henderson, where he observed them preying on a colony of pigeons; but he had never been able to get close enough to shoot one. Now he held one in his hands, an old bird, he said, but a beautiful one. It was almost as good a Christmas present as he could have received.

That night, they tied up fifteen miles above Natchez. No special celebration took place on board the flatboat, but before he went to bed Audubon wrote in his journal: "I hope that my family wishes me as good a Christmas as I do them. Could I have spent it with my beloved wife and children, the exchange of situation would have been most agreeable."

Then he fell asleep in the dark, dirty cabin of the flatboat, moored by the banks of the Mississippi River. The willows at the edge of the river were green, and the days were warm, almost like May in Henderson. As he closed his eyes, he could hear the water lapping against the sides of the hull and the creaking of the boat as it pulled against its moorings. Since leaving Cincinnati he had collected many new specimens and made many new drawings. More than that he had fought and, at least for the time being, conquered his severest fits of depression. But he was still lonely, still uncertain of himself, still not sure where he was really going and what he was really trying to do.

CHAPTER XIII

1820 — 1821

THE morning after Christmas Day, 1820, dawned beautiful and clear. On awakening, Audubon found the deck of the flatboat covered with frost and the grass along the riverbanks glistening white. As soon as he had eaten breakfast and it was light enough to enable him to work, he began drawing, determined to finish before he reached Natchez the pictures he had already started.

At eleven o'clock Audubon was still sketching feverishly when Captain Aumack brought his flatboat under the bluffs of the city and made it fast. What Audubon, like all other travelers arriving by water, saw first was Natchez-Under-the-Hill, one of the worst and most scandalous of all the settlements along the river, filled with drinking places, gambling halls, and houses of prostitution offering every entertainment wanted by the boatmen. On the way downstream, boatmen stopped at Natchez to celebrate; the most difficult part of the journey was over. On their way back, they stopped at Natchez again; it was the last town of any size before they struck out into the wilderness for the long walk home.

From this evil trade Natchez-Under-the-Hill prospered, although occasionally some boatman took revenge on the city. James Girty, for example, the nephew of the notorious renegade Indian fighter, came to Natchez on a barge called the *Black Snake;* and his crew, going ashore, were fleeced in one of the gambling houses. Girty therefore decided to raid it. In the ensuing fight several of the gamblers were killed; and the forces of law and order, intervening for once, arrested Girty and charged him with manslaughter. Things looked bad for him. After all, the city had to defend its own. The proprietress of a dance hall, however, came to Girty's assistance. By various means she persuaded all but one stubborn witness to leave town at the time of the trial, and she took care of the stubborn one with a dose of arsenic. Because no one was there to testify against him, Girty received an acquittal.

Jack Russel, captain of the steamboat *Empress,* was another of the few men able to meet and challenge Natchez-Under-the-Hill on its own terms. On one of his trips, Russel carried as a passenger a minister who was going west to buy land. At Natchez-Under-the-Hill the minister foolishly opened his purse in public; some gamblers noticed how much money he was carrying, beat him up, robbed him, and sent him limping back to the *Empress.* There he found a sympathetic listener in Russel.

Gathering together several of his crew, Russel went ashore and located the gamblers barricaded inside a building. He tried to force them to leave their stronghold and even lit fires to smoke them out, but soon realized this tactic would work only if he burned down the whole town. Not quite prepared to do that, he returned to the *Empress,* picked up a heavy rope, tied one end around the house and attached the other to the *Empress.* Taking his place in the wheelhouse of his steamer, he gave the order to back the boat away from the shore. The house began to rumble and creak as the rope bit into the flimsy timbers. One of the gamblers rushed out the door with an ax, cut the rope, and dashed to safety. Already annoyed, this new maneuver simply made Russel even more determined than before. Back he came, carrying a chain to fasten around the house. Once more he ordered the *Empress* to reverse its engines. The steamboat belched smoke, the water whirled around its stern, and the house strained on its flimsy foundation. This time the gamblers acknowledged they had lost. Before their building completely collapsed, they offered to return the minister's money.

Girty and Russel, however, were the exceptions. Most boatmen, although they liked Natchez-Under-the-Hill—indeed they loved it—knew they would find no justice in its dirty streets and alleys. All through the keelboat period, it festered at the edge of the river; and no historian has ever recorded the crimes that took place within its narrow limits. They were too many and too vicious.

On top of the bank the town took on an entirely different aspect. As Audubon wrote, "When, by a very rude causeway, I gained the summit, I was relieved by the sight of an avenue of those beautiful trees called here the Pride of China. In the Upper Town I found the streets all laid off at right angles to each other, and tolerably well lined with buildings constructed with painted bricks or boards. . . .

"The first circumstance that strikes a stranger is the mildness of the temperature. Several vegetables as pleasing to the eye as agreeable to the palate, and which are seldom seen in our eastern markets before May, were here already in perfection. . . . The country for many miles inland is gently undulated. Cotton is produced abundantly, and wealth and happiness have taken up their abode under most of the planters' roofs, beneath which the wearied traveller or the poor wanderer in search of a resting-place is sure to meet with comfort and relief."

Except for the slum down by the river, Natchez was a pleasant town and Audubon was glad to be there, although he thought Main Street too narrow to be handsome, the jail and courthouse only tolerable and the churches miserable-looking. But these were his only complaints. He was in the best mood he had enjoyed since leaving Cincinnati; and, to make things even better, he met, on the streets of Natchez, Lucy's brother-in-law from Shippingport, Nicholas Berthoud.

Berthoud, whom Audubon had always liked, immediately offered to take Audubon and Mason to New Orleans in his own boat, thus saving them from having to travel any longer with Aumack. Furthermore, he asked Audubon to come and stay as his guest at Garnier's hotel, which was the best in the town. The house was handsome and surrounded by a large veranda overlooking a fine garden; and Garnier himself proved friendly and interested in Audubon's work.

During that first day at Natchez, Berthoud also introduced him to James Wilkins, one of the men to whom Alexander Wilson had carried letters of introduction on his journey down the river. Wilkins told Audubon he was only a businessman and had relatively little interest in birds, but even he had noted several specimens that could not be found in Wilson's book. This was such good news that Audubon made a careful note of what Wilkins had said. Certainly, the remark substantiated Drake's opinion that many birds on the Mississippi flyway were still unidentified.

Audubon also took an hour or so to look at the remains of an old Spanish fort which lay a short distance from the town. About two years previous, a large portion of the hill near it had given way, sinking about a hundred feet and carrying many of the houses of the Lower Town into the river. The earthslide had left behind it a large basin, which the people of Natchez used as their dump. The vultures came here by the hundreds, and as Audubon watched them he saw a bald eagle appear, chase one of the vultures, knock it down, and feast on the entrails of a horse which the vulture had partly swallowed.

But unfortunately, even with Berthoud's hospitality, Audubon could not afford to devote all his time to birds and sightseeing. When he landed he did not have a cent in his pocket, and he was too proud to ask Berthoud for money. The only way to earn any was to do what he had done at Louisville and Cincinnati: find someone who wanted a portrait. Consequently, he stopped by to see a Natchez painter named Cook and ask his help in obtaining some commissions. "I assure you," Audubon noted in his journal, making a rather bad pun, "he was scarcely fit for a scullion." Yet Cook welcomed Audubon, listened to his request, and found him two commissions drawing portraits, each one at five dollars. "This," Audubon noted, "was fine sauce to our empty stomachs."

He finished the first picture quickly and received his money right away. With the second, however, his experience was less fortunate. He did his work just as expeditiously, but the subject of the portrait left town that night without giving anyone instructions to pay for the sketch. Thus Audubon was done out of his five dollars. "I merely put this down," he wrote, addressing his sons in his journal, "to give you the best advice a father can present you with. Never sell or buy without immediately paying for the same. A constant adherence to this maxim will keep your mind and person at all times free and happy."

Cook, pleased with both pictures and the speed with which

Audubon had executed them, suggested that perhaps he could join Audubon and Mason and travel down the river with them. Audubon agreed but on these terms: Cook was to assume one third of the expenses and the cost of all the materials he used. In addition, he was to give Audubon a daily salary of two dollars, payable in advance each month. In one day at Natchez, Audubon had lost his old faith in credit. Apparently these terms were not acceptable to Cook. He began to mumble something about joining them later; and Audubon, sensing no agreement would be reached, wasted no more time in returning to Garnier's hotel.

At dinner he discovered he had grown unaccustomed to such civilized surroundings. On board the flatboat, meals were both informal and irregular. Often, the hungriest person did the cooking merely because he himself was ready to eat, and the less hungry joined in if they felt like it. Sometimes the food consisted of a partridge or a duck, plucked and cleaned, then thrown onto the hot embers of the fire without any further preparation. At other times, a man would cut a slice of bacon from the side that hung by the chimney and eat it raw, perhaps with a hard biscuit. At the hotel that night, he found himself unconsciously lapsing into his flatboat manners, occasionally picking up his meat and vegetables with his fingers. Yet he was not in the least ashamed of his behavior and remarked in his journal that he was accustomed to a life of physical hardship and was no eastern "dandy" in high-heeled boots and wearing a corset. He did not like the poverty of his life, but he reveled in its physical toughness.

Through the intercession of Garnier, Wilkins the next day agreed to lend him his copy of Wilson's *Ornithology*, so he could compare the birds he had collected on his trip with those Wilson had already described. But he had a problem: Wilkins had not received the last volume. Without it, Audubon could be almost sure—but not absolutely sure—that any of his birds represented a new discovery. It was tantalizing, but he could do nothing about it because none of the other subscribers in Natchez had received the last volume either. (Wilson, of course, was dead, but a group of men in Philadelphia were continuing his work and attempting to complete the book.) Yet the time spent searching for the missing volume was not wasted. In his trips around town, he procured two more commissions to do pictures at five dollars each, finishing them just as quickly as he had done before but being certain to collect his money on the spot.

The attentions he received at Natchez were heart-warming to him. Once again he was a respected figure among his peers. In contrast with the desperate loneliness of his flatboat life, he now found himself welcomed by cultivated people who were anxious to help him with his work. In spite of his scorn for eastern dandies and his affection for the outdoor life, Audubon desperately needed the companionship of men and women with cultivated, educated minds. He found that companionship at Natchez.

On December 30, 1820, Aumack left for New Orleans. Audubon was not sorry to see him go, although he regretted parting with Cummings, whom he had grown to like more and more. Because Berthoud, too, was leaving the next day, he had only a little time left in Natchez and used it to study Wilson's book. Too poor now to buy one for himself, he must have regretted his unwillingness to purchase one from Wilson at Louisville. But he did the next best thing; he took copious notes, particularly on the water birds.

Early the next morning he packed his luggage and carried it down to the river where Berthoud's boat was tied up. Instead of drifting or rowing, Berthoud had made arrangements with the captain of the steamboat *Columbus* to tow his keelboat to New Orleans; and because the *Columbus* was not yet ready to leave, Audubon found he had time for breakfast. Leaving his luggage on the bank and asking one of Berthoud's men to store it on board, he returned to Garnier's hotel for his meal.

At one o'clock, its whistles blowing, its stacks smoking, the *Columbus* pulled away from the Natchez landing and moved toward the center of the channel. Berthoud's captain, meanwhile, had rowed the keelboat out to the middle of the stream and was waiting. As soon as the *Columbus* was in position, he tossed two lines to her waiting crew, who made them fast to the *Columbus*'s stern, and off they started. This, for Audubon, was the way to travel. No longer did he and Mason have to put up with Aumack's gibes and complaints. Instead, he had the company of his friend and relative, Berthoud. And instead of moving downstream slowly, the keelboat was going just as fast as the *Columbus* could pull it.

In a happy mood, Audubon spent all afternoon on deck making drawings and then went to the cabin to arrange his belongings. He put away his gun, his art materials, his clothing, his portfolios. But one portfolio was missing. It must be with Berthoud's luggage, he thought. It was not. He looked all through the cabin. No portfolio. He went on deck and searched there. No portfolio. Berthoud, hearing the news, joined in the hunt. They went through the keelboat from one end to the other. Still no portfolio. The crew members did not remember seeing it; neither did the man who had loaded the luggage on board; but Audubon knew he had brought it from the hotel that morning. Obviously it had been left on the riverbank.

As well he might, he fell into a fit of despair. The good he had gained from his stay at Arkansas Post and his visit to Natchez was undone. The portfolio contained fifteen drawings of birds—Audubon was sure three were new species—and the picture of Lucy. "I now must . . . try to find it again," he wrote in his journal, "but so dull do I feel about it that I am nearly made sick. . . . Should I not get it again, it may retard my return home very considerably." Immediately he wrote a letter to Garnier, asking him to advertise for the missing portfolio, and Berthoud, always friendly, prepared a letter to go to a business acquaintance at Natchez, but Audubon had little hope that any of these efforts would be successful. Natchez-Under-the-Hill was not a place that respected art, and Audubon could imagine what would happen when a boatman or a gambler found his pictures. They would end up, he was sure, pasted to the walls of a shack in Natchez-Under-the-Hill, filling the chinks of a flatboat cabin, or nailed to a steering oar to protect it from chafing against the stern.

All that night he worried about his loss. The next morning, in the most hopeless frame of mind since he had reached Arkansas Post, he wrote down in his journal that on New Year's Day, twenty-one years before, he had been at Rochefort, copying letters for his father. Then he continued, "What I have seen and felt since, would fill a large volume—the whole of which would end at *this day, January 1st, 1821. I am on board a keelboat going down to New Orleans, the poorest man on it,* and what I have seen and felt has brought some very dearly purchased experience; and yet yesterday I forgot that no servant could do for me what I might do for myself. Had I acted accordingly, my portfolio would now have been safely in my possession."

Then he added this pathetic note: "Not willing to dwell on ideal futurity, I do not at present attempt to foresee where my poor body may be this day, twelve months." The year 1821 had not started auspiciously.

In spite of this new discouragement, he found life on board Berthoud's boat far pleasanter than on Aumack's. The cabin was comfortable; the meals were not only regular, they were clean and served on plates; and Berthoud had a servant to wait on table. In addition, the boat moved on its journey swiftly, for Berthoud, besides being towed by the steamboat, also had a good crew "who dare not contradict orders."

At noon on New Year's Day, the keelboat reached Bayou Sarah, a small village on the left bank of the river near St. Francisville. Tied up at the landing were many flatboats, two brigs, and a steamboat, the *Alabama,* all of them loading cotton. About half an hour after their arrival, the *Alabama* left to go down to Baton Rouge, an action that placed the captain of the *Columbus* in a difficult position. If the *Alabama* reached there too far ahead of him, she would probably pick up all the available freight; but he could not hope to overtake her with the bulky, awkward keelboat still in tow. On learning this, Berthoud agreed to cast his lines free and follow after, while the *Columbus* went on ahead. The captain of the *Columbus* promised to wait for them for three hours at Baton Rouge, but when they arrived there at six in the evening, the steamboat was already gone.

In the succeeding days Audubon took time to paint the captain's portrait, for which he was paid in gold coin. He also shot several terns but, without a copy of Wilson's book, was unable to tell whether he had discovered a new species. All the while, they were slowly drawing closer to New Orleans and on the sixth of January moored to the shore about six miles above the city, planning to arrive early the following morning. For most of the night, Audubon heard the squeaking of wood against wood, the lapping of water, and the sound of men's boots as they trod the deck. He was almost at New Orleans, but he was so depressed by the loss of his portfolio that he wrote in his journal, "Tomorrow perhaps may take us there. Yet so uncertain is this world that I should not be surprised, if I was never to reach it. The further removed, the stronger my anxiety to see my family again presses on my mind. Nothing but the astonishing desire I have of completing my work keeps my spirits at par."

In spite of his morbid doubts, the keelboat did arrive at New Orleans the following morning, tying up to the shore in the great crescent of the river, which seems almost to enfold the city in its arms. Berthoud was the first ashore but Audubon soon joined him at the offices of Gordon & Grant, cotton commission brokers, where Berthoud introduced him to one of the partners, Alexander Gordon. Gordon had news that all was well with Lucy and the boys at Cincinnati and a letter from Lucy to Berthoud along with a pair of gloves she had made for her brother-in-law. He invited the two men for dinner; but when they later called on Felix Arnaud, an old friend of the Berthoud family, he persuaded them to break their engagement with Gordon and come to a party he himself was giving that night.

It was a gay evening. The food was good, the wine flowed freely, the men exchanged stories, and Arnaud brought out his pet monkey, which entertained the company with its tricks and pranks. For someone of Audubon's temperament and with his love of fun, it should have been a happy evening, but he was in no state of mind to enjoy it. "I thought myself in bedlam," he wrote. "Everybody talked loud and at once." He drank too much, finally left, paid a short call on Gordon, and then went back to the keelboat where, suffering from a severe headache brought on by the wine, he went to bed.

The next day was a holiday, the anniversary of the Battle of New Orleans, that curious battle in which a future President of the United States combined with a band of pirates to defeat the British in an engagement fought after the signing of the peace. In spite of his drinking bout the night before, Audubon was up early and visited the colorful, noisy market, brushing shoulders with wealthy Creoles, busy slaves, and middle-class housewives, all the time searching for some new bird among the heaps that were offered for sale. He found nothing of interest but was amazed at the prices, which he thought high—$1.25 for a pair of ducks, $1.50 for a goose, and even twenty-five cents for an owl, although he had to admit that the owl was cleaned, dressed, and ready to eat.

As the hour approached for the official revue to celebrate the holiday, he searched for a vantage point from which he could watch it. Alone and still depressed, he finally found a place where he could look over the heads of the crowd and even see the governor himself. It was a gay occasion and he let himself enjoy it to the utmost, forgetting for the moment all the troubles that besieged him. After the revue, he reached in his pocket. His pocketbook was gone.

Since leaving Cincinnati he had suffered a series of misfortunes: the man at Natchez had failed to pay him for the portrait; he had lost his portfolio with the fifteen drawings; now his pocketbook had been taken by a thief. It contained no money; he had little money to put in it. But it held all his letters of introduction, including one to the governor at New Orleans. This loss, he believed, meant that he would never be able to see the governor, never come closer to him than he had that day at the parade. Yet he wanted the governor's help and support.

Once again in despair, he walked aimlessly through the city streets, underneath the handsome iron balconies, past gateways leading into magnificent patios, through the shadows cast by St. Louis Cathedral, across the Place d'Armes, down the narrow alleys with their stone paving, and along the walls of the Cabildo where the Spanish governors had maintained their offices. Even in winter, when the doors are shut and the trees are bare, New Orleans has an air of sensuous mystery like a woman who may have sinned but is sure of forgiveness. Of all the cities in America, it should have appealed the most to Audubon, not only because of its French heritage but because it was New Orleans. Yet he saw nothing on his long walk. The crowds, still happily celebrating their victory over the British, passed him unnoticed. They and their laughter belonged to another world.

Except for Mason, he was alone. Mason kept him company, trying to comfort him—Mason who was nothing but a vagabond himself, an artist with no buyers for his work and no patron to support him. But Mason's friendliness could not compensate for this fresh disaster. No matter what Audubon did, it seemed to him, nothing worked.

As darkness closed over the city he turned his steps back to the waterfront and boarded the keelboat. He had nothing else to do; nowhere else to go. The crew members were drinking heavily, having their own celebration, as were the crews on the other boats. During the night one of the men became so drunk he fell overboard, not with a yell or a cry but quietly, resignedly, and would have drowned unnoticed if, by pure chance, a woman had not noticed him collapse and drop into the water. She gave the alarm. A nearby steamer put out a boat and pulled the sodden man from the river. On this sordid note Audubon ended his second day at New Orleans.

On the next, he fared no better. He looked up an old Shippingport friend, John B. Gilly, who was now a merchant at New Orleans; he visited John W. Jarvis, a popular and successful portrait painter of the time; and he saw George Croghan, a friend from Louisville. But no one had work for him; no one was able to encourage him. Even a letter from Lucy failed to raise his spirits. She had nothing cheerful to tell him. Finally he returned to the keelboat and spent the remainder of the day writing another letter to Garnier about his lost portfolio and wishing that he had never left Natchez.

For several days he searched the city for work, growing more despondent all the time. Ostensibly the purpose of his trip was to find and draw more birds, but he could not concentrate on this one activity alone, for he had to have an immediate means of supporting himself and Mason. He met an Italian painter who was employed by the New Orleans theatre and persuaded him to look at the drawing of the bald eagle. The Italian was delighted with it, brought Audubon back to the theatre, introduced him to the directors, and then thoroughly insulted him by offering him a job at $100 a month to paint scenery in the Italian style. He called on Romain Pamar, a crockery merchant, who had gone bail for him when he was arrested over the steamboat affair; but Audubon was now poor and Pamar's reception was uncordial. He again visited the portrait painter, Jarvis, and displayed his work. Jarvis looked at the pictures but refused to say whether they were good or bad. Instead he lectured Audubon on how he himself drew an eagle. "He made it resemble a lion," Audubon noted, "and covered it with yellow hair, not feathers." So much for Jarvis, but as Mason was packing up the pictures again, Audubon took Jarvis aside. Would the portrait painter be interested in an assistant? he asked. He would be willing to do such work as finishing the clothing and the backgrounds. Jarvis stared at him, but asked him to come back the following day and discuss the proposition further.

Having nothing better to do with his time, Audubon followed Berthoud on his business calls. Together they entered Pamar's warehouse. This time, to Audubon's great surprise, Pamar asked him what he charged for his portraits. Quickly Audubon replied twenty-five dollars, twenty more than he had dared charge at Natchez. Pamar had three daughters and said he wanted them all in the same picture. How much would that be? A hundred dollars. Before Pamar could say no, Berthoud turned to Audubon and told him to make a fast sketch of one of the Pamar girls who happened to be present. He wanted to give Audubon an opportunity to show what he could do. Sitting on a crate in the warehouse, Audubon drew as rapidly as he could. The results were good; the clerks smiled; Pamar was so pleased he immediately sent a servant to obtain Mrs. Pamar's approval of the project and, better yet, told Audubon he would leave the price up to him. Audubon needed the money so badly, he wanted to start work right away, but one of the daughters was out of town. Nevertheless the prospect of a commission cheered him.

Later in the day he called again on Jarvis, the painter. Jarvis said he had thought the matter over; he did not see how Audubon could be of the slightest use to him. Deeply hurt by the artist's bluntness, Audubon rose, bowed, and departed without another word and wandered down to the levee. Around him, he could hear the normal sounds of life: church bells ringing, billiard balls knocking together, hunters' gunshots at the river. Yet he felt remote from all human activity. Stunned by Jarvis's curt dismissal, he took his gun and a skiff and rowed out into the river, where he shot a fish crow and brought it back to the keelboat to sketch. In the evening, still alone, still restless, he went ashore for a short stroll and on the way back to the river passed a building where a quadroon ball was being held.

In the exotic life of New Orleans, the quadroon balls held a unique place. Each beautiful quadroon, carefully raised by her Negro mother and educated in every social skill, had only one purpose: to become the mistress of a wealthy, young white man in return for his protection. Once contracted, this liaison lasted until the man's marriage and sometimes afterward, while the quadroon continued the cycle by preparing her own daughters for the same career. At the quadroon balls, which rivaled and often surpassed the regular balls, the quadroons, accompanied by their protectors, made their appearance. Audubon longed to join the festivities. Fond of music and dancing, fond, too, of the company of women, he was weary of his dull, drab keelboat life. For one dollar, the cost of admission, he could have bought a few minutes of gaiety and fun, but he did not have a dollar to spend. Yet he could not tear himself away from the spot. A lonely figure, he stood in the street outside, listening to the sound of violins in the New Orleans night like a thirsty man who hears a cascade of water in the distance but cannot reach it. Then he sadly walked back to the keelboat—"home, as we are pleased to call it," he said.

For the next few days, his journal entries reflect more clearly than anything else his increasing desperation as he vainly looked for work. Here is what he wrote:

> "MONDAY 15th January 1821
> TUESDAY 16th   "   "
> WEDNESDAY 17th "   "
> THURSDAY 18th   "   "

"This is a way of cutting the matter short, but indeed the time has been so long and dull during these days that I think it a good riddance to use them thus."

He heard from Pamar about the portrait. Mrs. Pamar, it seemed, had her heart set on having their daughters' picture done in oils; Audubon worked only in black chalk. Pamar, however, gave him a small commission to draw one daughter, but because the girl was not ready to sit, Audubon thought the income would arrive too late. His friend, John B. Gilly, was also willing to sit for him. Although he was not to be paid, he could use the picture for advertising his work. He also received another letter from Lucy.

Instead of cheering him, Audubon noted that the letter "ruffled my spirits sadly." Lucy had been through much since leaving Flatland Ford. She had lived at the Indian Queen and in a log cabin. She had ridden horseback to Philadelphia. She had never interfered with his hunting, his fishing, or his long trips. But she had not made the mistakes. She had not invested their money in the store; she had not erected the steam mill; she had not purchased the steamboat. She had left these matters up to him and look how they had turned out. Lucy was courageous, but she lacked the ability to conceal her dissatisfactions. In his present mood, her complaints and pointed remarks were almost unbearable to Audubon.

Then suddenly, like the sun bursting through the clouds after a storm, things took a sharp turn for the better. Impressed by the portrait of Gilly, several people wanted Audubon to do their pictures. From Friday, the 9th of January, until the 17th, he received nine commissions, earning a total of $220. "I am," he wrote, "fatigued, wearied of body, but in good spirits, having plenty to do at good prices, and my work much admired. Only sorry that the sun sets." Employment and recognition were what he most needed, and when he received them, his spirits soared. Foolishly but lovingly, he went out and bought a set of chinaware to send to Lucy. This left him with more than $200, which he also gave her. Then, in his optimism, he hired a man named Smith to collect specimens for him at twenty-five dollars a month and a girl to wash and cook for himself and Mason at another ten dollars a month.

One problem, however, remained; he could not find a copy of Wilson's *Ornithology* to use. "The high value set on that work now," he said, "particularly lately, has rendered it extremely rare, and the few who possess it will not lend it." In some respects this was discouraging, because he needed the book so badly for his own work. On the other hand, it was promising that people were so much interested in birds.

Aumack's flatboat was now in New Orleans and so was Aumack. Relations between the two men had improved, and Aumack went out pelican hunting again. This time, however, he was dead sober and procured a fine specimen on a nearby lake. For the next few days Audubon busied himself drawing this one bird. In his remaining time, he solicited more commissions for portraits and went to see Alexander Gordon regularly. The cotton merchant, whom he had met through Berthoud, was becoming a close friend. He also was busy finding lodgings for himself and Mason, because Berthoud was about to return to Shippingport, taking his keelboat with him. Finally he settled on a room in a building located between two grocers on Barracks Street, near Royal Street. Being flimsily built, it was noisy, and he could hear everything going on in the stores as well as in his landlady's quarters, but the rent was within his means—ten dollars a month. The landlady, after speaking pointedly about the honesty of strangers, wanted a month's rent in advance but Audubon could not afford this. They settled on a half month, and he and Mason moved in. Except for his brief stay at Garnier's hotel in Natchez, it was the first time since leaving Cincinnati that he had lived ashore.

On February 15, 1821, he went down to the levee to see Berthoud off. In his arms he had a package to be delivered to Lucy. It contained twenty of his best pictures, including the bald eagle and eight birds that had not been described by Wilson. They were the most meaningful gift he could send to her.

CHAPTER XIV

1821

DURING his first days at New Orleans, when he was poor and lonely, Audubon had stood outside the closed doors of the quadroon ball, listening to the sound of violins in the nighttime and wishing he could spare a dollar for the admission charge. Now he was neither famous nor rich, but at least he had a little money in his pocket and something of a name as a portraitist, at least enough of a name to plunge him into an erotic adventure which added a touch of color to the dull routine of his life.

He was walking down the street shortly before Berthoud's departure for Shippingport, when he was stopped by "a femelle of fine form." (He was always sensitive to the appearance of the women he met.) Because she was wearing a heavy veil, he could not see her face; and without raising it or introducing herself, she abruptly began to interrogate him. Had he been sent over by the French Academy to portray the birds of America? she asked. No, he answered, he had no commission from the Academy. Was he the man who did portraits in black chalk? Yes, he was. With an air of mystery that enchanted him and without explaining herself further, the woman told him to wait for thirty minutes, then go to a certain address and walk upstairs. She would be there to greet him.

Puzzled but excited by this romantic invitation, Audubon passed the thirty minutes browsing in a nearby bookstore and then walked to the address the woman had given him. As he entered the room where she was waiting, she rose to greet him, stepped to the door and locked it with a double lock, after which she turned toward him and with a sudden movement threw back her veil. Audubon gasped in wonder. She had, he said, "the most beautiful face I ever saw."

Without telling him who she was, she began to bombard him with more questions. Was he married? How long had he been married? Was his wife in the city? So nervous that he visibly trembled, Audubon tried to answer each question as best he could. Finally the beautiful stranger told him to sit down and offered him a glass of cordial. "I drank it," said Audubon, "for I needed it." She went on with the questions, while he blurted out his answers. Was he capable of doing her portrait? He thought so. What did he charge for a picture? Usually twenty-five dollars. If by chance he learned her name, would he swear to keep it secret? Of course. Had he ever done full-length figures as well as portraits? Yes, he had. Still smiling sweetly at him, she asked him her next question: "Naked?"

"With a 48-pounder through my heart," Audubon said later, "my articulate powers could not have been more suddenly stopped." Yet that was precisely what the woman wanted, a full-length portrait of herself naked, and she hoped he could start work on it that very day. First, however, she suggested he take a short walk to recover himself. Stunned, he went out into the street. "I felt," he said, "like a bird that makes his escape from a strong cage. . . . Had I met a stranger on the stairs, no doubt I would have been taken for a thief. I walked away fast without looking behind me."

When he returned, she had everything ready for him to begin, chalks and paper laid out for his use and, in one corner of the room, a couch on which she planned to lie. In front of the couch were some curtains which could be closed, thus forming a dressing room. Stepping behind the curtains, she pulled them shut; and, as Audubon waited, he could hear the sounds she made as she undressed. "Stranger as she was to me," he said later, "I could not well reconcile all the feelings that were necessary to draw well, without mingling with them some of a very different nature."

Finally the sounds ceased, and she called to him that she was ready. Would he please draw the curtains open? He did so, and the sight of her beauty so startled him that he dropped his chalk, which clattered as it rolled across the floor. But the woman herself was perfectly calm. Did he like the pose? she asked. Would he like her to change it? Did she look well? Too well for his talents, Audubon mumbled in reply as he began work on the picture. For more than an hour he sketched, until the woman complained that she was growing chilly. Would he please close the curtains again? Pacing up and down the room, occasionally looking at his picture, and still filled with erotic excitement, Audubon waited for the woman to finish dressing. When she emerged from behind the curtains fully dressed, she behaved in the most matter-of-fact manner. Could he do some more work on the picture that day without her modeling for him? Yes, he said. He could correct his preliminary sketch. Pulling a bell cord, the woman summoned a servant, ordered cakes and ale and, while Audubon rested, asked him further questions about his life, his work, and his urge to paint birds. Afterward, while he made his corrections, she stood beside him; and from her comments, he knew she was a good artist in her own right.

The next day when he returned, she wanted to know how much he planned to charge her for the portrait. Still confused and bewildered, Audubon said he would leave the price up to her. What would she suggest? After a moment's consideration, she replied that a "souvenir" would, perhaps, be more suitable than money. How about a good gun? He warned her that his tastes in firearms were expensive, but she insisted that he take five dollars to make a deposit against one of his own choosing.

For several more days, Audubon went regularly to the mysterious woman's room. At the same time he kept up with his commissions for twenty-five-dollar portraits, all "a little at the expense of my eyes at night." Every time he returned to the woman's room, he found that she too had been working on the picture during his absence, adding a touch here or a line there; not, she explained, because she was dissatisfied, but because she wanted to mingle her own talents with his in the finished work.

On the last day, when the picture was completed, she herself signed it as though it had been her own, but she also placed Audubon's name in a dark corner of the drapery where it would be difficult to find. She then gave him the money to purchase the gun he had selected, asked him to think of her every

time he used it, and made him promise to keep her name,
which he now knew, a secret.

The adventure was over. Audubon took the money, bought
the gun, and had it engraved with an emblem that the woman
had designed for the purpose and also with the date, February
22, 1821. Then with his own hands he engraved her name in a
place "where I do not believe it will ever be found." But he
could not let the matter drop there. On several occasions he
went back to her house to call on her, but the servants always
informed him that madam was not at home. Yet for all her
subsequent coolness, she had done him a great service. At a
time when his self-confidence was shaken, her attentions helped
to restore his self-esteem. At a period when his life was dull and
uneventful with the drabness only the poor can know, she had
brought to him a touch of colorful, unexpected romance, entering his life for a few brief days like a brilliant butterfly
against a gray sky. Whatever abnormal impulse drove her to
employ him, whatever erotic tendency made her want to pose
nude in front of him, she revived his spirits and gave him new
strength. For a time afterward, although he was still weary of
New Orleans, his complaints were fewer, his discouragement
less acute.

Lucy, of course, heard about the episode right away. With
his usual candor, he sat down immediately and wrote her about
what had happened. When, naturally enough, she plied him
for further details, he responded with a full account of everything that had happened, warning her, however, to share the
information with no one except her brother, and with her
brother only if he promised never to tell anyone.

Three days before Audubon finished his picture of the beautiful woman, the Senate ratified a treaty which gave the United
States possession of a territory that was unusually rich in birdlife, for Spain, after two years of negotiations and the threat
of war, had finally ceded East Florida, the long peninsula of the
present state. Although this purchase greatly expanded the area
that would have to be included in any book on the birds of
America, for the moment Audubon had his hands full, trying
to make a living and collecting the specimens that were available to him near New Orleans.

A more exciting event for him than the purchase of East Florida was the arrival of the golden plovers, those mutely colored, long-legged shorebirds that suddenly appeared in New Orleans by the thousands. As news of the birds' approach reached the city, the hunters went out in parties of twenty to a hundred and took up their stands, ready for the impending slaughter. As the birds began circling overhead, the hunters called to them, luring them within gunshot in flocks of as many as a hundred at once. All day long the firing went on, and the toll was terrible. One man who was standing near Audubon shot by himself sixty-three dozen golden plovers that day, and Audubon thought it would be conservative to estimate that a total of 144,-000 were killed.

The adventure with the erotic woman had done much to raise his spirits and so had the sight of the golden plovers, but the best and most thrilling news came in March. One of Aumack's crew members, knowing Audubon's distress over the lost portfolio, had stopped at Natchez-Under-the-Hill on his way home and searched for it. Where Garnier, the hotel owner, and Alexander Gordon's friends had failed, the crew member succeeded. Perhaps he knew the slum section better, perhaps he was merely lucky. In any case, he found the pictures, took them to the local newspaper office, and sent word to Audubon that the editor would hold them until he received Audubon's instructions. Alexander Gordon immediately notified an acquaintance to forward the portfolio to New Orleans and, more important, guaranteed payment of any expense involved.

Yet this was practically the extent of his significant good fortune during that spring in New Orleans. The rest of the time he alternated between small triumphs and large defeats. The defeats were caused partly by circumstances—he had no readily salable talent or skill to offer the world—but they were also caused partly by himself. Under the strain of the life he was leading, he was becoming his own worst enemy, unduly sensitive to insults whether imagined or real, and overconscious of his position as half-servant, half-social equal of the people he met. Anxious to get ahead and desperate for money, he was willing to abase himself and play the role of sycophant. Then, in moments of revolt and disgust, he would strike down the hands extended to help him, rendering all his previous efforts useless.

He was particularly frustrated by his unsuccessful attempts to join a surveying expedition that he learned the United States planned to send to East Florida. He importuned the governor for an appointment on its staff, but the governor was not encouraging. As far as he knew, the expedition would not study the country; it would merely establish the line; and therefore only surveyors—and no draftsmen—were needed. Audubon remarked sarcastically that he could not believe "that a journey so interesting would be performed only to say that men had gone and come back." In his journal he said longingly, "My life has been strewn with many thorns, but could I see myself and the fruits of my labor safe, with my beloved family all well, on a return from such an expedition, how grateful would I feel to my country and . . . to my Author."

On the advice of friends, he wrote directly to President Monroe; he solicited the help of Nicholas Berthoud; he stooped so low as to sacrifice his self-pride by calling on an artist named Vanderlyn to ask him for an endorsement of his work. On entering Vanderlyn's studio, he told the artist what he wanted; and Vanderlyn "spoke to me," Audubon wrote bitterly, "as if I had been an abject slave, and told me, on walking away, to lay my drawings down . . . and that he would return presently and look them over. I felt so vexed that my first intention was to pack off, but the expedition was in view."

After thirty minutes, Vanderlyn returned, bringing with him an army officer, and invited Audubon into his private room behind the studio and told him to open his package of drawings. With sweat pouring down his face, partly from nervousness, partly from humiliation, Audubon untied his portfolio and laid the pictures on the floor. The officer immediately liked them; and Vanderlyn, after examining one closely, said it was handsomely done. "I breathed," Audubon wrote haughtily, "not because I thought him a man of superior talents . . . but because he was looked on as a very excellent judge, and because I had been told that a few words from him might be serviceable." In spite of his low opinion of Vanderlyn, Audubon was glad to take from him a note of recommendation and, and in his touchy state, even gladder to be followed out into the street by the army officer, who wanted to know how much he charged for his portraits.

While Audubon was relishing his small triumph over Vanderlyn, Lucy was visiting the Berthouds at Shippingport and from there wrote one of her cousins in England. "It is now a long, long time since I heard from you," she said, "though I have written several times without a reply, a circumstance which is a source of grief to me, for with my years, increases my attachment to old friends and the early scenes of my youth, and now I see the walks and the favorite spots I used to frequent in happier times as plainly before me, as if no time had elapsed since." Continuing in this plaintive vein, she wrote about her father's death—William Bakewell had died on March 6—saying that "his departure from this scene of trouble can hardly be regretted"; she discussed the deaths of her two daughters; and she wrote about "the various losses and misfortunes of my husband's affairs." She spoke, too, about money, emphasizing that she was forced to educate her two sons herself and mentioned that she might be compelled to return to Cincinnati, because living was cheaper there. To write to her cousin in this complaining tone was one thing; to send the letter to New Orleans so Audubon could add a postscript was quite another. But that was exactly what Lucy did.

Her letter reached him when he was wavering between brief periods of optimism and pessimism. He still hoped for an appointment with the government expedition to East Florida; he was giving regular art lessons to the young and attractive wife of a New Orleans physician, Dr. Heerman; he had discovered an inaccuracy in one of Wilson's pictures of a warbler (in his intense desire for success, he acted as though he were running a race with the dead Scotsman); and the steamboat *Columbus* had brought to New Orleans a number of old friends who were willing to order portraits. Best of all, the lost portfolio had arrived safely from Natchez.

On the other hand, as he wrote Lucy, he was deeply saddened by the news that Mason's father had died. Mason, who helped Audubon collect specimens, was also his student. According to Audubon, he could probably draw flowers now better than any man in America. And he was also concerned by

Lucy's increasingly bitter attitude. "I hope," he wrote her, "you will never be deceived or disappointed more by those to whom thou may have to give things in charge, but, my Lucy, thou must not be quite so hard on the world. There are a few yet who are good and do something for others besides themselves." Then, having admonished her, he gave vent to his own great well of bitterness. In his attempt to secure an appointment on the expedition to East Florida, he had asked Nicholas Berthoud for help but had received no reply. Perhaps, in those days of uncertain mails, his letter never reached Shippingport; perhaps Berthoud's answer never arrived at New Orleans; perhaps Berthoud was simply too busy to do anything at the moment. In any case, Audubon was sharply critical of Lucy's brother-in-law. Lucy, he said, was not to mention the expedition to Berthoud again. He could get along perfectly well without Berthoud's help, he wrote angrily of the man who had proved such a good friend to him.

Then, in a softer mood, he ended his letter with assurances of his love for his wife. "My future plans," he wrote, "are and will be forever, to do all in my power to enable thee to live with comfort and satisfaction. Wherever I may chance to be carried by circumstances, believe it, my dear Lucy, and I shall be happy and comfortable."

These remarks, however, did nothing to allay Lucy's growing disgust with him. Annoyed by his loss of her money and his inability to support her, irritated by his criticism of Berthoud and other members of her family, she made it clear in her next letter that she had no desire to accompany him on any further travels. In fact, she did not even want to see him again until he had some accomplishment to show for his efforts. In anguished bewilderment at this unexpected attack, he answered her in both sorrow and anger. "I am very sorry," he wrote. "that *thou* are so intent on my *not* returning to thee. If that country we live in cannot feed us, why not fly from it?" Then he lashed out at her family, whom he apparently considered a bad influence on her thinking. "If Mr. Berthoud has written me," he said, "it is more than *I* know of yet. Why, Lucy, do you not cling to your better friend, your husband? Not to boast of my intentions any more toward thy happiness, I will merely say

I am afraid *for thee.*" Then he wildly attacked her family once again. "If you have not written to your uncle [Benjamin Bakewell], do not," he said. "I want no one's help, but those who are not *quite* so engaged in their business." After making this comment, he returned to Lucy herself. "Your great desire that I should stay away," he wrote, "is, I must acknowledge, very unexpected. If you can bear to have me go on a voyage of at least three years [he had been thinking at various times of going to England] without wishing to see me before, I cannot help thinking Lucy would probably be better pleased should I never return—and so it may be."

But in his angriest, most desperate mood, he could not send a letter ending with those words. The next day, taking up his pen again, he added a penitent postscript. "My dearest girl," he said, "I am sorry for the last part I wrote yesterday, but I then felt miserable. I hope thou wilt look upon it as a momentary incident. I love thee so dearly, I feel it so powerfully, that I cannot bear anything from thee that has the appearance of coolness."

While he was trying to explain himself to Lucy, his other affairs were also deteriorating, and he found himself involved in a quarrel with the Heermans. For more than a month he had been giving art lessons to pretty Mrs. Heerman, an arrangement that had provided him with a steady source of income. But Mrs. Heerman liked to flirt, and so did Audubon. In no time at all, their relationship, although they certainly were not in love, had become more complex than that of student and teacher. Then Audubon somehow offended his pupil, and the doctor abruptly dismissed him. Once again Audubon realized that he was in that strange position he so much hated of being half-servant, half-equal. Mrs. Heerman could flirt with him, but her husband could discharge him like any employee. Furious at what he considered a fresh insult, he haughtily refused to ask for the hundred dollars he believed the Heermans owed him.

In spite of his efforts, he was failing in New Orleans as he had failed elsewhere. He had a few friends like the Pamars and Alexander Gordon, but he had been less than successful as a portraitist and art teacher, barely able to support himself and Mason and send any money to Lucy. Consequently, he decided to accept the offer of a wealthy woman named Mrs. Pirrie, who wanted him to come to her plantation at Bayou Sarah and teach art to her daughter, Eliza. At first Audubon demanded rather strict terms. He wanted room and board for himself and Mason, time to collect more specimens, and a hundred dollars a month in salary. Mrs. Pirrie agreed to everything but the hundred dollars. Sixty, she said, was enough. So sixty it was.

On June 6, 1821, with almost no regrets, Audubon and Mason boarded the steamboat *Columbus*. Disembarking at Bayou Sarah, he walked with Mason to the nearby town of St. Francisville. There he had dinner with a friend, but all the while kept thinking of the steamboat and wishing that he could continue with it back to Shippingport and Lucy. His melancholy, however, did not last long. After the meal, as they walked toward the plantation five miles away, he began to overcome his homesickness and take a fresh interest in his surroundings—the rich magnolias, the hollies, the beeches, and the thousands of warblers and thrushes.

At Oakley, the Pirries' plantation, he quickly became friends with James Pirrie, a delightful Scotsman and accomplished painter, who proved himself both generous and entertaining as Audubon's host and employer. That was when he was sober. When he was drunk, which according to Audubon was frequently, he became short-tempered and refused to associate with any of the other people at Oakley. Mrs. Pirrie, a wealthy, hard-working woman, rather henpecked her husband; and although generous too, she sometimes flew into violent rages. Her daughter Eliza was her idol, an adored child of fifteen with, as Audubon noted, a good figure, although she was not particularly pretty. The rest of the household was composed of Eliza's married sister, Mary Ann Smith, who lived on a nearby plantation and came to Oakley often, Mrs. Hardwood, a visiting Englishwoman, and Mrs. Throgmorton, whose home was in New Orleans.

Audubon and Mason had no difficulty fitting into this group; and, after the months he had spent in the city, Audubon was like a miser stumbling into a warehouse of gold. For several weeks he had no time to write in his journal anything but the birds he had seen or hoped to see. "Black Cap^d Titmouse, Parus atricapillus. Very plenty," he wrote. "Young quite grown middle of June. Crested Titmouse—Parus bicolor. The same." Entry followed entry, all in a similar vein. He watched the purple martins outside the plantation house; he studied a chuck-will's-widow, brought to him by Pirrie's overseer; and he captured alive two red-cockaded woodpeckers, which he had shot but only winged. The first of the two he caught easily; but the second, as soon as it fell to the ground, hopped to the nearest tree and started climbing it. Audubon rushed forward, reached out his hand, and grabbed the bird. The woodpecker dove at his fingers with its strong beak. Audubon jumped back and let it go, but before it escaped he was able to get hold of it again, this time by the back. His next problem was what to do with the two birds. He did not want to return to Oakley immediately. On the other hand, he could not carry a live woodpecker in each hand while he continued his hunting. Finally he thought of a solution. Taking off his hat, he placed both birds in it and clamped it tightly back onto his head. All the rest of the day, each time he fired his gun, the report was echoed by plaintive, alarmed cries from under his hat.

In this peculiar fashion, he went on hunting. On his return to Oakley, he took off his hat and found that although one woodpecker had died, the other was still healthy. Taking it up to his room, he thrust it quickly into a wooden cage, but almost as quickly, it sent chips of wood showering from its rapidly moving beak and in a few moments was free. Loose in the room, it ran across the floor and up the wall, searching for insects between the bricks, in every crack, and under every shelf, while Audubon drew its picture and noted with satisfaction, "Sorry I am to have to say that Mr. Wilson's drawing could not have been made from the *bird fresh killed,* or, if so, it was in very bad order about the head; he having put the small streak of red feathers of the head immediately over the eye, while a white line is there, the red being placed far back of the ear. And the whole of the wing not at all marked like that of the bird. The side of the breast is also badly represented. The lines in nature are longitudinal only and show more of a body."

During those happy weeks at Oakley, he gave lessons to Eliza.

Then, his duties finished, he and Mason went into the woods. While Audubon concentrated his attention on birds, Mason looked for plants. His drawings were now so excellent that Audubon sometimes let him do the backgrounds for his own pictures, an arrangement that provided good practice for Mason and saved Audubon endless hours of work that did not really relate to his principal subject. When the finished picture turned out well, both student and teacher took pride in signing their names to it in pencil; and, as Audubon told Mason, if the drawings were ever published, they could each take credit for their share of the work.

Not one sorrowful comment appeared in Audubon's journal for week after week. Then he ruined it all with his own foolishness. The first sign of approaching trouble came in his entry for August 20, 1821. He had killed a rattlesnake, one almost six feet long, and brought it back to Oakley, where he studied it carefully, posed it, and drew its picture. Then he noted that "my amiable pupil, Eliza Pirrie, also drew the same snake," and added, "It is with much pleasure that I now mention her name, expecting to remember often her sweet disposition and the happy days spent near her." For a tutor, married and thirty-six years old, with children of his own, this was an extremely romantic comment to make about a girl fifteen years of age. But Audubon was repeating the mistake he had made with Mrs. Heerman.

A few weeks later, Eliza became sick, and matters quickly reached a crisis. Mrs. Pirrie, worried about her daughter's health, kept her in bed and refused to let Audubon see her. When she was better, her doctor, whom Audubon suspected of being in love with her and therefore jealous, refused to permit her to continue with her art lessons. Audubon grumbled. The doctor, with Mrs. Pirrie's backing, stood firm. Finally as a compromise, Audubon was allowed to visit Eliza but only at set times. Just as he had done with Mrs. Heerman, Audubon became confused between his privileges as a social equal and the limitations imposed on him by his status as an employee. He insisted on seeing Eliza more often; the doctor remained firm; Eliza became touchy; and finally, on the tenth of October, Mrs.

Pirrie intervened. Like Dr. Heerman before her, she dismissed Audubon from her employ.

This was a blow to both his pride and his pocketbook. Once more he was without a job. Even more important, he had not finished all the collecting he wanted to do at Oakley. Would it be possible, he asked Mrs. Pirrie, for Mason and himself to stay on for ten more days as Mrs. Pirrie's guests? Generously Mrs. Pirrie agreed, and Audubon threw himself into his work, correcting and arranging his notes, and totting up the errors he had found in Alexander Wilson. "I tried to speak of them with care," he wrote condescendingly in his journal, "knowing the good will of that man and the hurry he was in, and the vast amount of hear-say he depended on."

The additional ten days, however, only made matters worse. In his sensitive state of mind, he became convinced that the women in the house were conspiring against him and he began to quarrel openly with Mrs. Pirrie. One day, as he finished a portrait of Mrs. Pirrie that Eliza had started, she suddenly spoke harshly of the work he was doing. Another time, while they were sitting at the table, she burst out laughing at him. Mr. Pirrie persuaded her to apologize, but Audubon was so angry he would not listen to her. Instead he rose and silently stalked out of the room.

Then came the question of the bill. Audubon included ten days during which Eliza had been sick, making the total $204. Mrs. Pirrie strongly objected to the ten days, flew into a rage, and accused Audubon of trying to cheat her. Audubon coldly insisted that he be paid in full. Mrs. Pirrie flatly refused. Audubon sent for Mr. Pirrie, who was on one of his drunks. Mr. Pirrie, anxious to stop the clamor in his household, instructed his son-in-law to pay the bill in full, sending, at Audubon's request, one hundred dollars to Alexander Gordon so that it could be forwarded to Lucy.

The following afternoon, Mrs. Pirrie, apparently regretting the quarrel, gave Mason a full set of clothes that had once belonged to one of her dead sons. It was a generous present and, because Audubon was supporting Mason, it was a gift to both men, not just one of them. But Audubon, his pride wounded, rudely rejected Mrs. Pirrie's overture. "I positively refused to acquiesce," he wrote, "knowing too well how far some gifts are talked of—and not willing that my companion should diminish the self-respect I think necessary for every man to keep towards himself, however poor, when by *talents,* health, and industry he is able to procure his own necessities."

After dinner, because he and Mason were planning to take the steamboat to New Orleans the next morning, he relented enough to leave his room and say good-bye to Mrs. Pirrie, Eliza, Mary Ann Smith, and the others. Even in performing this act of common courtesy, he behaved childishly. "My entry before the circle," he remarked coldly in his journal, "possessed none of that life and spirit I had formerly enjoyed on such occasions. I would gladly have wished to be excused from the fatiguing ceremonies. Yet I walked in, followed by Joseph, and approaching Mrs. Pirrie, bid her good-bye as simply as ever any honest Quaker did, touched slightly Mrs. Smith's hand, as I bowed to her. My pupil rose from the sofa and expected a kiss from me, but none were to be disposed of. I pressed her hand and, with a general salute to the whole, made my retreat—much to the great surprise of everyone present, who had heard those very women speak constantly before of me in the highest terms of respect, now scarcely deigning to look at me. As Joseph was following me, he received a volley of farewells from the three ladies of the house, put after him ridiculously to affect me. But the effect was lost, and it raised a smile on my lips." Thus on October 19, sneering and hurt, he walked out of the room where he had found so much happiness and out of the lives of the Pirries who, for three months at least, had done so much for him.

At ten o'clock the next morning, at Bayou Sarah, he and Mason boarded the steamboat *Ramaso.* Behind lay the beautiful countryside of St. Francisville where, in a moment of despair, he had found not only so many new birds and so many errors in Wilson, but relief from the miserable city life he had been leading. Ahead lay only New Orleans and a return to the same struggle which had so nearly defeated him before.

❦

CHAPTER XV

1821 — 1823

NEW ORLEANS is a city of water. It buys the products brought down the river by water and carried up from the Gulf of Mexico by water. It lives on the harvests gathered from fields that are almost swamps or, if they are dry, have been enriched through the centuries by the water sweeping over them. It even buries its dead in the water, for the most shallow grave becomes a pool almost before the coffin has been lowered. And when it rains at New Orleans, the water collects on the streets because it has no place to go. Every spot to which water might drain is already filled. On the Monday morning that Audubon returned to New Orleans, it was raining.

He walked off the steamboat *Ramaso* into the overcast, wet city, a lonely figure among the river gamblers, traders, planters, and planters' wives, all the busy, preoccupied people who, traveling back and forth on the great river, made up the majority of every passenger list. They had homes to go to, acquaintances to visit, offices where they could transact their business. Audubon, with the exception of a few remaining friends, had none of these, and his future looked as gray as the weather. He was determined, nevertheless, to succeed where he had once before failed, to wrest from the city the living it had previously denied him.

As he stepped onto the levee he cut a ridiculous figure among the well-dressed planters, and he knew it. At Oakley he had let his appearance go. His hair was long and shaggy, his suit of yellow nankeen cloth shabby and loosely fitting. As the first move in his renewed assault on the city's indifference, he decided to cut his hair and order a new suit. This, he rightly thought, would enable him to obtain pupils more easily. Next he planned to find temporary lodgings for himself and Mason, then permanent lodgings for himself, Lucy, and the boys. For Lucy had at last relented. She said she would come to New Orleans to live with him, although he did not know when.

Once on shore, he put his new plan of action into effect. He rented, for sixteen dollars a month, a small furnished room on the Rue St. Ann where he and Mason could stay. He cut his hair, ordered new clothes, visited his friends, and spent three days looking for a house for Lucy. He also worried about the hundred dollars he had asked Pirrie to give Alexander Gordon to send to her, because as yet she had not acknowledged them.

At the end of the first week, his sense of determination still strong, he took stock of himself and his accomplishments. A full year had elapsed since he had left Cincinnati—not the seven or eight months he had originally planned—but he had completed sixty-two drawings of birds and plants; he had three pictures of quadrupeds and two of snakes; in addition, he had done approximately fifty portraits; and, as a commercial undertaking, he had started a picture of Father Don Antonio, an unconventional but beloved New Orleans priest, which he hoped to be able to sell at a good price. Furthermore, although he had left Cincinnati penniless, he was able to note in his journal, "I have now forty-two dollars, health, as much anxiety to pursue my plans of accomplishing my collection as I ever had, and hope God will grant me the same powers to proceed." It was not a good record, but it was not bad, and he felt relaxed enough to wax philosophical about his own appearance. "My dress all new and my hair cut," he wrote with humor and some bitterness, "my appearance is altered beyond my expectations. ... When a handsome bird is robbed of all its feathering, the poor thing looks bashful, dejected, and is either entirely neglected or looked upon with contempt. Such was my situation last week. But when the bird is well fed, taken care of, suffered to enjoy real life and dress himself, he is cherished again, nay admired. Such is my situation this day. Good God, that forty dollars should thus be *enough* to make a *gentleman*. Ah, my beloved country, when will thy sons value more intrinsically each brother's worth? Never!"

But for all his brave resolution, he found his position in New

Orleans virtually unchanged. Only his handful of close friends wanted to see him; everyone else remained indifferent. Discouraged in his attempt to obtain individual art students, he tried to get a job as a schoolteacher. He visited several institutions, all of which, he thought, treated him impolitely. At one or two, the staff would hardly talk to him and made it clear that they regarded him as an adventurer who had to be treated with caution and suspicion.

As he struggled through those first weeks after his return to New Orleans, two friends, Mr. and Mrs. Brand, welcomed him warmly at their house and asked him to teach their son art at two dollars an hour. The day after this arrangement had been agreed upon, Mrs. Brand expressed an interest in joining the lessons herself, which meant an extra dollar an hour. Now at least he had a steady source of income. Shortly afterward he met John Gwathway, the proprietor of the Indian Queen, the hotel where he and Lucy had stayed at Louisville. Gwathway told him that Lucy's stepmother had died; and regardless of Lucy's feelings—although there is no reason to believe Lucy was fond of her stepmother—Audubon was delighted. He had never liked William Bakewell's new wife; she had never liked him. That score was now settled forever, and he noted the fact in his journal, calling her "my constant enemy," although he added piously, "God forgive her faults."

But still he had no word directly from Lucy herself, no acknowledgment of the hundred dollars he had sent her, no definite date when he might expect her in New Orleans. As the days slipped by and no letter came from her, entries like these began to appear in his journal: "Anxious to hear from my wife" and "No news from my wife yet." The silence into which she had fallen added to the growing depression that began to overtake him, as he saw himself again defeated in what he had hoped to achieve in New Orleans.

Then, unexpectedly, came an opportunity to do an unartistic, but commercially profitable, job. An attorney named Joseph Hawkins called one day when Audubon was out and left word with Mason that he would like to have Audubon make a copy of an engraving done by Vanderlyn, the artist whom he had so much disliked. This was the type of hackwork he had always tried to avoid, but he had reached the point where he could not afford to refuse the commission, lowly and insulting as it might be. He went to bed that night, making, as the final entry in his journal, this comment: "My feelings much harassed about my beloved wife from whom I have not heard for two weeks," and the next day he agreed to do the job for Hawkins at a price not to exceed fifty dollars.

Hawkins was not unkindly and even came to Audubon's lodgings expressly to look at the picture of the New Orleans priest. But in his heart Audubon resented the necessity that forced him to accept such assignments. He did turn down one, a request from a scene designer named Basterop to help him do a panoramic view of New Orleans. This, Audubon realized, would absorb too much of his time and prevent him from continuing with his own work. That night he again recorded his worries in his journal. "No news," he wrote, "from my beloved Lucy nor children. Very uneasy on their silence."

The next day, however, he at last received word but from an unexpected source. Once more he met John Gwathway, who seemed to know all the gossip of Louisville. Lucy, Gwathway announced, had been planning to leave for New Orleans on the first of the month, which meant she might arrive at any time. But why did not Audubon hear from her directly? The information from Gwathway, he remarked pathetically in his journal, "kept me nearly wild all day. No friend, no wife, near." He tried to draw; he visited his acquaintances, the Pamars, and the scene designer, Basterop, and in the evening wrote, "The nearer the moment that I expect to see my beloved Lucy approaches, the greater my impatience, my disappointment, daily, when evening draws on."

He was depressed further by a ghost which rose from the past to haunt him. A man who had once acted as an agent for Audubon & Bakewell learned that he was in New Orleans and presented him with a bill that the former firm had owed. Audubon was furious. Everything he had owned was in the hands of his creditors, even the grave of the daughter whom he and Lucy had buried near the goose pond. As he told the man flatly, he was in no position to assume old obligations that had been legally extinguished.

Indeed, he was so badly off that he decided to swallow his pride and send Dr. Heerman a bill for the hundred dollars still due on the lessons he had given Mrs. Heerman, the lessons that had ended so disastrously just before he left for Oakley. He could not bring himself to talk to Dr. Heerman in person or even go to Dr. Heerman's house. Therefore, he wrote out the bill and asked Mason to deliver it. To his surprise, Dr. Heerman said he would pay it the following week but within four days changed his mind completely and refused to give Audubon any money at all. Fortunately one of Audubon's pupils, Miss Dellafosse, decided to increase her lessons to one a day, much to his satisfaction. On November 24, he acquired another pupil—they were coming so slowly they could be counted one by one. This was Pamar's daughter, who, according to Audubon, "exhibited the brightest genius I believe I ever met with." At the same time he was also finding Miss Dellafosse "beautiful and extremely agreeable."

But still he received no word from Lucy. The scheduled arrival of every steamboat brought expectation; the actual arrival, only disappointment. Under the strain of waiting, he became morbidly sensitive, jealous, and bitter. He met a highly successful art teacher and, because the man did not know him, lashed out at him in his journal. The artist had as many pupils as he wanted, but Audubon was sure that the samples of his work that he showed to obtain them had actually been painted by someone else. That he could believe such nonsense about another man shows how he had lost his sense of proportion and was driven into fantasies by his lack of money and recognition.

Then he encountered what he considered fresh insults because of the Brands' daughter. For some time, he had been giving her lessons at Miss Dellafosse's house. Now Mr. and Mrs. Brand wanted him to go to the school that the girl was attending and continue her lessons there. The school was obviously prepared to give its students art lessons; yet the Brands were insisting that an outsider be employed for the purpose. Opposition to Audubon was inevitable, and in his state of hypersensitivity he was not equipped to handle the situation. Immediately he suspected that the headmistress was cool toward him, and he thought he overheard the other teachers speaking about him sarcastically. His nervousness made his pupil uneasy and the lesson was completely unsuccessful. Audubon left, vowing to himself that he would never return.

The Pirrie family, meanwhile, had returned to New Orleans for the winter; and the same day that Audubon felt himself ridiculed at the girls' school, he also thought himself mocked by Eliza. He happened to see her on the busy New Orleans streets, but she did not notice him. Instead of speaking to her and catching her attention or even nodding to her, Audubon went haughtily on his way without a word to his former pupil. That evening he wrote in his journal, "My lovely Miss Pirrie of Oakley passed by me this morning, but did not remember how beautiful I had rendered her face once by painting it at her request with pastelles. She knew not the man who, with the utmost patience and, in fact, attention, waited on her motions to please her. But," he added with a touch of scorn and defiance, "thanks to my humble talents I can run the gauntlet through this world without her help."

Audubon was now in serious trouble, not so much with the world at large as with himself. The crushing humiliation of his bankruptcy and the realization that no one wanted him had destroyed his self-confidence and his self-esteem, leaving no emotional defense to take their place, not even the illusions in which he had formerly found a refuge. All he had left was his pride, his naked, quivering pride, sensitive beyond belief to every word, to every intonation, to every movement or expression on the part of the people he met. And his pride was leading him into disastrous quarrels with Dr. Heerman, Mrs. Pirrie, the schoolteachers of New Orleans, the artists, almost all the people who could, and often would, have helped him. If they snubbed him, he was hurt; if they tried to assist him, he was hurt; if they paid no attention to him either way, he was hurt. And each hurt made him act foolishly and brought about a new disaster. Only one person could break the sequence, and that one person remained silent. "So anxious am I," he noted in his journal in an incoherent sentence, "during the whole of my present days, to see my family that my head is scarce at right with my movements. And yet I must feel my sad disappointments and retire to rest without the comfort of her so-much-wanted company." The next day he added, "It is now twenty-six days since the last letter I have had from my wife is dated. Three steamboats have arrived since from Louisville, and no news of her departure has reached me. My anxiety renders every moment painful and irksome."

Two events now occurred to help Audubon regain his balance. He was at the Brands' house one day when he unexpectedly met Eliza Pirrie face-to-face. To his surprise, she did not cut him. Indeed, she was friendly, gracious, and wanted to see him again. Then came the wonderful news that Lucy was on board the steamboat *Rocket,* headed toward New Orleans. The boat had been delayed on its journey but should arrive in four or five days more.

On December 18, 1821, when the *Rocket* drew alongside the New Orleans riverfront and lowered its ornate gangway, Audubon was standing on the levee, anxiously looking at the rows of faces that lined the rails. Some were friendly, some indifferent, some handsome, some ugly, but at a distance they were only faces, unattached to the bodies below and somehow impersonal. As he scanned them, Audubon wondered if that could be Lucy, half-hidden behind the man with the tall hat? No, she was prettier than that. There she was at the end of the row, the woman who was not waving. She was not waving because she had not seen him. No, that was not Lucy. She was taller than that. Perhaps she had not come after all. Perhaps his information was wrong. Once more he looked at the rows of faces, searching for the one face he wanted; and at last he found her, with Victor and John beside her.

Fourteen months had passed since they had seen each other, months marked by misfortunes and misunderstandings, each of which had left a scar on their relationship, scars that only they themselves could heal. For a moment or two they remained on the levee, the smoke from the steamboats rising in the background, the keelboats and flatboats with their crude, dirty crews moored on every hand, the crowd milling around them. Then, as the boys plied him with questions, Audubon led his wife to the Pamars' for dinner and, after the meal, to the house he had rented for her at 505 Dauphine Street. It was not a prepossessing house, only a small wooden building with a sloping roof, but it was home and the best he could offer her. That night, before he went to bed, he wrote with feeling in his journal, "After fourteen months absence, the meeting of what life renders agreeable to me was gratefully welcomed, and I thanked my Maker for this mark of mercy." Once more he was at peace with himself.

In contrast to the lonely months before, the days following Lucy's arrival were filled with happy activity for Audubon. He canceled some of his lessons so as to have more time with her. He took out all his pictures, including those he had sent to her by Nicholas Berthoud, and reviewed them with her one by one, the bald eagle, the terns, the pelican, every picture with its own individual story. But as he turned the sheets of paper with Lucy standing beside him, he was disappointed. He found they were not as good as he had expected.

Yet he was not downhearted and on Christmas Eve gaily welcomed an unexpected guest, Ferdinand Rozier, who was in New Orleans on a short visit. Outside, the weather was disagreeably cold. Ice an inch thick had formed in the water buckets and horse troughs, but inside the house on Dauphine Street everything was merriment as the former partners discussed what had happened to them over the years. The contrast between their positions must have been painfully evident. Rozier was prosperous; Audubon destitute. Rozier had tangible accomplishments to show for his time; Audubon, only the nebulous hope that his book might someday be published. Yet he probably talked well that night; and behind his gay manner, Rozier did not see the shadows of his fears and doubts.

The next morning, Christmas Day, when the Audubons woke up, they found it was snowing. All morning the flakes drifted over the city, covering the levee and the Place d'Armes with white, powdering the steeples of St. Louis Cathedral, and clinging to the niches of the ironwork balconies. As the noonday sun warmed the city, the snow melted and turned to slush, but the afternoon brought a new wave of cold. The slush froze; the streets turned to ice; the horses slipped on the pavements; and the wheels of carriages skidded dangerously. At their house on Dauphine Street, Lucy and Audubon were still talking. Audubon was in high spirits. With Lucy beside him, nothing could discourage him, not even the contrast between his position and Rozier's or the realization that his drawings were not as good as he had imagined them. Indeed, his spirits soared so high that on December 30 he resolved to do ninety-nine bird pictures in the next ninety-nine days and, to carry out his plan, he hired a New Orleans hunter to collect specimens. But enthusiasm was not money. On January 1, he started a new journal book and wrote as his first entry, "Two months and five days have elapsed before I could venture to dispose of one hundred and twenty-five cents to pay for this book, that probably, like other things in the world, is ashamed to find me so poor."

Nor did the succeeding weeks bring any improvement. Mrs. Brand, who was expecting a child, dropped out as an art student, but she did employ Lucy as a governess for the new baby. This gave Lucy steady work, but it also added twelve dollars a month in tuition to the family's expenses, because Victor and John could no longer be educated by Lucy at home. In fact, Lucy's arrival had not solved any of Audubon's basic problems; and by March, 1822, he was in another fit of depression. He was still unable to support his family in the manner he wanted to; he was not, in spite of his New Year's resolve, progressing with his book; and Lucy, who had criticized him by mail, was now criticizing him in person. As he often did when he was frustrated, he began to think of moving on again. Remembering the few pleasant days he had spent at Natchez, he decided to return there, but Lucy refused to accompany him. She had left Louisville to come to New Orleans. She was not going to leave New Orleans to move to Natchez, particularly when she had a steady job with Mrs. Brand. Consequently Audubon decided to go alone, although the money for his passage presented a problem. He simply did not have it.

He still possessed his skill at drawing, however. Could he trade it for a trip up the river? After a number of inquiries, he found that the captain of the steamboat *Eclat* was willing to carry him to Natchez in exchange for a portrait of himself and his wife. Audubon therefore gathered his few belongings—his drawings, a gun, some gunpowder packed in bottles, chalks, paper, and the other supplies he needed—packed them in a small chest, carried it down to the river, and, on March 16, 1822, boarded the *Eclat*. Once again, he saw around him the endless confusion of the city's waterfront, the colorful steamboats, the graceful sailing ships, the snub-bowed flatboats, and the waters of the Mississippi running through the marshes and flatlands to the gulf. Once more he was on the deck of a boat with his chest safely stowed away while the whistles blew, the engines rumbled, and the crowds on shore waved back at the passengers standing at the rails. As he had so many times before, he felt the quivering of the hull as the boat strained in turning against the current; and he saw New Orleans, the city from which he had hoped so much and received so little, disappear around the bend in the river.

On either bank, the foliage stirred in the spring breeze; Negroes with long poles sat on the levees angling for catfish; planters in broad-brimmed hats bargained at the landings with the captains of passing keelboats; and occasionally a squatter looked up from the team he was driving to watch the boat moving up the river. Again he saw the familiar sights, the spot where he had spent the night with Nicholas Berthoud just before they reached New Orleans, Bayou Sarah where he had believed himself the victim of indignities but where he had also recovered his lost gaiety. By now, steamboat life was routine to him. He knew what it was like to load and unload cotton and other crops, to watch the gangplanks lowered and raised, to see the crowds embark and disembark. Except for completing the picture of the captain and his wife and doing portraits of a few passengers, he had nothing to occupy him on the journey and could relax and enjoy it.

Three days out of New Orleans, he needed some additional supplies. Pulling his chest from its storage place, he unstrapped it, opened it, and started taking out the materials he needed. As he did so he noticed a stain on one of his drawings. He picked it up hastily and looked at it. The stain was bad. He picked up another picture. It too was stained. Then he noticed a shimmering piece of glass lying loose in the chest. To his horror, he saw that one of his bottles of gunpowder had shattered and the powder, pouring over his pictures, had stained some of them so badly that they were useless.

In spite of this new discouragement, he landed at Natchez in good spirits, determined to find there the success he had failed to gain in New Orleans; and for once he was not disappointed. Almost immediately he obtained some students and, through the intervention of friends, secured an appointment to teach art at Elizabeth Academy in Washington, a few miles from Natchez. Although Lucy still refused to join him, she agreed to let the two boys move to Natchez, where Audubon made arrangements for them to attend school.

Only one problem remained. He had set himself a schedule that strained even his enormous physical capacities. To teach his classes at Elizabeth Academy, he had to travel approximately seven miles. Yet he could not move to Washington because he needed the work he had obtained in Natchez. His life, therefore, became a frenetic dash between the two towns; and under the pressure he collapsed. One of his friends, Dr. William Provan, fortunately came to the rescue. He treated Audubon free of charge, paid the boys' tuition bills, and as soon as Audubon recovered, found him a job teaching at a school in Natchez. Thanks to Dr. Provan's efforts, he had steady employment and a steady income, all on a schedule he could keep. The only thing he did not have was time to complete his book. On the 8th of July he sadly wrote in his journal, "While work flowed upon me, the hope of completing my book upon the birds of America became less clear; and full of despair, I feared my hopes of becoming known to Europe as a naturalist were destined to be blasted."

So also were Joseph Mason's hopes. For long months, he had been following Audubon, keeping him company through one adversity after another, comforting him when he lost his pocketbook at New Orleans, sharing his anxiety over the missing portfolio, helping him collect embarrassing debts like Dr. Heerman's, and worrying with him over where they would find their next meal. All this time, he had worked on his drawings of plants and helped Audubon with the backgrounds of some of the bird pictures. But there was no point in continuing to do this if the book was never to be published. He decided, therefore, that he should return home. Audubon, of course, had no money to give him as a parting present, but he did the next best thing. He supplied him with enough paper and chalk to do pictures in exchange for his passage to Cincinnati, and he also presented him with a double-barreled gun that he had purchased years before in Philadelphia. In return, Mason left behind the drawings he had done for Audubon with their penciled signatures, "Plant by Jos. Mason." It was a case of two poor men giving to each other the best they had to give.

After Mason's departure, Audubon received word from Lucy that the Brands' baby had died. Because she no longer had a job in New Orleans, she was willing to come to Natchez. Happily he went down the steep hill on the day of her arrival, greeted her at the river's edge and, taking her by the hand, led her back through Natchez-Under-the-Hill, past the cheap frame buildings, the coarse women, and the shady gamblers to the handsome town at the top of the bluff. Looking around her, Lucy saw the graceful brick buildings, the broad streets, and the lovely gardens of this strange double-city which held forth hope of the best life they had known since leaving Henderson.

Through Audubon's friends she quickly obtained a position as governess to a minister's children, while Audubon went on with his teaching and the boys continued their schooling. With a home of their own and a reasonable income, they had their first moments of peace in years; and in his relaxed mood, Audubon thought less and less about his book on birds. For a short time he seriously considered joining a new business enterprise being set up in Mexico. At another, he listened carefully to the advice he received from a visiting English naturalist. "He called," Audubon wrote in his journal, "and spent the evening with me, and examined my drawings, and advised me to visit England and take them with me. But when he said I should probably have to spend several years to perfect them, and to make myself known, I closed my drawings and turned my mind from the thought." In place of either enthusiasm or despair, Audubon was overcome by weariness and numbness and was giving way to a desire to be reconciled with the world on its own terms, whatever the cost to his pride.

Just as he was about to give up all thought of the book, a fresh crisis smashed the routine of the Audubons' lives. The minister for whom Lucy was working became slower and slower about paying her salary until, fearful that she would receive no money at all, she decided to resign. Dr. Provan again came to the Audubons' assistance. He knew a widow, a Mrs. Percy,

who owned a plantation named Beech Woods near Bayou
Sarah. Mrs. Percy wanted to start a school for her own children and those of the neighboring plantations. Would Lucy be
interested in running it? Lucy certainly would be. The job
offered her more security than she had ever known. Audubon,
on the other hand, had struck up a friendship with an itinerant
portrait painter who offered to teach him how to use oils. Remembering his experience with Mrs. Pamar, who wanted her
daughters painted in oils, not drawn in black chalk, Audubon
was delighted to accept this offer. Lucy, therefore, was to go to
Beech Woods and start the school while Audubon remained in
Natchez to join the itinerant painter in a partnership and, at
the same time, take lessons from him.

But the new plan, at least Audubon's part of it, did not work
out. Like Louisville, Cincinnati, and New Orleans, Natchez did
not offer an endless market for portraits. Soon he and his partner were traveling farther and farther in search of commissions
and finally their travels brought them to Beech Woods for a
short visit. From there they went to Jackson, Mississippi, which,
Audubon said, "I found to be a mean place, a rendezvous for
gamblers and vagabonds. Disgusted with the place and the people, I left it and returned to my wife."

What Audubon most needed, if he were ever to finish his
book, was a patron; and Mrs. Percy was willing to play this
role on a temporary basis. She offered him a job teaching music
and drawing during the summer months with enough free
time to collect new specimens. It was a good offer and he accepted it immediately, but it placed him in a difficult position.
At Beech Woods, Lucy had the full-time job; Audubon the
part-time one. Lucy was the permanent member of the community; Audubon the transient. In other words, Lucy, in the
eyes of Beech Woods, was the success; Audubon the failure.
Already unduly sensitive, his position on the plantation made
him even more so and, in his nervous state, he soon quarreled
with Mrs. Percy. As part of his arrangement with her, he had
agreed to do a portrait of her children. Setting to work, he
gave their complexions a slight yellowish tinge. Mrs. Percy
wanted him to make the color a little lighter. Audubon said
he would only paint their complexions as he saw them. Mrs.
Percy insisted that the color be changed. Audubon refused. Mrs.

Percy argued more strenuously. Thereupon Audubon flew into a rage, stalked out of the house and into the woods. He spent a few days sulking by himself. Then, without returning to Beech Woods even to say good-bye to Lucy, he sent word asking Victor to join him. He was going back to Natchez.

Together, father and son returned to the city which Audubon now looked on as home, but he had no further plan. For a time he thought of moving to Philadelphia. Then he toyed with the idea of going back to Louisville and trying to re-enter the mercantile business, although he realized his lack of capital made this idea impractical. While he was attempting to decide what to do, he secured a commission to paint a large picture of Natchez for which he was to be paid three hundred dollars. But before the scene was finished, the woman who had ordered it died. Her heirs did not want it, and, for that matter, neither did anyone else. In desperation, Audubon hung it in a store where it remained unsold for years.

Then he and Victor both became seriously ill—the doctor said they had yellow fever—and Lucy had to take a leave of absence from her school, come to Natchez, and nurse them. When they were well enough to travel, she took them back to Beech Woods; she had no other place to take them. It was a final humiliation for Audubon to be forced to seek asylum at the plantation which he had left so haughtily only a short while before.

On his recovery, the question still remained, what should he do next? There was no point in his returning to Natchez. The idea he had once had of going to Europe was clearly impractical; he had neither the money nor enough pictures. New Orleans could offer him nothing further. Perhaps, he thought, he might find employment as a teacher in Philadelphia, a larger and more cosmopolitan city. Perhaps he could also find there a publisher for his book.

Therefore, in the beginning of October, as the early morning mists from the river became heavy with the approaching cold, Audubon again said good-bye to Lucy and, with Victor, who planned to accompany him as far as Shippingport, boarded the *Magnet*. Up the Mississippi puffed the steamboat, past Natchez and Arkansas Fort until it came to the village of Trinity near Cash Creek where, so many years before, Audubon had

camped with Rozier on their way to Ste. Genevieve. Here, because the water was too low to proceed farther, the boat was
forced to stop. Victor, having inherited all his father's enthusiasm and physical exuberance, suggested leaving the *Magnet* and walking to Shippingport rather than waiting for the
river to rise.

Audubon agreed, but before starting out he wanted to see
Cash Creek again and, with Victor, rambled over to the stream.
With his usual romanticism, he probably spun a glorious tale
about his former encampment, telling his son about the wolves
and the Indians and the swans and how he had been lost in
the woods. Victor, as he listened, could undoubtedly see the
figures huddled around the campfire and hear the sound of the
Indians laughing. For a moment at least, he was able to share
in the exciting life of his adventurous father. Then the two
returned side by side to the tavern at Trinity to spend the
night.

In later years, when time had mellowed his memories, Audubon wrote, "The very sight of the waters filled me with joy
as we approached the little village of Trinity," but that was
not his mood when, in the evening, he took up his pen to write
to Ferdinand Rozier. All the time he had been at Cash Creek,
he had been thinking about his former partner, and what he
wrote to him from the tavern at Trinity reveals a man who is no
longer on the brink of despair but has passed over the brink.

"I am yet, my dear Rozier," he said, "on the wing, and God
only knows how long I may yet remain so. I am now bound to
Shippingport to see if I can, through my *former friends* there,
bring about some change in my situation. I am now rather
wearied of the world. I have, I believe, been too much of it."

Aside from the few formal remarks that were customary in
the correspondence of those days and a brief introduction to
the bearer of the letter, he said nothing more; no pretense that
the book would succeed; no plans for the future, not even plans
to go to Philadelphia, just the bare hope that his friends in
Shippingport would help him.

Torn from his heart was the lonely cry of despair, the statement of complete disillusionment: "I am now rather wearied of
the world. I have, I believe, been too much of it."

CHAPTER XVI

1823 — 1824

In the little hotel at Trinity, his courage and faith exhausted, Audubon turned to Ferdinand Rozier, the man whom he had once badgered and mocked. Ripping away the veil of pride that concealed his true feelings, he revealed himself for what he was: an utterly defeated man. He had no choice, however, except to go on, to follow blindly and hopelessly the bleak path that lay ahead. The next morning, therefore, he set out on foot for Shippingport with Victor and two other passengers from the *Magnet.*

One of them was "a delicate and gentlemanly person" named Rose, who acknowledged that he might not be able to keep the pace set by Audubon; the other was "a burly personage" whom Audubon called "S." and who immediately aroused his antagonism by expressing fears that Victor, because of his youth, would hold them all back. To Audubon, consequently, the trip became a duel between his son and S., a trial of strength to prove which one was the better.

Three days later, Victor was limping like "a lamed turkey," but the rest of the group was not much better off. Their feet were sore, and they were tired. Then Victor began to get his second wind. Instead of lagging behind with the others, he kept up with his father; and by the morning of the seventh day, the duel was over. Both Rose and S. admitted that the pace was too fast for them. Perhaps it would be better, they suggested, if Victor and Audubon went on alone. The boy, who had all his father's physical endurance, laughed and thought the idea a good one; and Audubon, proud that his son had defeated S. —he had so little to be proud of those days—readily agreed.

During the brief interlude of this trip from Trinity to Ship-

259

pingport, Audubon had recaptured some of his old enthusiasm and his zest for frontier life; but in his present predicament it was an interlude that could not last. Each step of the way was bringing him closer and closer to a confrontation with reality. "I am yet on the wing," he had written Rozier from Trinity, "and God knows how long I may remain so." His hope lay with his friends in Shippingport. What they would offer him remained to be seen, and it turned out to be extremely little. When he arrived in Shippingport he had thirteen dollars in his pocket and needed a job desperately, but no one was anxious to have him. Ironically, Victor had less difficulty finding work than his father. Almost immediately he was hired as a clerk by the father of Nicholas Berthoud, Lucy's brother-in-law. At least this relieved Audubon of the necessity of supporting his son, but it was also another blow to his self-esteem. His fourteen-year-old boy was employable, but he himself was not. Lucy's family was willing to rally to the support of Audubon's wife and children but not to the support of Audubon. None of his former friends, none of his relatives by marriage, came forward with a job; none had a place he could occupy. Only a few months before, in Natchez, he had seriously expressed a desire to re-enter the mercantile business at Louisville or Shippingport. Now he faced the bleak reality; he could not even find a job as a clerk.

But he had not exhausted all his resources. He might have no standing as a merchant, a naturalist, or a teacher. But he was a painter, was he not? So he found work painting.

He painted the interior of a steamboat.

And that was that. That was the best either Louisville or Shippingport could give; and when the task was done, there was nothing else. Some friends suggested he do a picture of the Falls of the Ohio and sell it. He accepted the idea and, on November 9, 1823, wrote in his journal, "Busy at work, when the weather permitted, and resolved to paint one hundred views of the American scenery. I shall not be surprised to find myself seated at the foot of Niagara." But this plan, too, faded away as the days shortened and the cold crept over Kentucky. No one wanted Audubon's landscapes. All winter long, trying to keep alive, he searched for commissions, traveling back and forth between Shippingport and Louisville and obtaining just enough orders for portraits to keep going, but he was not in any way advancing his career. And he was lonely, too. His former friends were cool to him; and Lucy, with her steady job at Beech Woods, showed no interest in rejoining him; he had so little to offer her.

By springtime, he realized that he would have to move on again, but where could he go? He thought again of traveling to Philadelphia, perhaps to take art lessons himself and, at the same time, explore the possibility of having his book published. What made him revert to this idea was his growing realization that he had no alternative if he hoped to extricate himself from the depths to which he had fallen. Difficult as it might be to finish his book and to find a publisher, he had tried everything else without success. This hope was about all he had left.

As spring came to Kentucky and the trees by the river unfolded their leaves, he therefore said good-bye to Victor, who still had his job as a clerk; and on April 5, 1824, he arrived at Philadelphia, filled with the optimism he usually felt when he was on the threshold of a new venture. As his first act, he said later, "I purchased a new set of clothes, and dressed myself with extreme neatness," but a woman who met him said that he still looked like a backwoodsman with his hair long and his shirt unbuttoned at the collar. Next, he called on Dr. William Mease, one of the few people in the city whom he could ask for help, because in spite of his years at Mill Grove and his many business trips to Philadelphia, he knew almost no one of consequence.

Dr. Mease received him kindly and started him off well by introducing him to Thomas Sully, the painter. Sully looked at Audubon's portfolio of bird pictures and was well impressed. Through Sully, Audubon met other artists and was able to arrange a public exhibit of his pictures. He also succeeded in obtaining an introduction to Charles Lucien Bonaparte, a nephew of Napoleon. Bonaparte, who was a distinguished ornithologist, was then living in the United States and working on a four-volume bird book which would serve as an extension of Alexander Wilson's. He might, therefore, have regarded Audubon as a potential competitor and shunned him. Instead, he looked at the pictures, liked them, and suggested that they call on

Titian Peale, the artist, whom Bonaparte had engaged to do the illustrations for his own book.

Until then, everything had gone better than Audubon had had any right to hope. Starting with one friend, he had, in a matter of days, greatly widened the circle of his acquaintance-ship. Everywhere he went he had been well received; people admired his pictures; men like Bonaparte respected his opinions on ornithology. For someone who had been scorned for so long, treated almost like a beggar, his success came too quickly, and he stepped into Titian Peale's studio in a mood of overconfidence. At that moment his troubles started.

He took one look at the pictures Peale was doing for Bonaparte and later noted scornfully in his journal that "from want of knowledge of the habits of birds in a wild state, he represented them as if seated for a portrait, instead of with their own lively ways when seeking their natural food or pleasure." To hold these opinions privately was his artistic right, but to express them openly was dangerous and impolitic. Yet it is obvious that Audubon did not conceal his feelings. Anxious to make a name for himself and jealous of any competition, he was unwilling to give the artists and scientists of Philadelphia an opportunity to judge for themselves between his work and the work of others. Instead, in his haste and his overconfidence, he pronounced the judgment for them.

Regardless of Peale's reaction, Bonaparte was not offended by Audubon's attitude. Still friendly and still generously disposed toward the newcomer, he took Audubon to a meeting of the Philadelphia Academy of Arts and Sciences, introduced him to the members, and made arrangements for him to show his pictures. There Audubon promptly made his second enemy, a man named George Ord. Extremely nervous and high-strung, Ord had a personality made up of contradictions. He could be a brilliant conversationalist with his friends, yet with strangers he was reserved and shy. At times he was charming, delightful, and thoughtful; at others, he would fly into an unpleasant, un-reasonable rage. This curious man had, some years before, struck up an acquaintance with Alexander Wilson and had gradually forced himself on the ornithologist, offering him ad-vice, writing him letters, and setting himself up as Wilson's principal intimate. It was a curious impulse that drove Ord in this direction. Independently wealthy and well known in Philadelphia, he seemed to have everything in life he needed, but the association with Wilson apparently compensated for some basic lack. Even after Wilson's death, he continued to play the same role. He assumed responsibility for editing the last volumes of Wilson's work, although he was not particularly well equipped to do so; he collected and published Wilson's papers; and he wrote Wilson's biography. In short, he regarded Wilson and his work as his personal property.

Naturally Ord was at the meeting of the Philadelphia Academy of Arts and Sciences at which Audubon made his appearance, and what took place is easy to envision. Bonaparte led Audubon around the table where the members were seated and introduced him to the chairman, who asked him to speak and show his pictures. Audubon, confident that his audience would share his own opinion of his work, talked far too much and too boastfully. Since 1820 he had been striving to outdo Wilson, carefully noting every bird he discovered that did not appear in Wilson's book, every error he had found in Wilson's drawings. Now he had an opportunity to tell a scientific society just what he had accomplished, and he did so. On and on he went, trying to demonstrate the superiority of his own pictures; and with every word that he uttered, Ord grew angrier. Finally, Ord exploded into one of his rages.

Because Ord was a member of the academy and respected by the audience, the result of the conflict was a debacle for Audubon. As Ord's temper flared, so did Audubon's. The room rang with caustic remarks. Audubon, always somewhat tempted to exaggerate, made absurd comments. Ord pounced on them. By the end of the evening Audubon was shattered and disillusioned. He had expected friendship and received enmity; he had desperately wanted praise, praise to justify his misspent years and give him hope for the future. Instead, Ord tongue-lashed him; and many of the audience, out of friendship for Ord, joined in. With his short temper, Ord was not an easy man to handle, but neither was Audubon. The clash between them, each with their vested interest in a competing work, might have been avoided, but only with patience and tact on Audubon's part. These, however, were two qualities he lacked.

Nor did he learn anything from his experience at the meeting, because within a few more days, he made another enemy in much the same way. This was Alexander Lawson, the engraver who had done the plates for Wilson's book and therefore had a deep concern for its financial success. Audubon was introduced to him, and in no time at all the two men were at odds. Lawson said that Audubon's pictures were too soft, too much like paintings to be suitable for engravings. Audubon remarked sarcastically in his journal that Lawson's "figure nearly reached the roof, his face was sympathetically long, and his tongue was so long that we obtained no opportunity of speaking in his company."

Bewildered and hurt by the antagonism he was encountering after his initial success, Audubon now lost his head completely and started lashing out in every direction. Bonaparte, still admiring his skills and still anxious to help him, offered him a job doing bird pictures for his own book. Audubon set his price so ridiculously high that Bonaparte withdrew his offer. Rozier was in town and, doubtless remembering the pathetic letter Audubon had written him from Trinity, came to call. Audubon's temper was now so completely frayed, his sense of proportion so distorted, that he dismissed his former partner with the contemptuous comment that he was still thirsting for money.

But the disaster was not yet complete. Joseph Mason, Audubon's former student and partner, was now employed as an artist at Bartram's botanical gardens outside Philadelphia. Learning that Audubon was in the city, he too came to call. It should have been a pleasant occasion, but it was not. During the course of his visit, Mason asked to see the pictures they had worked on together, the ones they had each signed in pencil, sharing the honor for the completed work. Audubon brought them out; and Mason, looking at these drawings again, saw to his surprise that Audubon's signature now appeared in India ink, ready for the engraver, while his own signature remained in pencil or, in some cases, had even been erased.

To Mason, Audubon's intentions were all too clearly apparent. In spite of his teacher's earlier promises, Mason was to receive no credit for the plants he had drawn. Angry and hurt, Mason argued in vain that his name, too, should appear. Audubon was adamant. The birds were the principal subjects of the pictures. He, Audubon, had drawn the birds. He alone would sign the drawings. Morally, Audubon had done nothing wrong in accepting Mason's assistance in doing the backgrounds. More than one great artist, engaged in an immense project, has used the help of others, supervising their work and reserving the right to approve it or reject it. In this Audubon was merely following a time-honored custom. Where he was wrong, and badly wrong, was in refusing to acknowledge the assistance he had received. Yet he could not bring himself to do so. That slender stack of drawings represented his only accomplishment during those years of poverty and humiliation. He had to take full credit for every single one.

By acting as he did, he created another enemy in Philadelphia, one who was in a position to supply Ord and his friends with just the sort of information they wanted. Mason could prove to them that Audubon, in spite of his claims, had not done all the work himself, that he was to a certain degree a fraud. In his anger, Mason did just that.

By this time, any chance Audubon might have had of finding a publisher in Philadelphia was completely dissipated. He tried giving painting lessons at a dollar each, a price even lower than he had charged in New Orleans, but with little success. He exhibited his drawings but found the show did not pay for itself. Frustrated at every turn and having made many influential enemies, he realized he must look elsewhere, perhaps in New York, for the support he needed.

Yet his visit to Philadelphia had not been entirely wasted. Aside from Thomas Sully, who was a useful acquaintance and had also given him some instruction in handling oils, he had gotten along well with Bonaparte and had made several other important friends. One of them was Dr. Richard Harlan, a Philadelphia physician and a competent naturalist. Another was Charles Alexandre Lesueur, a distinguished French naturalist who happened to be in the city at the time. He also met Edward Harris, a wealthy young man who lived in Moorestown, New Jersey. Harris came to see Audubon, was much taken with his drawings, and offered to buy some. After Harris had selected some pictures, Audubon offered him the painting of the Falls of Ohio at what he thought was a sacrifice price. Harris recognized Audubon's generosity and responded with a generous act of his own. He refused to buy the picture but pressed a hundred-dollar bill into Audubon's hand. Counting that gift, he had $130 when he left Philadelphia. In addition, he had collected letters of introduction to several people in New York. Most important of all, however, he had learned a lesson: never try to take a city by storm without regard for the feelings or work of others. That hard-earned knowledge perhaps made the whole trip worthwhile.

A few days before he left for New York, he received an invitation from a friend to drive out to Mill Grove and call on the present owner, Samuel Wetherill. On the way, Audubon thought about the happy days he had spent there, about the opportunities he had missed, and the state to which his carelessness had brought him. The carriage turned off the road and down the drive. There in front of him was the handsome stone farmhouse, the sloping fields running down to the creek, and off in the distance the hemlock woods where he had so often wandered. The carriage pulled up at the door; Audubon and his friend stepped down; Wetherill came out to greet them and invited them in. Suddenly Audubon could stand it no longer. Overcome with emotion, he abruptly snatched up his hat and ran toward the woods, looking for the cave where he and Lucy had become engaged. Wildly he raced down the slope toward the creek, but the cave was gone. The stones surrounding it had been used to repair the mill dam.

Not much was left him, not even this one pleasure. He had acted foolishly at Mill Grove and, for years afterward, had continued repeating his first mistakes, taking Lucy and himself down a long, crooked road that seemed to run further and further away from the dreams they once had had. Now, following the fiasco in Philadelphia, the end of the road was again out of sight.

Sadly he returned to the city, packed his clothes, tied up his pictures in his portfolio, put his $130 in his pocket along with his letters of introduction, and on the last day of July boarded the stagecoach for New York. All night long, the wheels rattled over the roads of New Jersey. Occasionally a light glimmered in a farmhouse where a mother watched over a sick child or a sleepless old man sat by himself in his loneliness. There was light, too, wherever the coach stopped to take on passengers or change horses, light coming from the lanterns hung on the inn or held by the porters and stablemen. Otherwise, the world through which Audubon traveled was as black as the world of his own thoughts.

Yet when he arrived in New York he threw himself into the work of making himself known with all the energy he possessed. He went directly to his lodgings, left his luggage, and then set out calling on the people to whom he carried letters of introduction. Almost immediately, however, he learned that New Yorkers, then as now, transact little business in the middle of the summer and that most of the men he wanted to see were out of town. By the end of the day, he was so thoroughly discouraged that he wondered whether he had been wise to leave Philadelphia or whether it might not be preferable to move on to Boston or Albany. He decided, however, that he should stay a short while longer. On the second day of his visit he went to the natural history museum, where he "found the specimens of stuffed birds set up in unnatural and constrained attitudes." This was indeed true, because it would be many years before taxidermists learned to create lifelike displays, but he then went on with unbelievable arrogance: "The world owes to me the adoption of the plan of drawing from animated nature. Wilson is the only one who has in any tolerable degree adopted my plan." The shock of his reception in Philadelphia had not yet worn off; in his desperation, he would admit no rivals. His pictures, and his pictures alone, had to be the supreme authority.

The difficulty was that no one shared his opinion, and so the next day, having almost nobody else to call on, he swallowed his pride and went to see Vanderlyn, the artist for whom he had expressed such contempt in New Orleans. Once before, he had asked Vanderlyn to endorse his work and Vanderlyn had done so. Perhaps he would do so again. When he knocked at Vanderlyn's studio, Vanderlyn received him kindly, stopped painting, and took time to show him the pictures on which he was working. But that night when Audubon returned to his lodgings, he remarked sarcastically in his journal that he "was not impressed with the idea that he was a great painter."

Fortunately he did not neglect to call on Dr. Samuel L. Mitchill, the one person in New York most able to help him. During his long years in the West, he had made no effort to keep in touch with the doctor, thus letting lapse the single most important scientific connection he had. But this made no difference to Mitchill. He received Audubon graciously, examined his pictures, and then at Audubon's request, wrote a letter to the New York Lyceum, saying that Audubon would like to show his drawings and also be considered for membership. Nine days later, Audubon again unwrapped his portfolio before a gathering of an important scientific organization. Sobered by his experience in Philadelphia, he behaved more moderately and received an invitation to present a paper at a meeting to be held on August 11. For his subject he chose the migration of swallows, the topic that had so interested him in Cincinnati. The members were sufficiently impressed by it to order its publication, and it became the first writing of Audubon's to appear in print.

But that was the only accomplishment he achieved during two weeks in New York. The Lyceum appreciated his pictures but no one had the slightest interest in publishing them; and Audubon began to suspect, rightly or wrongly, that the Philadelphians who had invested in Wilson's book were spreading the rumor that Mason was responsible for much of what Audubon claimed to be his own. If, at that point, he had made a gracious acknowledgment of Mason's help, the rumor would have stopped; but he was in no mood to do so. Instead, realizing his book would not be published in New York, he again considered the possibility of going to Europe, and the thought of the expense threw him into despair.

For several days more, he hung around New York without either plan or purpose. Vanderlyn was doing a picture of Andrew Jackson and, to pass the time, Audubon agreed to model for the body. He also made some sketches of his landlady and her child. On August 14, he wrote a letter to Thomas Sully in which he made a brave effort to keep up appearances.

"My reception in New York has surpassed my hopes," he said untruthfully. "I have been most kindly received." Then after describing the beauty of the New York harbor, flattering Sully a little, and sending good wishes to his new acquaintances in Philadelphia, he ended with a postscript saying, "I leave for Boston tomorrow."

In the morning, however, he had changed his mind again and was on his way to Albany, hoping to see DeWitt Clinton, who had taken an interest in some aspects of ornithology. Clinton was not in town; and frustrated again, Audubon decided, on second thought, that he would gain nothing by going to Boston. Aimlessly, he went instead to Niagara Falls, which he wanted to see.

Entering the hotel, he walked to the register, signed his name, and, in a fit of romantic defiance, added the words: "who, like Wilson, will ramble, but never, like that great man, die under the lash of the bookseller." For all his proud words, he presented a curious and disreputable appearance as he stood in the lobby. According to the account of his visit that he wrote later, he arrived at Niagara Falls dressed "just like one of the poorer class of Indians, and was rendered even more disagreeable to the eye of civilized man by not having, like them, plucked my beard, or trimmed my hair in any way. Had Hogarth been living, and there when I arrived, he could not have found a fitter subject for a Robinson Crusoe. My beard covered my neck in front, my hair fell much lower at my back, the leather dress which I wore had for months stood in need of repair, a large knife hung at my side, a rusty tin-box containing my drawings and colors was wrapped up in a worn-out blanket that had served me for a bed, and was buckled to my shoulders. To every one I must have seemed immersed in the depths of poverty, perhaps of despair."

The landlord, however, was not put off by his strange looks and, on learning that Audubon was an artist, offered to give him any assistance that he might require. While Audubon was waiting in the lobby, however, he noticed several pictures of Niagara hanging on the walls "by which I was so disgusted that I suddenly came to my better senses. 'What!' thought I. 'Have I come here to mimic nature in her grandest enterprise, and add *my* caricature of one of the wonders of the world to those which I see here?' " And the sight of the falls themselves, tumbling over their great ledge in a cascade of water, reinforced his decision. One view of them, he wrote, "satisfied me that Niagara never had and never will be painted."

Even though he realized the falls were beyond his capacity as an artist, he found in their grandeur what he most needed after the stress of his visits to Philadelphia and New York. Hearing the thundering water, seeing the rainbows arch against the sky, and watching the current race at a quickening pace to the lip of the drop, he gradually shed the wild, uncontrolled feeling of resentment that had seized him. Like a man emerging from a delirium, he became his normal self again.

Refreshed, he returned to the village, bought dinner for twelve cents, and walked back to the hotel. There he spent the evening thinking about himself and his future, but no longer despairingly. His experiences in Philadelphia and New York had changed his attitude. In neither city had he found a job or a publisher, but his ambition had been stimulated by his appearances before the Academy of Arts and Sciences and the Lyceum. At least some of the members had shown respect for him and his work, and he had tasted the glory of recognition. Although he was still poverty-stricken, still without a publisher, he was now determined to become famous, to make himself known on his own merits. That night, in the hotel at Niagara, he "went to bed thinking of Franklin eating his roll in the streets of Philadelphia, of Goldsmith travelling by the help of his musical powers, and of other great men who had worked their way through hardships and difficulties to fame, and fell asleep, hoping, by persevering industry, to make a name for myself among my countrymen."

The following morning, he walked over to look at the falls again before he set out for Buffalo on foot. He had now completely abandoned his earlier plan of going to Boston and, instead of spending more time in the East, had decided to return to Kentucky or Louisiana. At Buffalo, he shaved his beard, purchased more presentable clothes, and bought deck passage on a schooner bound for Erie, Pennsylvania. By agreeing to provide his own bed and provisions, he obtained his passage for only a dollar and fifty cents but he might just as well have taken the most expensive accommodations available, because shortly afterward his pocket was picked, leaving him almost penniless.

On the schooner, he fell into conversation with the captain, who, much taken by this strange wanderer, invited him to sleep in the cabin. Audubon, however, refused. "I never encroach where I have no right," he smugly remarked in his journal. The night was clear, the lake smooth. Placing his buffalo robe and a blanket on the deck, he made himself comfortable, took out his journal, and wrote, "Even the sailors, ignorant of my name, look on me as a poor devil not able to pay for a cabin passage." In his new state of mind, he thought of himself as already famous, already recognized as the outstanding authority on American ornithology. All night the schooner moved across the waters of Lake Erie, the stars shining and the sails straining against their sheets. Occasionally a spar creaked in the darkness, or there was a footstep on the deck as the helmsmen changed watches, while Audubon, wrapped in his robe, dreamed contentedly.

But Lake Erie is treacherous. Shallow in proportion to its area, the wind can quickly churn it into a boiling cauldron of whitecaps; and on August 28 a gale blew in. The schooner smashed its way through the waves, lifting its bow to meet each crest and then crashing down into the following trough, until they passed the harbor at Presque Isle, Pennsylvania. By this time, the captain thought it dangerous to go farther and dropped anchor in order to ride out the storm. During the night the schooner pitched and tossed, its naked masts describing great arcs against the sky; and when morning came, the storm had not lessened. An officer at the naval base on shore, noticing the schooner's predicament, sent out his gig to inquire how they were faring. Although the boat was safe, Audubon and another passenger, weary of the storm, took the opportunity to return with the gig to the land, where they decided to pool their resources and travel on together.

After a two-day journey, they reached Meadville, Pennsylvania; between them, they had only a dollar and a half. After engaging a room at a tavern, Audubon immediately set about trying to obtain some commissions for portraits. "I had opened the case that contained my drawings," he said, "and putting my portfolio under my arm, and a few good credentials in my pocket, walked up Main Street, looking to the right and left, examining the different *heads* which occurred, until I fixed my eyes on a gentleman in a store who looked as if he might want a sketch. I begged him to allow me to sit down. This granted, I remained purposely silent until he very soon asked me what was *'in that portfolio.'* These three words sounded well, and without waiting another instant, I opened it to his view. This was a Hollander, who complimented me much on the execution of the drawings of birds and flowers in my portfolio. Showing him a sketch of the best friend I have in the world at present [Lucy, of course], I asked him if he would like one of himself in the same style. He not only answered in the affirmative, but assured me that he would exert himself in procuring as many more customers as he could. I thanked him, be assured ... and having fixed upon the next morning for drawing the sketch, I returned to the Traveller's Rest, with a hope that tomorrow might prove propitious."

Audubon, of course, had neither a studio nor money to rent one, but the Hollander permitted him to use the garret over his store. Reached by a crazy flight of stairs from the back, the room contained as furnishings two hogsheads filled with oats, a parcel of Dutch toys thrown carelessly on the floor, a large drum and a bassoon, fur caps hanging along the wall, and the portable bed of the merchant's clerk which swung like a hammock in the center. Unfortunately the room also had four windows, one on each side, and so no matter which way Audubon turned, he was always facing into the light.

By hanging blankets across all but one of the windows, Audubon focused the light in a single direction. Then he arranged a chair, posed his first subject, a young man, and took out his black crayons. As part of his salesmanship, he had gathered the largest possible audience to watch while he worked. In a short time the portrait was finished, and since it met everyone's approval, the merchant took his place in the chair. He too was pleased by Audubon's work; more people asked for pictures;

and within a few days he had enough money to continue on to Pittsburgh, where he received a pleasant surprise.

News of his appearances before the Lyceum and the Academy of Arts and Sciences had apparently reached the city before him. Although he had failed to find a publisher and had made many critics and enemies, he was no longer a complete nobody, and Pittsburgh recognized the change. As a result, he spent a month and a half in the city, making trips out into the countryside, collecting new specimens, and doing portraits. But Pittsburgh, like every other city, offered only a limited market for his talents; and, as the days shortened and the steep hills along the rivers turned red with the touch of fall, Audubon knew he must leave.

For some time, he had thought of going down the river in a skiff. Finding three people—a doctor, an artist, and an Irishman—who were willing to make the trip with him, he purchased a boat; and the four of them set out, taking turns at the oars. No sooner had they left Pittsburgh, however, than black clouds rolled across the sky, dropping sheets of rain, which rippled the surface of the water and drenched the travelers. As night fell, they pulled the boat ashore, turned it upside down, and huddled underneath it for shelter; but next morning it was still raining, and it rained until they reached Wheeling, where, wet and exhausted, they decided to give up. Audubon, who had left Pittsburgh with only a little money, was again in financial trouble. He picked up some cash by selling the skiff and then wandered through the streets of Wheeling, trying to peddle some lithographs of General Lafayette, which he had purchased earlier in the hope of reselling them at a profit. No one wanted them, however, and disgusted with his inability to find any buyers, he took the money he had and used it to purchase passage on a keelboat to Cincinnati.

There he visited the house where he and Lucy had once lived and called on his few friends, but he found himself hounded by creditors. Apparently a number of people had sold supplies to the Western Museum on Audubon's order and held him personally responsible for the nonpayment of their bills. For Dr. Drake's great plans for the museum had never materialized. Failing to obtain the necessary financial support, the trustees soon sold it to an entrepreneur who turned it into an amusement center. Instead of featuring natural history displays, as Dr. Drake had hoped, its principal exhibit became a waxworks depicting the "Infernal Regions," a composite of Dante's Inferno and Milton's Hell, which contained walking skeletons, imps with flaming eyes, and a female figure of Sin who at intervals leaped from her seat and howled. To make hell even more realistic, the owner had installed a device with which he could occasionally give the spectators an electric shock. Of the work Audubon had done, nothing significant remained.

Unable at Cincinnati to secure any commissions for portraits, he ran completely out of money, but he was too ashamed to ask for a loan. Finally he considered approaching a business office where he was known, but before he entered the door he lost his nerve. Several times he passed up and down the street in front of the building before he finally got up his courage, went in, and was given fifteen dollars to buy deck passage on a steamboat to Louisville.

As he walked up the gangway to go on board, he presented a truly pathetic figure. His hair was long, his clothes unkempt; he not only had no money of his own, he was in debt. Only as a special favor was he allowed to take his meals in the cabin; and at night, when he wanted to sleep, he lay on a pile of wood shavings that he had scraped together. On either side of the river, as night came, the houses lost their form and became mere spots of light in the darkness and the banks formed vague outlines against the sky. The steady chugging of the engine and the whistle blowing an occasional signal were the only sounds. Lying on his heap of shavings, Audubon appeared little more than a tramp. Yet his resolution was still firm and his spirits still high. Unlike his trip up the river, when he had written so gloomily to Rozier, this time he was happy. "The spirit of contentment," he noted in his journal, "which I now feel is strange, it borders on the sublime; and, enthusiastic or lunatic, as some of my relatives will have me, I am glad to possess such a spirit."

At Louisville, he found that Victor was still happy working for the Berthouds, but that he himself was not particularly welcome. His utter neglect of his personal appearance put some people off, but the worst trouble was their memory of his many misadventures. As he wrote in his journal, "I discover that my friends think only of my apparel, and those upon whom I have conferred acts of kindness prefer to remind me of my errors." He was learning that the act of bankruptcy had no effect on public opinion and was not enough to re-establish his reputation in Louisville and Shippingport, where his past was too well known and where too many people had suffered from his speculations. Weary of being preached at, tired of being universally scorned, unable to find work, he decided to move on again.

There was only one place left in the world where he could go. That one place was back to Mrs. Percy's plantation at Bayou Sarah.

CHAPTER XVII

1824 – 1826

As Audubon's steamboat approached the landing place at Bayou Sarah, night fell and the rain came pouring down, not a fresh, cleansing rain, but a sultry rain that spread its wet without bringing relief from the heat. Since it was nearly midnight, the captain decided it was too dangerous to touch shore with the steamboat and landed Audubon from a smaller boat.

The night was pitch black and the rain still coming down in torrents when he groped his way along the country road. Even the forms of the magnolia trees were lost in the descending sheets of water, but he knew the way well and soon entered the village. There he learned that the whole area lay under the dreaded scourge of yellow fever, but he was not badly alarmed; minor epidemics were rather common in those days. He walked on to the largest hotel. No lights were on in the building; not a guest was sitting up late in the taproom; but the door was open, and he went in. Fumbling his way toward the desk, he called for a clerk. No answer. He called again. Still no answer. He stood in the middle of the lobby and shouted, but the only sound was the echo of his own voice. The hotel was entirely deserted. No one was there, not even a member of the staff. Suddenly the truth struck him. This was no minor epidemic. This was a major outbreak of yellow fever, and everyone in the hotel had fled to the safety of the pine woods. Now greatly concerned about the health of Lucy and John, he walked rapidly to the post office and, in the dark night, knocked repeatedly on the door until the postmaster roused himself and came to speak to him. He was able to assure Audubon that Lucy and John were safe at Mrs. Percy's and also recommended a tavern where Audubon might find accommodations.

The landlord of the tavern refused to take him in but suggested he go to the house of a German living at the edge of the village. Once more Audubon walked through the lonely streets, trying to protect his pictures from the rain by sheltering them against his body. Finally, in the continuing blackness, he came to the German's house and again knocked on a dark, unfriendly door. Inside the house he could see a light being kindled, and heard someone fumble with the lock. Then the door was thrown open in his face. He told his story to the German, who, not in the least afraid of Audubon's strange and shabbily dressed appearance, invited him to come in, fed him, and offered to lend him a horse on which he could ride to Mrs. Percy's that night instead of waiting until morning. Wanting to reach his family as quickly as possible, Audubon accepted and set off immediately. Early in the morning, he reached Mrs. Percy's. Audubon found Lucy already up and giving a lesson to her pupils. "Holding her and kissing her," he said, "I was once more happy, and all my toils and trials were forgotten."

His odyssey was over; but although his meeting with Lucy was fleetingly romantic, the end of his journey was not a particularly happy event for her. More than a year had passed since he had marched out of Mrs. Percy's house in a tantrum, and now he was back again with nothing to show for his long absence. One look at him told her this. As he himself said, he arrived "with rent and wasted clothes and uncut hair, altogether looking like the Wandering Jew." What if he had appeared before the Academy of Arts and Sciences in Philadelphia or delivered a well-received paper to the New York Lyceum? Neither of these events had produced a single penny of income or a publisher willing to print the book.

Yet as she talked to him, she must have noted his new determination, his conviction that he would really become famous. His dreams may have seemed as impractical as ever, he himself as far removed from reality, but she certainly sensed an underlying strength that had not been part of his character before. He had had his trials and defeats, some of them crushing, but he had also had his moments of triumph; and as he told her about his plans for the future, she agreed to help him.

The first step was to repair the quarrel with Mrs. Percy. Because Mrs. Percy had a generous nature, this matter was soon settled. Audubon was asked to stay on at Beech Woods and therefore had, for the first time since leaving Henderson, a permanent home. The next step was to lay the groundwork for a trip to England. Clearly, no American publisher would undertake a book in direct competition with Wilson's, but a British publisher might. To go to England, however, required money. This meant Lucy would have to continue teaching school and Audubon would have to abandon his wild idea of a shortcut to success, settle down, save his money, and try to perfect his collection of bird pictures.

What was most unusual about his new program was that he stuck to it. For more than a year he remained with Mrs. Percy at Beech Woods, a period that was one of the happiest and least eventful in his life. Lucy continued to provide the family's major support by operating her school, and each time she received her pay, she put aside part of it for Audubon's European trip. He himself spent many days in the woods, shooting birds and making additional drawings. But his activity had more purpose than ever before. He knew now that the book would have to be better than anything he had envisioned earlier, and he tried to make it so.

To add to his pleasure at Bayou Sarah, he discovered that his former clerk, John Pope, had become a doctor and was living nearby. Without the least difficulty, the two men, now more sober and mature, picked up the thread of their old friendship and found it unimpaired by their long separation. But Audubon's renewed interest in birds and his enjoyment of his friend did not make him neglect his responsibility to earn money to supplement what Lucy brought in. He started by teaching art to some of the girls at Beech Woods, probably the same pupils Lucy had. Then he began to give lessons in French and music and finally added fencing, which he taught to the sons of the neighboring planters.

On Saturday nights, gay at heart and less troubled than he had been for years, he went to the dances which were held in the building containing the cotton gin. With his long hair flowing, he would play his violin, join in the dancing himself, and offer to teach new steps to anyone who wanted to learn them. As his fame as a dancer spread, he was asked to give lessons professionally, and he promptly accepted an invitation to hold a class at Woodville, Mississippi. "I went to begin my duties," he wrote in his journal, "dressed myself at the hotel, and with my fiddle under my arm, entered the ball-room. I found my music highly appreciated, and immediately commenced proceedings.

"I placed all the gentlemen in a line reaching across the hall, thinking to give the young ladies time to compose themselves and get ready when they were called. How I toiled before I could get one graceful step or motion! The gentlemen were soon fatigued. The ladies were next placed in the same order and made to walk the steps; and then came the trial for both parties to proceed at the same time, while I pushed one here and another there, and was all the while singing myself, to assist their movements. Many of the parents were present, and were delighted. After this first lesson was over I was requested to *dance to my own music,* which I did until the whole room came down in thunders of applause, in clapping of hands and shouting, which put an end to my first lesson and to an amusing comedy. Lessons in fencing followed to the young gentlemen, and I went to bed extremely fatigued."

After this success, he was asked back on a regular basis, and only once was his position threatened. An itinerant instructor arrived in Woodville and tried to depose Audubon, insulting him behind his back, deriding his pupils, and doing everything possible to undermine him. The women of Woodville preferred Audubon but the men, looking for amusement, tried to fan the quarrel into a duel. Playing on Audubon's short temper, they encouraged him to issue a challenge; but just before he did, one of Audubon's wiser friends realizing that the matter was becoming serious, took it upon himself to talk to the instructor. Audubon, he explained, was the best shot in the area. Why continue to irritate him? The newcomer took the advice, quietly packed his luggage, and slipped away.

Winter, the cold Louisiana winter that rarely freezes but never warms, came and went. The magnolias sprang into blossom, then faded; the cotton came into flower; the white bolls stood on the plants; the field hands picked them and carried

them to the gin; the bales were loaded on the passing steamboats; and the air took on the first cold tinges of fall. The deer
grew new antlers and raced before the huntsmen; the ducks
and geese flew south; and once more winter came, the cold,
damp wind blowing up from the river, the ground dead and
sterile underfoot. All this while, Audubon danced and hunted
and played his violin and added to the small accumulation of
savings he and Lucy were gathering until it amounted to
$1,700. This was enough to take him to Europe and redeem
the pledge he had made to himself more than a year before
in New York.

On April 26, 1826, he kissed Lucy good-bye and, leaving her
and John to the care of Mrs. Percy, went to St. Francisville to
spend the night with John Pope. The next morning he boarded
the steamboat for New Orleans, where he lost no time in purchasing passage to Liverpool on the *Delos,* a ship commanded
by Captain John Hatch from Kennebunk, Maine. Rather than
wait in New Orleans while Captain Hatch finished loading his
cargo of cotton for the mills of England, Audubon used the
time to return to Beech Woods to say good-bye to Lucy again.
Then he went back to New Orleans to collect a few more letters of introduction—one of them was from Vincent Nolte, the
European merchant with whom he had traveled years before—
and on May 17, 1826, boarded the *Delos.*

In his portfolio he had all the material he needed to continue
working for many months. Some of his pictures were finished
and ready for the engraver; some he had once considered
finished but now realized should be done over; some were
merely sketches on which he could base future pictures. In addition, he had his notes on birds because, like Wilson, he hoped
to publish a text to accompany his illustrations.

While he stowed these precious belongings away, the steamboat *Hercules,* which Captain Hatch had engaged as a tug,
maneuvered the *Delos* into the current and turned its bow
down the river, away from Lucy and Bayou Sarah and toward
Audubon's last hope for the future. Ten hours later, it brought
the ship through the pass that formed the channel into the Gulf
of Mexico, cast off its lines, and left the *Delos* to itself in a dead
calm.

The sails flapped in the windless air, the sheets hung slack,

the ship rose and fell on the ocean swell with no forward movement to steady it, and the wheel spun uselessly in the helmsman's hands. Overhead the sun burned ferociously, and under
its heat the ship smelled strongly of tar and hemp and old
cargoes. Almost immediately Audubon became violently seasick. He still remembered enough of the sea, however, to remain on deck, where the fresh air and the straight, firm line of
the horizon quiet a man's stomach. He exercised and even hung
his hammock on the deck, and in no time was feeling well
again and able to enjoy the voyage.

Like any traveler on a long ocean trip, he soon had his particular favorites among the passengers and crew. He liked the
two mates, both of them from Maine, and he became especially
fond of Captain Hatch.

Another particular friend was an Irish passenger, Benjamin
Swift, and in the company of these men Audubon found plenty
to do. After they had been out only a few days, they came upon
a school of dolphins "that glided by the vessel like burnished
gold by day, and bright meteors at night." Captain Hatch and
his mates proved skillful at luring the dolphins alongside the
ship with baited hooks and then spearing them with a five-
pronged fork called a "grain." They also caught a porpoise. "I
had never before examined one of those closely," Audubon
noted, "and the duck-bill-like snout, and the curious disposition of the tail, with the body, were new and interesting matters of observation to me."

All this time, the weather continued calm and the *Delos*
made little progress toward England. By June 4, they had been
at sea three weeks and were not within sight of Cuba. By June
17, they had finally seen the island but then, unable to move,
lay off its shores for long days in the excessive heat. Audubon,
still sleeping on deck where it was cooler, passed the time shooting birds and drawing them, making sketches of the sailors,
and going swimming. Outwardly he was calm and contented;
inwardly he was gnawed by doubts. Describing his feelings in
his journal, he wrote, "My leaving America had for some time
the feelings of a dream; I could scarce make up my mind fixedly
on the subject. I thought continually I still saw my beloved
friends, my dear wife and children. I still felt every morning
when I awoke that the land of America was beneath me, and

that I would in a short time throw myself on the ground in her shady woods, and watch for, and listen to the many lovely warblers. But now that I have positively been at sea since *fifty-one* days, tossing to and fro, without the sight or the touch of those dear to me, I ... look forward with an anxiety such as I never felt before, when I calculate that not less than four months must elapse before my wife and children can receive any tidings of my arrival on the distant shores to which I am bound. When I think that many more months must run from the life's sand-glass allotted to my existence before I can think of returning, and that my reunion with my friends and country is as yet an unfolded and unknown event, I am filled with sudden apprehension which I cannot describe nor dispel."

As Audubon paced the deck thinking these thoughts, the ship, at last free of the great calm, was moving northward. On July 4, it was off the Grand Banks in thick, foggy weather, its sails gray against the gray sky. A few days later, the temperature dropped sharply, "as if," Audubon noted, "we had just turned the summit of a mountain dividing a country south of the equator from Iceland." Onward the ship went, the winds blowing more strongly, and at three o'clock on the morning of July 18, the helmsman, standing his watch at the wheel, sighted Ireland; and finally, on July 20, the *Delos* dropped anchor in the Mersey River. Audubon was at last in Liverpool.

When he first went ashore, timid and lonely in the rain, a heavy blanket of smoke and fog enveloped the city. To Audubon, fresh from the Louisiana countryside, the smoke was oppressive, irritating his lungs and making his eyes smart. With his fellow passenger, Benjamin Swift, he had breakfast at an inn and went immediately to the office of the firm of Gordon and Forstall to see Alexander Gordon, whom he had known so intimately in New Orleans. Gordon was now living in Liverpool and furthermore was married to Lucy's sister, Anne. He was apparently away, however, and Audubon merely left some letters he had brought with him and went to the Liverpool museum, spending several hours there alone. For the next day or so, he busied himself finding lodgings, clearing his books and pictures through customs, visiting with Swift, who was leaving soon for Ireland, and spending much of the money he and

Lucy had saved. Unable to resist the lure of the Liverpool stores, he bought two watches, along with watch chains and seals, for a hundred and twenty pounds, almost a third of all the money he had. One of them he kept for himself; the other he sent to Lucy. Then he went to the firm of Rathbone Bros. & Co. and delivered the letters given him by Vincent Nolte. One of the brothers, William, immediately invited him for dinner on the following Wednesday to meet William Roscoe, an influential historian and botanist who might be able to help him; the other brother, Richard, asked him to have dinner with him that very day.

Between them, the Rathbones made him feel at home. They introduced him to the American consul, showed him around Liverpool, and took him out to the country to meet their father. Then came the important evening when he was to meet Roscoe. Nervously he sat through dinner, trying to keep up a conversation but wondering all the time what Roscoe would say when he saw the pictures. The meal over, Audubon brought out his portfolio. He felt unusually gloomy as he slipped the pictures one by one out of their case and waited for Roscoe's opinion. It came quickly. After seeing only a few of them, Roscoe expressed high admiration for them and invited Audubon to call the following day at his botanical gardens, located about a mile and a half outside of Liverpool.

Thanks largely to the Rathbones' efforts, word of Audubon's arrival had begun to spread across Liverpool. On returning to his lodgings after visiting Roscoe, he found the following note waiting for him: "Mr. Martin, of the Royal Institution of Liverpool, will do himself the pleasure to wait upon Mr. Ambro to-morrow at eleven o'clock." Although annoyed by the misspelling of his name, Audubon was ready when Martin came. A quick look at the pictures led Martin to offer to hold an exhibit for Audubon the following week at the Royal Institution.

Before that date, however, he had dinner with the Alexander Gordons, and Anne, taking one look at his appearance, threw up her hands in horror. Here he was in one of England's major cities with his hair long and flowing, his clothes unfashionable. She suggested that, as quickly as possible, he get a haircut and purchase a more normal coat. Certainly, he could not appear

at the Royal Institution looking like an uncultivated frontiersman. Fortunately Audubon resisted all her common-sense arguments. Either deliberately or by pure intuition, he had assumed, in a stroke of showmanship, the role of an American
woodsman, a role the British would find intriguing.

So the next day, in spite of Anne's scoldings, he appeared at
the Royal Institution with his hair still flowing down over his
shoulders. Promptly at noon the doors were thrown open, and
the viewers, mostly women, came flocking in. For the scheduled
two hours, Audubon talked with them and answered their
questions. Then, tired and worn out, he fled to the country
to visit some of his new friends but was back at the Royal
Institution the next day. Because the exhibit continued to be
successful, Audubon soon found himself lionized in Liverpool
and the center of a social whirl. He visited the Roscoes regularly, and the Roscoe daughters came to the Institution every
day the pictures were on exhibit. He visited the Rathbones and
found himself especially taken by Mrs. William Rathbone. He
also met Lord Stanley, a British statesman with wide interests
and powerful connections, who was so pleased with the pictures that he was soon kneeling on the floor to see them better.

His abrupt success made Audubon feel so confident that on
August 6, only a few weeks after the *Delos* dropped anchor at
Liverpool, he was able to write, "When I arrived in this city, I
felt dejected, miserably so; the uncertainty as to my reception,
my doubts as to how my work would be received, all conspired
to depress me. Now, how different are my sensations! I am well
received everywhere, my works praised and admired, and my
poor heart is at last relieved from the great anxiety that has for
so many years agitated it, for I know now that I have not
worked in vain."

Continuing to bask in his newly found eminence, he went
that afternoon to see Roscoe. The house was filled with Roscoe's relatives, and Audubon quickly found himself the center
of attention. The guests asked him to imitate the calls of wild
birds; they plied him with questions about his adventures in
the American wilderness; and when he returned to his room
that night, he delightedly wrote in his journal, "The *well bred*
society of England is the perfection of manners; such tone of

voice I never heard in America. Indeed, thus far, I have great reason to like England."

He certainly did have reason to. Never in his wildest dreams had he imagined such immediate success as this. In Liverpool he already knew all the best people and was invited to the best houses. With his strange appearance, his descriptions of the American frontier, his ability to make sketches on the spot, which he often did for his friends' amusement, he was a popular figure. More important, his pictures were highly regarded, and people were offering him as much as a guinea an hour for lessons. On the basis of this triumph, he was already making plans for the future. He would go to Manchester, then to Derbyshire to see Lord Stanley again, on to Birmingham, London for three weeks, Edinburgh, back to London, then over to the Continent to visit Paris and Nantes; and to help him in his travels he had, safely tucked away in his room, letters of introduction to some of the most notable people living in Britain, Sir Walter Scott and Maria Edgeworth among them.

But before he did any traveling, he had to give thought to making some money. For all his success, he had not earned a cent in Liverpool, and his supply of capital was dwindling. Roscoe, with unusual sensitivity, realized his predicament and kept advising him to charge admission to the exhibit. Strangely enough, Audubon hesitated to do so. At Philadelphia he had been willing, even glad, to accept an outright gift of a hundred dollars from a man he hardly knew; but in Liverpool, where he was famous—perhaps because he was famous—he found it difficult to take money. Roscoe understood this too and, with great tact, persuaded the committee of the Royal Institution to ask him to charge admission. "This request," Audubon wrote with relief, "must and will, I am sure, take off any discredit attached to the tormented feeling of showing my work for money."

As a special feature for the new exhibit, he began painting a picture of some turkey cocks. He had brought to England enough sketches and drawings of American birds so that he could continue working, sometimes doing additional pictures for his book, sometimes working on entirely fresh pictures which he hoped to sell individually, sometimes painting subjects he found in England. During this period, in spite of all his social engagements, he occasionally painted for as long as fourteen hours a day. But his spirits were high.

Best of all, his exhibit had proved to be a commercial success. By September 9, when a happy, reassured Audubon climbed into the stage for Manchester, the show had netted him about a hundred pounds, and he was feeling so prosperous that he even paid a pound for a seat inside the coach. What is more, the Royal Institution had packed all his pictures for him, thus saving him time and trouble, and had instructed their curator to travel with him to Manchester and set up the exhibit there.

One quick look at Manchester, however, made Audubon decide it was far less agreeable than Liverpool. He was astonished by the smoke, the narrow, crooked lanes, and by the noise, which kept him awake that first night. But his unfavorable impression of the city did not prevent him from setting to work immediately. He first called on the American consul and with his assistance arranged to rent an exhibition room. Then with the help of the Royal Institution's curator, he cleaned it up and put it in order, starting the job at five o'clock in the morning and finishing it at eleven. After that he went out and delivered some of his letters of introduction. Next he hired a man at fifteen shillings a week to watch the door and collect the admissions. This time, after his success at Liverpool, he had no hesitation about making a charge to see his pictures.

As the hour approached for the exhibit to open, however, he began to have misgivings. Manchester itself did not appeal to him, but more important, he did not underestimate the role that the Rathbones and the Roscoes had played in making him known in Liverpool. At Manchester, as he said, "My pictures must depend on their *real* value; in Liverpool I *knew* I was supported by particular friends."

Although the first day's audience was considerably smaller than his expectations, he remained undiscouraged and even wrote Lucy, rather untruthfully, that he was being received as well at Manchester as he had been at Liverpool and, still in a jubilant mood, told her to encourage their son John to begin a collection of drawings himself. The second day showed no improvement; and on the third day he noted that "my exhibition was poorly attended," but added hopefully, "those who came seemed interested."

About a week later, the attendance was still poor. While Audubon happened to be away from the exhibit, one of his Liverpool acquaintances dropped by, talked to the doorkeeper, examined the record book, and realized the exhibition was a failure. He later "told me," Audubon wrote, "he was sorry and annoyed at my want of success, and advised me to go to London or Paris. He depressed me terribly, so that I really felt ill."

Instead of going to one of the larger cities, he paid a short visit to some friends in the country outside Manchester. On his return, he found that the attendance still had not picked up and, instead of making money, he was not even covering his expenses. As he stood in the room contemplating his problem, he overheard two people talking. One said that the exhibit was worth a shilling; the other argued that Audubon was only a hoax and ought to be drummed out of town. By September 28, realizing that the situation was serious, he returned to Liverpool to seek the advice of his friends.

On hearing about his experience, they rallied around to help him draw up a better plan of action. Their first step was to introduce him to a London bookseller named Bohn, who chanced to be in town. Bohn had an immense store, carrying two hundred thousand volumes as his regular stock. What better person could be found to advise Audubon on the publication of his book? Although Bohn had never seen the best pictures, which were still in Manchester, he listened to Audubon's problem and advised him not to waste any more time holding exhibitions. In his opinion, they would not earn money—he had been merely lucky at Liverpool—and would not make him sufficiently famous to interest a publisher. What he should do instead was to go to London, talk to the leading naturalists, engravers, and printers, and attempt to determine the cost of producing the book. Then he should travel to Paris, Brussels and possibly Berlin and do the same. In this way, he would be able to judge when, where, and how the book should be produced. On second thought, however, Bohn advised having it printed in Paris but with two hundred and fifty copies bound in England with an English title page. Thus, to the English-speaking world, it would seem to be an English book. To this suggestion Audubon objected strongly. "No work of mine," he wrote, "shall be other than true metal—if copper, copper, if gold, gold, but not copper gilded." While the first volume was being printed, Bohn told Audubon he should begin corresponding with the leading scientific organizations, issue a prospectus, and publicize the book.

He had some other practical advice to offer. Audubon had planned to make each picture life-size, but Bohn argued against this idea. "Be governed by this fact," he said, according to Audubon's record of their conversation, "that . . . to have your book laid on the table as a pastime or an evening's entertainment, will be the principal use made of it, and that if it needs so much room as to crowd out other things or encumber the table, it will not be purchased by the set of people who are now the very life of the trade. If large public institutions only and a few noblemen purchase it, instead of a thousand copies that may be sold if small, not more than a hundred will find their way out of the shops; the size must be suitable for the *English market* (such was his expression) and ought not to exceed that of double Wilson." In other words, it could be twice the normal size of a book, but not nearly as large as Audubon had planned.

Before deciding definitely what to do next, Audubon thought he needed a rest and went to stay for a few days with the Rathbones in the country. When the time came to return to Manchester, Mrs. Rathbone and her daughter, Hannah, decided to accompany him. It was a clear fall day, and Mrs. Rathbone served lunch as the carriage jolted along. As soon as they reached Manchester, Audubon went directly to his exhibit room and found he had a new problem. His doorkeeper was drunk, so drunk, in fact, that he could not even understand that Audubon was discharging him.

During this second visit to Manchester, Bohn, the bookseller, arrived in town and attended the exhibit. On seeing the pictures, he became so enthusiastic that he retracted his earlier advice. They should, he said, be published life-size after all. Audubon, of course, was elated by this reaction, but instead of going directly to London as Bohn suggested, he took the short vacation he needed and spent it touring Derbyshire with Mrs. Rathbone and Hannah, visiting, among other places, the town where the Bakewells had once lived. Returning to Manchester

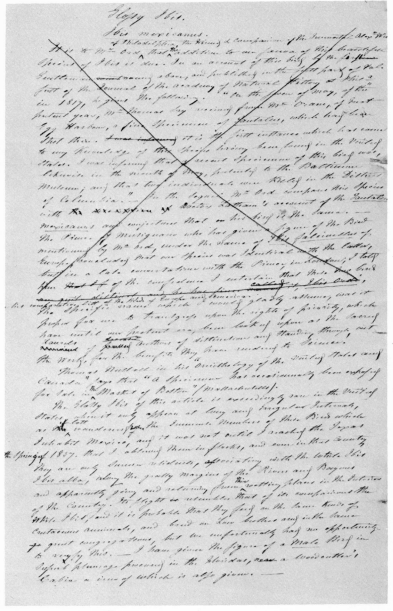

A manuscript page from the *Ornithological Biography*. Although Audubon employed an assistant to edit his material and help him with his grammar and certain scientific material, he was meticulous about preparing his original copy, striking out whole sections that did not satisfy him and making many corrections.

Double-crested Cormorant

PHALACROCORAX DILOPHUS

Double-crested cormorant by Audubon. When Audubon attempted to collect specimens of cormorants in Florida, he found to his surprise that the balls from his gun were unable to penetrate the birds' heavy nests. In order to shoot them, he had to wait until they took to the air.

Portrait of Audubon. This engraving, made after a painting done by John and Victor Audubon, appeared in Duyckinck's *National Portrait Gallery of Distinguished Americans*. It conveys the impression that Audubon attempted to make, particularly in England, of being a rugged outdoorsman who knew the frontier.

Audubon, painted by Victor and John. Audubon's two sons collaborated in this picture of their father. The painting was probably done around 1841 after Audubon had achieved his international reputation as a bird artist.

PANORAMIC VI

New York in 1844 by Havell. After completing the engravings for *Tʰ Birds of America*, Havell moved to the United States. This picture sho

Painting by John Wodehouse Audubon. Although John never attained his father's greatness, he was a competent artist in his own right and did many of the pictures for Audubon's book on animals. This oil painting shows a common meadow vole and a rice-field mouse.

he city at the time of Audubon's return to America and his decision to make his permanent residence in New York, where he lived until his death.

Photograph of Lucy Audubon. After Audubon's death and when the family's fortunes began to decline, Lucy sometimes gave art lessons in order to make a living. She so enthused one of her students, George Bird Grinnell, that he later founded the first Audubon Society for the protection of American birdlife.

Photograph of Audubon by Brady. Although Brady's great fame came during the Civil War, he had been an active photographer for many years before.

Minnie's Land, Audubon's New York home. Here Audubon supervised the production of his small edition of *The Birds of America,* worked on *The Quadrupeds of North America,* and lived out the rest of his days. It was the only house that he had been able to own since his bankruptcy in Kentucky years before.

at the end of the week, he went into a frenzy of activity, paying twenty calls in one day, collecting letters of introduction, and painting. Ever since he had been in England, he had been working on his pictures, adding some new ones like the painting of the turkey cocks that he did for his second exhibit at Liverpool and redoing many of the pictures he already had finished, changing them and improving them.

On October 24, he was ready to leave Manchester but not yet prepared to make an appearance in London. Instead, he had decided to go to Edinburgh, an important intellectual and cultural center but which, being smaller, might prove more friendly. On a clear and beautiful morning, with the comment, "I am leaving Manchester much poorer than I was when I entered it," he boarded the stagecoach.

It was after dark on October 25 when he came to a stop at the Black Bull Hotel in Edinburgh. All Audubon had been able to see were the buildings and streets in the shadows made by the gaslight, but he was already calling Edinburgh a "splendid city." The next day, on George Street, he located an apartment in a house belonging to a woman named Mrs. Dickie. From the window he had a view of the river and the boats plying back and forth, and since the charge was only a guinea a week, which Audubon thought was low, he quickly decided to rent it.

Then he returned to his inn to collect his luggage and ended up in a dispute with the porter he hired. The porter, a man with a tremendous beard, carried the trunk and portfolio to George Street, deposited it in Audubon's apartment, accepted his payment, and left with no argument. But a minute later he was back, holding out a brass shilling which he claimed Audubon had given him. In fact, he was ready to swear that Audubon had. Furious at being caught by such a trick, Audubon grabbed the coin, threw it in the fire, and gave the man another. Then he unpacked, settled his things in his rooms, took out his letters of introduction, and started off on a round of calls.

On the afternoon of October 26, 1827, Audubon, dressed in his western clothes with his hair still flowing down to his shoulders, began his effort to conquer the city of Edinburgh.

CHAPTER XVIII

1826 – 1827

BASED on his previous experience, the odds were against Audubon's being a success in Edinburgh. He had met open hostility in Philadelphia, indifference in New York and Manchester, and success only in Liverpool—one city out of four. At the end of his first afternoon in Edinburgh, it looked as though Liverpool would soon be one out of five. He had called on Professor Robert Jameson, the naturalist: not at home; James Hall, a lawyer: away in the country; Dr. Charles Henry of the Royal Infirmary: not available; another physician, Dr. Thompson: out; Dr. Andrew Duncan of the University of Edinburgh: away until six in the evening.

With his usual persistence, Audubon finally reached Jameson at the university, but the conversation between the two men was short. Although Jameson said he might be able to call on Audubon and see his pictures, he did not have time to do so right away. Audubon also delivered a letter of introduction to Dr. Knox, a distinguished anatomist and surgeon, who left his work and greeted him with bloodstained hands and wearing his surgical coat. Dr. Knox alone said he would try to help but he could do nothing at the moment.

The rest of the day Audubon rambled through the city looking at the sights. To some visitors, Edinburgh remains a gray, colorless, but clean city; to others, with different eyes, it is romantic, gay, and beautiful. Audubon was obviously one of the latter, for he immediately loved the city. Yet this did not prevent him from falling into one of his moods of bleak despair when he returned to the rooms he had rented so happily only a few hours before.

Outside was the handsome view of the Firth; inside every-

thing was arranged comfortably in the taste of that period: a
pair of stuffed pheasants on the buffet, a black haircloth sofa
and chairs, little cherubs on the mantelpiece, and some sweet-
smelling geraniums in pots. Mrs. Dickie had provided the best,
but even his cheerful quarters failed to brighten Audubon's
mood. "I unpacked my birds," he wrote, "and looked at them
with pleasure, and yet with a considerable degree of fear that
they would never be published. I felt one of those terrible attacks of depression to which I so often fall a prey overtaking me,
and I forced myself to go out to destroy the painful gloom that
I dread at all times, and of which I am sometimes absolutely
afraid."

Even the driving rainstorm and the cold wind blowing
through the city did not deter him from taking an early morning walk the following day. He wandered through the New
and Old Towns, visited the market, looked at the monument
to Nelson, and was back in his apartment in time to greet the
Patisons, who were thoughtful friends he had made on the
stagecoach. After they left, he paid two more calls. Still no one
was at home to him. He then visited Patrick Neill, a naturalist and horticulturist who operated a printing business. Neill
greeted him cordially, promised to come to see him, and walked
with him to the street. But that was all he accomplished.

Again the time lay heavy on his hands. To fight back his
loneliness he walked three miles to Leith where he hung
around the docks until the sun dropped below the horizon.
Only then did he dare to go back to his rooms. As he feared,
no letters or messages were waiting for him; no one had responded to his many calls. Unable to stay at Mrs. Dickie's with
nothing to do, he went out once more, browsed at a bookstore
and lost himself in a performance of *Rob Roy*. Afterward, in a
happier mood, he noted in his journal, "I would just as soon
see 'Le Tartuffe' in broken French by a strolling company, as
to see 'Rob Roy' again as I have seen it in Kentucky."

The next day, Saturday, was just as uneventful. No one came
to George Street; no one invited him to dinner; no one was the
least interested in his arrival in Edinburgh. The only mail he
received was a letter from Roscoe saying that Jameson and
Prideaux John Selby, a British ornithologist, were collaborat-

ing on a bird book. Why did not Audubon try to join them? Audubon reacted violently against the suggestion. "My independent spirit," he wrote, "does not turn to the idea with any pleasure, and I think if my work deserves the attention of the public, it must stand on its own legs, not on the reputation of men superior in education and literary acquirements."

Sunday, events took a slight turn for the better. The Patisons dropped around again with more friends; and a few other callers, including Duncan, the university professor, came around. Then Knox, the anatomist, arrived, bringing a friend. After looking at the pictures, Knox said they were the finest of their kind he had ever seen and that he would take it on himself to introduce Audubon to some of the scientists of Edinburgh. At least this was encouraging, but when Audubon went to call on the prominent critic and essayist Lord Francis Jeffrey, he was disappointed to find him out.

Increasingly, it became apparent that he was failing in Edinburgh as he had failed everywhere else except in Liverpool. The trickle of visitors to his rooms was inconsequential; and aside from Knox, they could not, or would not, help. But Audubon, unwilling to admit defeat, decided to remain a little longer.

On Monday he received the promised visit from Neill, the naturalist who ran the printing shop. Neill looked at the pictures, admired them, and offered Audubon the first practical advice he had received so far. The person to see, Neill said, was W. H. Lizars, the noted Scotch engraver who was doing the plates for the bird book by Jameson and Selby. Lizars knew how to produce illustrated books; he also had influence in Edinburgh. Moreover, Neill saw no point in wasting further time. They would go see Lizars immediately. Lizars listened as Neill described the pictures and agreed to go back to George Street with the two men and look at them himself. Knowing that this was a critical moment, Audubon worried every step of the way, and by the time the three men had reached his rooms he had entirely lost his confidence. He drew up one of the black haircloth chairs for each guest, brought out his portfolio, slowly unbuckled it, and with his "heart like a stone," to use his own words, held up one of his drawings. The effect on

Lizars was instantaneous. He leapt from his chair and explained that he had never seen anything like this before. Picture after picture delighted and astonished him, particularly a picture of some mockingbirds and a rattlesnake.

At last, after days of fruitless waiting, Audubon had found an influential friend. In a short time, at Lizars's urging, the visitors began to come. Jameson, the professor who had spoken to Audubon so coolly five days before, arrived. Lizars had him by the arm. Lizars invited Audubon to his house that night, Jameson invited him for breakfast the next morning. Dr. Thompson's sons knocked, offered their father's apologies for not seeing Audubon earlier, and invited him to breakfast on Thursday. Outside, the cold wind was driving the rain against the gray buildings, pools of water collected in the streets and on the castle's pavements, water fell in sheets from the gutters, and the wind whistled around the chimney pots; but Audubon was gay. He put on his coat and walked outside. Even in a storm, he wrote, Edinburgh "is surprisingly beautiful, picturesque, romantic." The tide had turned at last. How much it had turned is reflected in Audubon's comments after his breakfast with Jameson, who had at first been so indifferent to him. Jameson, Audubon wrote, "is no more the man I took him to be when I first met him. He showed me an uncommon degree of cordiality, and promised me his powerful assistance so forcibly that I am sure I can depend on him." And so it worked out. By noon the same day, Jameson was back at George Street with several friends. Until four o'clock in the afternoon, he made Audubon show them one picture after another. When he left, Audubon went out for another walk and dropped by to see Lizars, whose enthusiasm was growing greater and greater.

The next day Lizars was back at Audubon's lodgings, bringing with him Mrs. Lizars and some friends to look at the remainder of the pictures. He had liked the mockingbirds and the rattlesnake, but when he saw the turkeys—the cock, the hen and the brood of young—he decided that was the best. No, on second thought, he preferred the hawk pouncing on the seventeen partridges. That was the one he wanted to engrave. Yet there was also the whooping crane eating the newly born alligators. But when he saw the duck hawks with bloody tatters of meat in their beaks and the cruel looks in their eyes, he was silent for a moment. Then he announced formally to the room that he would definitely engrave and publish that picture.

Too many people were present for Lizars and Audubon to discuss the engraver's proposal, so at five o'clock Audubon went to Lizars's house, where Lizars repeated his offer to engrave the duck hawks and added that he wanted to promote Audubon's work. Unlike Bohn, the bookseller, he suggested having an exhibit; and when he learned that Audubon had letters commenting favorably on his exhibits in Liverpool and Manchester, he made Audubon get the letters and took him to see Jameson. Jameson agreed to arrange a similar exhibit in Edinburgh; and that night when Audubon went to bed, he thought of the future with some serenity. "Wealth," he wrote in his journal, "I do not crave, but comfort." Not since Henderson had he been able to dream that someday he would again find even comfort.

Lizars was the magician who worked the change. Almost as though he had raised a floodgate, the visitors thronged to Audubon's rooms. Arrangements were made to have John Symes, the portrait painter, do Audubon's picture for Lizars to engrave and distribute abroad. Presents of pears and apples appeared in his apartment. He received invitations to dinner. The Royal Institution invited him to hold an exhibit in their building. Wilson of the influential *Blackwood's Magazine* made a friendly visit. Even the famous phrenologist George Combe came to call. He desperately wanted to make a plaster cast of Audubon's head.

In spite of all these attentions, including the favorable notice he was receiving in the papers, Audubon suddenly plunged into one of his fits of gloom. For two weeks, while the gay life of Edinburgh whirled around him, he was lonely, dispirited, and melancholy. During this period, he failed to write in his journal, and on November 19, 1826, when he picked it up again, he said, "I do not know when I have thus pitilessly put away my journal for almost two weeks. My head and heart would not permit me to write, so I must try to *memorandum* now all I have seen. What I have *felt* is too much for me to write down, for when these attacks of depression overwhelm me life is almost unendurable." The cause of his emotional state was simply this: Lizars had decided not to publish just a single picture, but to undertake the first five plates of Audubon's projected book. In fact, he was already at work on two pictures, and that, wrote Audubon, "was enough to put all my powers of acting and thinking at fever heat. . . . I felt bewildered with alternate uncertainties of hope and fear."

Under their agreement, Lizars, in effect, was extending credit to Audubon to cover the cost of publication. When the first five plates, comprising a "number," came off the press, Audubon was to sell them and repay Lizars from the proceeds. But it was not the financial risk that concerned him; it was the final trial of the dream he had nurtured since 1820. Until the first number was published, he could continue exhibiting pictures and hoping for the future. If he was rejected by Manchester, he could go to Edinburgh; if Edinburgh rejected him, he could go to Glasgow; if Glasgow did not want him, he could try London. Even if one exhibit after another proved to be a failure, with no Liverpool to relieve the strain, total defeat would come slowly and be represented only by an accumulation of smaller failures. But once the first number was published, he would know definitely whether his book had a chance of success. Lizars's decision to produce it was exactly what Audubon wanted but, paradoxically, it destroyed his last emotional defense.

The decision also meant a considerable change in his plans, because he did not dare leave Edinburgh before the prints were completed. In those days before the discovery of photographic processes, the engraver was not compelled mechanically to follow the original. Working entirely by hand, he could, if he wished, add a line here, drop a line there, thus improving the original or making it worse. The colorists, too, worked by hand; and there was no mechanical means of controlling them either, no way of assuring their continued performance even after the initial standards were established. Under these circumstances, even with Lizars doing the work, Audubon had good reason to stay at Edinburgh and make certain that his pictures were reproduced exactly the way he wanted them to be.

On November 24, 1826, he outlined his new plans in his journal. He intended "to publish one number [a collection of five pictures] at my own expense and risk, and with it under my arm, make my way. If I can procure three hundred good substantial names of persons or associations or institutions, I cannot fail doing well for my family; but, to do this, I must abandon my life to its success, and undergo many sad perplexities, and perhaps never again—certainly not for some years —see my beloved America. The work, from what I have seen of Mr. Lizars's execution, will be equal to anything in the world at present, and of the rest the world must judge for itself. I shall superintend both engraving and coloring personally, and I pray my courage will not fail; my industry, I know, will not."

Then, being far more realistic about business matters than he had been in the days when he considered himself a businessman, he discussed the price he would have to charge. "It is true," he went on, "the work will be procured only at great expense, but then, a number of years must elapse before it is completed, so that renders the payment an easier task. This," he added, summing up his thoughts, "is what I will *try;* if I do not succeed I can return to my woods and there in peace and quiet live and die. I am sorry that some of my friends, particularly Dr. Traill [another of his Liverpool friends], are against the pictures being the size of life, and I must acknowledge it renders the work rather bulky, but my heart was always bent on it, and I cannot refrain from attempting it."

This was an astonishingly shrewd and practical analysis of his problem and showed the effect of Lizars's teaching, for he recognized that the price he would have to charge limited his potential market but that he would, in effect, be selling the book on the installment plan. Also, deciding once and for all to make the pictures life-size, he was taking a calculated risk but one that might be essential. Although he did not say so, Wilson's book was now well known in England. To overcome the competitive advantage it enjoyed as a result of being first, he had to do more than merely add a few more birds; he had to bring out a work that was much more spectacular. To achieve this goal, the larger size was important. Even if it made the book bulky, it would show his pictures to better advantage. He also discussed with Lizars the printed text that would accompany the pictures, because, like Wilson, he wanted to produce a book that not only portrayed the birds but also told about them. Lizars advised him to publish the text separately. To secure a British copyright, he would have to deposit eleven free copies at the Stationer's Office. By separating the inexpensive, easily pirated printed material from the costly, hand-colored illustrations, he could save considerable money and still secure the protection he needed.

Lizars was also taking a firm hand in other arrangements. For the portrait he wanted for publicity purposes, he insisted on Audubon's wearing a wolf-skin coat, not the dress of an English gentleman. Contrary to Anne, he realized that Audubon would attract attention as an American woodsman. He also hired another artist to finish the sky in a picture Audubon was painting. His purpose was not only to help Audubon with his technique and to hurry the work along; he wanted to show him that the engravers did not need a completely finished picture. As long as Audubon gave them the central figures of the birds and the general composition, they could add the minor details in the backgrounds. In short, Lizars was giving Audubon an intensive course in the practical aspects of book publishing.

And Audubon was learning quickly. He was painting more intensely than he had ever painted before, understanding now that practically every picture had to be done over and that he had to keep working on new pictures. He was also realizing more than ever the value of publicity and, as a consequence, let himself be swept up in a whirl of activity. He agreed to have a cast of his head made for the use of the phrenologist George Combe. He discussed a possible article on turkey buzzards with the editor of *Jameson's Philosophical Review,* became involved in trying to recover one of his paintings which had been stolen from the exhibit (the case was solved when the thief, after a warrant had been sworn out, returned it anonymously), read the announcements of his book which were beginning to appear, delivered several papers before scientific groups, applied for admittance to the Royal Academy, did a picture of two house cats fighting over a dead squirrel, received the promise of a subscription from the University of Edinburgh, dined out regularly, met most of the consequential people in Edinburgh, and, although he sometimes complained of being tired, enjoyed himself immensely.

By December 21 he had so recovered from his earlier depression that he was able to write Lucy a jubilant letter. "My situation in Edinburgh," he wrote her, "borders almost on the miraculous. Without education and scarce one of those qualities necessary to render a man able to pass through the throng of the learned here, I am positively looked on by all the professors and many of the principal persons here as a very extraordinary man," and added proudly, "What different times I see here, courted as I am, from those I spent at Beech Woods."

He also discussed the practical aspects of what he was doing. "It will now be a month," he wrote, "since my work has been begun by Mr. W. H. Lizars of this city. It is to come out in numbers of five prints, all the size of life and on the same size paper as my largest drawings—it is called double elephant. They will be brought up and finished in such superb style as to eclipse all others in existence. The price of each number is two guineas, and all individuals have the privilege of subscribing for the whole or any portion of it. Two of the plates were finished last week. Some of the engravings, colored, are now up in my exhibition rooms and are truly beautiful. I think that by the middle of January the first number will be completed and under way to each subscriber. I shall send thee the very first, and I think it will please thee. It consists of the male turkey, the cuckoos in the pawpaws, and three little drawings that I doubt thou dost remember, but when thou seest them, I am quite sure thou wilt. The little drawings in the center of those beautiful large sheets have a fine effect and an air of richness and wealth that cannot help insure success in this country. I cannot yet say," he added a little more soberly, "that I will ultimately succeed, but at present all bears a better prospect than I ever expected to see. I think this under the eyes of the most discerning people in the world—I mean, Edinburgh.

"If it takes here, it cannot fail anywhere. It is not the naturalist that I wish to please altogether, I assure thee. It is the wealthy part of the community. The first can only speak well or ill of me, but the latter will fill my pockets. The Univeristy of Edinburgh having subscribed, I look to the rest of them—

eleven in number—to follow. I have here strong friends, who interest themselves considerably in my success ... but I cannot do wonders at once, I must wait patiently until the first number is finished and exhibit that, for although my drawings are much admired, if the work itself is inferior, nothing can be done; and until I have it, I cannot expect many subscribers. As soon as it is finished, I will travel with it over all England, Ireland, and Scotland, and then over the European Continent, taking my collection with me and exhibiting it in all the principal cities."

Turning to the future, he went on, "In the event of ultimate success, I must have either my son or some other person to travel for me to see about the collection of payments for the work and to procure new subscribers constantly. As I conceive my Victor a well fit man for such business, and as it would afford him the means of receiving a most complete education and a knowledge of Europe surpassing that of probably any other man, in case of success, I will write for him immediately, when I hope no more constraint or opposition will be made to my will." The last few words, appended to his optimistic plans for the future, contained a note of bitterness. Audubon and Lucy were again having differences.

Ever since he had been in Great Britain, he had counted the mails coming from America and frequently complained, just as he had done in New Orleans, about Lucy's failure to write. Sometimes, he noted, a ship would make the round-trip passage between the two continents without his hearing a word from her; sometimes, he said, he would write to a man in the United States and obtain an answer to his letter without receiving a single word from her in the meanwhile. Clearly, she was busy and preoccupied at Beech Woods and had neither the time nor the inclination to write frequently, but what really bothered Audubon was her unwillingness to discuss with him any joint plans for the future. He wanted her to think about coming to England; she refused to give the idea the slightest consideration. He wanted to work out a program whereby someday they could be together again; she was content to remain right where she was at Beech Woods.

On that December day in Edinburgh, he went on plaintively,

"I am now better aware of the advantages of a family in unison than ever, and I am quite satisfied that, by acting conjointly and by my advice, we can realize a handsome fortune for each of us. It needs but industry and perserverence. . . . It is now about time to know from thee what thy future intentions are. I wish thee to act according to thy dictates but wish to know what those dictates are. Think that we are far divided and that either sickness or need may throw one into a most shocking situation without either friend or help, for as thou sayest thyself, 'The world is not indulgent.' Cannot we move together and feel and enjoy the natural need of each other. Lucy, my friend, think of all this very seriously. Not a portion of the earth exists but will support us amply, and we may feel happiness anywhere, if careful. When you receive this, sit and consider well. Consult N. Berthoud, thy son, Victor, or such a person as Judge Matthews. Then consult thyself, and in a long, plain, explanatory letter, give me thy own heart entire."

While he waited for an answer from Lucy, he continued the busy schedule that might, in time, lead to his return to America. He gave drawing lessons to Sir William Jardine and to Selby, trying to help them with their pictures of birds. He went out so often that on many days he changed his clothes at least three times, wearing not his old frontier dress, but stockings and pumps and finely tailored jackets and trousers, or, as he put it, "all the finery with which I made a popinjay of myself in my youth." Every morning he shaved carefully; but, as he told Lucy, his hair was still long and curly and, with a shrewd appraisal of his own showmanship, he noted that it did as much for him as his skill at painting. All this activity—and almost all of it was necessary—placed tremendous pressure on his time. He could permit himself only four hours of sleep at night and finally hired a painter to help him with some of his detail work. Even with this assistance, he was falling behind schedule as the year 1826 came to a close. On December 23 he noted in his journal, "I had to grind up my own colors this morning; I detest it, it makes me hot, fretful, moody, and I am convinced has a bad effect on my mind. However, I worked closely, but the day was shockingly short." On Christmas Day he woke with a bad headache which disappeared only after a long walk; and the following day his extreme fatigue caused him to write, "My steady painting, my many thoughts, and my brief nights bring on me now every evening a weariness that I cannot surmount or command. This is, I think, the first time in my life when, *if needed,* I could not rouse myself from sleepiness, shake myself and be ready for action in an instant; but now I cannot do that, and I have difficulty often in keeping awake as evening comes on." That night he was so exhausted that he suddenly excused himself from a dinner party he was attending, went back to his room, and without undressing, fell asleep on the sofa. Around midnight he woke up, cold and hungry, ate some food, and then forced himself to lie down again, because he wanted to be rested the following day. He had been invited to stay with Earl Morton; and Earl Morton, former Chamberlain to Queen Charlotte, was a person whom he wanted to impress.

Promptly at one o'clock, the Earl's coach rolled down George Street and stopped at Mrs. Dickie's front door. Audubon was waiting, his portfolio and valise already packed. Preceding the servant down the stairs and into the street, he put his foot gracefully on the step of the handsome coach standing by the curb, swung himself inside, and settled back on the purple morocco seat. Down George Street the coach went, the fine horses arching their necks, the coachman and footman remaining aloof above the crowds of ordinary people, past the castle, through Charlotte Square, and onto the Glasgow Road. For eight miles, Audubon rode in elegance, enjoying every minute of it but, like a schoolgirl at her first dance, torn between the two extremes of delight and fear. Lady Morton he already knew and liked, but what would the Earl be like? As he wondered, the carriage turned off the road and up a drive, raced around a great circle, and stopped in front of a large, turreted building, ornamented with stone lions and Lord Morton's heraldry. A liveried servant opened the door; Audubon handed him his gloves, hat and sword cane (carrying a sword cane had become one of his affectations), and went up the stairway into a large drawing room which was decorated with pictures by Rembrandt, Van Dyke, Claude Lorraine, and Titian. The tables, Audubon noticed as the Lady Morton came forward to greet him, were covered with books and drawings, and a telescope stood at one end of the room. Then Audubon was introduced to the Earl. To his surprise, instead of the immense, imposing man he had expected, the Earl was small, slender, and decrepit, so weak that he was barely able to stand alone, so sick he could hardly speak, and so emotional that he welcomed Audubon with tears in his eyes. Then, unable to remain on his feet any longer, he sank back into his chair.

At lunch, to which the Earl was pushed in a wheelchair, Audubon met two other guests; and afterward the entire company returned to the drawing room, where Audubon unbuckled his portfolio and exhibited his pictures one by one. Everyone was awed by the beauty of the birds, Audubon's composition, and his masterful handling of color; and Lady Morton complimented him by asking him to give her a lesson. When the group broke up, Audubon went for a walk, returning in time to dress for dinner. The meal, he noted, was served by four men who "were powdered and dressed in deep red, almost maroon liveries, except the butler, who was in black, and who appeared to me to hand fresh plates continuously."

Up early, Audubon walked into the drawing room the next morning and surprised the maids, who were busily at work doing the cleaning. Rather than upset the household routine, he went out for a walk, looking at the spacious grounds, the beautiful Abyssinian horses, the gamekeeper with his dogs, the hothouses filled with roses, and all the other appurtenances of a wealthy estate. After breakfast, he gave Lady Morton the lesson he had promised, and she, in turn, entered a subscription for his book. She offered to pay in advance for the first number, but Audubon, for the time being, was beyond the need for such help and was pleased that he could decline. Before long the coach was again at the door, Audubon's portfolio and valise were brought out, and, saying good-bye to his new friends, he was on his way back to Edinburgh. His first overnight visit at the home of a British nobleman had been a complete success.

His next formal party, however, was not. One of his close

friends in Edinburgh was Captain Basil Hall, a former naval officer who had served as a midshipman on the British frigate *Leander* when its attack on American shipping off Staten Island forced Audubon's ship to enter New York by way of Long Island Sound. Hall had arranged a dinner on New Year's Eve at which Audubon could meet Francis Jeffrey, a man of letters and a regular contributor to the powerful *Edinburgh Review*. Although Audubon had shown himself adept at the social graces —he could wander with ease and grace through the most distinguished circles in Edinburgh—he still retained, underneath it all, the same sharpness of temper, the same resentment of a snub, that he had always had; and by his terms he had been insulted by Jeffrey. When he had first arrived in Edinburgh, he had called on Jeffrey; Jeffrey had never returned the call. He had sent him a free card of admittance to the exhibit of his pictures; Jeffrey had not used it. Therefore, as far as Audubon was concerned, "He never came near me, and I never went near him; for if *he* was Jeffrey, *I* was Audubon, and felt quite independent of all the tribe of Jeffreys in England, Scotland, and Ireland, put together." Basil Hall, good-natured, gregarious, and open-minded, was attempting the impossible when he brought the two men together.

Audubon was the first guest to arrive; Jeffrey and his wife, the last. Jeffrey, Audubon said, "was a small man with a woman under one arm and a hat under the other. . . . He bowed very seriously, so much so that I conceived him to be fully aware of his weight in society. His looks were shrewd, but I thought his eyes almost cunning. He talked a great deal and very well, but I did not like him; . . . Mrs. Jeffrey was nervous and very much dressed. If I mistake not, Jeffrey was shy of me, and I of him, for he has used me very cavalierly." In order to give Audubon a chance to talk, Hall repeatedly mentioned the United States; Jeffrey kept turning the conversation away from the subject. After dinner, Hall asked Audubon about his work. Audubon answered as briefly as possible and at ten o'clock rose and said good night, although it was New Year's Eve.

The change in the calendar brought no change in his daily routine. Aside from starting a new journal book, the early months of 1827 were, for Audubon, like the last months of 1826, a continual effort to meet more people and to become better known, to finish more pictures, sell more subscriptions to his book, and when the first number came out, to be ready to travel to London, a city which would inevitably have a critical effect on the outcome of his entire effort.

He attended the meetings of the Society of Arts and, for the first time in public, demonstrated how he mounted his birds on wires so that he could draw them. He read a paper on alligators to the Wernerian Society and had a plaster cast taken of his face. He was elected an associate member of the Society of Scottish Artists and, in return, painted for them a picture of a black cock. And on January 22 he realized a great ambition. He at last met Sir Walter Scott.

Scott's position was unique. He was not only one of the most widely read authors of his day, one who had introduced many modern concepts into the art of storytelling; he was also a man of unusual personal qualities, unassuming, dignified, and honorable—in his time, a figure of international consequence and a hero to millions.

Captain Hall, who had befriended Audubon in so many ways, arranged the meeting. He arrived at George Street one morning and announced that Scott would see Audubon right away. Together they went to Scott's house; and that evening Audubon wrote in his journal, "My eyes feasted on his countenance. I watched his movements as I would those of a celestial being; his long, heavy, white eyebrows struck me forcibly. His little room was tidy, though it partook a good deal of the character of a laboratory. He was wrapped in a quilted morning-gown of light purple silk; he had been at work writing on the 'Life of Napoleon.' He writes close lines, rather curved as they go from left to right, and puts an immense deal on very little paper. After a few minutes had elapsed he begged Captain Hall to ring a bell; a servant came and was asked to bid Miss Scott to see Mr. Audubon. Miss Scott came, black-haired and black-dressed, not handsome but said to be highly accomplished, and she is the daughter of Sir Walter Scott. There was much conversation. I talked little, but, believe me, I listened and observed, careful if ignorant."

Scott's own account of the meeting shows the impression Audubon created in Europe when he played the role of an American woodsman. He had studied ornithology, Scott wrote, "by many a long wandering in the American forests. He is an American by naturalization, a Frenchman by birth, but less of a Frenchman than I have ever seen,—no dash, no glimmer or shine about him, but great simplicity of manners and behaviour; slight in person and plainly dressed; wears long hair, which time has not yet tinged; his countenance acute, handsome, and interesting, but still simplicity is the predominant characteristic."

Two days later, at Scott's request, Audubon called again, bringing with him his portfolio of pictures. Scott remarked on them favorably and later wrote, "This sojourner of the desert had been in the woods for months together. He preferred associating with the Indians to the company of the settlers; very justly, I dare say, for a civilized man of the lower order—when thrust back on the savage state—becomes worse than a savage." Scott's phrases, such as "sojourner of the desert," "many a long wandering in the American forests," and "great simplicity," explain much of Audubon's appeal abroad, how he fitted himself neatly into the Old World's preconceived and romantic notions of the New. Like many another artist, he sensed intuitively that by selling himself, he could better sell his work; and in searching around for a means, he found one at hand in his own past experiences and Europe's emotional involvement with what it imagined to be the frontier. Adroitly Audubon played on his knowledge of the West, adding a touch here and a highlight there. His trips on the rivers assumed almost the proportions of explorations; his casual meeting with Daniel Boone imperceptibly grew into a warm friendship. To every man belongs the right to alter somewhat his own past, and in Audubon's case, these subtle changes helped to sell his pictures.

But during those Edinburgh days, he was not only trying to publicize his art, he was also trying to perfect it. He had great talent, obviously, but essentially he was untrained. Most of what he knew, he had taught himself, slowly and haphazardly at first, then, as art became the center of his life, seriously and with concentration, looking at the work of other artists and talking with them about their techniques. Indeed, he had already developed his own philosophy of art, and he stated it clearly, although indirectly, in his criticism of other painters in Edinburgh. For example, at the Royal Institution, he studied a painting of the death of a stag by Landseer. "I saw much in it of the style of those men who know how to handle a brush and carry a good effect," he wrote, "but nature was not there, although a stag, three dogs, and a Highlander were introduced on the canvas. The stag had his tongue out and his mouth shut! The principal dog, a greyhound, held the deer by one ear just as if a loving friend; the young hunter had laced the deer by one horn very prettily, and in the attitude of a ballet dancer was about to cast the noose over the head of the animal. To me, or to my friends [in Kentucky] ... such a picture is quite a farce; not so here however." Although personally a romantic, as an artist Audubon was a realist. His aim was to represent his world as he actually saw it.

There was nothing lazy about his effort. He drove himself continually; and although he was dissatisfied with Landseer's picture, he was not at all content with a picture of his own hanging in the same exhibit. "I know well," he wrote, "that the birds are drawn as well as any birds ever have been; but what a difference exists between drawing one bird or a dozen and amalgamating them with a sky, a landscape, and a well adapted foreground. Who has not felt a sense of fear while trying to combine all this?" Only a few weeks earlier, he had made a similar comment. "My painting," he wrote of the picture he was currently doing, "has now arrived at the difficult point. To finish highly without destroying the general effect, or to give the general effect and care not about the finishing? I am quite puzzled. Sometimes I like the picture, then a heat rises to my face and I think it is a miserable daub. This is the largest piece I have ever done; as to the birds, as far as *they* are concerned, I am quite satisfied, but the ground, the foliage, the sky, the distance are dreadful. Today I was so troubled about this that at two o'clock, when yet a good hour of daylight remained, I left it in disgust...."

In his development as an artist, he had at first concentrated

on individual birds, attempting to capture their color and shape
as accurately as possible. As long as he did this, he was competing on an equal basis with Wilson and other ornithologists.
The next step was to achieve the naturalism that he thought
Landseer lacked, to make his birds real, not merely feather by
feather and color by color, but also in their postures and motions. The last, and most important, stage was to create, not
just a picture of birds, but an entire picture, taking each realistic detail and making it contribute to the whole effect. He
was striving for more than scientific accuracy; he was striving
to create art out of scientific elements. This concept carried
him far beyond his time and made him more closely related to
the spirit of the middle twentieth century than to the art of
his own contemporaries like Landseer, whose objective was to
make the romantic even more romantic.

Yet his concentration on general aims did not cause him to
neglect the techniques necessary to attain them. Toward the
end of January, he was puzzling over his colors and wrote in
his journal, "A man may do a good deal of painting in eight
hours provided he has the power of laying on the true tints
at once, and does not muddy his colors or need glazing afterwards. Now a query arises. Did the ancient artists and colorists
ever glaze their works? I sometimes think they did not, and
I am inclined to think thus because their work is of great
strength of standing—a proof with me that they painted clean
and bright at once, but that this *once* they repeated, perhaps, as
often as three times. Glazing certainly is a beautiful way of
effecting transparency, particularly over shadowy parts, but I
frequently fear the coating being too thin, and that time preys
on those parts more powerfully than on those unglazed, so that
the work is sooner destroyed by its application than without it.
I am confident that Sir Joshua Reynolds's pictures fade so much
in consequence of his constant glazing."

This concern with techniques and composition made him
anxious to meet and talk with other artists. Consequently, when
Joseph B. Kidd, who at nineteen had already obtained something of a reputation as a landscape artist, came to call, Audubon received him warmly. The two men conversed at great

length, and Audubon invited Kidd to come to his apartment every day for meals and to help him with his painting. As a man, he was foolishly proud; as an artist, he was humble enough to seek assistance.

While January passed into February and February turned into March, Audubon remained in Edinburgh. He met more of the city's famous men; he delivered more scientific papers, including one on passenger pigeons; he watched Lizars and his staff at work; and he kept on painting like a man possessed with the idea of making up for a lost lifetime.

And one by one he received from Lizars the five prints that would make up the first number of his book. First, not the duck hawks as Lizars had originally suggested, but the wild turkey cock. Next the yellow-billed cuckoo. Then the prothonotary warbler, the purple finch, and finally the Canada warbler— five different birds, each done life-size, each printed on a sheet of paper large enough to contain a full-scale picture of the biggest American birds. Wilson's pictures were good; these were magnificent. Wilson's book was small enough to fit on a bookshelf; this book was so enormous it could be placed only on a table. Looking at the sheets, Audubon, although questioning his ability to sell subscriptions, was content and ready, at the age of forty-one, to leave for London with the first number. His friends, however, were not yet willing to let him go.

Before he went, they insisted that he absolutely must cut his hair. His long curls had, as he believed, helped him when he first arrived in Edinburgh, but ever since then had been growing longer and longer, while he himself had been reverting to the stylish dressing habits of his youth and gaining a reputation as a serious artist and scientist. His flowing locks, therefore, were becoming increasingly incongruous. Yet on the subject of his hair, Audubon was incredibly vain and refused either to cut it or trim it. His friends formed a conspiracy. They called on him, they wrote him notes, they did everything possible to make him abandon this posturing; until finally, on March 19, 1827, he yielded to their entreaties, called in the barber and ordered him to cut away.

When the ordeal was over, he sat down at his table, took out his journal, and selected a fresh, blank page. Carefully, he drew an inch-thick black band of mourning in the form of a rectangle, and in the center, he wrote:

Edinburgh
March 19th, 1827

This day my hair was sacrificed, and the will of God usurped by the wishes of man. As the barber clipped my locks rapidly, it reminded me of the horrible times of the French Revolution when the same operation was performed upon all the victims murdered at the guillotine; my heart sank low.

At the bottom he signed his name with his usual flourishes, JOHN JAMES AUDUBON.

He was now ready to move on to London.

CHAPTER XIX

1827

ON April 5, 1827, with the sun shining and the first touches of spring warming the cold hills of Scotland, Audubon boarded the stagecoach and started on his trip to London. The first number of the book was out. Now he faced the supreme trial: could he obtain enough subscribers to make it profitable?

Only a few weeks before, he had told Lucy that he was sending her a copy of the first number along with some prospectuses and asked her to make arrangements to solicit the two leading libraries in New Orleans. He warned her, however, against selling subscriptions to people whose credit was not good. Indeed, he continued, he might limit the book's distribution to Great Britain where the subscribers would be geographically concentrated, thus keeping to a minimum the amount of traveling time necessary to reach them. With Victor's help, he thought—he was returning to the idea of having Victor come to Europe as his assistant—he could settle down in one of the large cities without letting the job of collecting his bills interfere with his painting.

On his way he stopped at Belford in Northumberland and stayed with the ornithologist Selby, and then visited Selby's brother-in-law, Captain Mitford, who lived at Mitford Castle near Northumberland, but that, for a time, ended the social aspects of his journey. Instead of going to London directly, he had decided to solicit subscriptions and, for this purpose, went to Newcastle.

At first sight the city, with its shabby appearance and smoky atmosphere, reminded him of Manchester, but he did not let this deter him from going to work. By now he had an established method for making himself known. First, he rented a suitable room; second, he delivered his letters of introduction as quickly as possible; finally, he waited in his lodgings for visitors to appear so that he could talk to them and show them his pictures. However much Newcastle may have looked like Manchester, the reception it gave Audubon was quite different. He soon was receiving calls from men like John Adamson, the secretary of the Literary and Philosophical Society, and an invitation to have tea with Thomas Bewick, whose woodcuts were world-famous.

Bewick, he wrote, "welcomed me with a hearty shake of the hand, and took off for a moment his half-clean cotton nightcap tinged with the smoke of the place. He is tall, stout, has a very large head, and his eyes are further apart than those of any man I remember just now. A complete Englishman, full of life and energy though now seventy-four, very witty and clever, better acquainted with America than most of his countrymen, and an honor to England." Bewick showed Audubon "the work he was at, a small vignette cut on a block of box-wood not more than three by two inches, representing a dog frightened during the night by the false appearances of men formed by curious roots and branches of trees, rocks, etc. The old gentleman and I stuck to each other; he talked of my drawings, and I of his woodcuts, till we liked each other very much. Now and then he would take off his cotton cap, but the moment he became animated with the conversation the cap was on, yet almost off, for he had stuck it on as if by magic. His eyes sparkled, his face was very expressive, and I enjoyed him much more, I am sure, than he supposed."

After tea and coffee, Bewick's son, Robert, brought out a new type of bagpipe and played Scotch and English airs, while Bewick himself produced a copy of his book on animals as a present for Audubon to send to his family. Soon after ten the party broke up, and Audubon walked back to Newcastle through the deserted, crooked streets, sure that he had made another friend.

For thirteen more days, he remained in the city. Bewick came to see his pictures and admired them as did many others who arrived at Audubon's inn. Some visitors were cordial like Adamson, who arranged to have a special seat reserved for Audubon at St. Nicholas Church and treated him with every consideration. Others, however, were not so courteous. When callers arrived at his room, he would unstrap his portfolio, hold up his pictures one by one, answer his visitors' questions, and hope that before they went out they would enter their names in his subscription book. It was the best method available to him, although it was physically tiring, nerve-racking, and left him open to insults. For example, a girl and her brother arrived, spurred and booted and whips in their hands, while their groom remained outside walking their fine horses. Arrogantly and with hardly a word to Audubon, the girl pre-empted the best seat in the room for herself and sat down. The brother took his place beside her and insolently fired one question after another without regard for the other people in the room. Then, having taken up Audubon's time and attention, the girl and her brother rose and stalked out together without expressing any interest in the pictures or any appreciation for Audubon's hospitality.

In spite of such unpleasant episodes and the difficulties involved in showing his pictures individually to strangers, Audubon secured several new subscribers. Best of all, he had gained the friendship of Bewick, whom he went to see again, writing afterward that "the old man set to work to show me how simple it was to *cut wood!* But cutting wood as he did is no joke; he did it with as much ease as I can feather a bird; he made all his tools, which are delicate and very beautiful, and his artist shop was clean and attractive." Before Audubon left Newcastle, Bewick performed a particularly gracious act. Audubon went to take tea with him. "The old gentleman," he said, "was seated as usual with his night-cap on, and his tobacco pouch in one hand ready to open; his countenance beamed with pleasure as I shook hands with him. 'I could not bear the idea of your going off without telling you in written words what I think of your "Birds of America"; here it is in black and white, and make whatever use you may of it, if it be of use at all,' he said, and put an unsealed letter in my hand."

With this gesture of Bewick's still fresh in his mind, Audubon took the coach to York, where he planned to solicit more subscribers. His first morning in York, the weather continued bitterly cold although it was nearly the end of April. As he looked from his window Audubon could see snowflakes falling, snowflakes that turned to rain and mist and then back again into snow, but he had no time to waste. Taking out his packet of letters to people in York, he made his rounds in the storm and returned to the inn shortly before noon. There he received a call from a friend, who kindly brought with him the curator of the museum. In the afternoon Audubon took a long walk alone, first going to the cathedral. Then he followed a road into the country, past an old castle, or abbey, which was covered with ivy and so disintegrated that Audubon thought it was ready to fall down. From there, still by himself, he walked along the edge of the Ouse, stopping to throw pebbles across it, then through some fields and, since it was raining hard, came back to the inn drenching wet.

The following day, nothing happened. Audubon sat in his room once more, hoping for visitors who did not come, his pictures still strapped in his portfolio, his subscription book devoid of new names. The endless waiting in an empty room was unbelievably difficult to bear, the expectation that every footfall in the hallway might be a visitor arriving, the realization that the sound was made by another guest who had no interest in birds. Unable to stand the suspense longer, Audubon went to the museum and tried to sell a subscription to the curator. But the curator refused, pleading a shortage of funds. After this unsuccessful effort, Audubon returned to the inn. No one had called during his absence; no one came during the rest of the day. All his letters, it appeared, were merely pebbles dropped into the ocean of York's indifference. In the evening, he accepted an invitation to an acquaintance's house, but the other guests were not interested in either art or birds and spent the evening discussing politics and criticizing the United States. Completely discouraged, Audubon returned to the inn and wrote in his journal that "tomorrow may be fairer to me in every way; but this 'hope deferred' is a very fatiguing study to follow."

After he had taken his customary morning walk, the visitors did start to arrive, some fifty of them altogether. Audubon went through his regular routine, the tiresome process of holding up his pictures one by one as his guests inspected them. But when he was finished, no one seemed at all interested; and by the end of the day he began to think that he might not make a single sale in the city. One of his acquaintances suggested that since York would not come to him, why did he not go out and call on the nobility and gentry himself? Audubon was offended by the suggestion. "I thanked him," he wrote, "but told him my standing in society did not admit of such conduct, and that although there were lords in England, we of American blood think ourselves their equals." Although willing to be a traveling salesman and to work with an intensity he had never shown in Henderson, he would not become a door-to-door peddler.

During the next few days, York gradually warmed to him. More visitors came, and several subscribed. One resident took Audubon on an extended tour of the cathedral, going out on the roofs with him to see the view, and Audubon by himself had an adventure which he carefully recorded. Walking along the Ouse one morning with his sword cane in his hand, he noticed a large butterfly belonging to a species he did not recognize. He whirled quickly with his cane and struck at it, attempting to knock it down. With this motion, the scabbard of the cane flew off, arched through the air, and landed in the water more than halfway across the stream, leaving Audubon standing on the bank with the bare blade in his hand as though he were about to fight a duel. Feeling thoroughly foolish—a number of people were out walking and noticed him—he watched his scabbard floating with the current. For a moment, he thought of diving in after it but then realized this would make him even more ridiculous. Finally he located a boatman who recovered it for a sixpence. In many respects, this incident was symbolic of his entire visit at York. Regardless of the subscribers he had obtained, he had felt silly, waiting in his room for visitors who did not come and hoping for honors that were never given him. It was with a sigh of relief, therefore, that he rose at five o'clock on Sunday, paid what he considered an exorbitant bill to his landlady, and boarded the stage to Leeds, his next stop.

Even though he arrived on a Sunday, he lost no time starting out again with his letters and, unlike his experience at York, did not have long to wait for results. The next morning, the visitors began coming to his inn, looking at and admiring his pictures, and bringing with them the naturalist John Backhouse, whom Audubon immediately liked. He was not, Audubon wrote, "a *closet naturalist,* but a real true-blue, who goes out at night and watches owls and night-jars and water-fowl to some purpose, and who knows more about these things than any other man I have met in Europe."

His second day in Leeds marked the anniversary of the day he had parted from Lucy at Bayou Sarah; and looking back on that date, he wrote, "How uncertain my hopes ... were as to the final results of my voyage,—about to leave a country where most of my life had been spent ... to enter one wholly unknown to me, without a friend, nay, not an acquaintance in it. Until I reached Edinburgh I despaired of success; ... Now I feel like beginning a New Year. My work is about to be known. I have made a number of valuable and kind friends. I have been received by men of science on friendly terms, and now I have a hope of success if I continue to be honest, industrious and consistent." What gave him the most hope were the twenty-one subscriptions he had sold since leaving Edinburgh.

His stay at Leeds was short, but he took time to visit the large mills operated by a man named John Marshall, who had become a subscriber. "The first thing to see was the great engine," Audubon wrote, "150 horse-power, a stupendous structure, and so beautiful in all its parts that no one could, I conceive, stand and look at it without praising the ingenuity of man. Twenty-five hundred persons of all ages and sexes are here, yet nothing is heard but the *burr* of the machinery. All is wonderfully arranged." Then he added, somewhat wryly, "A good head indeed must be at the commander's post in such a vast establishment." He had learned much since leaving Henderson.

He sold five more subscriptions at Leeds before he pushed on to Manchester, where his reception was different than it had been before. The Natural History Society immediately offered him exhibit space. So did the Royal Institution. He could not find a room in an inn, and an acquaintance promptly invited him to stay at his house. Friends from his previous visits flocked around him. The first day he sold five subscriptions and stayed up until two o'clock being entertained. At the end of the week, as he prepared to move on to Liverpool, he wrote in his journal, "Manchester has most certainly retrieved its character, for I have had eighteen subscriptions in one week, which is more than anywhere else."

On reaching Liverpool he walked immediately to the Royal Institution to see the curator, who had been so helpful to him in the past, and the next day went to stay with the Rathbones. After the stresses of his trip, he took a week's vacation at Liverpool, seeing his friends and having long conversations with the Rathbones, telling them everything that had happened to him. He even lent his journals, which he kept primarily for Lucy, to Mrs. Rathbone and her daughter to read. He also saw Roscoe who, he wrote sadly, "has much changed. Time's violent influence has rendered his cheeks less rosy, his eye-brows more bushy, forced his fine eyes more deeply in their sockets, made his frame more bent, his walk weaker; but his voice had all its purity, all its brilliancy." Audubon also visited his brother-in-law, Alexander Gordon, but Gordon was out. Then when Audubon saw him, he admitted he had lost a letter which Lucy had sent to him to forward. Since the two men had first become friends in New Orleans, their relations had deteriorated badly, probably as a result of Gordon's marriage into the Bakewell family. But Audubon took his revenge in the way family members often do. Anne, he wrote to Lucy about Gordon's wife, looked better than when he was there before but, he added slyly, she appeared unhappy.

He also took time to give a full report on his activities to Lucy, who was still teaching school at Bayou Sarah, although she had left the Percys and was living with a family named Hall. He had been careful, he said, to have the smallest practical number of copies printed. This, Lizars had told him, was fifty. These had all been sold, his costs recovered, and he had ordered another fifty. His intention for the future was never to have many extra copies on hand, but to print only enough to keep up with the demand. He then calculated his potential profit. A hundred subscriptions would earn for him more than forty-two pounds; two hundred subscriptions, more than a hundred and seventy-four pounds; and five hundred subscriptions would bring him more than ten thousand dollars a year, enough to enable the entire family to live in a grand style.

How like, and yet unlike, Audubon this report was. In his old speculative manner, he had calculated the profit on a hundred subscribers, then doubled the number and portrayed the life of ease he and Lucy could lead, then more than redoubled it again and saw himself as a wealthy man. This was in the spirit of the businessman of Henderson who had built the steam mill, invested in boats and followed the rainbow of his imagination into bankruptcy. But the new Audubon was shown by the element of caution in his calculations. Only fifty copies were to be printed at a time; all deliveries were made on a cash basis; one hundred subscriptions were planned to carry the venture beyond the break-even point. These were the figures of someone who knew exactly what he was doing. From his past disasters Audubon had learned a great deal, but this did not fully account for his sudden shrewdness. He had also learned much from Lizars.

Moreover, a deep friendship had sprung up between Audubon and his engraver. In Edinburgh, he could always count on a warm welcome at Lizars's house, and after leaving Scotland, he made it a point to write Lizars every Saturday, giving him a full report on what had taken place during the week. Audubon's affection was fully reciprocated. In spite of his many other commitments, Lizars continued to advise Audubon, suggesting, for example, that it would be more practical for him to have new prospectuses printed wherever he happened to be than to reorder them from Edinburgh. In this way, Lizars pointed out, Audubon could make any changes he wanted and, at the same time, save shipping costs. During this critical period, Lizars was filling many roles: the trusted friend, the confidant, and the respected business adviser.

With the production of his book in such good hands, Audubon could devote his full attention to selling it, going from city to city and repeating over and over again the same tiresome routine. His only concern, he wrote Lucy, was to collect his bills promptly and obtain enough subscribers, so that he could pay Lizars and keep him at work. To do this, he planned to visit London and afterward make a tour of the principal towns of England, Scotland, and Ireland, giving exhibits and selling oil paintings to cover the cost of traveling.

Then he spoke about his and Lucy's future in terms that were, for him, unusually realistic, particularly when his wife was involved. He admitted to her that his program would be difficult to carry out and that it was risky, but he stressed the caution with which he was acting. As far as Lucy was concerned, he wanted her to remain in Louisiana until at least the end of the year. By that time, he hoped he would have made sufficient progress to enable her to come to England and live in comfort. How much he had been tempered by experience was revealed by his emphasis on being careful and prudent.

In this sober frame of mind, he made the critical trip to London, hopeful for the best, fearful of the worst. Fortunately he was accompanied by Bentley, one of his Liverpool friends, because the trip was long and tiresome. They left Liverpool on Sunday morning and, after traveling all night, rolled through the tollgate that marked the outer limits of London at ten o'clock in the morning. He felt, he wrote, as though he were entering "the mouth of an immense monster, guarded by millions of sharp-edged teeth, from which, if I escape unhurt, it must be called a miracle." His trepidation was justified. London represented the supreme test. Among the cities of Great Britain, it was the most sophisticated, the one most likely to withhold its approval. Yet within its blocks and blocks of buildings, it contained enough potential subscribers to make the book a success. Without London's support, however, failure was a probability.

Weighed down by this knowledge, he took rooms with Bentley at the Bull and Mouth, the regular stopping place of the Liverpool coach. The next day, Monday, he walked with Bentley through the city, Bentley leading and "I following," Audubon wrote, "as if an ox led to the slaughter." It was, he noted, "positively a day of gloom to me." The first order of business was to find permanent lodgings, and he settled on rooms at 55 Great Russell Street. The next was to start delivering the endless supply of letters. He had them from people in Edinburgh, Manchester, Liverpool, any place he could collect them.

Some of them were even letters he had obtained in the United States more than a year before and kept with him ever since.

Around the city he went with those slips of folded paper that might, or might not, open the necessary doors. Yes, John Children, Secretary of the Royal Society, was at home to Mr. Audubon. Would Mr. Audubon show some of his pictures at a meeting of the Linnaean Society that evening? Mr. Audubon would. Yes, Sir Thomas Lawrence, the portrait painter, would see Mr. Audubon. After reading a letter from Thomas Sully—one of the few benefits Audubon had reaped from his visit to Philadelphia years before—Sir Thomas agreed to come on Thursday at eight A.M. to look at Mr. Audubon's pictures. Yes, Mr. Albert Gallatin, the American Minister, would call on Mr. Audubon at his lodgings.

So it went for the first full week. Up one street and down another Audubon went, locating addresses in the unfamiliar city, raising and then lowering brass door knockers attached to formidable-looking doors, hearing the echo of the rapping in unknown halls, speaking to stern-looking servants, handing over the letters, and hoping always that the written word would make the recipient act on his behalf or at least show an interest in his work. "I have," Audubon wrote, "been about indeed like a post-boy, taking letters everywhere.... I returned to my rooms, being worn out; for in one day alone I must have walked forty miles on those hard pavements, from Idol Lane to Grosvenor Square, and across in many different directions, all equally far apart."

Slowly his efforts took effect. Gallatin came to Great Russell Street, looked at the pictures, and invited Audubon to the Embassy to meet Mrs. Gallatin and their daughter; John Children invited him to supper; Sir Robert Ingalls of the East India Company asked him for the night at his house in Clapham. Sir Thomas Lawrence examined some of his pictures and pronounced them "very clever, indeed"—slighting praise, but Audubon was glad to receive it. He met Nicholas Vigors, First Secretary of the Zoological Society of London, and Vigors told him he would be elected a foreign member of the Athenaeum. Best of all, as he was walking down the street one day he suddenly came face to face with young Kidd, the artist whom he had liked so well in Edinburgh. The meeting was by pure chance. Kidd had not known Audubon's itinerary after leaving Scotland; Audubon had had no idea Kidd was planning to come to London. Together, they visited an art exhibition and Audubon invited Kidd to use his room at Great Russell Street as his own studio. "His youth, simplicity, and cleverness," Audubon wrote, "have attached me to him very much."

Then, without any previous warning, a blow fell.

Sorting through his mail one day, Audubon came upon an envelope written in Lizars's bold but rather scrawly handwriting, handwriting that was in direct contrast to the delicacy of his engravings. On opening the letter, Audubon discovered that its contents did not reflect Lizars's usual good nature. Instead, Lizars reported that all his colorists had gone out on strike. Production on the book, therefore, had come to a complete standstill. This meant that Audubon could not fill any orders he received in London. The only thing to do, Lizars wrote him, was to take a supply of the black and white engravings, find his own colorists, and let them do the work until the strike was over.

The news, Audubon wrote, "was quite a shock to my nerves." Already depressed by the sheer immensity of London and facing the most critical gamble in his whole venture, he found himself stripped of his supply of books and therefore cut off from his major source of income. With enormous courage, he decided his only course was to keep his predicament a secret, see all the people with whom he had appointments, and receive Charles Lucien Bonaparte, who was in town.

He had not met Bonaparte again since his visit to Philadelphia years before, when Bonaparte had treated him kindly and offered to employ him as an artist; but "in a moment," Audubon wrote, "I held him by the hand. We were pleased to meet each other on this distant shore. His fine head was not altered, his mustachios, his bearded chin, his keen eye, all was the same. He wished to see my drawings, and I, for the first time since I had been in London, had pleasure in showing them. Charles at once subscribed, and I felt really proud of this."

As soon as Bonaparte left and as soon as he was able to dismiss several other visitors who had arrived the same day as

Lizars's letter, Audubon dashed into the streets of London, and for three days did nothing but look for colorists. He went here and there like a man possessed, talking to art stores, to dealers, to printers, to anyone who might tell him about colorists. Finally, on the recommendation of the proprietor of a print shop, he went to see a young engraver, Robert Havell, who was in partnership with his father. After a short conversation, Havell persuaded Audubon he could maintain Lizars's high standards. What is more, he agreed to color the prints for less money than Lizars was charging.

Satisfied and relieved by this arrangement, Audubon took time to visit Sir Thomas Lawrence again. Sir Thomas, a pale and pensive man, invited him into his studio and showed him some of his unfinished work, which Audubon studied carefully in hopes of improving his own techniques. But even the chance of seeing Sir Thomas in his studio did not make the day a happy one, because Havell, having agreed to do the coloring, suddenly disappeared. No one, not even his family, knew where he was. Five times Audubon went to his shop and asked for him. Five times he was told that Havell had gone out of town without leaving word where he would be. "I am full of anxiety and greatly depressed," Audubon noted in his journal that day. "Oh! how sick I am of London."

After a short absence, Havell returned and began his work, which proved highly satisfactory. But the crisis over the colorists had tragically affected the relationship between Lizars and Audubon. Instead of the stream of friendly letters that had once passed between the two men, each apparently began to suspect the intentions of the other. On June 21 Audubon noted in his journal, "I received a letter from Mr. Lizars that was far from allaying my troubles. I was so struck with the tenure of it that I cannot help thinking now that he does not wish to continue my work." And this may well have been Lizars's attitude. When he had befriended Audubon in Edinburgh, Audubon had been a hopeful, but struggling artist, sorely in need of a patron. Recognizing that need, Lizars decided to fill it, not because he wanted more business for his shop, but because he admired Audubon's work.

Audubon, on the other hand, regarded their arrangement in

an entirely different light. At first he had felt nothing but gratitude toward Lizars; but as he sold more subscriptions he became more preoccupied with the book, and his attitude changed. Instead of thinking of himself as receiving a favor from Lizars, he fancied that he was conferring one on the engraver and demanded more and more service. As he complained to Lucy from London, he had planned to leave the city three weeks earlier on another trip, but Lizars had been late in delivering the first number to the subscribers. He then went on to say that the second number had not arrived when he had expected it, completely forgetful that Lizars had already told him how much other work he was handling—work for which he was presumably paid cash on delivery. Now Lizars had a strike to contend with. Even this would not have caused a break between the two men if Havell had not started to sing a siren song. Thoroughly competent but not yet fully established, he underbid Lizars. From the start he had offered to color the prints more cheaply. Now he said that he would do the plates too at a price less than Lizars's, and he pointed out that his location in London was advantageous because he was closer to the supply of copper and paper. He also probably played on Audubon's vanity by emphasizing the importance of the book.

If Havell had been incompetent, his overtures might have had a disastrous effect on Audubon's work. But Havell actually was a skillful engraver and the offer he made was really an improvement on the arrangement with Lizars. As Audubon explained to Lucy, he had already given Havell the pictures for the third number and, with his new business acumen, he showed how Havell's prices would affect his earnings. Instead of a net profit of just over forty-two pounds on a hundred copies of a number, he would now make almost twice as much. Because the price of the first hundred copies included the cost of the engravings, which could be used for a total of 1,500 copies without repairs, the difference was extremely favorable to Audubon. No wonder he made the change, and it reflects no discredit on Lizars that Havell underbid him. What is sad though is that Audubon parted from Lizars without the slightest sign of regret or apparently any memory of those days in Edinburgh when he had sat alone in his apartment on George

Street waiting for the visitors who never came until Lizars brought them. Nor did he seem to recall his excitement when Lizars had announced that he would engrave and publish at least one picture and then had increased the number to five, or his own comment only a few months before when he had written at Leeds, "I wish I had some one to go to in the evenings like friend Lizars."

Instead, he permitted Havell to obliterate Lizars's name from the ten plates Lizars had already engraved and substitute his own. Except for the volumes already sold and the few that might be still in stock, all trace of Lizars was eliminated from Audubon's life, work, and plans.

CHAPTER XX

1827

W HILE Audubon was making his arrangements with Havell, the uncertainty of his situation plunged him into another of his fits of despair. Toward the end of June he wrote in his journal, "I have no longer the wish to write my days. I am quite wearied of everything in London; my work does not proceed, and I am dispirited"; and in the beginning of July he added, "I am yet so completely out of spirits that in vain have I several times opened my book, held the pen, and tried to write. I am too dull, too mournful. I have finished another picture of rabbits; that is all my consolation. I wish I was out of London."

As he gained confidence in Havell, however, his spirits began to recover. During August, in one of his long letters to Lucy, he described his way of life. London, he explained to her, was an expensive place in which to live, and he had to be extremely careful with his money. On the other hand, he was not relying entirely on the proceeds from his book. From time to time, he was able to sell individual pictures and had earned more than twenty-two pounds doing some drawings for a Scottish lady. With this money he purchased six gilt frames for pictures that he intended putting up for sale at Liverpool. Because he was now charging twenty to thirty guineas for a painting—quite different from the five dollars he had once been glad to accept at Natchez—the sale of these pictures would give him all the ready cash he needed.

Then, like any provincial visiting a large city for the first time, he boasted to Lucy of the might of London. Edinburgh was a village compared to it. As for Louisville! Why the Duke of Bedford alone owned more property in London than made up the entire town of Louisville. And the sights! At the Equestrian Theatre, he had seen one man handling twelve horses at the same time, all racing at a full gallop. And crime! It was hardly safe to go out at nights, the streets were so filled with robbers and prostitutes.

Turning to the future, he told her that he thought he would have to spend five years more in England. That was during the first week of August. Two weeks later, without any further explanation, he told her that he might have to stay for eight years, and perhaps even longer. No wonder that Lucy remained distrustful of her husband's planning. Five years, eight years, which would it be?

In a letter to Victor, Audubon said he thought Lucy might come to England in January, bringing the two boys with her. Victor himself could find employment with a commercial firm in Liverpool; John, who was younger, could remain with his mother and father and complete his education at the University of Edinburgh. As for his own circumstances, Audubon said that the city was almost empty, the nobility and the wealthy people having gone out of town until November. He had arrived much too late and, as a consequence, had sold many fewer subscriptions than he had expected.

Although his stay in London was during the off season and although much of his time had been spent in his negotiations with Lizars and Havell, Audubon had achieved some tangible accomplishments. For one thing, Charles Lucien Bonaparte, coming to Audubon's rooms one night with a number of outstanding scientific men, had noticed among Audubon's pictures many birds that he and the others had never seen recorded before. By tradition, the original discoverer of a bird has the right to name it, but tact prevented Audubon's naming his own birds after himself. Realizing this, Bonaparte, as Audubon recorded in his journal, offered to do so for him. With a pencil, he gave names to some fifty birds and urged Audubon to publish them at once in manuscript at the Zoological Society.

On his way down to London, Audubon had jocularly commented that he might be presented to the King and perhaps sell him a subscription. Among his subjects, George IV was not widely admired. As a prince, he had married Mrs. Maria Fitzherbert—an alliance that was illegal under the Royal Marriages Act—and had then married Caroline of Brunswick, whom he later attempted to divorce in squalid and much-publicized proceedings. Through the aid of governments led by men like Wellington, Canning, and Peel, England had not suffered from his reign, but the King himself, dissolute and gross, was an unworthy monarch and quite unlike the future Queen, Victoria, who was then playing with her dolls. Nevertheless, the King's approval was important; and Audubon was excited when he was able to write Lucy that although he had not met the King personally, the King had become a subscriber. Indeed he had also been instrumental in obtaining the subscription of the Duchess of Clarence, later Queen Adelaide.

In spite of the poor timing of his visit to London, he had made an inroad on the city's indifference and obtained the patronage of royalty; but he could not remain there indefinitely or, for that matter, even into the fall, because he now had a complicated business to manage. In addition to being his own artist, his own production manager, and his own salesman, he had to serve as circulation manager, collection agent, and bookkeeper—no small task in an era when the mails were uncertain and the methods of transferring funds still cumbersome. Each subscriber had agreed to take five numbers a year, paying two guineas apiece on delivery. This meant that Audubon had to make certain that each number was received by the subscriber in good condition, the money collected immediately and deposited with a commercial house on which he could draw for funds, and the appropriate records kept. For every hundred subscriptions, therefore, he had to make five hundred deliveries and collections a year. To handle this business, he had established centers at Edinburgh, Newcastle, York, Leeds, Manchester, Liverpool and London, appointing agents who were sometimes friends, sometimes business acquaintances. When he was in London, however, he realized that his system was not functioning efficiently. As he noted in his journal, "I attended to my business closely, but my agents neither attended to it nor to my orders to them; and at last, nearly at bay for means to carry on so heavy a business, I decided to make a sortie for the purpose of collecting my dues, and to augment my subscribers."

With these objectives, and not as a vacation or an excuse for escaping London, he went on a flying visit to Manchester. From there, he wrote Lucy, he intended to go to Liverpool, then northward through Leeds, York, Newcastle, and on to Edinburgh, where he would settle his account with Lizars. Afterward, he would return to London, hoping to arrive back in the city by the middle of November. In the course of the trip, he expected to sell some new subscriptions—he now had the third number to show to prospects—but he was particularly anxious to collect some four hundred and fifty pounds which were already due him.

Once more he discussed his plans for the family's future; but this time, instead of pleading with Lucy to join him, he was advising caution. "I am doing as well as I could expect," he wrote, "and wait patiently for the first of January next, as I hope *then* to be *positively assured* that I can have thee with me on such terms as will render you happy." For emphasis, he underlined the words "positively assured" twice. He wanted no chance of failure in satisfying her demands. In terms that would be pathetic if they were not so disarmingly honest, he also confided his thoughts to Victor. He hoped soon to have a hundred and fifty subscribers. Then he would have acquired the "pecuniary means ... to have your Mamma and John over with me, and the ensuing season, I will also write for you to come. I have but little doubt now of all this being effected, but still I wish not to blunder any more; and when I do write your Mamma to come, it will be in full assurance that I can make her comfortable for life." "I wish not to blunder any more." Those words, written to his son, reveal the intensity of his remorse for the mistakes at Henderson.

During his two weeks in Manchester, he saw some of his old friends, personally delivered copies of the third number to his subscribers, collected the money already due to him, and obtained ten new subscriptions. Then he dashed off to Leeds, and on to York, where he discovered that his agent had done almost nothing for him, not even delivering the numbers. From York, where he collected fifty pounds and obtained two more subscribers, he pushed on to Newcastle. There he took time to call again on Thomas Bewick, the artist whose woodcuts he so much enjoyed. "I found the good gentleman as usual at work," Audubon noted, "but he looked much better, as the cotton cap had been discarded for a fur one. He was in good spirits, and we met like old friends. I could not spend as much time with him as I wished, but saw sufficient of him and his family to assure me they were well and happy." Then he stopped off for a short visit with Selby, the ornithologist, and on October 22 rose early to start for Edinburgh. All day long the rain poured down and, as Audubon looked out the window, he could see the ocean, "agitated, foaming and dark on the surface in the distance," and was "scarce able to discern the line of the ocean." Although at the end of his journey he was "cold, uncomfortable and in low spirits," he wasted no time in settling down to business.

The first step was to call on Lizars, who did not return Audubon's animosity. He invited Audubon to dine with him and, at Audubon's request, presented his bill, which Audubon promptly paid. Lizars examined the copies of the third number which Havell had produced, thought they were competently done, and to Audubon's delight offered to meet Havell's price if he were permitted to do part of the work. Audubon enjoyed what he regarded as this triumph, but his enjoyment did not blind him to the advantageous position in which he found himself. Shrewdly he remarked to Lucy that with two engravers now anxious to work for him, he had a check on them both.

His next step was to obtain an Edinburgh agent. For this purpose, he called on Lizars's brother, Donald, who was a leading bookseller and who accepted the assignment. Lizars himself, however, was dubious about the outcome; and Audubon wrote that he "has dampened my spirits a good deal by assuring me that I would not find Scotland so ready at paying for my work as England, and positively advised me not to seek for more subscribers either here or at Glasgow." This was sound, not malicious, advice, for, as Audubon quickly noted, "It is true. Six of my first subscribers have abandoned the work without even giving me a reason; so my mind has wavered. If I go to Glasgow and can only obtain names that in the course of a few months will be withdrawn, I am only increasing expenses and losing time, and of neither time nor money have I too great a portion; but because I know that Glasgow is a place of wealth, and has many persons of culture, I decide to go."

But the trip to Glasgow was hardly worth the effort. For four days he wandered through the city and at the end of that time had obtained only one new subscriber, the university. Yet he was able to report to Lucy that, since leaving London, he had obtained sixteen new subscribers, including the Marquis of Londonderry and the Earl of Kinnoul. The fifth number was completed, and he had paid for the work done so far.

In the middle of November, he left Edinburgh for Liverpool, stopping at York and Manchester on the way. His first thought was to see the Rathbones again, and the morning after his arrival he walked out to their country place, where he felt so much at home. "When I reached the house," he wrote in his journal, "all was yet silent within, and I rambled over the frozen grass, watching the birds that are always about the place, enjoying full peace and security. The same black thrush (probably) that I have often heard before was perched on a fir-tree announcing the beauty of this winter morning in his melodious voice; the little robins flitted about, making towards those windows that they knew would soon be opened to them. How I admired every portion of the work of God. I entered the hothouse and breathed the fragrance of each flower, yet sighed at the sight of some that I recognized as offsprings of my own beloved country. Henry Chorley [an old friend] . . . now espied me from his window, so I went in and soon was greeted by that best of friends 'Lady' Rathbone. After breakfast Miss Hannah opened the window and her favorite little robin hopped about the carpet, quite at home." At the Rathbones' house he found relief from the dreary, repetitive business of selling subscriptions—stopping at a strange inn in an alien town, delivering his letters, waiting for the verdict of the community, then moving to another city. Never in his Henderson days had he worked so hard or so persistently. Yet now, even after his journey, he did not believe he could afford to remain long with the Rathbones and that same day went back to Liverpool.

There he made an effort to repair his relations with the
Bakewell family by calling on Alexander Gordon. Gordon,
however, was not in; and Anne, to Audubon's surprise, admitted that she had never seen a single number of his book. Returning to his room immediately, he brought her copies of the
first numbers and asked her to look at them herself and also
show them to Gordon. Before he left Liverpool, Anne had
agreed to purchase two caps for Lucy on his behalf and he was
able to tell Lucy that he had seen Gordon, who had received
him in more friendly fashion than before.

But in spite of his improved relations with the Gordons and
the promise that his book would eventually be successful, a
slight note of despondency marked his letters to Lucy at this
time. For one thing, he was becoming thoroughly disillusioned
with his oil paintings and, with candor, admitted that neither
their composition nor the total effect he achieved was good.
Then he added the bitter truth: the pictures he was selling
were being purchased only by his friends. What he needed, he
said, was another lifetime to perfect his technique with oils.

Another matter that bothered him was the dishonest role he
was playing. Partly out of pride and partly because he sensed
the truth might count against him, he had never confessed to
anyone the precariousness of his financial position. Even the
Rathbones did not know, and when Audubon, at their request,
asked Lucy to write them, he had to remind her to say nothing
of their financial affairs. His friends all thought that he and
Lucy were well off, and Lucy must keep his secret. Then he
ended his letter by telling her that he would decide by the first
of January whether or not she should join him.

By the first week of December, he realized that his hesitations
about his plans were causing misunderstanding at home. Every
time he wrote Victor he asked Victor to send the letter, or a
copy, to Lucy; and one of these letters, written from London,
had apparently disturbed her greatly. In reply to her questions,
Audubon poured out his heart to her, and his words tore away
all pretense from the apparently debonair, jaunty, and persist-
ent artist who seemed in Liverpool to have no cares but the sale
of his book. "The letter I wrote to Victor," he said to Lucy,
"and which he sent to thee was written, when indeed, *although*

I was in London, I had the blues with a vengeance. But it would take twenty sheets to explain the reasons why I had the blues; and I am sorry, quite sorry, my dear wife, that thou shouldst feel uncomfortable. I would wish thee for *once* and for *ever* to believe that I *never* mean to cause thee pains whatever I say or do. But often when quite alone and feeling as if forsaken, my heart as well as my spirits give way, and I commit these errors with which, it seems, I have filled up my letters to Victor. However, *generally* I try to look at the bright side of everything, and, I assure thee, my hopes are still good. . . . Only think in what situation I came to England, without friends and with but little money, and compare with that the success I have met with. Then think again of the expense I have been at continually and the travelling I have had to perform and the cares I have been at continually to promote my views. . . .

"I have wished for thee every day, every moment; and at my present age I have postponed daily, through what *thou* callest prudence, to write for thee *positively to come*. I feel quite convinced that it is thy wish to join me. Did I think differently for a moment, my spirit would cease, and my happiness would be only a vapour. No, my dear wife, I assure thee, I have never doubted thy goodwill towards me, but have more than once sighed, and deeply, too, at thy extraordinary fears of *suffering as much as me* by being together. But do, my dear girl, again recollect that I am unwilling to give thee a moment of uncertainty and that the very instant I feel myself firm, I will write for thee. . . .

"Wert thou here, I only would have to work a very little harder than I do now; and the comfort I would really feel, I am afraid, my Lucy, I *will never feel*. How often have I told thee how dearly I love thee? Well, my Lucy, I am convinced that I feel now more attached and truly devoted to thee than ever. Honors, hopes of wealth, even the education of our children, all is in my soul for thy own sake, and for thy own only; come or stay, I must live thy friend, thy lover, thy faithful husband."

What more could any husband say to any wife?

He wrote to her again the day before Christmas, this time in a more cheerful mood. He opened by wishing her a merry

Christmas and expressed the hope that "I will not spend that day in 1828 *quite so far* from thee." Originally, he explained, he thought he could leave Liverpool earlier, but his fifth number had not arrived. According to the reports he had received from Havell, the shortness of the winter days and the heavy fogs in London had made it difficult for the colorists to work. Turning his thoughts once more to the future, he added, "I have little doubt that next year will be much better than this, and I wait with impatience my return to London to adjust all in my business in such a way as to enable me to write to thee positively to come. . . . Mr. Gordon, thy sister, Anne, and all the Rathbones think well of my business and are of my way of thinking, that it must improve rather than diminish." The news that even the Gordons now approved of his work must have somewhat reassured her.

The day after Christmas, which he found "dull—silent—mournful," he wrote again. His exhibitions at Liverpool and Edinburgh, he reported to Lucy, had netted him about two hundred pounds, but his living costs had used up this amount. Nevertheless, from the paintings and subscriptions he had sold, he had managed to pay the money he owed Havell and Lizars, and he had more than seven hundred pounds due him from his subscribers. He had also purchased all the clothing he would need during the coming year, had some cash in his pocket, and had finished several paintings that he was sure he could sell.

As he added up his assets at the end of 1827, he had reason to be proud; but he was not sufficiently confident to ask Lucy to join him in England. Carefully he explained to her all that he had done but warned her that the first year she was with him might not be as comfortable as she would wish. And once more he postponed the time when he would write to her and say definitely that she should come to England. Earlier he told her he would let her know the first of the year. Now he said he would write to her after he had returned to London.

On New Year's Day he was in Manchester; but instead of setting a definite date for Lucy's trip to England as he had once intended to do, his first resolution for 1828, as he entered it in his journal, concerned an entirely different worry. "Now, my Lucy," he wrote, addressing his entry to her, for his journal

was a record written especially for her, "when I wished thee
a Happy New Year this morning, I emptied my snuff box,
locked up the box in my trunk, and will take *no more*. The
habit within a few weeks has grown upon me, so farewell to it;
it is a useless and not very clean habit, besides being an expensive one. Snuff! farewell to thee. Thou knowest, Lucy, well that,
when I will, I *will*." Yet his real concern at the start of the
new year was not snuff; it was the controversy stirred up by
some of his comments on American wildlife.

In his journal entry for December 10, 1827, he had written,
"I received a letter from Thomas Sully [the artist in Philadel-
phia], telling me in the most frank and generous manner that
I have been severely handled in one of the Philadelphia newspapers. The editor calls all I said in my papers read before the
different societies in Edinburgh 'a pack of lies.' " Those papers,
five in all, had dealt with turkey vultures, alligators, black vultures, wild pigeons, and rattlesnakes and had been subsequently
published in various magazines, reaching the United States in
this form.

For the most part, these papers were accurate reports made
by a careful observer; but two of them in particular provided
Audubon's enemies in Philadelphia with ammunition to attack him. In one, Audubon claimed that carrion eaters located
their food by sight, not smell. This conclusion was correct, but
it was contrary to the general belief of the time and therefore
subject to argument. But the real object of contention was Audubon's discussion of rattlesnakes. In picking these snakes as
a topic, Audubon had entered dangerous ground. Although
not much was known about them scientifically, they had captured the imagination of the public, both in the United States
and Europe. Snakes with rattles that they shook to warn their
enemies! This alone was enough to stimulate interest and excitement. And Audubon, the man who had told the European
traveler about the skunk and had drawn pictures of nonexistent
fish for Rafinesque, could not resist the obvious temptation.

"The mode of copulation used by these reptiles is so disgust-
ing," he had said in part, while the sedate audience in Edinburgh shivered deliciously, "that I would refrain from any mention of it"—more shivering—"were it not my chief purpose to

record any facts regarding them that may be uncommon or little known. Early in spring, as soon as the snakes have changed the skin that contained their last year's growth, they issue brightly coloured, glistening with cleanliness and with eyes full of life and fire. The males and the females range about, in open portions of the forest, to enjoy the heat of the sun, and, as they meet, they roll and entwine their bodies together, until twenty, thirty, or more, may be seen twisted into one mass, their heads being all turned out, and in every direction, with their mouths open, hissing and rattling furiously, while, in the meantime, the secret function is performed.

"In this situation," he continued dramatically, "they remain for several days on the same spot, and the danger of approaching such a group would be very great; for, at sight of any enemy to disturb them, they all suddenly disengage, and give chase." What a picture! It was enough to set the savants of Edinburgh shaking their heads over the horrors of living on the American frontier and the serious risks run by the speaker for the meeting. It was also enough to send any informed herpetologist, amateur or professional, into guffaws of laughter.

But that was not all. Audubon repeated, with all the solemn, but vague, verifications that accompany a story of this sort, one of the oldest folk tales about rattlesnakes, the legend of the tooth left in the boot. For sheer power of storytelling and as a model of its type, Audubon's version bears repeating. "To give you an idea of the long time this poison retains its property," he said, "I shall relate a curious but well authenticated series of facts, which took place in a central district of the State of Pennsylvania, some twelve or fifteen years ago." The yarn, as Audubon told it, complies perfectly to the tradition of the campfire. It is, the teller says, "curious," but also "well authenticated." Even the date and the location are according to the traditional style: "a central district of the State of Pennsylvania," which sounds specific, but is not; and "twelve or fifteen years ago," not "a number of years ago" or some other loose term. Obviously Audubon had learned his lesson well in Kentucky, for here is the boatman spinning a yarn while the Ohio River rolls by in the darkness and the rain pelts down on the roof, the water occasionally seeping between the cracks in the boards and dripping down the walls of the hot, smoky cabin. "A farmer was so lightly bit through the boot by a rattlesnake as he was walking to view his ripening corn fields," Audubon told his audience, "that the pain felt was thought by him to have been from the scratch of a thorn, not having seen nor heard the reptile; upon his return home, he felt, on a sudden, violently sick at his stomach, vomited with great pain, and died in a few hours. Twelve months after this, the eldest son who had taken his father's boots, put them on and went to a church at some distance. On his going to bed that night, whilst drawing off his boots, he felt slightly scratched on the leg, but merely mentioned it to his wife, and rubbed the place with his hand. In a few hours, however, he was awakened by violent pains, complained of general giddiness, fainted frequently, and expired before any succour could be applied with success; the cause of his illness also being a mystery."

But the horror was not nearly over. "In the course of time, his effects were sold, and a second brother, through filial affection, purchased the boots, and, if I remember rightly, put them on about two years after." Again, with the phrase "if I remember rightly" Audubon followed the ritual groping after truth that characterizes this type of story. "As he drew them off, he felt a scratch and complained of it, when the widowed sister being present; recollected that the same pain had been felt by her husband on the like occasion; the youth went to bed, suffered and died in the same way that his father and brother had died before him. These repeated and singular deaths being rumoured in the country, a medical gentleman called upon the friends of the deceased to inquire into the particulars, and at once pronounced their deaths to have been occasioned by venom. The boots that had been the cause of the complaint were brought to him, when he cut one of them open with care, and discovered the extreme point of the fang of a rattlesnake issuing from the leather, and assured the people that this had done all the mischief. To prove this satisfactorily, he scratched with it the nose of a dog, and the dog died in a few hours from the poisonous effect it was still able to convey."

A true story? There was not a grain of truth in it. The poison remaining on one tooth stuck through a piece of leather would be imperceptible; and the poison of a rattlesnake, Audubon to the contrary, quickly loses all its potency when exposed to the open air. But even without the benefit of scientific knowledge, the story is a palpable falsehood, and Audubon should have known it or, what is more likely, actually did know it.

Yet his article was not composed entirely of falsehoods; he also included some of his own accurate, firsthand observations. But even these were suspect in the light of his obvious story-telling; and his critics especially objected to his references to the climbing abilities of rattlesnakes, which were not well known at the time. They went up trees and attacked bird nests, Audubon said, and indeed the first picture in his fifth number showed some mockingbirds nesting in a yellow jessamine with a hideous rattlesnake wrapped around its trunk. Its jaws are open, its tail and rattle silhouetted against the white back-ground, and it looks as though it is ready to devour one of the frightened birds. It is a dramatic picture and artistically a good one. Furthermore, in spite of Audubon's critics, it is absolutely truthful. For rattlesnakes, as he claimed, do climb trees. They do not climb as frequently or as well as, for example, black-snakes; but canebrake rattlesnakes, such as the one Audubon pictured, have been observed ten feet above the ground.

Although part of what he had said was folklore, most of it was true. But at such a distance, he could not answer his critics personally. So during those busy weeks in Liverpool and with so much else on his mind, he sat down and wrote a long letter to Thomas Sully, trying to extricate himself from his difficulty. Most of his life, he said, had been spent observing nature and making careful notes of everything he had personally seen. He had friends and relatives who could vouch for that. Further-more, why should he risk his reputation at this point in his career by telling stories? He had more common sense than that. In addition, no one at the Wernerian Society had doubted his word, and neither had the members of the other societies to which he belonged.

It was a long letter, but it was not a good letter. Certainly common sense and self-interest should have prevented him from telling fables before a scientific audience, but he had been unable to resist the frontiersman's temptation to spin yarns to the tenderfeet. This, of course, he hesitated to admit, although his foolishness undermined his standing as a serious naturalist. But he did not even present an adequate defense of those statements that he knew were true, failing to cite a single date or a specific place where he had made his observations. All that he relied on was the strength of his own assertion that he had kept notes and that he was believed by the best scientists in Europe, arguments that hardly went to the heart of the criticism.

He was just as stubborn as he had always been. Having said it was so, it must be so. No further proof was needed, even though his reputation as a competent, accurate observer had been impaired.

CHAPTER XXI

1828

O N New Year's Day, 1828, Audubon went to Manchester for a short visit before starting back to London on the evening of January 4. Having dropped off to sleep in his seat shortly after a nine o'clock supper, he woke up some four hours before daybreak. Overhead the moon shone brightly, gradually sinking to the west as the sun rose in a cloudless sky and its rays flashed on the white frost that covered the ground. His three fellow travelers suggested a game of cards to pass the time, and Audubon agreed, provided they did not play for money. While he might gamble on a Kentucky steamboat or a venture as hazardous as publishing *The Birds of America,* he would not gamble on the turn of a card. The time went pleasantly enough, although he was beginning already to regret his New Year's resolution. "I missed my snuff all day," he noted in his journal, "whenever my hands went into my pocket in search of my box, and I discovered the strength of the habit, thus acting without thought. I blessed myself that my mind was stronger than my body."

Back in his lodgings on Great Russell Street, he wrote, "I am again in London, but not dejected and low of spirits and disheartened as I was when I came in May last; no, indeed! I have now *friends* in London, and hope to keep them."

In this mood of optimism, he plunged into the work that lay ahead of him. First he unpacked all his pictures, sorted them out, examined them, re-examined them, and finally picked out the twenty-five that would make up the five numbers to be published in 1828. Next he named several of his new birds, diplomatically calling them after important men who had befriended him. Then he made a particularly wise decision. Still rankling under the criticism of his articles and speeches, he decided to discuss the problem with John Children, secretary of the Royal Society. Being both a naturalist and a physicist, Children was thoroughly conversant with the demands of scientific publication. His advice was simple and direct. Except for the text to accompany *The Birds of America*, Audubon should not publish anything at all. Now that five numbers of pictures had been printed and distributed, he no longer needed the sort of publicity that came from magazine articles; and by limiting himself to his major and really important work, he avoided the danger of falling into errors that might seriously jeopardize his entire reputation. Audubon accepted the advice, although somewhat reluctantly and sadly.

Having made that important decision, he spent what he called "a long morning" with Havell settling their finances for 1827. At the conclusion of their session, he noted in his journal that "it is difficult work for a man like me to see that I am neither cheating nor cheated. All is paid for 1827, and I am well ahead in funds." Looking back on his own past, he added, "Had I made such regular settlements all my life, I should never have been as poor a man as I have been." But he still had some learning to do, because on February 7, less than three weeks later, he found himself charged for fifty more copies of numbers than he could account for. This, he calculated, meant a loss to him of nearly a hundred pounds, but rack his brains as he might, he could not figure how the shortage had occurred. Unwilling himself to accept the blame for the faulty accounting, he commented in his journal that "it seems strange to me, that people cannot be honest, but I must bring myself to believe many are not, from my own experiences."

This bleak attitude was partly the outcome of another fit of depression induced by a bad cough and a sore throat, both of which made him feel utterly miserable and also alarmed him about his general condition. For several days he stayed in the house on Great Russell Street, not even going out for the early morning walks that usually brought him physical and emotional relief. Gradually his health came back, but his exuberance did not. As January, a cold, damp, miserable time of year in London, slowly dragged out its days, he wrote in his journal, "Oh! how dull I feel, how long am I to be confined in this immense jail? In London, amidst all the pleasures, I feel unhappy and dull; the days are heavy, the nights worse. Shall I ever again see and enjoy the vast forests in their calm purity, the beauties of America? I wish myself anywhere but in London. *Why* do I dislike London? Is it because the constant evidence of the contrast between the rich and the poor is a torment to me, or is it because of its size and crowd?"

His discouragement was deepened by the galling news that the British Museum, on the specific recommendation of Sir Thomas Lawrence, had refused to subscribe to his work. Sir Thomas, the painter on whose words of faint praise Audubon had clung so avidly only a short time before, privately believed that the drawings were mediocre, the coloring and engraving bad. A further insult came from the Earl of Kinnoul. In Edinburgh, Audubon had boasted to Lucy about having obtained the Earl's subscription. Now the Earl asked him to call, only to tell him that all his pictures looked alike and that his work was a swindle. There were other disappointments too, such as the news from Donald Lizars in Edinburgh that four subscribers had decided not to continue.

Yet even in London he had moments of happiness. A friend in York sent him two caged wood larks that added to the cheeriness of his room. He walked frequently in Regent's Park, a favorite spot, and one night, as he suddenly looked up, he saw two flocks of wild ducks silhouetted against the new moon. Often, as he wandered through this oasis in the heart of the city, he heard a blackbird singing or watched the starlings, which in England were not the nuisance they have since become in the United States. He received a perpetual ticket of admission to one of the London zoos and another to the Zoological Gardens. He was elected to membership in the Linnaean Society and the Zoological Society, and he was given by one of his Liverpool friends what he called a "curiosity,—'a double penny' containing a single one, a half penny within that, a farthing in that, and a silver penny within all." He was delighted and, with the boyish enthusiasm that he had not yet entirely lost, said, "Now, my Lucy, who could have thought to make a thing like that?" His relationship with Lucy had entered a quieter period. Having passed the deadline of January 1 which he had originally set as the date for deciding when she should come to England, he realized the time was still far off. As he put it in a letter he wrote in early February, "I am deferring still to write to thee to come to England, but I hope it will be for the best at last."

March 3 found him on another selling expedition, this time to Cambridge. After the confinement of London, he was delighted to be in the country again; and the pageantry of the university, its customs and rituals, the beauty of the trees set against the darkening stones of the old buildings, the River Cam winding its way under the arched bridges, and the warm-heartedness of the university community—all these made a profound impression on him. By the end of the first day, he had sold one subscription and had the promise of another sale; by the end of the second, he had met many of Cambridge's important professors but had sold no more.

When he woke on the third morning, the snow was blowing through the narrow streets and piling up on the window ledges. That day he visited the library and the Philosophical Society and dined once more in a college hall. The conversation after each of the meals intrigued him, and for the first time he began to wish that he had a college education. At the end of the day, however, he had received no additional subscriptions, but, as he wrote in his journal, "I must not despair; nothing can be done without patience and industry, and, thank God, I have both." The very next day his patience was rewarded; he received a subscription from the son of Lord Fitzwilliam, who was a student; and when he returned to London on March 15, he had obtained a total of five.

Nevertheless, he could see no possibility of Lucy's coming to England for a time longer. "At present, my dear wife," he wrote her, "I must acknowledge that I do not feel quite justified yet. However, I have *no reason* to think that I will not do well at last. Therefore, be patient and happy, as much as in thy power." He had, however, devised a method of setting aside a sum of money for her. "I have determined," he wrote her, "not to touch any money from the public institutions that subscribe to my work, except those that subscribed early, and then to deposit these amounts in the *Bank of Scotland for thy sole use and benefit* forever. It may amount to two or three hundred pounds per annum; and if ten years of this takes place, thou will be perfectly independent of the world for life, *leaving thee to will it* to our sons. These, my dear wife, are my plans. May our God grant me life to accomplish them and thou life to enjoy the result." This, of course, was for the future. For the present, he wrote to her that he had been out buying gifts for her, six dresses, some handkerchiefs, and a pair of French gloves.

After remaining in London only a few days, he started off for Oxford, arriving there "shrunk to about one half my usual size by the coldness of the morning, having ridden on top of the coach, facing the northern blast, that caused a severe frost last night, and has, doubtless, nipped much fruit in the bud." In Oxford he again set out with his letters of introduction, and almost immediately obtained a subscription from the Anatomical School. Then he visited the Radcliffe Library, which had purchased the first number. "When I saw it," Audubon wrote, "it drew a sigh from my heart. Ah, Mr. Lizars! was this the way to use a man who paid you so amply and so punctually? I rolled it up and took it away with me, for it was hardly colored at all." Impressed by the pictures Audubon had brought with him and by his insistence on quality, the Radcliffe Library agreed to subscribe to the whole set. But that was the end. No one else in Oxford subscribed. "There are here," he noted in his journal, "twenty-two colleges intended to promote science in all its branches; I have brought here samples of a work acknowledged to be at least good, and not one of the colleges has subscribed. I have been most hospitably treated, but with so little encouragement for my work there is no reason for me to remain." Disillusioned, he returned to London.

All through the month of April, as spring crept slowly through the parks and gardens of London, his depression continued. "Whenever I am in this London, all alike is indifferent to me," he wrote, and then again, "I cannot conceive why, but my spirits have been much too low for my own comfort." Finally, on April 21, he wrote, "The same feelings still exist this year that I felt last, during my whole stay in London. I hate it, yes, I cordially hate London, and yet cannot escape from it. I nei-

ther can write my journal when here, nor draw well, and if I
walk to the fields around, the very voice of the sweet birds I
hear has no longer any charm for me, the pleasure being too
much mingled with the idea that in another hour all will again
be bustle, filth, and smoke."

One cause for his gloom, in addition to his dislike for London, was the slow pace at which Havell was progressing. Havell
was not shirking his work, but it took time to engrave each
plate by hand and then color every print separately. The last
part of the process particularly worried Audubon. He haunted
Havell's workrooms, checking and double-checking the efforts
of each employee. One colorist so concerned him, he asked
Havell to deliver an ultimatum to the employee: either improve your work or be dismissed. Thereupon all the other
colorists, fearful for their own jobs, went on strike, and work
on the seventh number came to a complete stop. For ten days
the shop lay idle and vacant while Havell assembled a whole
new crew.

With production again underway, Audubon was able to enjoy to the utmost a review of his book that appeared in *Loudon's Magazine of Natural History*. At first, Loudon had approached Audubon himself, asking him to write some articles,
but Audubon clung to his earlier resolve never to write articles again. Loudon was not to be put off so easily, however.
A week later he was back again, ready to offer eight guineas for
a single article. Audubon still refused, although he could have
used the money. Loudon then did the next best thing. He com-
missioned William Swainson, a British naturalist and writer, to
review Audubon's book; and the review was excellent. After
reading it, Audubon wanted to meet the author and eagerly
accepted an invitation to visit the Swainsons at their house outside of London. Mrs. Swainson, who received him warmly,
shared his interest in music; Swainson, his interest in birds.
During the four-day visit, they talked of little else; and Audubon showed Swainson how he used wires to pose a dead bird
in a lifelike position. For the first time since he had left Liverpool, Audubon felt himself among friends, not people on whom
he had to make an impression or whom he was trying to enroll
as subscribers.

Aside from this visit, he hardly left his lodgings during June, July, and the first part of August except to take the exercise he desperately needed and to visit Havell's workrooms. Sometimes he went there several times a day, examining each plate in process, studying the black and white prints, and checking the work of every individual colorist to be sure that the proper standards were maintained. Back in his room, he spent many hours keeping up with his correspondence, which had now swollen to enormous proportions. In addition to his frequent letters to Lucy, he had tried to stay in touch with almost every person of consequence he had met, in this way enlarging the circle of his acquaintances; but he did not let any of these tasks interfere with his painting. Every morning, he was up at four o'clock and painted until dark.

During this lonely summer, when most of the people he might ordinarily have seen were away from London, he gave considerable thought to his own future and how he could better handle his work. With each successive number, the task became greater and greater. There were more records to keep, more prints to inspect, more deliveries to make, and he was bothered by the fact that he was rapidly using up the best of his pictures. He was a serious artist now, determined to make art his way of life, and he thought that many of his earlier paintings did not measure up to his new, professional standards. But the only way he could obtain new pictures was to return to the United States. In May he had commented in his journal on the problem that he faced. "I have been summing up the pros and cons respecting a voyage to America, with an absence of twelve months. The difficulties are many, but I am determined to arrange for it, if possible. I should like to renew about fifty of my drawings; I am sure that now I could make better compositions, and select better plants than when I drew merely for amusement, and without the thought of ever bringing them to public view." But here, as he saw it, was the problem. "To effect this wish of mine, I must find a true, devoted friend who will superintend my work and see to its delivery—this is no trifle in itself. Then I must arrange for the regular payments of twelve months' work, and *that* is no trifle."

As he wrote to Lucy, if she were in England she could take

charge of his business while he was away. He was convinced that he could obtain subscriptions in several European countries, including Germany and Russia, but how could he possibly make the necessary trip? This, in effect, was his problem. To continue the book, he needed a staff, but he could not pay for one because his subscription list was not expanding. Bleakly he noted in his journal on August 9 that "the number of my subscribers has not increased; on the contrary, I have lost some."

During the remainder of August, he slowed his pace somewhat. He met a Mr. Parker whom he had known formerly in Natchez, and agreed to sit while Parker did a picture of him as a woodsman. This took more time than he had expected, time that he resented having to give up, but he was pleased with the final results. He also happily accepted another invitation to visit the Swainsons and was just starting out to see them when a stranger gave him a paper bag containing a live passenger pigeon. At that time, and for many years later, amateur and professional scientists liked to import new birds, animals, and plants in the hope of establishing them in areas where they were unknown. The man with the paper bag was one of these, and he wanted Audubon to take the pigeon with him and release it in the country. Audubon, of course, was glad to do so, and this unexpected touch of America in the heart of London, this thin echo of the wingbeats of passenger pigeon flocks, augured well for the visit with the Swainsons, which indeed proved to be everything that Audubon expected. At the end of it, they had become such good friends that the Swainsons decided to accompany him on the trip to Paris he planned to take early in September.

The France to which they traveled that fall was different than the country from which Audubon had escaped in the uncertain times of 1806. The Treaty of Vienna had ended the continuing warfare which Jean Audubon had foreseen when he obtained passports for his son and Ferdinand Rozier; but with Napoleon gone, the Bourbons were back on the throne, and Charles X, having learned little from his family's experiences, was leading the country directly toward another revolution. Within months of Audubon's visit, the barricades would again be erected in the streets of Paris. It was not, therefore, an auspicious time to sell a costly book like *The Birds of America.*

Audubon, however, was unaware of the political problems besetting France, and just as soon as they had unpacked, he and Swainson visited the Jardin des Plantes briefly and then went to the Natural History Museum to pay a call on Baron Georges Cuvier. Of all the naturalists he had talked to so far, none approached Cuvier in stature or fame. The son of a retired army officer, Cuvier had early shown signs of genius and by the time Audubon reached Paris held many high positions: perpetual secretary of the National Institute, professor of natural history in the Collège de France, member of the Council of the Imperial University, and chairman of a commission to study certain aspects of higher education in France. The list of his publications was long and impressive. He had written a definitive work on mollusks, a book on fishes that contained identifications of some five thousand species, and pioneering books on paleontology, and was considered the world's leading authority on the structures of living and fossil animals. Never before had Audubon met a scientist whose praise could mean more to him professionally.

At the museum, he and Swainson were told that it would be absolutely impossible to see Baron Cuvier. He was much too busy. So they waited a few moments, knocked again, and insisted on having their names taken to Cuvier. The attendant, when he returned, led them upstairs and ushered them into the Baron's room. This was the critical moment, and Swainson played an important role because Cuvier, although he had never heard of Audubon, knew about Swainson. For a short time he talked to the two men, then invited them for dinner on the coming Saturday. After the dinner, Cuvier singled out Swainson and Audubon, discussed ornithology with them, and asked the price of Audubon's book. When Audubon and Swainson went back to their hotel late that night, they felt well satisfied with themselves and with their introduction to the scientific society of France.

So far it had been a wonderful trip, and it became even better the next day when he and Parker, his friend from Natchez who had also joined him, went to Saint-Cloud to attend the fete. "We saw on a platform a party of musicians, three of whom were Flemish women, and so handsome they were surrounded by crowds. We passed through a sort of turnstile, and in a few minutes an equestrian performance began, in which the riders showed great skill; jugglers followed with other shows ... the same show in London would have cost three shillings; here, a franc. We saw people shooting at a target with a crossbow. When the marksman was successful in hitting the center, a spring was touched, and an inflated silken goldfish, as large as a barrel, rose fifty yards in the air—a pretty sight, I assure thee. ... We had an excellent dinner, with a bottle of Chablis, for three francs each, and returning to the place we had left, found all the fountains were playing, and dancing was universal."

The first shadow fell across Audubon's visit to Paris when the King's librarian, a small white-haired gentleman, assured Audubon that it was out of the question for the King to subscribe to such a work. He did, however, give Audubon a card of introduction to Barbier, who managed the King's private library at the Louvre. Barbier was not hopeful but suggested that Audubon write to Baron de la Bouillerie, Intendant of the King's Household. Although Audubon was having a good time in Paris, and although his book was widely admired, he still was not obtaining the subscriptions he had expected. The members of the Royal Academy of Sciences looked at the pictures and admired them, but thought the price too high. The government, too, seemed reluctant to subscribe; and Audubon, in spite of his earlier enthusiasm, wrote in his journal, "Poor France! thy fine climate, thy rich vineyards, and the wishes of the learned avail nothing; thou art a destitute beggar, and not the powerful friend thou wast represented to be. ... Had I come first to France my work never would have had a beginning; it would have perished like a flower in October"; and two days later he added, "There is absolutely nothing to be done here to advance my subscription list." But he still refused to give up hope.

The Minister of the Interior, he learned, had the authority, on behalf of the government, to subscribe to any number of copies of any number of publications, so he wrote for an appointment. While he waited, he spent as much time as he could with Cuvier, who had agreed to sit for a portrait to be done by Parker. Those were pleasant hours, because Audubon had found in Cuvier a warmhearted admirer and a good friend. Nor did Cuvier forget his earlier promise to write a review of Audubon's book. He asked Audubon to bring his pictures to the Royal Institute on the afternoon of September 22, so that he could examine them again. Audubon arrived promptly at one thirty, the time set by Cuvier, but Cuvier was not there. "I sat opposite the clock," Audubon wrote, "and counted the minutes, one after another; the clock ticked on as if I did not exist; I began the counting of the numerous volumes around me, and as my eyes reached the center of the hall they rested on the statue of Voltaire; he too had his share of troubles. . . . The clock vibrated in my ears, it struck two, . . . I tried to read, but could not; now it was half past two; I was asked several times if I was waiting for the Baron, and was advised to go to his house, but like a sentinel true to his post I sat firm and waited." In spite of Audubon's fears, however, the Baron had not neglected the appointment. "All at once I heard his voice," Audubon continued, "and saw him advancing, very warm and apparently fatigued. He met me with many apologies, and said, 'Come with me'; and we walked along, he explaining all the time why he had been late, while his hand drove a pencil with great rapidity, and he told that he was actually *now* writing the report on my work! I thought of La Fontaine's fable of the turtle and the hare; and I was surprised that so great a man should leave till the last moment the writing of a report to every word of which the . . . critics of France would lend an attentive ear. For being on such an eminence he has to take more care of his actions than a common individual, to prevent his fall, being surrounded, as all great men are more or less, by envy and malice."

Although unpunctual, Cuvier had the ability to work quickly. "My enormous book lay before him," Audubon wrote of this crucial moment, "and I shifted as swift as lightning the different plates that he had marked for examination. His pencil moved as constantly and rapidly. He turned and returned the sheet of his manuscript with amazing accuracy, and noted as quickly as he saw, *and saw it all.* We were both wet with perspiration. It wanted but a few minutes of three when we went off to the Council room, Cuvier still writing, and bowing to everyone he met." The interview ended, Audubon left, glad to get into the open air, and wondering what the Baron would say in print.

For several days after, his uppermost desire was to see a copy of what Cuvier had written. The manuscript was out of the hands of the Baron, who had not shown it to Audubon, and was either at the printer's or the editor's, but which one? He called on both offices three times without success but finally caught up with the manuscript at the printer's, after it had been set in type. In order to see the proofs before publication, Audubon suggested that he might be of some help in correcting them, and the printer agreed. At last he had a chance to read the critical analysis of his work by one of the foremost, if not the foremost, naturalists in Europe. He had believed Cuvier was friendly to him; he had believed Cuvier admired the pictures; but, as he knew, a wide difference can exist between the opinion a man expresses as a private individual and the opinion he expresses publicly as a world authority. Spreading out the proofs, Audubon began reading them and quickly discovered that his fears had been unfounded. Cuvier called the work one of the finest books on birds that he had ever seen. Yet Audubon felt a slight twinge of disappointment. Having first worried whether the review would even be favorable, now that he knew it was, he was not satisfied. "It is a great eulogium certainly," he remarked in his journal that day, "but not so feelingly written as the one by Swainson; nevertheless, it will give the French an idea of my work."

He could turn his full attention back to getting new subscribers. At the King's library, he learned that the book had been inspected by the committee in charge of purchases and had received a favorable report. But he was informed that even if the King finally added his name to the list, he must appoint a French agent with power of attorney to receive his payments. Otherwise, he would not be able to collect a penny. "The librarian, a perfect gentleman, told me this in friendship," Audubon wrote, "and would have added (had he dared) that kings are rarely expected to pay." But Audubon's temper had been worn thin by procrastination and red tape. "I, however, cut the matter short," he wrote, "knowing within myself that, should I not receive my money, I was quite able to keep the work."

Audubon was no longer impressed by kings and their vacillating habits, but he was swept off his feet by the Duke of Orléans. Through the French artist, Pierre Redouté, he received an invitation to visit the Duke at one o'clock on the afternoon of September 30. "Kentucky, Tennessee, and Alabama," he wrote, "have furnished the finest men in the world, as regards physical beauty. I have also seen many a noble-looking Osage chief; but I do not recollect a finer-looking man, in form, deportment, or manners, than this Duc d'Orléans. He had my book brought up, helped me to untie the strings and arrange the table, and began by saying that he felt great pleasure in subscribing to the work of an American, for he had been most kindly treated in the United States, and should never forget it."

Baron Cuvier could put on Audubon's work the imprint of scientific approval. The Duke of Orléans could render an even more practical service, because he knew the right people. He promised immediately to send letters to the Emperor of Austria, the King of Sweden, and other crowned heads. He also urged Audubon to write immediately to the Minister of the Interior, implicitly suggesting that he would use his influence on Audubon's behalf. He also subscribed himself, adding his name to the list in his own large and legible hand.

The Duke evidently kept his promise to intercede with the Minister of the Interior, for the very next day Audubon received an invitation to come to the minister's office. After some questions and a little conversation, the minister asked Audubon to write to him again, setting forth his terms, and said he would reply as soon as possible. Audubon had wanted some definite subscriptions, but, he wrote, the minister "looked at me very fixedly, but so courteously I did not mind it. I tied up my portfolio and soon departed."

Still the days slipped by one after another, and no word came from the government. Audubon alternated between sightseeing and trying every device he knew to stir the officialdom of France. He attended the distribution of prizes at the French Institute, spending three hours watching the impressive ceremonies. He saw the King and the royal family get out of their carriages at the Tuileries. He obtained a subscription from Baron Cuvier, which particularly pleased him because of Cuvier's standing as a naturalist. He called on Count Joseph Jérôme Siméon, Minister of State, who also advised him to see Baron de la Bouillerie, Intendant of the King's household, and told him he should add to his list Baron de Vacher, secretary to the Dauphin. The Baron, he wrote, "promised me to do all he could, but that his master was allowed so much (how much I do not know), and his expenses swallowed all." On October 15, frantic over the slow action of the French government, he wrote bitterly in his journal, "Not a word from the minister, and the time goes faster than I like, I assure you. Could the minister know how painful it is for an individual like me to wait nearly a month for a decision that might just as well have been concluded in one minute, I am sure things would be different." More important even than the suspense was the loss of time and money, for during his six weeks in Paris, he had been unable to continue with his work.

A few days later, he called on two more ministers and saw the Baron de la Bouillerie, who promised to speak to the King but asked Audubon to put his conditions in writing again. From the Baron's, Audubon walked to the office of Count Siméon, the Minister of State, to see whether he had any news. "It was his audience day," Audubon wrote, "and in the antechamber twenty-six were already waiting. My seat was close to the door of his cabinet, and I could not help hearing some words during my penance, which lasted one hour and a half." What struck Audubon was that the Count greeted every person with the same words, "Monsieur, I have the honor to salute you," and said good-bye to each one with the words, "Monsieur, I am your very humble servant." "Conceive, my Lucy," Audubon wrote, "the situation of this unfortunate being, in his cabinet since eleven, repeating these sentences to upwards of one hundred persons, answering questions on as many different subjects. What brains he must have, and—how long can he keep them?" The Count assured Audubon that the subscription was being seriously considered and gave his word that Audubon would receive a definite answer on the coming Tuesday.

Having exhausted every resource at his disposal and with nothing to do but wait, Audubon spent the next day watching the King review the troops outside of Paris. But reviews, ceremonies, and sight-seeing were merely ways of passing time. They did nothing to bring an answer to the real question: Would the nobility and the government subscribe? October 20 came. "Nothing to do," Audubon wrote, "and tired of sight-seeing. Four subscriptions in seven weeks." October 21: one subscription from the young Duchess of Orléans. October 22, and Audubon had made up his mind. "The second day of promise is over," he wrote, "and not a word from either of the ministers. Now, do these good gentlemen expect me to remain in Paris all my life? They are mistaken. Saturday I pack; on Tuesday morning, farewell to Paris."

Four days later, just as he was about to leave Paris, he received a letter from Baron de la Bouillerie, announcing that the King had subscribed to the book for his private library. This, said the secretary of the Duke of Orléans, meant that Audubon could expect subscriptions from most of the royal family, because none of them liked to be outdone by any of the others. "Good God! what a spirit is this," Audubon commented. "What a world we live in!" He interviewed a bookseller who had been recommended to him as a possible agent by Cuvier and received a letter from Count Siméon, saying the Minister of the Interior would take six copies for various French towns and universities.

For two months he had been in Paris, two months that he could ill afford to waste. He had spent forty pounds and gained only thirteen new subscribers. He had, however, received a rest and a change, both of which he needed badly as he returned to London to wrestle with the same old problems: producing more numbers, selling more subscriptions, and, most important of all, making up his mind when he could safely ask Lucy to join him.

CHAPTER XXII

1828 – 1829

As soon as he returned to London, Audubon took up the first order of business: selecting the pictures for the eleventh number, which had to be delivered to the subscribers early in 1829. To keep up with his schedule, he had to place these in Havell's hands well before the beginning of the year.

By the seventh of November this task was out of the way; and Audubon turned his attention to filling the orders he had received in Paris. This meant painting two pictures for the Duke of Orléans and shipping the back numbers of his book to his new subscribers. The weather turned bad—one day it was so foggy and dark that men carried torches in the middle of the day—and this, of course, deprived him of the light he needed for painting. But whenever the weather permitted, he rushed to finish his commissions, not even stopping to copy the pictures, a practice that he often followed with paintings that he liked. As for the back numbers of his book, he did not have enough copies already colored, so these had to be prepared; and Audubon, of course, inspected each number before it was shipped. On examining them, he discovered that one colorist had performed an inadequate job. Therefore the entire number had to be redone, delaying the shipment and greatly annoying Audubon. But, as he noted in his journal, "Depend upon it, my work will not fail for the want of my own very particular attention."

He also had to consider the sales end of his business. Toward the end of the year, he calculated that he had a hundred and forty-four subscribers, a sizable number but still far short of his goal. Although he had originally counted on making most of his sales in Europe, he had also written his friend Dr. Richard Harlan about the possibility of obtaining subscribers in the United States, particularly in Philadelphia.

"I know of no society here," Harlan replied, "likely to subscribe to so costly a work. They have been too accustomed to enlarge their libraries by presents and begging. Besides, men of natural science are scarce here, and those not able to purchase many expensive works on their own account. Nevertheless, I think a few copies could be sold here, were they actually on the spot. I should be happy to make the effort, on trial." Harlan, friendly as always, was willing to help but unwilling to raise false hopes. What he said, in effect, was that Audubon would have to continue to depend largely on his European sales. This meant, as Audubon saw it, the need for more of his exhausting trips.

On his return from Paris he also took steps to make himself more comfortable, because it looked as though he would have to remain in England for a long time. Giving up his lodgings at Great Russell Street, he took three rooms with the Havells at 79 Newman Street, at a hundred pounds a year rent. There he passed most of his time, for he was too busy to go out much. He saw a few close friends like the Swainsons and those of his Liverpool acquaintances who happened to be in London, but he took a respite from his frantic efforts to meet more and more people.

The biggest problem of all, however, was what to do about Lucy. Earlier she had agreed to come to England, but she had continually demanded assurance that her life there would be comfortable, not a repetition of her existence at Henderson and New Orleans. Her terms, in other words, had become higher and higher. He had therefore given up his previous hope that she might bring John with her and have Victor follow shortly after. This, he began to think, was impossible. If Lucy came at all, she would have to come alone. But should he invite her; and would she come if he did? These two questions were constantly uppermost in his mind.

He wanted her desperately. Nothing else in life would satisfy him, but he was torn between living without her or asking her to join him and then not being able to give her what she wanted. To say, as he did, that she required him to earn a great fortune was unfair and an exaggeration, but she had been extremely positive in stating that she would not exchange the security of Bayou Sarah for the remotest possibility of uncertainty. She had found a niche for herself, and she was not going to surrender it for anything less safe.

He described to her his eagerness to have her come, the rooms he had rented, the sort of life they would lead, and what his financial prospects were. But he could not bring himself to take the responsibility for saying that she should definitely come, because such a statement implied that he could provide for all her wishes. "I do long so much for thee, my dearest Lucy," he wrote on November 10, "that I am sick at heart and weary of our long separation, and I would write to thee [about coming], if I thought that thou wouldst be content with my fare, my rooms, and the company of thy husband. But I cannot write to thee that I am rich. It is not so. Therefore, I will not deceive thee." A week later he wrote her again. "Although I have not accumulated that *wanted fortune*, which, on thy account, I wish so much to possess, I think that we might live together tolerably comfortably. I am particular in my expressions, because I do not, in any point of view, wish thee to expect too much, and to see thee unhappy and discontent would now infringe on my faculties. Should thou determine on coming, *thou wilt be welcome*, and thy husband will do his very best to render thy days and thy nights comfortable." Gradually he was taking the position that it was not up to him to set a date for Lucy to come abroad; it was up to Lucy to decide if she wanted to come, for in the same letter he spoke to her of the great joy it would give him to have her *"willingly* with me," and he underscored the word "willingly."

Two days before Christmas, still struggling with the problem, he wrote in answer to a letter of hers, "I am glad to read of thy being happy and comfortable, but I am dreadfully fatigued at our separation. Whenever I lay my head on the pillow to rest, I feel a fear that we will never meet again, and many of my nights are sleepless." He would like, he told her, to visit America, but thought it was in his best interests to remain in England "until the completion of my extraordinary work." Then he hoped he could dispose of the plates and the copyright, come back to the United States, and live with her comfortably wherever John and Victor happened to be working. Meanwhile, since he had so little else to offer her, he was sending her his latest prospectus. It contained the review written by Baron Cuvier and she might take pleasure in translating it.

Right after the first of the year, however, he received another letter from Lucy, and for two weeks, working alone in his rooms in Havell's house, he kept debating what he should do next, because her letter reinforced his growing belief that she would probably never join him in England. Sensing the widening gap between them and understanding the futility of trying to bridge it by mail, Audubon suddenly decided to go to the United States in the early spring, talk to Lucy, and try to persuade her to return to England with him. Otherwise, he thought they ran the risk of never meeting again. His decision was a grave one. He had intended to make a trip to America in the future in order to collect more birds, but this was not the time. Not only did he have no one to supervise his business while he was away, he was fearful that some of his subscribers would think that he was abandoning the work and therefore discontinue their subscriptions. Yet he was prepared to take this risk for the sake of his relationship with Lucy. He planned, however, to travel under an alias, so that his subscribers would not know he had gone.

As soon as John Children, secretary of the Royal Society, heard about his idea, he raised objections. In place of Audubon's plan, he offered a much more practical alternative. Havell, in whom Audubon had implicit faith, would take all the pictures needed for the numbers coming out in the next twelve months and all of Audubon's unsold paintings. Every Sunday, he would write a full report to Audubon on the progress of the book and whether he had been able to sell any individual pictures. Children himself would act as Audubon's agent and would also take all the remaining pictures, seal them, and deposit them with the British Museum, thus keeping them absolutely safe and ensuring the book's continuance. William Rathbone, too, would play a role. He and Children were to correspond regularly and serve, in effect, as co-trustees. This plan was highly practical, and Audubon readily agreed to it.

As for his arrangements with Lucy, Audubon told her that he would write to her as soon as he reached New York. He hoped she would then go at least as far north as Louisville, where he would meet her. He could not in letters explain what he had accomplished, but in an hour's conversation she would understand. He emphasized, however, that he could not make the trip merely to solve their personal problems; he also had to collect enough material to enable him to finish the book. This meant that every day he spent in America he would be either collecting specimens or drawing pictures. He could not otherwise afford to make the journey.

During the winter and early spring of 1829, he was in good spirits over the prospect of seeing Lucy and the children. At last he concluded his arrangements as satisfactorily as he could, left England on April 1, and arrived in New York early in May. During the three years he had been away, he had achieved remarkable success. Although he had not made the money he had wanted to, he was now a man of some means with a hundred and fifty British pounds in his pocket, two hundred dollars of American money, sizable amounts owed him in Europe, plenty of clothes (in contrast to the rags he had worn formerly), an important publication to his credit, and a well-established reputation in England and the Continent. Inwardly he was changed, too. When he had last been in New York, he had just suffered the debacle in Philadelphia, was almost unknown and extremely insecure. Now he had measured himself against the world and the world's marketplace and found that he was not entirely wanting. This gave him a quiet self-assurance he had never possessed before.

The change was reflected in the manner in which he was received in New York. The Collector of Customs permitted him to bring in his books and gun without paying duty. People like Major Long, whose expedition had passed through Cincinnati while Audubon was there, were interested in talking to him; the Lyceum invited him to display his book, which was highly praised by the members; and the president of the Lyceum personally invited him to stay on for a few more days than he had originally intended.

But nowhere was the change in Audubon more apparent

than in the letter he wrote to Lucy shortly after his arrival. In it he showed that he knew exactly what he intended to do and how he was going about it; and so clear was he in his own mind that he went to the unusual expedient of numbering his paragraphs.

First, he told Lucy, he planned to stay in the United States as long as he could without endangering the publication of his book, perhaps as long as eleven months. Second, he wanted to make it clear that he had to spend every possible moment drawing plants and birds. This meant remaining in a few places where he could find the largest number of subjects, not traveling around the country. Third, he gave Lucy an up-to-date report on his finances. As he had promised, he had balanced his books before leaving England. In addition to the funds and supplies he had brought with him, he possessed in Europe assets totaling more than fifteen hundred pounds, including his cash, numbers ready for sale, and the debts due him. As he pointed out, this total would increase, even while he was in America, as each new number came out.

So far he had been practical, almost stern, in the tone of his letter. Then he broke down. All his emotions, all his regrets for the past and his hopes for the future tumbled from his pen one after another. To Lucy he offered himself and everything he possessed, his talents, his industry, what money he had, and, above all, his devotion. And what did he want from her? A frank and direct answer to the question, would she come to England with him? Then, his patience exhausted by her indecision, he raised the threat whose execution he dreaded. If she answered "no," he would never ask her again and they would be separated forever.

After this outburst he reverted to the formality of his numbered paragraphs. Victor, because he was already happily employed in Louisville, should remain there. John should too, unless he wished to be a painter. Then Audubon took up his sixth and last point, which was simply that she must make up her mind promptly and decisively.

Never before had he written to Lucy in quite such terms, but during the years in Europe he had been unable to impress her with the changes that occurred both in his financial situation and in his own character. Almost desperate over her apparent blindness and unwillingness to understand, he was delivering what amounted practically to an ultimatum.

But he could not end the letter on such a note. Passing on to other matters, he told her that he would wait in Philadelphia for her answer, because Philadelphia might provide a good market for his book and was a place where he could find the bird specimens he needed. He gave her news of his visit to New York, the friendly relations that had at last developed between himself and the Gordons, and the thrill he had felt when a packet arrived in New York from New Orleans after a passage of only twelve days. It was the closest he had been to Lucy in three years.

Having finished his business in New York, on May 14 he left for Philadelphia, where he visited a few of his friends like Dr. Richard Harlan and the painter Thomas Sully. But as he wrote to a friend, he was "scarcely able to tell you why I felt a dampening chill run through me as I walked along its fine streets," so after a few days he went to New Jersey. There he visited the swamps and collected some two hundred specimens, including a large number of whippoorwills and nighthawks, the skins of which he carefully prepared. He had, he thought, done pretty well for a fortnight.

His next collecting trip was to Great Egg Harbor, where the Great Egg Harbor River runs into a bay formed by the offshore bars southwest of Atlantic City. Audubon quickly found a fisherman who was glad to take him in. At daybreak on the morning he arrived, Audubon started to work. He shouldered his double-barreled gun, the fisherman had a fowling piece and a pair of oyster tongs, and the fisherman's wife and daughter brought a seine. Together they started out in a small boat. Audubon was particularly anxious to find what he called "lawyer" birds, black-necked stilts, which nested in New Jersey until about a hundred years ago. The fisherman knew where to find them, so, after setting their net across a channel, they rowed down an inlet for several miles and came to the center of a vast marsh. There Audubon found the birds he was searching for and collected all he wanted. By the time they returned to the main channel, the tide was out, and their seine was full

of fish. They cooked some of them and ate them on the spot;
one Audubon regarded as a curiosity and preserved it to send
to Baron Cuvier. While they waited for the tide to come back
in, they dried the net and wandered through the marshes, where
Audubon obtained more specimens. When the water was sufficiently high again, they rowed back to the fiisherman's house
with Audubon tired and contented.

This was a happy period for him. Before he left Philadelphia, as he wrote Lucy, he had heard that everything was progressing well in London, so that for the moment he had no
worries about his book; and he could not expect an answer to
his stern letter to Lucy for another week. The only shadow was
Victor's silence. "I have not had a word from Victor since my
arrival," he wrote, "and I must think it very astonishing."
Other than that, he was happy. Once more, he could "do as I
am fond of doing, i.e. eat, walk, shoot, draw, get up or lie
down when it suits my purpose."

In this manner, he wrote later, "I passed several weeks along
those delightful and healthy shores, one day going to the woods,
to search the swamps in which the herons bred, passing another amid the joyous cries of the marsh hens, and on a third
carrying slaughter among the white-breasted sea gulls; by way
of amusement sometimes hauling the fish called the sheep's-
head from an eddy along the shore, or watching the gay terns
as they danced in the air, or plunged into the waters to seize
the tiny fry. Many a drawing I made at Great Egg Harbor,
many a pleasant day I spent along its shores." But all good
things must come to an end. When his collection was finished,
Audubon returned to Philadelphia expecting to find Lucy's
answer.

But there was no answer. She had not written to him.

On July 15, still relatively cheerful, he wrote to her again,
telling her that he had received only one letter from her since
his arrival in the United States and not a single letter from
Victor or John. "I might say," he wrote, "I am most baffled in
my expectations in coming over the Atlantic." Once every week,
he had made it a point to write to her. Why did she not answer
him? Then, changing his tone, he told her that Thomas Sully
"does not think that thou wouldst know me, if presented to

thee now. I laugh at him and answer that my tall figure would be remembered at a glance. I am very stout and, what is surprising at my age, have grown a full *inch* taller than when I left thee. Dr. Harlan says that I look as if I should live forever." But before closing, he returned to his former plea. "Do write to me, my dearest Lucy," he said, "and let me know thy intentions and plans fully."

To Victor, however, he was not so gentle. Three days after writing Lucy, he sent a long letter to his eldest son, taking him sharply to task. He had been in America for two months and thirteen days, he said. Immediately on his arrival in New York, he had sent Victor his address and he had written several times since. But not a letter had he had from Victor. This was conduct unbefitting a man or a son. Did Victor think that he was going down the river to Kentucky or Louisiana in spite of having said that he could not take the time? Then, for Victor's benefit, he reviewed once more what he had been able to accomplish in Europe, which, he explained, had been more than he could have expected in his most enthusiastic moments. When he had reached New York, he went on, he had happily written Lucy about his plans, but all he had received in return were two letters; and they had both been unsatisfactory. In them, she had only expressed her fears and doubts.

Taking Victor into his confidence, he described the situation in which he and Lucy found themselves. She said she could not come north because she did not have enough money; he could not go south because he could not take the time. Lucy failed to understand the pressure under which he was working. All that she did was complain about his lack of affection and said that his failure to go to Louisiana proved that her doubts were well founded.

In an effort to enlist Victor's help and understanding, he added that she had never told him how much or how little she earned from her school. From the way she expressed herself, he had always thought that she was moderately well off. So there perhaps was the answer to one of their problems. Although her indecision had bothered Audubon, although she was timorous about many matters, and although her letters had often left him depressed and unhappy, Lucy might have hidden her financial circumstances from her husband, not wishing to burden him with the knowledge that she was not as well off at Bayou Sarah as he had thought. This might have been her contribution during those long three years of absence; but against the background of her many fears and her complaints about Audubon's lack of affections, it had increased, rather than diminished, the misunderstanding between them.

Now Audubon, with the practical sense he had acquired abroad, was ready to take decisive steps. He wanted Victor to write her and persuade her to wind up her affairs as quickly as possible, collect as much of the money due her as she could, and arrange to have the rest paid to Victor later. Then she was to come to Louisville and from there to Pittsburgh or Wheeling, where he would meet her. If she needed funds, she could draw on a firm in Philadelphia for two hundred dollars.

Because of the difficulties that were developing, he told Victor, he had delayed his planned departure for England, writing to both his engraver and Children, his agent, that he might have to remain in the United States until April or May of the following year. He was trying to do everything that was best for his family. Could they not understand that it was his work, not lack of affection, that kept him from going south?

Finally, he said that although his work schedule made it difficult for him to travel as far as Louisiana, he could perhaps go to Kentucky, although he did not like having to face his former friends and relatives there, all those people who had scorned him as a bankrupt and refused even to correspond with him as he worked his way back up in the world. He had brought some of them, like Nicholas Berthoud and William Bakewell, presents, but now that he was in the United States, he was not sure that he wanted to see them.

As things stood, Lucy could not—or would not—come north either to Louisville or Pittsburgh; Audubon thought he could not afford to take the time to go to Louisiana. By trying to enlist Victor's help, Audubon had for the time being done everything he could to break the deadlock. Nothing remained but to wait and see what came from his latest effort. In the meanwhile he had a good deal to do—writing to Havell, worrying about the subscribers he had lost, and encouraging Children to be firmer with his agent in Paris, who had refused to answer his correspondence. This particularly concerned Audubon, because a thousand dollars was still due him from France.

His life at that time was not especially happy. He had selected Philadelphia as his headquarters, not because he liked it, but because he could collect birds that he had been unable to obtain in Kentucky and Louisiana. At the same time, the city was close enough to New York so that he could receive his European mail promptly. While he was there, he concentrated hard on his drawings and once more found himself with a larger burden of work than he could carry by himself. He therefore employed a young German named Lehman whom he had known a number of years before in Pittsburgh. Lehman's assignment was to help Audubon with the backgrounds of his pictures, just as Joseph Mason had once done. This arrangement permitted Audubon to leave on August 1 to visit the Great Pine Swamp about a hundred miles away in Northumberland County, Pennsylvania, an area which was particularly rich in birdlife.

He stayed there at the house of a man named Jediah Irish; and on the first morning after his arrival, "the woods," he wrote, "echoed to the report of my gun, and I picked from among the leaves a lovely Sylvia [hemlock warbler], long sought for, but until then sought for in vain. I needed no more, and standing still for a while, I was soon convinced that the Great Pine Swamp harbored many other objects as valuable to me." Taking the dead bird in his hand and asking Mrs. Irish's nephew, who had gone with him, to pick some laurel twigs to use as a setting, Audubon returned to the house and started drawing immediately.

After a few more days in which Audubon hunted and sketched, Irish, who had been away when Audubon arrived, returned home. He was the sort of man whom Audubon particularly liked, strong, independent, and an excellent woodsman. "The long walks and the long talks we have had together I can never forget, nor the many beautiful birds which we pursued, shot, and admired. The juicy venison, excellent bear flesh, and delightful trout that daily formed my food, methinks I can still enjoy. And then, what pleasure I had in listening to him as he read his favorite poems of Burns, while my pencil was occupied in smoothing and softening the drawing before me!"

Even in these idyllic surroundings, however, he could not dismiss his troubles with Lucy. On August 24, he finally received his first letter from Victor; and it was entirely unsatisfactory. It was pointless, Audubon replied, to write any more words expressing his affection for his wife and children or explaining why he could not go to Louisiana. The letter was short and somewhat curt, but he was relenting. Instead of Pittsburgh or Wheeling, he said that he was again willing to go as far as Louisville. To Lucy, he wrote the same day that "I do wish thee to make all the cautious *haste* in thy power and leave Bayou Sarah for Louisville as soon as in thy power." As he explained to her, he especially trusted Captain Delano with whom he had come to America, and he wanted to make the journey back across the Atlantic with him. This meant being in New York before the first of the following April. Three days later, he wrote to her again, expressing himself in stronger terms. "I wrote to thee twice on the twenty-fifth instant," he said, "but I do so again. I feel so very unhappy and uncomfortable that I have not had a line from thee saying, '*I will leave Bayou Sarah; and will be at Louisville in Kentucky about such time or thereabouts.*' I have been in America now four full months; and although I expressed my extreme wish to have thee join me as soon as thou could settle thy affairs and arrange thy business to the best advantage and at thy convenience, not a word have I yet that is at all satisfactory. Let me beseech thee, my dearest Lucy, not to panic away and make up *conjectures* and all sorts of imaginary fears. Let me beseech thee also to be assured that my not going to Louisiana is *much more to our mutual advantage* than if I had done what my heart thoroughly dictated. I do wish thee to come. Have no fears whatever. I am thy friend and thy husband, as fond of thee as ever, as ever anxious, devotedly anxious, to render thee comfortable. Come, confide in me. Throw thy heart in my care." To Victor, the same day, he repeated what he had said before: "*I will be with you and John* as soon as your dear Mamma will write to me that she will meet me at Louisville. Depend upon this, that had it not been to the *particular advantage of us all*, I would not have remained east of the mountains. . . . I wish you to write to Mamma, who is always full of fears and of doubts, to *urge her* to come to Louisville as soon as she can *conveniently*. I will be there to meet her."

Audubon was like a man struggling in the throes of nightmare from which he cannot waken himself. Whatever he said, his family did not believe him; and all he could do was repeat the same words and the same phrases over and over again. Why could he not make them understand that he was staying in Pennsylvania, not because he liked it—he disliked Philadelphia—but because he had to? Why could he not make them understand that, although not rich, he was doing well? Why could he not make them believe that he was no longer the irresponsible man who had frittered away their money in Henderson?

Burned deep in their hearts was the humiliation of those last days in Kentucky, the desperate strivings in Cincinnati, the lonely, poverty-stricken months in New Orleans, the failure of the trip to Philadelphia and New York. Against these memories, they could only weigh the letters he sent them and the other evidence, such as the newspaper reports, the printed prospectuses, and the copies of the book itself. These should have been convincing, but they were not. Had he not been given to exaggeration in the past? Had he not entranced them with stories of the fortune they would make from the mill and the steamboats? Had he not talked many others, including members of Lucy's family, into affairs that proved disastrous? Why trust him now? Before Lucy would leave Bayou Sarah, she needed to see him with her own eyes; and before Victor was ready to help, he had to sense greater assurance on the part of his mother. She was the parent he loved, not this strange father who had been out of the country for three years.

Yet Audubon had little time to lament over the situation in which he found himself. He had too much work to do. Before the end of August, he had completed ten drawings in the Great Pine Swamp, which, added to the twenty he had done in New Jersey, gave him thirty new pictures to take back to England. In the Great Pine Swamp, he spent several days hunting for a pileated woodpecker, one of those enormous birds that fly like ghosts through the deep shadows of the heavy forests, and finally shot one so that he could compare it with some he had obtained previously farther south. In addition to the hemlock warbler he had discovered his first day, he also found the nest of a winter wren, a nest he had never seen before.

He spent approximately four weeks in the Great Pine Swamp before he returned to Philadelphia, to resume the routine he had followed during the previous winter in London. Every morning he woke up before daybreak, dressed, and went out for a walk. Then he returned to his room, worked until nightfall, when he took another walk. Shortly before bedtime he had a glass of grog, read for a while, and went to bed ready to follow the same schedule the next day. Except for the members of the household where he was living and his assistant, he saw hardly anyone, preferring to stay by himself and work. In four months he had completed forty-two drawings; enough, as he figured it, to keep Havell busy for two years. In these pictures he had included ninety-five birds and sixty different eggs. In addition, he had collected thousands of insect specimens to send to Children in England. He had also been in constant correspondence with Havell, checking his progress and advising him. When he had told Lucy and Victor that he was staying in Philadelphia only to work, he had truly meant it and was living up to his intentions. Best of all, Lucy had come to believe it. Forgetting her doubts and fears and convinced at last that he truly loved her, she had agreed to come to Louisville.

Toward the end of October he started out to meet her, making the journey he had made so many times before. West on the Lancaster Pike, which he had first ridden with Ferdinand Rozier; up over the mountains and down the other side to Pittsburgh, where he stopped briefly; on to Cincinnati, where he paused just long enough to visit the museum (he was distressed by the changes that had occurred); then to Louisville and his meeting with Lucy.

But Lucy was not at Louisville. She had changed her mind.

Victor and John, however, were there. When Audubon walked into the countinghouse where Victor was working, he barely recognized his own son. Three years had passed and Victor was no longer a child but a man. Audubon was pleased by the change and pleased, too, with John. Also he found his

welcome in Louisville warmer than he had expected. Gradually his friends and Lucy's family were becoming convinced
that he had written them the truth, not lies fashioned out of
the stuff of his old exaggerations. His book, although not yet
finished, was truly recognized as an authority in its field; he
did have new clothes and money in his pocket again. More
than anything else, probably, they were impressed by his self-
assurance, the assurance of a man who knew what he was doing,
not the cocky arrogance of youth. This quality they were unable to sense in his letters but they recognized it when they
saw him.

Then he was on his way again.

If Lucy would not come to him, he would go to her. If
he could not make her understand why he could not afford to
take the time to travel to Louisiana, then he would go to
Louisiana anyway. No matter if he failed to collect specimens,
no matter if he endangered his book by making the trip. What
was the book without Lucy? What was fame without Lucy?

So he took the steamboat from Louisville. On either side lay
the old familiar places: Henderson, planted in the curve of the
river and little changed since he had lived there; Cash Creek,
where he had camped with Rozier; Trinity, where, in the
depths of his distress, he had written his despairing letter to
his former partner; Natchez, where he had first learned to use
oil paints. The river was the same river, eternally flowing and
changing and yet never changing, digging away the banks here
but silting a channel there. Each spot the steamboat passed
was a place he had known in happy days or unhappy days. Yet
he was not thinking so much of the past and the memories it
evoked as he was looking forward to the future and what his
meeting with Lucy might hold for him.

Once again, the steamboat drew near the landing at Bayou
Sarah. Once more, Audubon disembarked in the sultry darkness of a Louisiana night. Once more, he found the town
ravaged by yellow fever which had again risen from the swamps
to lay its ghastly threat over the community. Once more, he
knocked on the doors of empty, deserted houses, their occu-
pants fled before the sickness; and once more, he finally found
a friend, who lent him a horse. "It was so dark," he wrote,

"that I soon lost my way, but I cared not. I was about to rejoin my wife. I was in the woods, the woods of Louisiana, my heart was bursting with joy!" At six o'clock on the morning of November 17, he reached the house of William Garrett Johnson, where Lucy was then staying. A servant came to take his horse, and Audubon walked quietly to the room where he knew Lucy would be. From outside the half-open door, he could hear the sound of a piano playing, not the way Lucy played, but the way a child would. Without saying a word, he looked into the room. Beside the piano stood Lucy, framed against the early morning light which flowed through the windows, while one of her pupils ran her young fingers across the keys.

For a moment Audubon watched them in silence. Then he gently murmured the one word, "Lucy." She looked up. He stepped forward. He held his arms open to her. She came to him.

Writing of this meeting, he said simply, "We were both overcome with emotion, which found relief in tears."

They were tears that washed away the years of misunderstanding, the suspicions bred of Lucy's fears and Audubon's unreliability, the doubts and the wonderings that could not be explained by letter. As they looked at each other, he saw again the woman to whom he had pledged his heart so many years ago; she saw the man to whom she had given her love in the cave down by the creek. Gone were the memories of the lead mine, the steam mill, the unsuccessful trading ventures, the steamboats, the lonely nights in the log cabin at Henderson. Gone, too, were the memories of the cruel letters that had come from Cincinnati to New Orleans, the threats that she would never see him again, the scoldings, the beratings. All these vanished like a stormy night before the rising sun of a fresh dawn.

CHAPTER XXIII

1829 – 1831

REGARDLESS of Audubon's feelings after three years of separation from his wife, Lucy would not leave Bayou Sarah immediately. Although she had had months in which to prepare herself to go, she still was not ready. One of the tasks she had to attend to—and one with which Audubon tried to help her—was finding somebody to take her place. He wrote a detailed description of the job to Havell, hoping that Havell's sister might be interested. For the most part, however, he was busy with his own work. The first week, he spent almost all his time catching up with his correspondence which he had neglected during his trip down the rivers. Then he began collecting again, because he still needed more specimens.

He also had several commissions to perform for his friends. The president of the Zoological Gardens in London had wanted some opossums, so, Audubon wrote, "I offered a price a little above the common and soon found myself plentifully supplied, twenty-five having been brought to me. I found them extremely voracious, and not less cowardly. They were put into a large box, with a great quantity of food, and conveyed by a steamer bound to New Orleans. Two days afterwards I went to the city to see about sending them off to Europe; but to my surprise I found that the old males had destroyed the younger ones, and eaten off their heads, and that only sixteen remained alive. A separate box was purchased for each, and the cannibals were safely forwarded to their destination." For the Gordons, with whom he was again on friendly terms, he obtained a male turkey; and for various other acquaintances, he collected and shipped abroad 1,150 young trees.

On January 1, 1830, Lucy was at last ready to leave; and

after a short visit to New Orleans, they took the steamboat *Philadelphia* to Louisville. Although Audubon had traveled many times on the Mississippi and the lower stretches of the Ohio, never before had he made the trip with Lucy; and he must have spent much of his time pointing out to her the places where he had had adventures she had been unable to share. At Louisville they stayed with the Berthouds and the Bakewells and saw their sons before leaving for Europe. On March 7, they started north again. Leaving the river at Wheeling, they went overland to Washington, where Lucy had a taste of the new life her husband could give her. President Andrew Jackson received them both cordially. Audubon's pictures were exhibited in the House of Representatives, which, as a body, became a subscriber; and Audubon obtained more letters of introduction and several new subscriptions. At Philadelphia, their next stop, he picked up his passport, which in the unflattering language of this type of document described him as "46 years, 5 feet 8½ inches, common forehead, hazel eyes, prominent nose, common mouth, pointed chin, greyish hair, brown complexion, oval face," hardly the picture of a man who had just gone the length of the United States on a lover's errand.

Before leaving New York, Audubon went to the market and purchased, for four cents apiece, three hundred and fifty passenger pigeons, which he carried to England as gifts for the London Zoological Society and several noblemen, including the Earl of Derby. Like the stranger who had thrust the pigeon into his hands in London, Audubon was interested in introducing the birds in England. The Earl alone had some success in breeding them and distributed them to his friends. In the process a few escaped, but fortunately they did not survive. It might well have been tragic if the pigeons, once so glorious in the clouds they formed over the American wilderness, had reproduced in such numbers in Great Britain, because they might well have blotted out many other forms of English birdlife. "But," as Audubon commented, "that the passenger pigeon should have a natural claim to be admitted into the British fauna appears to me very doubtful."

On arriving at Liverpool, Audubon and Lucy stayed with the Gordons. Anne was sick, and Lucy chose to remain behind to nurse her while Audubon went to Manchester, arranged another brief exhibit there, and dashed on to London, where he found he had been elected a fellow of the Royal Society. This was the good news; the bad news was that he had lost many of his subscribers. As each new number came out, a few people would decide they did not wish to continue paying ten guineas a year for such a publication and canceled their subscriptions. By the end of May, therefore, he was on the road selling again. After a week of hard work in Manchester, he gained one new subscriber and persuaded four more who had dropped their subscriptions to take them up again. From Manchester he raced to Liverpool to see Lucy, and after a short visit returned to Manchester, where he worked hard to bring the total number of his subscribers there back to the original thirty, then pushed on to London. From London he went to Birmingham, taking with him a copy of the seventeenth number and a hundred and twenty drawings, which he planned to exhibit at the Society of Arts. By June he was low in spirits for several reasons. Lucy, instead of joining him, insisted on remaining with Anne; the political situation in France was rapidly deteriorating, as liberal opposition to Charles X and his chief minister, the Prince of Polignac, increased; and to add to his disappointments, he found that Birmingham was not interested in his pictures. "My time here," he told Lucy, "had been of the dullest; I have only one subject in Birmingham. The good people will hardly give themselves the trouble of seeing 'The Birds of America,' much less to subscribe to this publication. However, I never give up the ship, and if Birmingham does not meet my expectations, I must go elsewhere." Yet there seemed little point in returning to London. George IV had died, still wearing around his neck a miniature of Mrs. Fitzherbert; and his brother, William IV, had succeeded him. William's wife, as the Duchess of Clarence, had subscribed to Audubon's book, a fact that must have been gratifying to Audubon. But while the capital was officially mourning its past and dissolute King, he could accomplish nothing there. In the midst of all these worries, Lucy had decided that, although Anne no longer needed her, she could not travel to Birmingham by herself. To this statement Audubon wearily replied, "I will say that I will find it rather inconvenient to go to Liverpool for thee, but if I cannot get thee without, I must do so." Worst of all were the number of complaints he was receiving about the quality of the pictures in his recent volumes. Charles Lucien Bonaparte, still friendly and interested, took him sharply to task for letting some of the recent prints pass inspection. In addition, Audubon reported to Havell from Birmingham that he had received many complaints from his subscribers. The quality of the prints was uneven; Havell was just not taking the time he should to examine each individual number as it went out. As far as he himself was concerned, he found it hard to bear the criticism. Perhaps he should give up trying and return to the American frontier.

His fears about staying too long in the United States had been fully justified, for during his absence one problem after another had accumulated. But in spite of what he wrote to Havell, Audubon had no intention of discontinuing publication of his book. Instead he threw himself energetically into the task of recouping his losses. To Havell, he was kindly but firm; the quality of the pictures had to be maintained. Furthermore, the inferior prints had to be replaced, and Havell was to recheck particularly all the pictures in number seventeen, the colorists having failed to do their job adequately. From Manchester he went to Liverpool, saw Lucy and Anne, who was now sufficiently well to let her sister depart, and then back to London for another visit.

Not satisfied with all he had accomplished, he began making plans for preparing the text to accompany the first hundred pictures. This was an undertaking that he did not feel qualified to handle by himself. For though he had lived in the United States for years and his English had greatly improved since the days when even Benjamin Bakewell could not understand what he had written, he still was not a fluent writer and needed an editor to help him with his grammar and punctuation. But the editor also had to be a scientist, someone capable of helping with the technical aspects of the book. Audubon, however, did not want a co-author. This was to be his own book, containing the results of his investigations in the United States.

In considering possible candidates for the position, he naturally thought of his friend Swainson, the naturalist with whom he had traveled to Paris. He and Swainson had become increasingly close, so close in fact that after their return from France Swainson had asked Audubon for a loan of eighty pounds. With some hesitation, Swainson had written, "But that my regard for you may be evinced, I will bring myself to lay under an obligation, which I would only ask from one of my own family. I was that moment thinking to which I should write, to ask the loan of 80 pounds for a few months, and now I will ask it of *you*. If you were aware of the peculiar feelings which we Englishmen have on such occasions, perhaps you would smile, but so it is that we never ask anyone, from whom we have the least idea of a refusal. Now, did I not believe you to be a sincere friend, do you imagine I should have told you I was in want of money, much less have asked you to lend me some?" It was obvious to Audubon that Swainson regarded him as being almost a member of his own family. This intimacy continued while Audubon was in America. Swainson kept writing Audubon, several times requesting him to obtain shells for him, asking him to bring back two live squirrels and several species of birds, and, at the same time, informing him about events in England; George Ord, for example, was in Great Britain and, still angry with Audubon and jealously maintaining the superiority of Wilson, had been casting aspersions on *The Birds of America;* several members of the Royal Society had been opposing Audubon's admittance as a member; a number of other persons had also been quietly raising questions about Audubon's work. Swainson, however, was defending his reputation. It was obvious that Swainson was a man to be trusted and, with his greater scientific knowledge, would be able to supply the skills that Audubon lacked.

Swainson had already expressed some interest in such a joint undertaking, so Audubon approached him with a definite plan that they work together on the book and that, during the process, the Audubons live with the Swainsons. Swainson immediately objected to most of what Audubon proposed. Swainson had already told him how delicately the English asked for a loan; it was only as evidence of his friendship that he had asked Audubon for eighty pounds. Now he told him about the English attitude toward paying guests. "As to boarding with us," he wrote sharply, "you do not know, probably, that this is never done in England, except as a matter of necessity or profession, in which case the domestic establishment is framed accordingly. But this consideration would have no influence with me in *your* case did the other circumstances allow of it. It would however be attended with so many changes in our every-day domestic arrangements, that it becomes impossible." Audubon was a member of the family when Swainson wanted money, but not when he suggested they live together while they were working on a common undertaking.

Furthermore, Swainson continued, he had no intention of serving merely as Audubon's editor; he insisted on being Audubon's co-author. As he explained, "Our parts are totally distinct, and we have no occasion to consult with each other what we should say at every page. Where our views may differ, I shall not, of course, say anything. My own remarks had better be kept distinct, in the form of 'Scientific Notes' to each letter. . . . It would of course be understood that my name stands in the title page as responsible for such portion as concerns me."

This proposal was completely alien to what Audubon had in mind. What he wanted was a scientist to help with the scientific aspects of the work, not one that would write a supplement to his own field observations. At this point, both men should have realized that no possibility existed of their reaching an agreement. Audubon was determined to take full credit for the final book, just as he had taken full credit for Joseph Mason's backgrounds; Swainson was equally insistent on keeping his contribution separate from Audubon's and receiving full acknowledgment for it. Nevertheless, Audubon still hoped that he could persuade Swainson to change his mind and wrote him to that effect.

While waiting for Swainson's reply, he started off on another selling trip, taking Lucy along with him. In rapid succession, they revisited all the places he had been to before as well as several new ones: Leeds, where he sold a subscription to the Marchioness of Hertford; York, where he had an exhibit at the Philosophical Society and wrote Havell promising to try to obtain for him the contract for Selby's and Jardine's bird book; Hull, where the Philosophical Society refused to subscribe but where Audubon collected a long-overdue bill from a former subscriber; Scarbrough, which he described as poor; Whitby, where he could not obtain a single subscriber; and finally Newcastle. He was also worrying about Lucy. These trips, with the pressure of meeting new people and attending to all the business details, had strained the physical strength of Audubon; Lucy found the pace even more difficult to maintain.

His greatest concern, however, was the collapse of his negotiations with Swainson, who had made it abundantly clear that he would not withdraw from the position he had taken. In a letter to Audubon he had stated his position bluntly. "Either you do not appear to have understood the nature of my proposition on supplying scientific information for your work," he wrote, "or you are very erroneously informed on the manner in which such assistance is usually given. Dr. Richardson [an ornithologist for whom Swainson had already worked], and a hundred others, similarly situated, might with equal justice say that no name should appear but their own, as it would rob them of their fame. . . . Your friends would tell you, if you enquired of them, that even *my* name would *add* something to the value of the 'The Birds of America.' You pay me compliments on my scientific knowledge, and wished you possessed a portion; and you liken the acquisition of such a portion to purchasing the sketch of an eminent painter—the simile is good. But allow me to ask you, whether, after procuring the sketch, you would mix it up with your own, and pass it off to your friends as your production?"

Waxing still angrier, Swainson went on, "Few have enjoyed the opportunity of benefitting by the advice and assistance of a scientific friend so much as yourself; and no one, I must be allowed to say, has evinced so little interest to profit by it. When I call to mind the repeated offers I have made you to correct the nomenclature of your birds [Swainson fancied himself an expert in this field] from the first time of our acquaintance, and recollect the dislike you appeared to have of receiving any such information or correction, I cannot but feel perfect surprise at your now wishing to profit by that aid, you have hitherto been so indifferent about." In closing, he remarked acidly that he was glad Audubon had not agreed to his original proposal because, in the meanwhile, he had accepted a more congenial offer from Sir William Jardine to help prepare a new edition of Alexander Wilson's book. Obviously, Audubon would have to look elsewhere for the help he needed.

From Newcastle, he took Lucy to visit Selby, the ornithologist, and then on to Edinburgh, where, completely exhausted by the journey, she took to her bed with a bad case of rheumatism in her right arm. While she stayed in their rooms on George Street—they were living with Audubon's former landlady, Mrs. Dickie—he plunged into his work.

As usual, he had some complaints to settle. For example, he wrote Havell that he had met a Miss Maria Woodruff, who, after comparing her numbers one through nine with those received by her friends, was so discontent with their quality that she had discontinued her subscription. It was the same old problem; the copies had not been checked carefully. Audubon talked to her at length, told her that he would replace all the numbers in her possession, and finally persuaded her to resume.

With her subscription attended to and Havell given his instructions, he turned his mind to his other business with his engraver. Would Havell send six copies of the nineteenth number to the following addresses in York? Would he send one copy to a woman at Leeds, but not before checking her past payments? Would Havell send numbers eighteen and nineteen to the agent for the Library of Congress, collect the money due, and give him a receipt? Would Havell find out whether Children would lend Audubon a copy of Pike's journal of his expedition? (Audubon had to keep up with the explorations of his own country.) Would Havell send him some of the bird specimens he had collected and had stored in London? Had Havell reinsured the plates for the engravings? Would Havell pay the man who supplied Audubon with art materials and also obtain two ounces of ultramarine which he had recommended? Audubon, who had never succeeded as a storekeeper, was now holding hundreds of facts and figures in his mind, jotting them down on envelopes, in his journals, in his subscription book—addresses, names, quantities of numbers delivered, quantities of numbers which had to be exchanged, people whose credit was good, people whose credit was poor, how much he was owed and by whom, what bankers he could draw on to collect certain bills, what funds were needed in London to pay for the work underway—all the many, but essential, details necessary to a business such as his.

He was also concerned about the deteriorating political situation in Europe. Charles X had abdicated the French throne, being replaced by the Duke of Orléans, who had received Audubon so warmly during his visit to Paris. That the man he admired was now King of France must have pleased Audubon, but it did not alleviate his worries. Practically all his French subscriptions had been taken by either the government or the nobility. Many of these were now lost. Furthermore the revolutionary movement was sweeping across Europe, with unrest occurring in Belgium, Poland, Italy, and Germany. This meant that Audubon could not look forward to expanding his list in Europe.

Yet he did not allow all this to overwhelm him or to divert him from preparing the written text to accompany his pictures. Immediately after his arrival in Edinburgh, he therefore set about finding a man who would take the editorship that Swainson had refused. Among those he talked to was James Wilson, a naturalist, who recommended a young scientist named William MacGillivray. Although competent and able, MacGillivray was not yet recognized and did not insist, as Swainson had done, upon the position of co-author. "He had long known of me as a naturalist," Audubon wrote. "I made known my business, and a bargain was soon struck. He agreed to assist me, and correct my manuscripts for two guineas per sheet of sixteen pages, and that day I began to write the first volume." His terms were also more reasonable than those offered by Swainson, who had wanted twelve guineas a sheet as well as additional pay for correcting the proofs.

Even if MacGillivray had asked for more money, Audubon probably would not have argued with him, because he was now in a great hurry to get the text into print. In the last few weeks, he had learned that Professor Jameson, who had befriended him in Edinburgh, was preparing to bring out a new edition of Wilson's work, Sir William Jardine another, and a Captain Brown was ready to publish a book on American birds with materials pirated from both Wilson and Audubon. The competition, consequently, was intense, but Audubon noted philosophically in his journal, "Most persons would probably have been discouraged by this information, but it only had a good effect on me, because since I have been in England I have studied the character of the Englishmen as carefully as I studied the birds in America. And I know full well, that in England novelty is always in demand, and that if a thing is well known it will not receive much support. Wilson has had his day, thought I to myself, and now is my time. I will write and hope to be read; and not only so, but I will push my publication with such unremitting vigor, that my book shall come before the public before Wilson's can be got out."

When Audubon wrote with such confidence about British taste, he was merely encouraging himself; when he recognized the importance of finishing his book promptly, he was being realistic. He had to produce his book as quickly as possible; and during that winter in Edinburgh, he spent most of his time working on the text. As he said, "Writing now became the order of the day. I sat at it as soon as I awoke in the morning, and continued the whole long day, and so full was my mind of birds and their habits, that in my sleep I continually dreamed of birds. I found Mr. MacGillivray equally industrious, for although he did not rise so early in the morning as I did, he wrote much later at night (this I am told is a characteristic of all great writers); and so the manuscripts went on increasing in bulk, like the rising of a stream after abundant rains."

MacGillivray proved to be the perfect assistant. Audubon got up every morning at four o'clock and worked by himself preparing the drafts of his part of the text. At ten, MacGillivray got up and began editing the work done by Audubon, correcting the grammar and punctuation and improving the language, for although Audubon was a forceful writer, he was not a disciplined writer. Often his grammar, punctuation, and spelling were completely wrong, or he became involved in long and unclear sentences; MacGillivray made all the necessary changes but, like a good editor, did so without altering Audubon's basic style or meaning. In addition, he wrote the anatomical descriptions of the birds and helped with the nomenclature. At ten or eleven o'clock at night, Audubon, exhausted after his long day, would go to bed. MacGillivray, however, would continue working until two o'clock the following morning. In addition to the material on birds, Audubon decided to include descriptions of his own life and adventures, one such "episode," as he called them, for every five articles on birds. His purpose was to provide variety and thus make the book more readable. So during those cold winter mornings in Edinburgh, as he sat writing in his rooms on George Street, he not only dealt with the birds of America, he also described on paper how he and Lucy had traveled down the Ohio in the skiff from Shippingport to Henderson; he told how the regulators enforced the law in the West; he recounted his adventures in the Great Pine Swamp of Pennsylvania, his feelings during the year of earthquakes in Kentucky and his sensations when he stood close to the path of the tornado. Because these articles did not relate to his scientific work, he spent less time checking the accuracy of his facts. At times he became confused in his chronology; at others, he made erroneous statements. For example, in describing his adventure with the European traveler and the skunk, he said that the skunk "as it made its retreat towards its hole, kept up at every step a continued ejectment," which no skunk is capable of doing. He also leapt to unwarranted conclusions. Having seen the paths of tornadoes in Ohio and in the Great Pine Swamp of Pennsylvania, he assumed that they were all caused by the storm he had seen in Kentucky, which was clearly an impossibility. He also used the episodes, consciously or unconsciously, to create an impression of himself as both an ornithologist and a man. In them he mentioned that he had taken lessons from the French painter David, and, forgetting his disastrous business experiences, indicated that he had never had any ambition except to produce *The Birds of America*. Yet these digressions from the truth and the errors he permitted to creep in were inconsequential. Taken as a whole, the episodes presented a dramatic and vivid picture of life on the frontier and a valid description of many of Audubon's adventures and journeys.

With the manuscript for the *Ornithological Biography*—that was the title he chose—accumulating rapidly, he tried to find a publisher, but the first two he approached turned him down. He then went to see Patrick Neill, the printer who had originally introduced him to Lizars. Neill had helped him once before and was willing to do so again. If Audubon wished to be his own publisher, Neill would print the book and extend to him the terms of credit usually offered to booksellers. On this basis Audubon ordered from him seven hundred and fifty copies. Commenting on this arrangement, Audubon noted in his journal, "Most happy is the man who can, as I did, keep himself independent of that class of men called the 'gentlemen of the trade.' Poor Wilson, how happy he would have been, if he had had it in his power to bear the expenses of his own beautiful work!"

As his own publisher, however, Audubon had personally to take steps to print the book in the United States and secure the American copyright, a matter that was of considerable concern to him. As he often did, he wrote to Dr. Harlan in Philadelphia to ask his advice and also consulted another Philadelphian, Dr. McMurtrie. After the customary salutations of the period, Dr. McMurtrie, a businesslike man, replied, "To the point. The booksellers [who were also publishers] are all ... so occupied with prior engagements that you will find it a difficult matter to do anything with them. They have their opposing interests in various books: Bonaparte's *Ornithology*, the new book on American birds by Nuttall now-printing, etc. etc."

After that discouraging news, he continued by telling Audubon that he could, on the other hand, serve as his own publisher. For approximately seven hundred dollars he could have five hundred copies printed "on very fine paper," but he warned Audubon to allow at least fifty dollars more for "extras." In the same practical vein, he added, "If you send *printed copy,* there will be a saving of thirty to forty dollars. *Let me advise you to do so, if possible.*" Then he dealt with the important question of obtaining the American copyright. *"Keep back the publishing of your London copy till the American edition is nearly ready* and the copyright secured. Depositing the manuscript won't do. A copy of the *printed book* must be deposited at the office at Washington within three months after taking

out the copyright." In other words, the doctor was wisely telling
Audubon in those days before the international copyright law
to keep his British edition out of the hands of the public until
he was prepared to obtain protection in the United States.
Otherwise, a copy could be taken to America, the book pirated
by an American publisher, and the copyright lost forever.

Dr. McMurtrie was ready to supervise the publication, but,
as he explained, "Time is my only *stock*. I am compelled to
make it yield me *interest*." For his work, therefore, he asked a
fifty-dollar fee, or, if Audubon sent a manuscript instead of
printed sheets, a hundred dollars. Audubon immediately responded by appointing McMurtrie his agent and by arranging
the business details. To Dr. Harlan he sent a hundred pounds
sterling, or something over four hundred dollars. The balance
needed to make up the estimated seven-hundred-dollar cost
would be paid to Harlan either by a Philadelphia firm or by
William Bakewell. (His relations with the Bakewell family were
rapidly improving, as his success became better appreciated.)
Lucy had already started to make a duplicate of the manuscript
by hand, but Audubon had become too practical to permit the
waste of time and money involved. He sent McMurtrie the
first twelve printer's sheets immediately and arranged to have
him receive the rest as promptly as possible.

He also wrote to Dr. Harlan that the copyright should be
taken out "in the name of my eldest son, Victor Gifford Audubon, of Louisville, Kentucky." He did not explain himself any
further to Harlan, but he did do so in a letter to Victor; he
did not want to have possessions in his own name in the United
States. In spite of his success, he was still scarred by the memories of Henderson and of the creditors who had approached
him in both New Orleans and Cincinnati. Perhaps he had nothing further to fear, but perhaps he did. In any case, he would
be easier in his mind if he owned no property that could be
attached.

All during March, he worked furiously. He still worried
about the political situation in France and the effect it would
have on his subscription list; he found a publisher for his *Ornithological Biography*, an Edinburgh bookseller named Adam
Black (in spite of his earlier assertions, he had obviously been

troubled by serving as his own publisher); he was arranging for the distribution of the book and setting its price—twenty-five shillings a copy to the general public, twenty-one shillings to subscribers to *The Birds of America;* and he was also making plans to return to the United States in the late summer. Once again, he needed to obtain more specimens in order to continue his work, this time from the south Atlantic coast, which he had not visited before. This, however, was to be a more extensive and elaborate trip than any he had taken. Now that he was a recognized artist and scientist and was making some money, he could afford to plan ahead and in March was already corresponding with Harlan about his projected journey. For one thing, he had decided that he would like to have an assistant to travel with him. Would Lehman, the artist who worked with him during his last visit to Philadelphia, be available? Would Harlan talk to Lehman? If Lehman was not free, then he would attempt to employ an artist in England and take him to the United States. As if all this were not enough, he embarked at the same time on another money-making venture. Kidd, the artist whom he had known and liked so well, was back in Edinburgh, and Audubon made an agreement with him to copy some of his drawings in oil paints and offer them for sale.

By April, Volume One of the English edition of the *Ornithological Biography* was out, and the American edition nearly so. Audubon remained in Edinburgh for a few weeks after the book's publication, impatiently waiting for the next set of prints from Havell. As soon as they arrived and he had approved them, he and Lucy packed their luggage and were off again on another of his exhausting trips, stopping at Newcastle, York, Leeds, Manchester, and Liverpool on their way to London. From London he dashed to Paris to collect some of the money due to him, then came back to London in time to read the reviews. Blackwood's influential *Edinburgh Magazine* particularly pleased him by its comments. In a two-part article, it quoted liberally from the *Ornithological Biography,* described Audubon as one of the world's great ornithologists, and compared him with Wilson. To Wilson, it conceded the better writing ability of the two, but it immediately added, "When or where the world ever saw or may see, we know not, a painter of birds in water colours or in oils superior or equal to Audubon."

He had been with Lucy in England for a little more than a year, and on the whole it had been a good year. Summing up what he had accomplished, he wrote in his journal, "I have balanced my accounts with the 'Birds of America,' and the whole business is really wonderful; forty thousand dollars have passed through my hands for the completion of the first volume. Who would believe that a lonely individual, who landed in England without a friend in the whole country, and with only sufficient pecuniary means to travel through it as a visitor, could have accomplished such a task as this publication?"

Certainly his accomplishments had been great. Yet he had never come close to the ambitious goals he had originally set for himself in Edinburgh when Lizars had given him the fifth print for the first number and he had started out for London. Then he had dreamed of having perhaps five hundred subscribers; his minimum goal had been two hundred. Altogether, since that day, he had obtained only a hundred and eighty, of which fifty had been discontinued. Sadly he closed the entry in his journal with the remark, "With all my constant exertions, fatigues, and vexations, I find myself now having but one hundred and thirty standing names on my list."

He definitely had to do better than that; and on July 31, he and Lucy boarded the *Columbia* at Portsmouth for their return journey to the United States. In addition to collecting more birds, he hoped he could obtain in America the additional subscribers he needed so badly.

CHAPTER XXIV

1831 — 1832

O N September 3, after five weeks at sea, the *Columbia*
sighted Sandy Hook, came into the wind, picked up the
pilot, then entered the Narrows, passed through the Lower Bay,
and came to dock in the East River. Almost twenty-eight years
had passed since Audubon, as a young emigrant from France,
had first seen New York City and wandered through its streets
a wide-eyed boy. Since that time, the city had changed almost
as much as he had. Then it had been struggling to surpass
Philadelphia as the nation's largest municipality; now, helped
by the completion of the Erie Canal, it had clearly won. Then
not a steamboat was to be seen in the river. In 1831, when he
returned with Lucy, the city was the home port of almost
eighty. Some of them, the fastest ones, ran up to Albany in
ten hours or less, and they carried the mail to Quebec in
ninety-six.

But Lucy and Audubon were not lonely in the now bustling
city. In addition to Audubon's numerous scientific acquaintances, they also had the Berthouds, for Nicholas had opened an
office in New York and was living there. Since Audubon had
redeemed himself in the eyes of the Bakewell family and Lucy
no longer had reason to be ashamed of him, they stayed with
the Berthouds for "a week in great comfort" and then went on
to Philadelphia, where Audubon found a more cordial reception than he had expected. The Philosophical Society subscribed to *The Birds of America,* as did John Wetherill, a member of the family that now owned Mill Grove, and Audubon's
good friend, Dr. Harlan. In addition, Audubon learned that
Congress was expected to pass an act during the coming winter
that would permit his book to enter the country free of duty,

an important advantage as far as his American subscription list was concerned.

Victor met them at Philadelphia—a change since Audubon's last visit to the United States—and together the family traveled to Baltimore. There they separated, for Victor was taking Lucy back to Louisville, while Audubon continued south on his collecting expedition. Lucy could accompany him on his selling trips, but he now intended to explore the whole southern coast and perhaps go to New Orleans and on out west. After seeing Lucy off, he took the steamboat for Norfolk, Virginia, wth his assistant, Lehman, who had agreed to make the trip with him, and a taxidermist, Henry Ward, whom he had brought with him from England. But that very first night, in spite of his excitement over his new adventure, he was homesick for Lucy.

From Norfolk, Audubon intended to go directly to Charleston, South Carolina, but the stagecoach office could not make change for Audubon's hundred-dollar bill—a contrast to the day in Cincinnati when he had to borrow fifteen dollars for his passage to Louisville. So instead of buying a ticket to Charleston, he stopped at Richmond, where he had letters to four of the residents. (Altogether, he told Havell, he had collected two hundred letters of introduction before leaving Philadelphia and expected to obtain more along the way.) From there, he went to Fayetteville, North Carolina, and finally reached Charleston, South Carolina, on October 16.

In spite of the beauty of the city, with its handsome buildings and magnificent gardens, he had a poor first impression of Charleston. He thought his boardinghouse overcharged him— ten dollars and fifty cents for three meals and two nights' lodging for himself and his two assistants—and the first person to whom he delivered a letter of introduction was polite but hardly friendly. Then he met the Rev. John Bachman, a Lutheran minister and an amateur, but skillful, naturalist. Bachman insisted that the entire party stay with him.

For the next three weeks, using Bachman's house as their office and headquarters, the three men worked furiously. Henry Ward skinned and preserved two hundred and twenty specimens of sixty different species of birds; Audubon drew fifteen birds; and Lehman completed five pictures by putting in the plants and landscapes needed for the backgrounds. They accomplished all this in spite of the extremely hot weather and the sand fleas that tormented them every time they went out collecting. While the three men were working, Bachman personally tried to sell some subscriptions and was so optimistic that Audubon thought his visit to Charleston would prove a most profitable one indeed.

In addition to Bachman, many other people made Audubon's visit to Charleston a success. They showered him with presents —one man gave him a bird dog and a silver snuffbox; they invited him out to dinner; they came to call on him; and the newspaper editors praised him and his work. He also, during those weeks at Charleston, received word that the Society of Natural Sciences in Philadelphia had at last elected him a member. In view of his past difficulties in the city, he regarded this as a great triumph.

By the middle of November, however, Audubon realized that his timing had been wrong with respect to the migrations of the birds that he most wanted to collect. At that season of the year, he should either have remained in Pennsylvania four to six weeks longer or gone farther south. He decided, therefore, that he could not afford to stay in Charleston and went on to St. Augustine.

There he immediately set about collecting birds, but the town so depressed him that he became obsessed by the curious and morbid thought that Havell might die. If this occurred, he wrote Lucy, he would have to stop his work in America and return to England. On the other hand, perhaps Victor was equipped to go to London and take his place. Or was he? Maybe Victor should join him in New Orleans the first of June, and the two of them could go farther west together. This would give Victor a chance to learn ornithology and enable him to continue the book if Audubon himself should die. As for John, he wished now that he had taken him to Florida. He would have been useful, and he too would have learned about birds and how to help with the publication of the book.

As a result of his past experiences, Audubon had a strong sense of isolation. When he had desperately needed assistance from his friends, they had deserted him. At least that is what he

believed, and he told Lucy that the family could never expect
help from anyone but themselves. What they should do was
act as partners—the father, the mother, and the two children.

This was increasingly his dream: to make *The Birds of America* a family enterprise with Lucy and the two boys helping him
supervise the production of the plates, handling the book-
keeping and the subscriptions, and assisting him by collecting
new specimens and working on the drawings. Yet he realized
that the dream might not be practical, for in the same letter
he said that if John and Victor were offered better opportunities, they should seize them. He particularly hoped that William Bakewell would take Victor in as a partner.

Victor's future, therefore, was to be decided for him; but
John had ideas of his own. Like every young boy growing up
on the Ohio and Mississippi rivers, he had his own heroes,
and they were not ornithologists; they were steamboat captains.
He did not want to become a merchant like his Uncle William
or an artist like his father. He wanted to spend his life in the
wheelhouse of a boat, and who could blame him? Certainly not
Audubon, although John's desires created some family com-
plications. But Audubon did not care what William thought.
Indeed, when it came right down to it, he was in favor of letting both sons do what they wanted to do. All he asked was
that they be capable at the business of their choice and that
they be honest.

As he worked in Florida, he complained frequently about the
irregularity of the mails and the difficulty of obtaining news
about the progress of his book. He was, however, encouraged
by the news he did receive. From Charleston he had written
Lucy that the newspapers had treated him well. Now many
other American publications were doing the same, and he
thought that the current of public opinion had changed in his
favor. His optimistic attitude was justified. Although he still
had many detractors and although George Ord could still be
counted an enemy, the publication of his two books and their
distribution in the United States, combined with growing interest in his southern journey, had brought him favorable attention. *The American Quarterly Review* in its December issue said of *The Birds of America* that it was "on so magnificent

a scale, that its expense puts it beyond the means of any but the richest, individually considered; public libraries and societies may however be able to purchase it; and we trust to their patriotism to encourage an ingenious man, whose labors reflect honor on their common country." It thought equally well of the accompanying text, but expressed the wish that a new edition would be illustrated with woodcuts. "This," the *Review* said, "will render the *Ornithological Biography* increasingly valuable, without being likely to operate prejudicially to the sale of the other" because of the difference in the cost of the two publications.

The editor of *The Monthly American Journal of Geology and Natural Science* was also friendly. Not only did he print the correspondence Audubon sent him from Florida about the progress of his work, he also spoke out strongly against Audubon's critics. Discussing the slights Audubon had received during his earlier visit to Philadelphia, the editor wrote that they are "by no means to be imputed to his countrymen at large, to whom he was comparatively unknown. The transaction grew out of a spirit of jealousy, which is always illiberal and the frequent parent of misrepresentation and calumny. Some of the friends of Wilson did not view, with the most cordial spirit, those evidences of transcendent merit, which others willingly accord to Audubon's drawings; then arose the spirit of party, and with it malevolence. A few small minds, who knew little or nothing of nature, and who had officiously intruded themselves into this matter, endeavored to make up for their want of knowledge on the subject, by excess of bad zeal. Opinions were industriously circulated, that Audubon had, in many instances, attempted to impose upon the credulity of the world, by inventing stories which had no foundations in truth, because they were contrary to the known habits of the animals they concerned; as if the habits of the animals of this vast continent, could possibly be known to any other class of men, but that adventurous one, which, like Audubon, has passed their whole lives in observing them." After more comments in the same vein, all leveled at George Ord and his supporters, the editor turned his attention to the rattlesnake controversy. "This Journal," he continued, "has always been prompt to repel unfriendly imputations directed against Audubon.... There is a communication from Col. Abert, of the U. S. Topographical engineers, where the most conclusive evidence is given from officers of high rank in the U. S. service, that the rattlesnake has those habits of climbing, and has been seen by others, in the situation depicted by Audubon. These gentlemen have been able to offer their testimony of his fidelity to nature, because they too have had rare opportunities of observing the habits of animals, in the distant and unfrequented territories of our country." With support such as this, Audubon was able to write joyfully to Lucy that he was overcoming his enemies.

By the first of the year, he and his two helpers had left St. Augustine and moved forty miles south to the plantation of a wealthy young man named John J. Bulow, who provided them with boats and assistants. He reported to Lucy that he now had five hundred and fifty bird skins, two boxes of shells, some curious seeds, and twenty-nine drawings of birds, eleven of which were completely finished. To help him finish his task, he was relying more and more on Lehman. He would set the birds up for his assistant, but once this was done, he found that Lehman could execute the drawings beautifully. He was also happy with the work performed by Henry Ward. But he was extremely bothered by the scarcity of birds and once more lamented that he had not remained longer in the North.

From Bulow's plantation he made an expedition overland to the headwaters of the St. John's River, which, for most of its course, runs almost parallel to the coast and therefore can be easily reached from the shore. "The weather was pleasant," he wrote later, "but not so our way, for no sooner had we left the 'King's Road,' which had been cut by the Spanish government for a goodly distance, than we entered a thicket of scrubby oaks, succeeded by a still denser mass of low palmettoes, which extended about three miles, and among the roots of which our nags had great difficulty in making their footing. After this we entered the pine barrens, so extensively distributed in this portion of the Floridas. The sand seemed to be all sand and nothing but sand, and the palmettoes at times so covered the narrow Indian trail which we followed, that it required all the instinct of sagacity of ourselves and our horses to keep it. It seemed to us that we were approaching the end of the world. The country was perfectly flat, and, so far as we could survey it, presented the same wild and scraggy aspect."

In another twenty miles, "all at once, however, a wonderful change took place:—the country became more elevated and undulating; the timber was of a different nature, and consisted of red and live-oaks, magnolias and several kinds of pine. . . . We now saw beautiful lakes of the purest water, and passed along a green space, having a series of them on each side of us. These sheets of water became larger and more numerous the further we advanced—some of them extending to a length of several miles, and having a depth of from two to twenty feet of clear water; but their shores being destitute of vegetation, we observed no birds near them."

After spending a few days with a planter named Colonel Rees and visiting a large spring nearby—Audubon estimated that it gave forth almost half a million gallons an hour in the rainy season—he returned to Bulow's plantation and back to St. Augustine on January 14. There he hoped to make use of a letter he had received from Louis McLane, Secretary of the Treasury, instructing the commanders of the revenue cutters sailing in the Floridas to provide Audubon and his party with transportation. This meant that Audubon could make two trips that he had in mind, one up the St. John's River and the other down the coast to the Florida keys. Because there were no revenue cutters at St. Augustine, he persuaded the commander of the naval schooner *Spark* to carry him and his two assistants up the St. John's River. He took great pride in this recognition by the government and wrote Lucy of the contrast between his life now and those days when he could not get a job even as a clerk on a river steamboat.

In this triumphant mood, Audubon set sail from St. Augustine at noonday, but the triumph was short-lived. The wind was fair, and the commander expected to be anchored inside the bar at the entrance to the St. John's River before dusk. But at four o'clock the wind suddenly moved to the northeast, clouds blew across the sky, and by eight o'clock, although they had sighted the St. John's light, they were not safely inside the bar, and the storm had become a hurricane. Audubon, as usual, became desperately seasick. All night long, the wind tore at the shortened canvas, the waves crashed across the deck in the darkness, and by morning, although the storm had somewhat abated, the *Spark* had been blown to the southeast, and the commander decided to return to St. Augustine rather than attempt to make the St. John's River. That night the wind blew up again and the temperature dropped below freezing, but the *Spark* rode out the storm comfortably.

On their next attempt, they reached the mouth of the river without difficulty; the pilot answered their signal and guided them across the bar, and, as Audubon wrote, "On the tide we proceeded apace. Myriads of cormorants covered the face of the waters, and over it fish crows innumerable were already arriving from their distant roosts. We landed at one place to search for the birds whose charming melodies had engaged our attention, and here and there some young eagles we shot, to add to our store of fresh provisions."

By February 12, they were almost a hundred miles up the river. The weather was hot, ninety degrees on shore, and the insects so thick that they extinguished Audubon's candle while he was writing in his journal. Occasionally he had an opportunity to go ashore, and he watched with concern the lumbermen who were cutting the live oaks. They would fell an enormous tree, then examine it closely for white rot. If the wood was free of disease and had not been distorted by the wind, they would cut it into timbers. Otherwise they would leave it lying on the ground. "Perhaps every known hummock in the Floridas is annually attacked," Audubon wrote in alarm, "and so often does it happen that the white rot or some other disease had deteriorated the quality of the timber, that the woods may be seen strewn with trunks that have been found worthless, so that every year these valuable oaks are becoming rarer. The destruction of the young trees of this species caused by the fall of the great trunks is, of course, immense, and as there are no artificial plantations of these trees in our country, before long a good-sized live-oak will be so valuable that its owner will exact an enormous price for it, even while it yet stands in the wood. In my opinion, formed on personal observation, live-oak hummocks are *not quite* so plentiful as they are represented to be."

Audubon was also fascinated by the alligators. They were "extremely abundant," he wrote, "and the heads of the fishes which they had snapped off, lay floating around on the dark waters. A rifle bullet was now and then sent through the eye of one of the largest, which, with a tremendous splash of its tail, expired. One morning we saw a monstrous fellow lying on the shore. I was desirous of obtaining him to make an accurate drawing of his head, and accompanied by my assistant and two of the sailors, proceeded cautiously towards him. When within a few yards, one of us fired, and sent through his side an ounce ball which tore a hole large enough to receive a man's hand. He slowly raised his head, bent himself upwards, opened his huge jaws, swung his tail to and fro, rose on his legs, blew in a frightful manner, and fell to the earth. My assistant leaped on shore, and, contrary to my injunctions, caught hold of the animal's tail, when the alligator, awakening from its trance, with a last effort crawled slowly towards the water, and plunged heavily into it. Had he thought once of flourishing his tremendous weapon, there might have been an end of his assailant's life, but he fortunately went in peace to his grave, where we left him, as the water was too deep.

"The same morning, another of equal size was observed swimming directly for the bows of our vessel, attracted by the gentle rippling of the water there. One of the officers, who had watched him, fired, and scattered his brain through the air, when he tumbled and rolled at a fearful rate, blowing all the while most furiously. The river was bloody for yards around, but although the monster passed close by the vessel, we could not secure him, and after a while he sank to the bottom."

But the voyage was not successful. One of the sailors accidentally shot himself through the forehead—an event that sickened Audubon—and he was also becoming discouraged both by his surroundings and his continuing inability to obtain the specimens he wanted. Hardly any birds were to be seen, he wrote Lucy, and those only common species. The river smelled foul; the food was bad—they were eating possums and young alligators; and he was beginning to disagree with the commander. Finally he decided there was no point returning down the river with the *Spark,* so he left the schooner and traveled back to St. Augustine by land.

There he took passage on the schooner *Agnes* for Charleston, where he hoped to find a revenue cutter that would carry him to the keys. On this journey, too, he met with a heavy storm. The boat was within forty miles of Charleston when a gale rose and blew it back to Savannah, Georgia, where the people he called on immediately told him that no one in the city would subscribe to *The Birds of America.* The next morning, however, a merchant, William Gaston, suddenly changed his mind. He not only paid two hundred dollars then and there for the first volume, he also agreed to act as Audubon's agent in the city. The same day, two more people subscribed, each of them paying cash; and on March 12, two days after Audubon arrived back in Charleston, he received a letter from Gaston saying that he had just obtained a fourth. Joyfully Audubon wrote Lucy that he now had twenty-two subscribers in America.

Unfortunately, no revenue cutters arrived in Charleston during his first week there; and although he sold three more subscriptions, he was growing more and more concerned by his failure to obtain additional specimens. His original schedule was now completely upset. As he wrote Lucy, he had come to the United States to collect more birds, so that he could continue with his book. But everything had gone wrong; and as a result of his poor timing, he had failed to obtain the specimens he wanted. There was no point now trying to go farther south than Key West; all hope of meeting her in New Orleans had vanished. What he had now decided to do was to remain in Charleston until the first of April. If no revenue cutter showed up by then, he would return to the Middle Atlantic States and search for seabirds there.

He changed his mind, however, about his deadline; and on April 14 the schooner *Marion,* which was attached to the revenue service, entered the Charleston Harbor. Audubon immediately called on its commander, Lieutenant Day, who readily agreed to take him to Key West, provided he could obtain permission from the Collector of the Port of Charleston. The collector read Audubon's letters from Washington and, in effect, placed the *Marion* at his disposal for two months.

Down the coast he went again, past the mouth of the St. John's River and St. Augustine, and by the end of April had reached Indian Key, some fifty miles south of Miami. During this voyage, Audubon had succeeded in collecting only a few birds; but at Indian Key he found just the person to help—a pilot named Egan, who worked for the deputy collector there. Egan, "besides being a first-rate shot, possessed a most intimate acquaintance with the country. He had been a 'conch diver,' and . . . to seek for curious shells in their retreat seemed to him more pastime than toil. Not a cormorant or pelican, a flamingo, an ibis, or heron had ever in his days formed its nest without his having marked the spot; and as to the keys to which the doves are wont to resort, he was better acquainted with them than many fops are with the contents of their pockets. In a word, he positively knew every channel that led to these islands, and every cranny along their shores." Furthermore, the deputy collector agreed to release him to accompany Audubon for the rest of the journey.

First, Egan took Audubon pelican hunting; and unlike Captain Aumack, who had ventured after pelicans during that stormy night on the river so many years before, the pilot knew exactly what he was doing. He borrowed a boat and had Audubon's party rowed to a sandy point. Then, telling the two sailors to ship their oars, he himself sculled the boat quietly "until suddenly coming almost in contact with a thick shrubbery of mangroves, we beheld, right before us, a multitude of pelicans. A discharge of artillery," Audubon continued, "seldom produced more effect; the dead, the dying, and the wounded, fell from the trees upon the water, while those unscathed flew screaming through the air in terror and dismay."

After they picked up the dead birds and stacked them under the gunwales, Egan next took Audubon half a mile farther and showed him a spot where four hundred cormorants were nesting. Audubon and the others fired a volley, and Audubon said that "the number that dropped as if dead and plunged into the water was such, that I thought by some unaccountable means or other we had killed the whole colony." But Egan only laughed. As the birds raised their heads from the water, hardly a one proved to have been injured. The men had fired too soon, Egan explained. Their shots had simply lodged in the tough, dry twigs from which the comorants made their nests. In shooting cormorants, he said, the gunner should wait until the birds took to the air. Under his instruction, they brought down a score of the birds ten minutes later.

For several days they remained at Indian Key, exploring the beaches and shores. Egan continued to be helpful in collecting specimens, Henry Ward was kept busy preparing skins, and both Lehman and Audubon, when they were not hunting, drew the birds and the necessary backgrounds for the pictures. Then they rowed to Sandy Island, which lies just six miles from the extreme point of South Florida. There they made camp, and "when we laid ourselves down in the sand to sleep," Audubon wrote, "the waters almost bathed our feet; when we opened our eyes in the morning, they were at an immense distance. Our boat lay on her side, looking not unlike a giant whale reposing on a mud bank. The birds in myriads were probing their exposed pasture-ground. The great flocks of ibises fed apart from equally large collections of godwits, and thousands of herons gracefully paced along, ever and anon thrusting their javelin bills into the body of some unfortunate fish confined in a small pool of water. Of fish crows, I could not estimate the number, but from the havoc they made among the crabs, I conjecture that these animals must have been scarce by the time of the next ebb. Frigate pelicans chased the jaeger, which himself had just robbed a poor gull of its prize, and all the gallinules ran with spread wings from the mud banks to the thickets of the island, so timorous had they become when they perceived us."

This, at last, was the Florida Audubon had hoped to see, and with the help of Egan he secured many of the specimens he had wanted. Nor was Egan merely a good hunter and fisherman; he was also skilled at handling a small boat. On their way back to Indian Key, "the sun was descending fast, when a black cloud suddenly obscured the majestic orb. Our sails swelled by a breeze that was scarcely felt by us; and the pilot [Egan], requesting us to sit on the weather gunwale, told us that we were 'going to get it.' One sail was hauled in and secured, and the other was reefed, although the wind had not increased. A low murmuring noise was heard, and across the cloud that now rolled in tumultuous masses, shot vivid flashes of lightning. Our experienced guide steered directly across a flat toward the nearest land. The sailors passed their quids from one cheek to the other, and our pilot having covered himself with his oil jacket, we followed his example. 'Blow, sweet breeze,' cried he at the tiller, and 'we'll reach the land before the blast overtakes us, for, gentlemen, it is a furious cloud yon.'

"A furious cloud indeed was the one which now, like an eagle on outstretched wings, approached so swiftly that one might have deemed it in haste to destroy us. We were not more than a cable's length from the shore, when, with an imperative voice, the pilot calmly said to us, 'Sit quite still, gentlemen, for I should not like to lose you overboard just now; the boat can't upset, my word for that, if you will but sit still—Here we have it!'...

"Our light bark shivered like a leaf the instant the blast reached her sides. We thought she had gone over; but the next instant she was on the shore. And now in contemplation of the sublime and awful storm, I gazed around me. The waters drifted like snow; the tough mangroves hid their tops amid their roots, and the loud roaring of the waves driven among them blended with the howl of the tempest. It was not rain that fell; the masses of water flew in a horizontal direction, and where a part of my body was exposed I felt as if a smart blow had been given me on it. But enough—in half an hour it was over. The pure blue sky once more embellished the heavens, and although it was now quite night, we considered our situation a good one."

They made a camp among the mangrove trees, and the next day rejoined the *Marion* and continued south. Down the coast of Florida the schooner went, with Audubon still collecting birds, Henry Ward skinning them, Lehman making drawings, and Egan serving as guide. This was nothing like Audubon's previous experiences in Florida. Except for an unprofitable visit to the Mule Keys, Audubon was pleased with the results of his expedition. Finally, they cleared Key West and headed toward the Dry Tortugas, some seventy miles away. "They consist of five or six extremely low, uninhabitable banks, formed of shelly sand, and are resorted to principally by that class of men called wreckers and turtlers. Between these islands are deep channels, which, although extremely intricate, are well known to those adventurers, as well as to the commanders of the revenue cutters, whose duties call them to that dangerous coast. The great coral reef, or wall, lies about eight miles from these inhospitable isles, in the direction of the Gulf, and on it many an ignorant or careless navigator has suffered shipwreck. The whole ground around them is densely covered with corals, seafans, and other productions of the deep, amid which crawl innumerable testaceous animals, while shoals of curious and beautiful fishes fill the limpid waters above them."

On these islands, the great sea turtles came ashore to lay their eggs; and Audubon had a chance to observe them. "On first nearing the shores, and mostly on fine moonlight nights," he wrote, "the turtle raises her head above the water, being still distant thirty or forty yards from the shore, looks around her, and attentively examines the objects on the shore. Should she observe nothing likely to disturb her intended operations, she emits a loud hissing sound, by which such of her many enemies as are unaccustomed to it are startled, and so are apt to remove to another place, although unseen by her. Should she hear any noise, or perceive indications of danger, she instantly sinks, and goes off to a considerable distance; but should everything be quiet, she advances slowly towards the beach, crawls over it, her head raised to the full stretch of her neck, and when she has reached a place fitted for her purpose, she gazes all around in silence. Finding 'all well' she proceeds to form a hole in the sand, which she effects by removing it from *under* her body with her *hind* flippers, scooping it out with so much dexterity that the sides seldom if ever fall in. The sand is raised alternately with each flipper, as with a large ladle, until it has accumulated behind her, when, supporting herself with her head and fore part on the ground fronting her body, she, with a spring from each flipper, sends the sand around her, scattering it to the distance of several feet. In this manner the hole is dug to the depth of eighteen inches, or sometimes more than two feet.

This labor I have seen performed in the short period of nine minutes. The eggs are then dropped one by one, and disposed in layers, to the number of a hundred and fifty, or sometimes nearly two hundred. The whole time spent in this part of the operation may be about twenty minutes. She now scrapes the loose sand back over the eggs, and so levels and smooths the surface that few persons on seeing the spot could imagine anything have been done on it. This accomplished to her mind, she retreats to the water, leaving the hatching of the eggs to the heat of the sand."

The vast numbers of animals and eggs on the Dry Tortugas had created a business for many men who made their living by harvesting this crop from the sea. Some took rods and walked the beaches. When they came on turtle tracks, they probed the sand with their rods until they located the nests and could recover the eggs. Others, searching for meat, captured the turtles themselves. "To upset a turtle on the shore," Audubon wrote, "one is obliged to fall on his knees, and, placing his shoulder behind her fore-arm, gradually raise her up by pushing with great force, and then with a jerk throw her over. Sometimes it requires the united strength of several men to accomplish this; and, if the turtle should be of very great size, as often happens on that coast, even handspikes are employed. Some turtlers are so daring as to swim up to them while lying asleep on the surface of the water, and turn them over in their own element, when, however, a boat must be at hand to enable them to secure their prize. Few turtles can bite beyond the reach of their fore-legs, and few, when once turned over, can, without assistance, regain their natural position; but, not withstanding this, their flippers are generally secured by ropes so as to render their escape impossible." Others harpooned the turtles, and Egan showed Audubon how this was done and told him that one man he knew had killed eight hundred green turtles this way within twelve months. In later years, the slaughter of green turtles brought them to the verge of extinction, but in Audubon's time the supply seemed inexhaustible.

In the Dry Tortugas, Audubon also met many of the Florida wreckers, seamen who made their living by sailing up and down the coast looking for wrecks they could salvage and also serving occasionally as pilots. He had expected them to be like pirates, but instead found them well-disciplined and friendly. Indeed, they took him on several expeditions and, before he left, presented him with a collection of shells, corals, and several live turtles.

They also offered to capture some rare birds for him, but time was running out and the *Marion* was due back in Charleston. So the commander ordered the sails hoisted and the anchor raised. The bow of the schooner cut a small wave in the surface of the water as it headed on the course that would take them north along the coast again. Audubon had enjoyed those days on the cutter, but he still did not have the birds he needed so desperately.

CHAPTER XXV

❧❧

1832 – 1833

A T the conclusion of his Florida expedition, Audubon looked on his future in the United States with more confidence. Not only had the days on the *Marion* in the company of men like Egan and the commander done him good; the use of the *Marion*, with the official recognition it implied, had stimulated him. He had collected some of the specimens he had wanted. Then, too, he had acquired a considerable number of American subscribers in recent months; and although George Ord was continuing his attacks, Audubon now had many supporters. As he had written Lucy earlier, the tide at last seemed to have turned.

He therefore decided to remain in the United States to obtain more subscriptions and collect more birds. He did not have sufficient funds, however, to continue supporting a full-time staff, so he separated from Ward at Charleston, where Ward found a job with the Natural History Museum, and from Lehman at Philadelphia. Then he sent for Lucy and the two boys—he was realizing his dream of having his whole family together to work on the book—and with them went to New York and on to Boston, which he had never visited before. His reception there justified his new self-confidence. Jubilantly he wrote Harlan, "Our success at Boston has been of the best kind. We have *now here* eight subscribers! And we hope to have a few more."

He left Boston on the fourteenth of August on the steamer *Connecticut* for Portland, Maine, with the intention of continuing up the coast to the Bay of Fundy. A week later he was in Eastport on the Canadian border, but, as he wrote Harlan, "*Birds* are very, very few and far between."

Because the water birds had not yet made their appearance, he spent about a fortnight farther inland. Then, not content with the results of his northern trip, he decided to take his family up the St. John's River, which starts running northeast in northern Maine, loops around in a giant U, and enters the Bay of Fundy at St. John in New Brunswick. Traveling overland, they reached the river at Fredericton, the province's capital, and took passage on a boat towed by two mules to Woodstock in New Brunswick. There they crossed the border to Houlton, Maine, and went down to Bangor. But Audubon was disappointed by his trip. He had again missed many of the birds he wanted and brought back relatively few specimens; but he had not lost his self-confidence, and he had not changed his mind about making the publication of his books a family business. On October 10, therefore, Victor sailed for England on the packet ship *South America* to serve as his father's business representative, while Audubon, Lucy and John planned to remain in Boston for the winter. On November 6, remembering his own arrival at Liverpool, Audubon wrote his son, "We are in full hope that by this day you are safely landed in hospitable England and that you have already met with friends as willing to render your time agreeable and useful as they were wont to be with me." And Lucy added the motherly postscript, "I have only time, my blessed child, to say God bless you! And may every success attend you. Write often to us and tell us everything about yourself. John is quite well and coming on pretty well in all things, but he will write to you himself very soon."

Harlan, who had made an extensive tour of Europe that fall, sent the Audubons a report on Victor's behavior as soon as he returned to the United States. "Nothing could exceed the kind attentions which your worthy son paid me when last in London," he wrote comfortingly. "He is rapidly improving himself and loses no opportunity in perfecting his education. He is respected and loved by all who know him." Greatly concerned about the success of his son, Audubon kept up a steady correspondence with him and, in addition to showering him with specific requests and suggestions, offered him a father's encouragement. Victor should keep his spirits up and remember the reputation now enjoyed by the name of Audubon; he should realize how much better off he was than Audubon had been when he first arrived in England; he should read good books and look at good paintings, thus keeping his mind occupied. Above all, he was not to forget that he was there to advance the family's interests; but, Audubon said mildly, he was sure that if any mistakes occurred, they would not be Victor's fault.

Yet he was not uncritical of his son. The quality of the plates, he thought, was falling off. Victor would have to pay closer attention to his responsibility for supervising Havell's work. He expressed concern, too, at the slowness with which the American subscribers were receiving their prints; he was discontented with Victor's accounting of the production costs; and he thought that his list of the copies delivered might be inaccurate.

He also complained that Victor did not seem to understand the accounts Havell submitted and therefore took time to describe how he himself analyzed and checked them. After each number was delivered, he had Havell give him an itemized list showing the subscribers and their addresses. This Audubon compared with his own subscription book and sometimes found an error. He also took pains, when he was traveling, to talk to his agents and ask to see a list of the shipments they had received from Havell. In this way, he had a further check on his engraver. Victor was now twenty-three years old, in those days an age when men operated businesses and commanded ships; he had had several years of experience in a mercantile house and had, indeed, aspired to a partnership; it was about time he learned some of the rudiments of accounting and auditing, if he was to be, as Audubon intended, the business manager of the family.

John, on the other hand, had abandoned his idea of becoming a steamboat captain, and was staying close to his father learning about birds and art. Audubon had become so pleased with John's progress that he was permitting him to draw some of the birds that were sent to Havell and challenged Havell to tell the son's pictures from the father's. With this division of labor—John handling the art, Victor the business—Audubon thought there could be no end to his books on birds.

In spite of the help he was receiving from his children, Audubon himself was busy during the winter of 1832–1833. He sold a number of additional subscriptions; he kept on drawing and providing Havell with new pictures (he even considered increasing the total pictures in each number from five to six or seven); he paid brief visits to New York and Philadelphia; and he made a number of influential friends—Dr. George Parkman and Dr. George Shattuck, both prominent Boston physicians; Thomas Nuttall, the botanist and ornithologist who had preceded him to the Arkansas Post in those days when he himself was unknown. He also kept up a constant correspondence with the Rev. Bachman, his Charleston friend, who was supplying him with new specimens and additional information about birds. Having finally tasted success, he did not intend to let it escape him through lack of attention or work on his part.

His continuing need, however, was birds. No matter how many subscriptions he sold, no matter how well Victor handled the business matters of the family, no matter how ably John drew pictures, the book could not be continued without more birds. These were the essential raw material on which everything else depended. He had now been the length of the Ohio and Mississippi rivers and had covered the Atlantic coast, although perhaps less successfully than he might have with better timing, from the Bay of Fundy to the Dry Tortugas. The Far West was still untouched by him, but to make a trip west of the Mississippi River would be a time-consuming and expensive venture, one that was clearly impractical for a while longer. He therefore decided to try the northeast coast again, starting earlier in the year and moving farther north than he had done before.

On the fourth of May, having left Lucy in New York, he sailed east from Boston down the prevailing wind and arrived in Eastport, Maine, three days later. There he found the weather so cold that there was no point attempting to go farther, so he decided to remain in Eastport a fortnight longer, making a trip back to Dennysville, which he had visited the year before. He still had his letters of introduction to the Revenue Service, and the Collector of the Port at Eastport treated him hospitably, so he took John on an expedition in a revenue

cutter around the mouth of the Bay of Fundy, a bay which is
justly noted for its tides. "Cape after cape, forming eddies and
counter currents far too terrific to be described by a landsman,
we passed in succession," he wrote, "until we reach a deep cove,
near the shores of White Head Island, which is divided from
Grand Mahan by a narrow strait, where we anchored secure
from every blast that could blow." They spent the night there
while Audubon searched for gulls, spent three days at Point
Lepreaux, a few miles east of the Canadian-American border,
then started west again to Eastport. The weather was cold, the
wind strong, the waves high, and the sails of the cutter reefed.
Racing along, they passed a heavily laden schooner going across
their course under full sail. As the other boat dropped astern,
they suddenly saw it caught by a wave or an extra-strong gust of
wind. Already strained to the utmost, the schooner swung far
to the leeward under the impact, but instead of straightening
up again, overturned. Spars, canvas, and rope floated in a mass
on the water as the ship, suddenly converted from a graceful,
handsome vessel to a floating hulk, lay lifeless on the water.
The crew of three may have been foolish about overloading
their schooner and failing to shorten sail, but they kept their
heads during the disaster and, disentangling themselves from
the floating debris, grabbed the keel. Quickly the commander of
the cutter ordered the helm swung over and worked his way
back against the wind, close enough to the schooner to toss
a line to the survivors. With the help of a fishing boat, he
brought the three sailors on board and towed the schooner into
a nearby harbor before turning back to Eastport. Audubon
"felt much sorrow at the sight of the dreadful accident" but
was greatly impressed by the skillful seamanship of the cutter's
commander.

Safely back in Eastport after a short, but successful, trip—
he had collected four rare birds—Audubon began to make more
definite plans for his journey farther north. He already had
John with him. Now they were joined by Dr. Shattuck's son,
and word had come that Thomas Lincoln, the son of one of
Audubon's friends in Maine, would also make the trip. This
gave him a staff. Now what he needed was transportation, and
he decided to charter a schooner. Knowing Lucy's propensity

for questioning his expenditures, he immediately explained to her that Shattuck and Lincoln would bear part of the expense and this would therefore be an economical way to make the voyage. Furthermore, he was sure that he could learn enough to make him the leading ornithologist in the country. This knowledge would enable him to earn more money for his family.

He chartered the schooner *Ripley,* whose owners expected it momentarily in Eastport and assured Audubon that in two days they would have it unloaded, ballasted, and ready for sea again. While he made these arrangements, Audubon was also busy purchasing the clothing and other equipment the travelers would need: ammunition, oilskin jackets, fishermen's boots, and other paraphernalia. In doing this, he was assisted by Dr. Parkman, who bought in Boston what was not available in Eastport. He was also joined by another medical student, William Ingalls.

By May 31 everything was practically ready—it had all taken more time than Audubon had expected—and, as he often did when he was on the verge of an expedition, he became apprehensive and emotional. To Victor, he wrote a long and almost pathetic note, begging him to continue with *The Birds of America* in the event of his own death. To Lucy, he said that he was in tears at the thought of leaving both her and the United States and prayed to God that he would return safely. After this outburst he calmed himself again and was ready to depart.

Long ago, in Henderson, when Audubon had been defrauded by the Yankee woodcutters who stole his equipment, he had shared the southern frontier's opinion of New Englanders. Now that he knew many of them personally, he had changed his mind and often referred to them as friendly and industrious and wrote with admiration of their seamanship. On June 6, when the *Ripley* weighed anchor, the many friends he had made at Eastport came down to see him off. Everybody shook hands all around; the batteries of the garrison and the cannon of the revenue cutter each fired a four-gun salute; and the *Ripley,* under a light breeze but running with the tide, left the harbor.

During the voyage, "we agreed to follow certain regulations intended for the general benefit," Audubon wrote. "Every morning the cook was called before three o'clock. At half-past three, breakfast was on the table, and everybody equipped. The guns, ammunition, botanical boxes, and baskets for eggs or minerals were all in readiness. Our breakfast consisted of coffee, bread and various materials. At four, all except the cook, and one seaman, went off in different directions, not forgetting to carry with them a store of cooked provisions. Some betook themselves to the islands, others to the deep bays; the latter on landing wandered over the country till noon, when laying themselves down on the rich moss, or sitting on the granite rock, they would rest for an hour, eat their dinner, and talk of their successes or disappointments. I often regret that I did not take sketches of the curious groups formed by my young friends on such occasions, and when, after returning at night, all were engaged in measuring, weighing, comparing, and dissecting the birds we had procured; operations which were carried on with the aid of a number of candles thrust into the necks of bottles. Here one examined the flowers and leaves of a plant, there another explored the recesses of a diver's gullet, while a third skinned a gull or a grouse. Nor was one journal forgotten. Arrangements were made for the morrow, and at twelve we left matters to the management of the cook, and retired to our roosts."

Generally speaking, the men paired off. Emery, the captain of the *Ripley,* joined up with Coolidge, the mate; Ingalls and Shattuck, both medical students, worked well together; Lincoln and John, being the strongest and most determined hunters, made the third pair. Audubon himself went with one or other of the groups, according to the circumstances.

On the port side of the *Ripley,* as it proceeded northeast, Audubon could see the coast of Nova Scotia, indented with hundreds of small harbors. Occasionally they paused to collect birds, but Audubon was anxious to move north as quickly as possible, and on June 10 they reached Canso, where they found twenty fishing boats all bound for Labrador. "As we dropped anchor," Audubon said, "we had a snowfall, and the sky had an appearance such as I never before recollect having seen. Go-

ing on shore we found not a tree in blossom, though the low
plants near the ground were all in bloom; I saw azaleas, white
and blue violets, etc., and in some situations the grass looked
really well. The robins were in full song; one nest of that bird
was found; the white-throated sparrow and Savannah finch
[Savannah sparrow] were also in full song."

At four o'clock the next morning they were under way again,
passing through the Strait of Canso, which divides Cape Breton
Island from the rest of Nova Scotia. "The land locked us in,"
Audubon wrote, "the water was smooth, the sky pure, and the
thermometer was only 46°, quite cold; indeed, I was more
grateful to see the sunshine whilst on deck this morning, and
to feel its warmth, than I can recollect before at this season.
After sailing for twenty-one miles, and passing one after
another every vessel of the fishing fleet, we entered the Gut of
Canso, so named by the Spanish on account of the innumerable
wild geese which, in years long past and forgotten, resorted to
this famed passage. The land rises on each side in the form of
an amphitheater, and on the Nova Scotia side, to a considerable
height. Many *appearances* of dwellings exist, but the country is
too poor for comfort; the timber is small, and the land, very
stony. Here and there a small patch of ploughed land, planted,
or to be planted, with potatoes, was all we could see evincing
cultivation." The schooner, now in the Gulf of St. Lawrence,
turned north along the coast of Cape Breton, which Jean Audubon had visited years before as a young seaman.

After a short stop at Jestico Island, three miles off the coast
of Cape Breton, the *Ripley* headed for the Magdalen Islands,
which lie between Cape Breton and the Gaspé Peninsula, reaching them on June 12. They spent one day there collecting birds
and would have remained longer, but the wind on June 14 was
so perfect for the rest of their voyage that they decided they
should take advantage of it. Their pilot, a Nova Scotian named
Godwin, wanted to show Audubon what he called the "Bird
Rock," where gannets bred in great numbers. "At eleven
o'clock," Audubon wrote, "I could distinguish its top plainly
from the deck, and thought it covered with snow to the depth
of several feet; this appearance existed on every portion of the
flat, projecting shelves. Godwin said, with the coolness of a man

who had visited this rock for ten successive seasons, that what we saw was not snow—but gannets! I rubbed my eyes, took my spy-glass, and in an instant the strangest picture stood before me. They were birds we saw,—a mass of birds of such size as I never before cast my eyes on. . . . The fishermen who kill these birds to get their flesh for codfish bait ascend in parties of six or eight, armed with clubs; sometimes, indeed, the party comprises the crews of several vessels. As they reach the top, the birds, alarmed, rise with a noise like thunder, and fly off in such hurried, fearful confusion as to throw each other down, often falling on each other till there is a bank of them several feet high. The men strike them down and kill them until fatigued or satisfied. Five hundred and forty have been thus murdered in one hour by six men. . . . So great is the destruction of these birds annually that their flesh supplies the bait for upwards of forty fishing-boats."

Audubon wanted to land on the rock but the wind was too high, so they set their course almost due north for the coast of the Canadian mainland. After three days of sailing they sighted a fleet of some thirty codfishing boats opposite the mouth of the Natashquan River, which flows southeast through Quebec and where the Hudson's Bay Company had a fishing establishment. Since no American ships were allowed to enter, they sailed westward and anchored in a small bay. Although they were actually in the Province of Quebec, Audubon considered the coast part of Labrador, "farther north than I ever was before. But what a country! When we landed and passed the beach, we sank nearly up to our knees in mosses of various sorts, producing as we moved through them a curious sensation. These mosses, which at a distance look like hard rocks, are, under foot, like a velvet cushion. We scrambled about, and with anxiety stretched our necks and looked over the country far and near, but not a square foot of *earth* could we see."

While they lay at anchor collecting birds a Canadian cutter, the *Gulnare*, entered the harbor, and Audubon called on the commanding officer, who promised to assist him in any way that he could. After obtaining as many new specimens as he thought possible, Audubon wanted to press on, but for five more days the wind was so unfavorable they remained in the harbor. Finally it changed, moving to the northwest. A heavy rain came down, and the swell rocked the *Ripley* so violently that Audubon could not draw. After dinner, the wind went to the southwest, and the captains of both the *Gulnare* and the *Ripley* thought they might be able to get free of the harbor at last. Everyone on the two ships worked fast, making ready; and, with its sails close hauled, the *Ripley* cleared the outer cape.

In spite of the heavy surf on the following day, Audubon landed on a group of rocks covered with guillemots and found that two "eggers" had landed before him. The eggers made a business of collecting the eggs of seabirds and selling them on the commercial market, and their actions disgusted and infuriated Audubon. They would kill as many birds as possible both for meat and for eiderdown, then strip the island entirely of eggs. "So inconsiderate are they," Audubon wrote, "that they kill every bird that comes their way. The eggs of gulls, guillemots, and ducks are searched for with care; and the puffins and some other birds they massacre in vast numbers for the sake of their feathers. So constant and persevering are their depredations that these species, which, according to the accounts of the few settlers I saw in the country, were exceedingly abundant twenty years ago, have abandoned their ancient breeding places, and removed much farther north in search of peaceful security. Scarcely, in fact, could I procure a young guillemot before the eggers left the coast, nor was it until late in July that I succeeded, after the birds had laid three or four eggs each, instead of one, and when, nature having been exhausted and the season nearly spent, thousands of these birds left the country without having accomplished the purpose for which they had visited it. This war of extermination cannot last many years more. The eggers themselves will be the first to repent the entire disappearance of the myriads of birds that made the coast of Labrador their summer residence, and unless they follow the persecuted tribes to the northward, they must renounce their trade." The commander of the *Gulnare* was equally appalled at the destruction, writing in his log that he had had no idea of the extent of the business.

By the middle of July the *Ripley* had worked approximately a hundred miles up the coast to the mouth of the Little Meca-

tina River; and the wind having died, Audubon took one of
the smaller boats and went ahead. As they approached the river
mouth, he was surprised "to see how small some of the ducks
looked which flew between us and the rocks, so stupendously
high were the rough shores under which our little bark moved
along. We doubled the cape and came to the entrance of the
Little Mecatina Harbor, but so small did it appear to me that
I doubted if it was the harbor; the shores were terribly wild,
fearfully high and rugged, and nothing was heard but the
croaking of a pair of ravens and their half-grown brood, mingling with the roar of the surf against the rocky ledges which
projected everywhere, and sent the angry waters foaming into
the air." After the *Ripley* was safely anchored and everybody
had had supper, Audubon, John, and Shattuck climbed to the
highest crest. Looking around them, they could see "nothing
but rocks—barren rocks—wild as the wildest Apennines anywhere; the moss only a few inches deep, and the soil or decom-
posed matter beneath it so moist that, wherever there was an
incline, the whole slipped from under our feet like an ava-
lanche, and down we slid for feet or yards. The labor was excessive; at the bottom of each dividing ravine the scrub bushes
intercepted our way for twenty or thirty paces, over which
we had to scramble with great exertion, and on our return we
slid down fifty feet more into an unknown pit of moss and
mire."

From Little Mecatina, the *Ripley* worked its way along the
northern shore of the Gulf of St. Lawrence, sailing when the
wind and weather were favorable, stopping for days in small
harbors while the men hunted and skinned birds and Audubon drew. It was difficult, intense work in a hardy country; and
by the middle of July, Audubon wrote in his journal, "Indeed
I now dread every change of harbor, so horribly rugged and
dangerous is the whole coast and country, especially to the inexperienced man of either sea or land." Yet as long as the
season lasted he refused to turn back, because this was the expedition that was to help make him the country's leading authority on water birds and, as he was not likely to make the
trip again, he intended to reap the greatest possible benefit
from it.

By August 1, they had reached the Strait of Belle Isle, which divides the island of Newfoundland from the mainland and marks the beginning of Labrador itself. "At noon," Audubon wrote, "we were visited by an iceberg, which has been drifting within three miles of us, and is now grounded at the entrance of the bay; it looks like a large man-of-war dressed in light green muslin, instead of canvas, and when the sun strikes it, it glitters with intense brilliancy." But although he was fascinated by the iceberg, he thought the time was coming to end the voyage. "I have determined," he wrote, "to make a last thorough search of the mountain tops, plains and ponds, and if no success ensues, to raise anchor and sail towards the United States once more; and blessed will be the day when I land on those dear shores, where all I long for in the world exists and lives, I hope." Under the pressure of constant work, his great strength was being exhausted. A few days later he wrote in his journal, "I now sit down to post my poor book, while a heavy gale is raging furously around our vessel. My reason for not writing at night is that I have been drawing so constantly, often seventeen hours a day, that the weariness of my body at night has been unprecedented, by such work at least.

"At times I felt as if my physical powers would abandon me; my neck, my shoulders, and, more than all, my fingers, were almost useless through actual fatigue at drawing. Who could believe this? Yet nothing is more true. When at the return of dawn my spirits called me out of my berth, my body seemed to beg my mind to suffer it to rest a while longer; and as dark forced me to lay aside my brushes, I immediately went to rest as if I had walked sixty-five miles that day, as I have done *a few times* in my stronger days. Yesternight, when I rose from my little seat to contemplate my work and to judge of the effect of it compared with the nature which I had been attempting to copy, it was the affair of a moment; and instead of waiting, as I always like to do, until that hazy darkness which is to me the best time to judge of the strength of light and shade, I went at once to rest as if delivered from the heaviest task I ever performed. The young men think my fatigue is added to by the fact that I often work in wet clothes, but I have done that all my life with no ill effects. No! no!" he continued sadly, "it is that I am no longer young."

He was forty-eight years old. By the standards of his time,

when men lived less long, he was getting on. He had been tired before but never as tired as now. More than once he had exhausted himself following a superhuman schedule, but never when the men working with him were not. As he himself said, he was "no longer young," and it was time to end the journey. The following day, the *Ripley* headed across St. John Bay toward the island of Newfoundland on the course that would take it home. As he watched the mainland of Canada disappear, Audubon wearily wrote in his journal, "Seldom in my life have I left a country with as little regret as I do this; the next nearest to this was East Florida, after my excursions up the St. John's River. As we sailed away, and I saw probably for the last time, the high rugged hills partly immersed in masses of the thick fog that usually hovers over them, and knew that now the bow of our truly fine vessel was turned toward the place where thou, my Lucy, are waiting for me, I felt rejoiced, although far away."

They raced down the coast—having made up his mind to go back, Audubon was in a hurry—and on the morning of August 13 they entered St. George's Bay at the southwest end of Newfoundland. Audubon decided to stay here a few days while they collected more specimens. Some of the men tried their hand at lobstering—they caught ninety-nine—and they all went to a dance. But this time it was not Audubon who played the violin; it was John. Audubon himself left the party at eleven o'clock "and slept soundly until the young men hailed for a boat."

After they left St. George's Bay, they were caught in a gale which carried them off course to the northeast; and when they tried to beat back to the Strait of Canso, the wind failed. Audubon then thought they might be able to reach the Nova Scotia town of Pictou, which faces Prince Edward Island, and that he could then continue the journey by land. But even this proved impossible, so he asked the captain to put him ashore on a nearby island. Catching a boat to the mainland, he soon reached Pictou and, after a few days of travel in Nova Scotia, went to Windsor on the Bay of Fundy. There Audubon watched the famous tides in the Windsor River "and saw the mass of water accumulating with a rapidity that I cannot describe. At half-flow the water rose three feet in ten minutes, but it is even more rapid than this. A few minutes after its greatest height is attained, it begins to recede, and in a few minutes the whole bed of the river is again emptied."

A steamer carried him from Windsor across the bay to St. John in New Brunswick, and down to Eastport. From there Audubon went to Boston, where he stayed several weeks, and on to New York. Although he had been exhausted by the trip, he was pleased with its results. He had, he told Victor, obtained eight new birds; he had made twenty-five drawings; and he had enough material to complete the second volume of *The Birds of America*. Although the trip had been expensive—it had cost about two thousand dollars—he was satisfied. He was sure now that his would be the best book on North American birds, and he the best ornithologist.

He needed that superiority and all the prestige that he had gained from his Florida expedition as well, because while he had been away he had come under the most vicious personal attack yet. For some time George Ord, Audubon's enemy in Philadelphia, had been in correspondence with a strange Englishman named Charles Waterton, author of the book *Wanderings in South America, the North-West of the United States, and the Antilles*. Not only was Waterton a traveler and an author, he was also an amateur naturalist; and at one time Audubon had admired him. Indeed, three years before, in a letter to Harlan, Audubon had criticized naturalists like Jardine for staying at home too much and avoiding the hardships of field work. Then he had added, "Waterton is the exception to this. His wife died in childbirth, and he has gone to seek once more in the wealthy forest of Guinea the pleasures he had felt before, and I sincerely hope that he will meet with great success."

This feeling, however, had not been reciprocated. Waterton had taken a violent dislike to Audubon, and had read Ord's letters avidly. "If I possessed any important information about this man," Ord wrote about Audubon, "I certainly should give it to you, but all my inquiries have one result, viz. that 'he is a well meaning sort of a man, though a great liar.'" Casting reflections on Audubon's professionalism, he continued, "For the greater part of the time in which he resided in the United

States, he was occupied in shopkeeping. He was thus employed when Wilson saw him at Louisville, Kentucky." Or, "He told the late Baron Cuvier that he had resided for twenty years in the woods of America, living in a rude hut constructed by himself, for the purpose of studying birds.... Now it is not necessary to inform a real naturalist that it is not in the depth of an American forest that the habits of birds can be studied.... But the story was well calculated to arouse the curiosity of John Bull, who is wonderfully taken with prodigies." On and on Ord ranted, picking apart detail after detail in Audubon's life, calling him untruthful for saying that rattlesnakes climb trees, accusing him of lying for claiming that carrion-eating birds were guided to their food by sight, not smell. There was no end to it: "Mr. A. has been pronounced the greatest ornithologist that has ever appeared; and to convince the world that there is no mistake in their estimate of his uncommon acquisitions, he seemed determined to make a display of his knowledge upon all occasions"; "I have been repeatedly solicited to review Audubon's great work, and his history or biography of our birds, but I have foreborn, for the sake of peace, as I am confident that I should have a swarm of hornets about my ears, were I to proclaim to the world all that I know of this impudent pretender, and his stupid book"; and again, "The time for displaying all this man's incompetency and mendacity to the world is not yet come." Sometimes Ord stated the truth —for example, Audubon's Bird of Washington, which he had been so excited to discover when he was living in Henderson, was nothing but an immature bald eagle; sometimes he invented half-truths and outright libels. One of these was particularly vicious. "When Swainson published his frothy puff about Audubon and his plates," Ord said, referring to the review that had appeared in *Loudon's Magazine*, "it was clearly understood between them that the former was to write the history of birds [the *Ornithological Biography*]; this was well known in London. The reason why Swainson did not write the work, as told me by himself, was that Audubon insisted upon his unknown name being given to the world as author! Mr. Swainson, upon this, very properly declined having anything to do with the affair."

It was partly true, partly fabrication—a strange mixture con-
cocted from Ord's jealousy and Swainson's injured pride. Waterton accepted it at face value, mulled over it, and in the
May issue of *Loudon's Magazine,* published while Audubon was
in Eastport, came out with a statement on the *Ornithological
Biography.* "Without leaving behind him in America any public reputation as a naturalist," Waterton wrote, repeating his
old complaints, "Mr. Audubon comes to England, and he is immediately pointed out to us as an ornithological luminary of
the first magnitude. Strange it is, that he, who had been under
such a dense cloud of obscurity in his own western latitude,
should have broken out so suddenly into such dazzling radiance,
the moment he approached our eastern island. I ask, what production of Mr. Audubon's is it that has called forth such rap-
turous applauses from our naturalists, who, not content with
their own prostration, would fain persuade the public to bow
submissive to the stranger?" It could not be Audubon's pictures, Waterton argued. They were "solely a work of art." It
could not be the article on vultures. That article was "lamen-
tably faulty at almost every point." It must, therefore, be the
Ornithological Biography.

And what about that book? Waterton repeated Ord's version
of his conversation with Swainson without mentioning names
but claiming that he possessed "undeniable proof" of its truth.
He compared the style of the *Ornithological Biography* with
the style of Audubon's article on vultures. And he came to the
conclusion that "in fine, the whole work, from beginning to
end, bears evident and undeniable marks of being the product
of one pen. One hand alone has directed that pen. Has this
hand been that of the reputed author?—No. . . . I request the
English reader to weigh well in his own mind what I have
stated; and I flatter myself that he will agree with me, when I
affirm that the correct and elegant style of composition, which
appears throughout the *whole* of the *Biography of Birds* cannot
possibly be that of him whose name it bears."

So Audubon had not written a word of his own book.

That was the charge leveled at him publicly on his return
from the exhausting expedition on board the *Ripley.*

❧❧

CHAPTER XXVI

1833 – 1836

As a younger man, Audubon had been quick to give way to his anger. When he thought that Dacosta had tricked him, he was ready to return to Philadelphia and murder his father's agent; at Henderson, he had been prepared to fight the man who purchased the steamboat; and when he believed himself mistreated in Philadelphia, he lashed out even at his friends. But now that he was older, he had learned to restrain himself. Instead of replying personally to Waterton, he ignored the article.

Victor, however, did not. In the July issue of *Loudon's Magazine,* he rose to his father's defense by saying, in a short communication, that he had proof from the person cited by Waterton that "Mr. Audubon, and no other person, is the *bona fide* author of the *Ornithological Biography.*" In closing, he added with a touch of his father's former sarcasm, "I shall not notice Mr. Waterton further, except to express my thanks for his generous conduct, in withholding his attacks on Mr. Audubon for two years after the book in question was published, and during the time the author was in England, and bringing these charges forward when my father has returned to the forests of America."

Others, too, joined in defending Audubon against Waterton and Ord. Among them was Swainson. Swainson's pride may have been hurt; he may have written sharply to Audubon; but he was not willing to let Waterton's statements pass unchallenged. "In reply to the questions and inquiries of that gentleman," he told the readers of *Loudon's Magazine,* "regarding the assistance I should have given to my friend Mr. Audubon, in the *scientific* details of his work, my reply was, that the nego-

tiation had been broken off from an unwillingness that my
name should be printed in the title page. I was not asked to
write the work, nor did Mr. Audubon 'insist upon his own
name being given to the world as the author' of such parts
as he wished me to undertake."

When Victor wrote to his father about the controversy, Audubon replied philosophically that he was sorry that Victor
should bother himself over Waterton's attacks. After all, the
world knew that he would not have to travel incessantly at great
expense if he only wanted to tell falsehoods. All he would have
to do was stay in his London apartment and write down whatever occurred to him. What really counted was not Waterton's
comments, but the quality of his book. If his book continued
at the same high standards, his detractors would automatically
be forced to retreat.

Then he went on with greater emotion that he was proud
of what he had done, he was proud of his wife and sons, of
the recognition that he had received from the United States
government, and of the circle of learned friends that he had
attracted. In that desperate period after his bankruptcy in Henderson, no one had wanted him and he was not sure what he
himself wanted. He had been confused in his mind then. Now
he was clear. He cared about his family and his book—nothing
else, not even the unfair charges made by Waterton.

After partially recovering from the exhaustion of his cruise,
Audubon laid out his plans for the coming winter. He intended
to remain in New York a while longer, then travel south, selling subscriptions and collecting more information about birds,
until he reached Charleston, where Bachman had invited the
whole family, Audubon, Lucy, and John, to spend the winter.
Before he left, however, he wanted to settle a problem that
was bothering him. In the first two hundred plates, making up
Volumes One and Two, he knew he had repeated three species.
This left the total number of species shown three short of what
it should have been. He now thought he should add three small
pictures to the last number of the second volume, thus fulfilling the promise he had made in his prospectus. The expense
concerned him, but he believed his repution would be enhanced. Actually he owed his subscribers more than three addi-

tional pictures. During those frenzied days of painting in London, he had included in his book three nonexistent birds which he called a carbonated warbler, Selby's flycatcher, and Cuvier's regulus. Apparently he had made errors in his original sketches and notes; these birds, although they resemble real species, have never been identified since. He had also duplicated more species than he thought by failing to distinguish between different phases of the same birds; and because he depended in part on specimens sent him by friends, he had also added what he called a Columbia jay to his collection of North American birds, thinking it had come from the Columbia River, when actually it was a magpie-jay from Mexico. Such mistakes, however, were completely understandable in terms of the knowledge of his time. He was pioneering, and his errors were those of a pioneer. What was truly significant, aside from the magnificence of his plates, was his successful effort to present more birds, including more new species, than anyone had done before and also his conscientious attempt to live up to the promises he had made in his prospectus.

Now that *The Birds of America* was well under way, he began thinking about two other money-making ventures, one of them old, one of them new. The old one was the arrangement whereby the artist Kidd copied some of the oil paintings Audubon had made in England and then sold the copies. Obviously this was working out well, because Audubon advised Victor to keep Kidd working as much as possible. The new venture was one he had been considering for several years: to reproduce *The Birds of America* in a reduced size. Bohn, the bookseller whom he had met in Liverpool, had strongly advised him against the mammoth publication on which he had set his heart, pointing out that both its cost and its cumbersome bulk would greatly curtail its sales. But even Bohn had eventually agreed that the pictures should first be produced as Audubon had envisioned them, and certainly their spectacular appearance helped Audubon gain the initial recognition he needed. It was equally certain, however, that the format Audubon chose had greatly limited the book's distribution. Despite all his efforts, he was still selling only one subscription here, another there.

Audubon had some definite thoughts on the new edition. The book absolutely must not come out before the large edition was completed and in the hands of the subscribers; until then his plans should be kept secret. But once the first book was finished, he should be prepared to start on the second almost immediately, because it would produce the greater profits. He also thought that the text of the *Ornithological Biography* should be included with the pictures, using the format adopted by Wilson. On the other hand, he had not made up his mind on many points and wanted Victor's advice. Would it be better to reduce the size of all the pictures or leave the small plates as they were? Should the engravings be done on copper or steel? Would woodcuts be acceptable? Could the book be produced more inexpensively in Germany or France than in England?

He stayed on in New York for several days, hoping for the arrival of twenty volumes which Victor was sending him and which he thought he might be able to sell on his trip south. But when they failed to come, he began his journey without them. At Philadelphia he called on his old friends but was unable to obtain any additional subscriptions. He was, however, so well known and reputedly wealthy that a former creditor, discovering that he was in town, served papers against him to collect an old debt. He was "on the point of being taken to prison, had I not met with William Norris, Esq. [one of his Philadelphia supporters], who kindly offered to be my bail." The experience, of course, revived the horrible memories of Henderson, and he wrote sadly, but not quite accurately, in his journal, "This event brings to my mind so many disagreeable thoughts connected with my former business transactions, in which I was *always* the *single* loser, that I will only add I made all necessary arrangements to have it paid."

After a brief visit in Baltimore he went on to Washington. To make *The Birds of America* complete, he would sometime have to go west. Because such a journey would be an extremely expensive private undertaking, he hoped he could be included on the staff of any future expedition sponsored by the government. But at the office of the Secretary of War, he "met with a reception that nearly discouraged me." After listening to

Audubon, the Secretary "said in an indifferent and cold manner that any request of that sort must be made in writing to the Department."

Before he left Washington, however, he received help from an unexpected source. "I was revolving in my mind how I might get to the Rocky Mountains without the assistance of the Secretary of War," Audubon wrote, "when I suddenly met with a friendly face, no less than Washington Irving's. I mentioned my errand to him and the answer I had received, and he thought I was mistaken. I might have been: but those eyes of mine have discovered more truth in men's eyes than their mouths were willing to acknowledge. However, I listened to good Irving with patience and calmness, and he promised to see the Secretary of War; and he also at once accompanied me to Mr. Taney, the Secretary of the Treasury, who received me well, and at once kindly gave me a letter, granting me the privilege of the revenue cutters along the coast south of Delaware Bay."

Returning to Baltimore from Washington, he retraced his former route south, taking the boat to Norfolk, stopping at Richmond, and by October was in Charleston, where John, who had gone ahead of Lucy and Audubon, met them. During that fall, Audubon was again hard at work, finishing the pictures of water birds and at the same time preparing the manuscript for the second volume of the *Ornithological Biography*. He had also been mulling over the criticisms of Waterton and Ord and had decided to refute them. With the assistance of Bachman, who was equally interested in the subject, he was conducting a new set of experiments to prove that carrion-eating birds located their food by sight, not smell; and when the experiments were finished, he intended to repeat them in the presence of witnesses. In addition, he was collecting all the material he could on the climbing habits of rattlesnakes and planned to publish a paper demonstrating the truth of what he had originally said in Edinburgh. Having told Victor to ignore Waterton's attacks, he now congratulated him on his reply, saying that it stated his own views exactly.

But during those months at Bachman's house, although he was comfortable and felt at home, he was disturbed and restless.

Always before, he had been able to recover his strength quickly, but he still felt the effects of the cruise on the *Ripley*. Instead of returning to his work with vigor, he began to wonder if he would live long enough to finish. That would be seven years, he wrote Victor, and he was getting old quickly. He could not do all that he should be doing. He drew all day, but when night came, he was so tired that he often went to bed when he ought to have been up writing.

To add to his troubles, Victor, apparently overwhelmed by his responsibilities in spite of Audubon's constant praise, now wanted his father to return to England as early in the spring as possible. This meant that Audubon had to put aside all thought of visiting the Floridas again or making a trip to the West. Yet he could not leave for England right away. Lucy was too delicate to make the trip until at least the first of May, when the water was calmer and the air warmer. He decided, consequently, to stay at Charleston with Bachman, then move slowly northward, arriving in New York in the spring, ready to leave for England.

During this interval of relative idleness—he was still working hard by ordinary standards but not by his—he gave himself over to worry. He was concerned about Victor's financial situation, because Victor kept asking for more and more money without specifying why he needed it. Audubon promised to try to raise between two and four hundred pounds and even went so far as to ask Dr. Parkman to collect advances against the undelivered second volume, something he had not previously done. But President Jackson had withdrawn the federal government's deposits from the Bank of the United States, thus forcing the country into a financial crisis. Indeed Dr. Parkman wrote from Boston that, under the circumstances, he thought it highly unlikely anyone would pay for the second volume before receiving it; and even Harlan was hard pressed. He had borrowed twenty pounds from Victor during his trip to England, and it was only with great difficulty that Audubon was able to collect the debt. He was worried also about twenty-eight drawings of seabirds that he had sent to Victor but which had failed to arrive in England. From January to April, when he finally learned that they were safe in Victor's hands, he fretted about them.

Out of these worries grew a variety of doubts. He had enough drawings, he told Victor, to finish the third volume but wondered if the fourth volume would contain a hundred plates: he was fearful that he just could not obtain enough specimens. He also looked at the future with considerable questioning. He was convinced that *The Birds of America* and the *Ornithological Biography* would someday be pre-eminent but thought this would not occur in his lifetime. Only after his death would Victor and John reap the benefits of what he had done.

Yet in spite of his recurrent pattern of fears, the winter of 1833–1834 was not all gloom. He made substantial progress on the manuscript of the *Ornithological Biography* to accompany the second volume of *The Birds of America;* he liked living with the Bachman family; and he was especially pleased with the success of John Bachman's experiments with the vultures and the article he wrote reporting the results. "It has been the long established belief of all civilized nations, since the time of the Romans," Bachman said, "that vultures were possessed of extraordinary olfactory powers by which they were enabled to scent their food at the distance of many miles. . . . All the writers on American ornithology have ascribed to the vultures of the United States the same extraordinary powers of smell with the single exception of Mr. Audubon, who in a paper published in *Jameson's Journal,* Edinburgh, 1826, detailed a series of experiments made in America several years previous from which he came to the conclusion that these birds were guided to their food altogether by the eye. . . . The sentiments thus expressed by Audubon, were at the time, and still are, treated with a good deal of severity, both in Europe and in his native country. . . . The lovers of American ornithology, who feel under many obligations to the man who has devoted so many years of his life to this interesting and beautiful department of natural science, will not condemn him unheard."

He then went on to tell how he had proved Audubon right. "On the sixteenth of December, 1833, I commenced a series of experiments on the habits of our vultures, which continued until the end of the month, and these have been renewed at intervals till the fifteenth of Jan., 1834. Written invitations were sent to all the professors of the two medical colleges in this city and to the officers and some of the members of the Philosophical Society and such other individuals as we believed might take an interest in the subject. Although Mr. Audubon was present during most of this time and was willing to render any assistance required of him, yet he desired that we might make the experiments ourselves—that we might adopt any mode that the ingenuity or experience of others could suggest, at arriving at the most correct conclusions."

By these preparations, Bachman hoped to eliminate any suggestion that Audubon himself had influenced the experiments. The results, of course, were convincing, because Bachman's tests were carefully planned and Audubon's thesis was correct. Furthermore, Bachman did not rely on his own word alone to carry weight with the scientific world; he had six leading citizens attest his report. Audubon was jubilant over the findings and the manner in which they were presented by Bachman. He sent an advance copy of the report to Harlan and to a few other people. Then he had two hundred copies printed and circulated in both the United States and England. It was read before the Academy of Natural Sciences in Philadelphia and published in their annals; Loudon, too, printed it along with some additional remarks by Bachman in Audubon's defense. Waterton, however, was not a man to give up easily. He immediately replied in *Loudon's Magazine of Natural History* by questioning the validity of Bachman's experiments, then again raised his doubts about the authorship of the *Ornithological Biography*, and ended challenging the truthfulness of Audubon's accounts of the passenger pigeons. The viciousness of his attacks was not abated, but in order to sustain them he was being forced to shift his ground to include some new subjects and he was also being driven to ridiculous lengths. As part of his experiment, Bachman had set out a rough picture of a sheep, "skinned and cut open. This proved very amusing—no sooner was this picture placed on the ground than the vultures observed it, alighted near, walked over it, and some of them commenced tugging at the painting. They seemed much disappointed and surprised, and after having satisfied their curiosity, flew away. This experiment was repeated more than fifty times with the same result." If this were so, Waterton contended, and vultures are attracted to their food only by sight, then he was "quite prepared to receive accounts from Charleston of vultures attacking every shoulder-of-mutton sign in the streets, or attempting to gobble down the painted sausages over the shop doors, or tugging with might and main at the dim and faded eyes in some decaying portrait of the immortal Doctor Franklin." Nothing, and certainly not reason, could extinguish Waterton's hatred or convert him into a friend, but Bachman's report did the next best thing: it made him appear as illogical as he actually was.

By spring Audubon was also encouraged by the state of his finances. In spite of his worries during the winter, he found that he was able to send Victor seven hundred and fifty-two pounds and still have enough money left to pay his family's passage across the Atlantic. Yet his prosperity created its own problems. Now that he was well known and presumed to be wealthy, he had been arrested in Philadelphia on the complaint of one of his former creditors. In Charleston, he had to contend with another who brought suit against him. Resignedly he wrote to Bachman after he left for New York that he had given everything he owned to his creditors, had gone to jail in Louisville, and had taken the oath of insolvency before the judge. If necessary, a copy of the record could be procured from the court. That was that. There was nothing further he could do about it, nothing further he intended doing. He hoped his lawyer would put a stop to this new suit just as quickly as he could. His uneasiness over this new onslaught did not improve his state of mind, and he wrote Bachman's sister-in-law from New York that since leaving Charleston, he had dreamed at night of sinking or burning ships. By day, he had thought only of the possibility of losing some of his drawings or having more subscribers discontinue. His mind was in a turmoil and he was obsessed by gloomy thoughts as he prepared to leave for England.

For the trip across the Atlantic he selected the largest ship he could find, one that would ride easily in heavy seas, and engaged the best stateroom. With himself and John both there to nurse her, he was able to give Lucy a comfortable journey. After landing in Liverpool, he went to Manchester to collect some money that was due him and then on to London, where the family was again united. Compared to the life he had led when he was living alone in London, this was a quiet existence. Lucy, he told Bachman, mended their socks and read out loud to them. John and Victor were hard at work; he had them both studying, John learning to do portraits in the familiar black chalk, Victor trying his hand at landscapes in oil when he was not traveling abroad to sell subscriptions or engaged in some other aspect of the family business.

But the pleasant domesticity of life in London did not divert Audubon from his own work. All winter long he had been busy with the manuscript for the second volume of the *Ornithological Biography*, but it still was not finished. This, then, was of first importance; and for two months he wrote constantly, putting the final touches on one hundred articles about birds and concluding thirteen "episodes," those short autobiographical sketches that he used to enliven the book. He also attended to some miscellaneous business.

During his travels in the United States, he always collected more bird specimens than he needed, finding that he could readily sell his extras in England. On his return to London, he earned in this way more than seventy-five pounds from the British Museum and received from an individual collector twenty pounds for a wild turkey cock. These birds were so valued, he wrote Bachman, that he could sell fifty more at the same price if Bachman would collect them and ship them to London. He also heard from Joseph Kidd, the painter, who sent to him all the copies of pictures he had on hand, and delivered some letters of introduction he had obtained from a banker in the United States to various bankers in England. One of these was to Baron Rothschild. "We found no difficulty in ascertaining the place of business of the great usurer," Audubon wrote in his journal. "Business in London is thoroughly matter of fact; no external pomp indicated the counting-house of the Baron; there was nothing to distinguish it from those of men with less enormous capital; and we walked into his private office

without any hindrance, and introduced ourselves without any
introducer.

"The Baron was not present, but we were told by a good-
looking young gentleman that he would come in in a few
minutes; and so he did. Soon a corpulent man appeared, hitch-
ing up his trousers, and a face red with the exertion of walking, and without noticing any one present, dropped his fat
body into a comfortable chair, as if caring for no one else in
this wide world but himself. While the Baron sat, we stood,
with our hats held respectfully in our hands. I stepped forward,
and with a bow tendered him my credentials. 'Pray sir,' said
the man of golden consequence, 'is this a letter of business, or
is it a mere letter of introduction?' "

By now Audubon was thoroughly annoyed with the Baron.
"Had a man the size of a mountain spoken to me in that arrogant style in America," he wrote, "I should have indignantly
resented it; but where I then was it seemed best to swallow
and digest it as well as I could. So in reply to the offensive
arrogance of this banker, I said I should be *honored* by his
subscription to the 'Birds of America.' 'Sir,' he said, 'I never
sign my name to any subscription list, but you may send in
your work and I will pay for a copy of it. Gentlemen, I am
busy, I wish you good-morning.' We were busy men, too, and
so bowing respectfully, we retired, pretty well satisfied with
the small slice of his opulence which our labor was likely to
obtain."

A few days later, Audubon sent the first two volumes of *The
Birds of America* to the Baron's office with a brief note out-
lining the contents of the next two volumes and ending, "Mr.
Audubon begs the powerful influence of the Baron Rothschild
in recommending 'The Birds of America' to his friends." The
Baron immediately ordered the bearer to take them to his
house; but when he received the bill, he "looked at it with
amazement and cried out, 'What, a hundred pounds for birds!
Why, sir, I will give you five pounds, and not a farthing more!'
Representations were made to him of the magnificence and expense of the work, and how pleased his baroness and wealthy
children would be to have a copy; but the great financier was
unrelenting. The copy of the work was actually sent back to

Mr. Havell's shop, and as I found that instituting legal proceedings against him would cost more than it would come to,
I kept the work, and afterwards sold it to a man with less money
and a nobler heart." To Victor, who was on a business trip in
France, Audubon wrote tartly, "Rothschild has returned the
work . . . I think it best for us to take it and let the Devil take
his, the Dutchman."

Between selling bird specimens to the British Museum, dealing with Baron Rothschild, and finishing his manuscript, Audubon was busy all the summer of 1834. In the early fall, he
went on another selling trip to places like Manchester, Leeds,
York, and other towns where he was known, but without much
success. Then he left Lucy and the boys in London and went
to Edinburgh. He had tried to persuade MacGillivray to come
to London to go over the manuscript with him, but MacGillivray was tied down by his duties at the College of Surgeons.
Much as MacGillivray regretted it, if the work were to proceed
without further delay, Audubon would have to come to Edinburgh. Actually, he pointed out, this might be a better arrangement anyway, because it would enable Audubon to be near
the printer's.

In Edinburgh he and MacGillivray quickly resumed their
efficient working relationship. MacGillivray had already edited
much of the material Audubon had sent him in advance, and,
at Audubon's request, Lucy joined them in order to give her
assistance. This was not a social visit to the city Audubon knew
so well. As Lucy wrote to a cousin, "We have not paid one
visit since we came, though we have many valuable acquaintances here, for the correction of the proof sheets occupies all
my husband's time." By December 3, Audubon was able to report to Bachman that the second volume of the *Ornithological
Biography* would be off the press in less than a week and that
many of the printer's sheets were on their way to Boston, where
the American edition would be published. He was pleased with
the book and pleased also with himself for not having used it
to rebut his enemies. "The reviewers here," he wrote Bachman, "are all agog for my volume, and I understand on the
watch for general defense or attack on Waterton, Ord, and
others. What shocking disappointment! Not a word is there in

the whole book even in allusion to these beetles of darkness!"
Bachman's article had been effective, and he knew enough to
let it stand by itself and not to stir up another hornets' nest by
carrying the controversy further himself.

As soon as the second volume of the *Ornithological Biography* was off the press, he returned to London to begin work
on the third. He was making more money than he could perhaps have expected, but Lucy was not yet content. As she had
written from Edinburgh to a relative, "Believe me, dear cousin,
the expenses we are now obliged to defray make it a matter
of necessity to consult economy." She wondered if she could
afford even to visit the former Bakewell home at Derby. Lucy's
unsatisfied desires provided one incentive to make Audubon
keep working at the stiff pace he had set for himself; the other
incentive was his own ambition and his growing fear that he
was aging rapidly. Every morning he was up at five o'clock
and, unless he was interrupted, worked steadily for the next
twelve hours, then had dinner, took a walk, conversed awhile
with Lucy and his two sons, after which he went to bed, to
rise the next morning and repeat his routine.

That summer he was back in Edinburgh again, once more
working with MacGillivray over the preparation of his manuscript for the printer and leading a secluded life. Having spent
so much time making himself known, he was now concentrating almost entirely on the production of his books. John, too,
was busy in Edinburgh. He had become sufficiently proficient
as a portraitist to paint professionally and in Edinburgh handled five sittings a day. Writing about his son to Bachman,
Audubon cast light on his own regrets for the opportunities he
himself had wasted. John, he said, "is more industrious than I
used to think he ever would be. Had I been as much so at his
age, I might have become a great man, but I had no one to
point out the way to me. I left my father too early or too late
and unfortunately had too much money at my command in
those days. I am now trying hard to make honorable amends
by laboring from morn to night every day." As a result of these
labors, he was able to write Bachman on December 1 that "this
is to inform you that my third volume of 'Ornithological Biographies' is finished and published; it consists of 639 pages with-

out the introduction. A copy thereof will be forwarded to you
in about a week.... And now, my dear friend, I have done
rather more towards the completion of our ornithology than
ever Alex^r Wilson! My episodes are very so so indeed, but I
think that the *information* connected with the *Birds* is 'pretty
fair'! At all events, I feel wonderfully relieved relieved once
more, for to me the preparing of such volumes is a matter of
great labor, not because I do not understand the subject itself,
but because every thing described will pass through the ordeal
of many a critic, all of whom I feel desirous to convince that
all I have said, and may yet add, is as pure and true as Nature
herself on a May Day!"

In December he returned to London, stopping along the
way at many of the towns where he had friends and subscribers.
All the time he had been in England, he had been urging his
friends in the United States to collect more specimens for him.
Letters went out to Edward Harris, the man who had helped
him when he was first in Philadelphia, Harlan, Bachman, and
Dr. Parkman in Boston, begging for more and more birds. He
even suggested to Bachman that he advertise for specimens in
the Charleston newspapers. But the combined efforts of his
friends were not an adequate substitute for his own. To continue
the book, he had to have more birds. This meant he must go
to the United States himself, and he urged Havell to finish
more of the plates for the fourth volume of *The Birds of America* so that he could leave.

Originally he had hoped to make the trip in the spring, perhaps by the first of April, but he had left many of his possessions, including his guns, in New York, and they had been
destroyed by fire. This made it necessary for him to delay his
journey while he purchased new supplies, and so it was not until September 4 that he and John arrived in New York. While
he was there, he received a letter from Harlan inviting him to
come to Philadelphia for a visit and, most important, to look
at the birds sent to the Academy of Natural Sciences by Thomas
Nuttall and John Kirk Townsend. Nuttall, of course, was an
old acquaintance of Audubon. An experienced botanist and
ornithologist, he had been one of Audubon's friends during his
winter in Boston. Townsend was an ornithologist, and the two

men had made an expedition to the Columbia River on the West Coast. Although neither of them had yet returned, the expedition, according to Harlan, had already forwarded about a hundred new species of birds taken from the far side of the Rocky Mountains.

To Audubon this was exciting news, but he received it with uncertain feelings. As he said to Bachman, "Harlan writes me that this collection belongs to the Academy of Natural Sciences. . . . Now I am anxious to portray all those and to publish them as an appendix to my present work. But I have some doubts that those gents will allow me to do so." Although Audubon had many friends in Philadelphia, the city, and particularly the academy, was the stronghold of George Ord.

Nevertheless, he went to Philadelphia to see the collection. He was allowed to examine it and found that it contained "about forty new species of birds, and its value cannot be described." Here in one spot were enough birds to make up almost half a volume of *The Birds of America,* birds that Audubon could not collect for himself without traveling across the continent on a trip that would be inordinately expensive.

But his worst fears were justified.

He received permission from the academy to look at the birds briefly, but he was refused permission to draw them.

CHAPTER XXVII

1836 – 1839

I N his earlier days, Audubon might have flown into a rage at the academy's refusal; but time had mellowed him and taught him to control his temper. Nothing could be gained by making a frontal attack on either Ord or the academy. On the other hand, he had friends as well as enemies. The proper course, therefore, was quietly to enlist their support.

He returned to New York, and almost at once the first offer of assistance was forthcoming. Edward Harris said he would give Audubon a hundred dollars toward the outright purchase of the entire collection from the Academy of Natural Sciences. "Is this not a noble generosity to show for the love of science?" Audubon remarked in his journal. But the academy had no interest in such a sale.

From New York, Audubon went to Boston. He saw his old friends like Dr. George Shattuck; he called on the governor; he paid a short visit to Salem in search of subscribers; he met Daniel Webster, who bought a subscription and gave him some free legal advice—Webster "thought it likely," Audubon told Lucy, that "a copyright of our great work might be secured to you and our children"; he visited Thomas Brewer, a young ornithologist of considerable merit, and sold a subscription to the Natural History Society with Shattuck paying much of the cost. Best of all, while he was there he learned that Nuttall had just arrived back from the West. "I sent Mr. Brewer after him," he wrote, "and waited with impatience for a sight of the great traveller, whom we admired so much when we were in this fine city. In he came, Lucy, the very same Thomas Nuttall, and in a few minutes we discussed a considerable portion of his travels, adventures, and happy return to this land of happiness." Nuttall, when he learned about Audubon's experience in Philadelphia, immediately gave him the skins of six new species and promised to help him obtain all the duplicates in the possession of the Academy of Natural Sciences. By his patience, Audubon had secured the best ally he could have, for Nuttall's influence far outweighed Ord's. On October 23, Audubon, having returned to Philadelphia and entered into negotiations with Nuttall's support to buy the duplicates, wrote to Bachman, "Now, good friend, open your eyes! Aye, open them tight!! [When excited, Audubon still sometimes lost control of his English.] Nay, place specks on your proboscis if you chuse. Read aloud!! quite aloud!!! I have purchased *ninety-three bird skins!* Yes, 93 bird skins!—Well, what are they? Why nought less than 93 bird skins sent from the Rocky Mountains and the Columbia River by Nuttall & Townsend! Cheap as dirt, too—only one hundred and eighty-four dollars for the whole of these, and hang me, if you do not echo my saying so when *you see them!!* Such beauties! such rarities! Such Novelties!"

Having won this victory, he went on to Washington. For a long time, he had wanted to re-enlist the assistance of the government in making another expedition down the Florida coast and then follow the shoreline of the Gulf of Mexico at least as far west as the Sabine River, which divides Texas from Louisiana, and perhaps even to the newly formed Republic of Texas. He was now so well known and had so many friends in the government that he had no difficulty gaining access to everyone he wanted to see, including President Jackson, who was serving the last months of his final term. Jackson invited both Audubon and John to an informal dinner. "I sat close to him," Audubon wrote in his journal. "We spoke of olden times, and touched very slightly on politics. . . . The dinner was what might be called plain and substantial in England; I dined from a fine young turkey, shot within twenty miles of Washington. The general drank no wine, but his health was drunk by us more than once; and he ate very moderately, his last dish consisting of bread and milk. As soon as dinner was over we returned to the first room where there was a picture, aye, a picture of our great Washington, painted by Stuart, when in the prime of his age and art. This picture, Lucy, was found during the war with England by Mrs. Madison, who had it cut out of the frame, rolled up, and removed to the country." But, added

Audubon, speaking as an artist, "It is the only picture in the whole house—so much for precious republican economy."

Backed by his own growing reputation and armed again with enthusiastic letters from people like Washington Irving, Audubon had no problem securing the cooperation of the Secretaries of the Treasury and War Departments and quickly received permission to travel on their ships. But, for the time being, an expedition to Florida was clearly out of the question. The previous December, Major Francis L. Dade had been sent with a force of a hundred and twelve men to reinforce Fort King, about a hundred and thirty miles east of Tampa Bay. Until he reached open country, Dade had carefully maintained flanking parties; but on December 28 he had discontinued them, thinking that he was safe from ambush. It was a cold morning and his soldiers buttoned their overcoats tightly over their ammunition boxes, so when the Indians attacked from behind patches of palmettos, they were unable to defend themselves immediately. At the day's end, only four soldiers were left alive; and the Indians had delivered, as forcibly as possible, their answer to the whites' demands that they move west to Arkansas. By the time Audubon came to Washington, all of Florida was in a state of war; and the ships assigned to its coasts were not available for scientific expeditions.

Indeed, there was some question whether he could even make a trip westward along the shoreline of the coast, for the United States was also engaged in hostilities with Mexico. In April of that year General Sam Houston had faced the Mexican general, Santa Anna, at San Jacinto and turned what had been a series of defeats into a major victory. Santa Anna was forced to surrender, and Texas won its independence. The result was freedom for the new republic, but the battle did not improve relations between the United States and Mexico. Consequently, their warships were harassing each other in the western waters of the Gulf. Under such circumstances, no one was certain whether ships could be spared for Audubon's planned trip to the Sabine River. There was nothing he could do, therefore, but go to Charleston and wait for the outcome of the fighting. If the Indians in Florida were defeated as quickly and easily as everyone thought they might be, perhaps he could make his trip to the keys in the spring.

The Secretary of the Treasury told him that the cutter *Campbell* was just about to sail and he could ride on it as far as Charleston. But Audubon, never a good sailor, refused, remarking in his journal, "The vessel is only fifty-five tons; and although Columbus crossed the Atlantic in search of a new world in a barque yet more frail, and although thy husband would go to the world's end after new birds on land, he would not like to go from Baltimore on such a vessel carrying three guns and twenty-one men."

So he traveled overland to Charleston, where he spent part of the winter with John Bachman. For Audubon, this was a pleasant way to pass the time. He enjoyed Bachman as a friend and liked working with him on their joint studies. For John, it was even a pleasanter time; he was deeply in love with Bachman's daughter, Maria. In fact, Audubon used to complain jokingly from England that John heard far more often from Maria than he himself did from Bachman. But enjoyable as the visit was, by the middle of February Audubon was growing restless. Edward Harris, his friend from Philadelphia, had joined them, and he was anxious to get started on his southern expedition because, as soon as it was completed, he had to get back to England to finish *The Birds of America* and the remaining volumes of the *Ornithological Biography*. Therefore, when no cutter had arrived that he could take to Florida, he decided to bypass that section of the country and go directly to Mobile, Alabama.

From Charleston he went to Augusta, Georgia, by railroad (he had learned to use this new, and increasingly popular, form of transportation), then took the stagecoach to Montgomery, Alabama. Until then, the Seminole War had been little more than an inconvenience to him, merely an event that interfered with his plans, but on his way across Alabama he saw a hundred Creek warriors who were confined in chains and, a few miles farther on, two thousand more. Here, after reading newspaper reports and talking to government officials, was the hard reality, and the sight upset him greatly. He could hardly abide looking at these pitiful people, some with tears in their eyes, some carrying their kitchen utensils and bits of furniture, and all moving from the land they knew to one that was unknown. By the time he had reached Mobile, Alabama, he had spent two hundred dollars on expenses, had not yet found a ship free to carry him and his party, and, as he wrote Bachman, his spirits were not good. He was also suffering from what he called "drinking Alabama water."

On the Gulf Coast, he searched unsuccessfully for several weeks trying to find an available ship. He even went to Pensacola to see the commodore stationed there, but the Seminole War still occupied the full attention of most of the armed vessels stationed on the Gulf. Finally, he went to New Orleans and on March 23, approximately two months after leaving Charleston, boarded the cutter *Campbell* for a trip to Galveston Bay in Texas. Although this was the same cutter on which he had been offered transportation to Charleston, an offer he had turned down, he was glad to be on his way.

Early in April in the company of the small schooner *Crusader,* which was to serve them as a tender, they came to Barataria Island on the coast of Louisiana, west of the mouth of the Mississippi. This had once been the headquarters of Lafitte, the pirate. They stayed there for several weeks, exploring the low-lying countryside, visiting with the few inhabitants, and collecting specimens. Then they pressed westward along the coast, always watchful for Mexican naval ships, and on April 24 reached Galveston Bay in the Republic of Texas.

Audubon was unimpressed by the appearance of both the town of Galveston and the soldiers stationed there. "We passed through the troops," he wrote, "and observed the miserable condition of the whole concern; huts made of grass, and a few sticks or sods cut into square pieces composed the buildings of the poor Mexican prisoners, which, half clad, and half naked, strolled about in a state of apparent inactivity. We passed two sentinels under arms, very unlike soldiers in appearance. The whole population seemed both indolent and reckless. We saw few fowls, one pig, and a dog, which appeared to be all the domestic animals in the encampment. We saw only three women, who were Mexican prisoners. The soldiers' huts are placed in irregular rows, and at unequal distances; a dirty blanket or coarse rag hangs over the entrance in place of a door. No windows were seen, except in one or two cabins occupied by Texan officers and soldiers. A dozen or more long guns lay about on the sand, and one of about the same calibre was mounted. There was a look-out house fronting and commanding the entrance to the harbor, and at the point where the three channels meet there were four guns mounted of smaller calibre. We readily observed that not much nicety prevailed among the Mexican prisoners, and we learned that their habits were as filthy as their persons."

Audubon's attitude toward this important port of the new republic was in part affected by his own health. He had been badly annoyed by the mosquitoes and on May 1 wrote, "I was much fatigued this morning, and the muscles of my legs swelled until they were purple, so that I could not go on shore." In some respects, this was a repetition of his voyage up the coast of Canada when he had pushed himself to keep pace with younger men. Along the Gulf Coast he was doing the same thing, and his physical strength was no longer equal to the test. Nevertheless, he busily collected birds at Galveston, found many that he thought interesting, and even came across a swordfish that had somehow grounded itself on a sandbar.

After more than two weeks at Galveston, he left the cutter *Campbell* and boarded the smaller tender *Crusader* to make the trip up Buffalo Bayou, which leads to the city of Houston. "This bayou," he wrote, "is usually sluggish, deep, and bordered on both sides with a strip of woods not exceeding a mile in depth. The banks have a gentle slope, and the soil on its shores is good; but the prairies in the rear are cold and generally wet, bored by innumerable crayfish, destitute of clover, but covered with coarse grass and weeds, with a sight here and there of a grove of timber, rising from a bed of cold, wet clay."

For the two days they ascended the bayou, it rained almost continuously. The water rose "about six feet, and the neighboring prairies were partly covered with water; there was a wild and desolate look cast on the surrounding scenery." Part of the way, the current was so strong that, even with the help of the *Crusader*'s gig, it took them eight hours to move twelve miles. By the time they reached Houston, Audubon, John and Harris were soaking wet from the rain, but the captain of a steamboat invited them to come aboard, change their clothes, and have a meal with him.

Texas was then less than a year old, still largely unsettled and poor, but still freshly proud of its victory over Mexico. Rhodes Fisher, the Secretary of the Texas Navy, had met Audubon in Galveston and agreed to introduce him to Sam Houston, the President of the new republic. Going ashore at Houston, which was then the capital, Audubon walked toward the President's house with Rhodes. "We saw before us," he wrote, "a level of far-extending prairie, destitute of timber, and rather poor soil. Houses half finished, and most of them without roofs, tents, and a liberty pole, with the capitol, were all exhibited to our view at once.

"We approached the President's mansion, however, wading through water above our ankles. This abode of President Houston is a small log-house, consisting of two rooms, and a passage through, after the Southern fashion. The moment we stepped over the threshold, on the right hand of the passage we found ourselves ushered into what in other countries would be called the ante-chamber; the ground floor, however, was muddy and filthy, a large fire was burning, a small table covered with paper and writing materials was in the center, camp-beds, trunks, and different materials were strewn around the room. We were at once presented to several members of the Cabinet, some of whom bore the stamp of men of intellectual ability, simple though bold, in their general appearance."

Although Houston, they learned, would be glad to see them, they would have to wait, and to while away the time they walked to the capitol, "which was yet without a roof; and the floors, benches, and tables of both houses of Congress were as well saturated with water as our clothes had been in the morning."

On the way back to Houston's house, Audubon and his friends stopped for a drink of grog and "first caught sight of President Houston as he walked from one of the grog-shops, where he had been to prevent the sale of ardent spirits. He was on his way to his house, and wore a large gray coarse hat; . . . he is upwards of six feet high and strong in proportion. But I observed a scowl in the expression of his eyes that was forbidding and disagreeable.

"We reached his abode before him," Audubon continued, "but he soon came in, and we were presented to his excellency.

He was dressed in a fancy velvet coat and trousers trimmed in broad lace. . . . He received us kindly, was desirous of retaining us for a while, and offered us every facility within his power. He at once removed us from the ante-room to his private chamber, which by the way was not much cleaner than the former. We were severally introduced by him to the different members of his cabinet and staff, and at once asked to drink grog with him, which we did, wishing success to his new republic. Our talk was short; but the impression which was made on my mind at the time by himself, his officers, and his place of abode, can never be forgotten."

Walking back to the boat in Buffalo Bayou, Audubon was again struck by the raw crudeness of the new capital and what he described as "a melee of Indians and blackguards of all sorts." The next day he left for Galveston, sailed directly for New Orleans, stayed there a few days, and returned to Charleston.

On the whole, it had not been a satisfactory journey. True, he had obtained some additional specimens, but by the time he reached Charleston, he was just as exhausted as he had been when he arrived back from Canada. As he later wrote to his friend Dr. Shattuck, "My late journey and voyage westward has proved a very trying one to my body and mind. I have lost fifteen pounds weight." He had been depressed by the captive Indians; he had not particularly liked Galveston; he had enjoyed meeting Houston but did not care for the city named after him; he had found New Orleans oppressively hot and disagreeable and had disliked every step of the journey from Mobile to Augusta. "If New Orleans appeared prostrated," he wrote, "Mobile seemed quite dead. We left in the afternoon for Stockton, Alabama, forty-five miles distant, where we were placed in a cart, and tumbled and tossed for one hundred and sixty-five miles to Montgomery; fare twenty-three dollars each, miserable road and rascally fare. At Montgomery we took the mail coach, and were much relieved; fare to Columbus, twenty-six dollars each. Our travelling companions were without interest, the weather was suffocating, and the roads dirty and very rough; we made but three miles an hour for the whole journey, walking up the hills, and galloping down them to Augusta, and

paying a fare of thirteen dollars each." This was not the energetic traveler who had ridden horseback from Henderson to
Flatland Ford or outwalked Mr. S. on the trip from Trinity.
This was a man who was beginning to feel the effect of his
years and who no longer responded gleefully to the physical
challenge of traveling.

In Charleston, however, he had a chance to restore himself
among friends. He and Bachman were becoming closer and
closer and were not only collaborating on the study of birds,
they were also making plans to produce a book together on
the animals of North America. Bachman was to do the text;
Audubon, the pictures. To add to Audubon's pleasure and to
the bonds between the two families, John married Maria Bachman that spring. Always a man of intense emotions, whether
likes or dislikes, Audubon received Maria as his daughter-in-
law with all the great affection of which he was capable. After
leaving Charleston and starting north with Maria and John,
he wrote Bachman, "Never in my whole life have I enjoyed
travelling so much as I have with my beloved daughter. Everything has been new to her senses. Hills and dales, trees and
fruits, bridges, rail cars, and highly fashionable circles have
danced before her alternately like so many novelties of nature
and of the world, and her own descriptions of the feelings
which have accompanied these transitions are so simple and,
meantime, so truly poetical and just, that I have envied her
situation a thousand times!"

At Philadelphia, Audubon separated from Maria and John.
The newly wed couple went ahead to New York and then to
Niagara Falls for their honeymoon. Certainly, Audubon must
have thought of the day he had visited the falls, dressed in his
wornout clothing, without a cent to his name, yet cherishing
dreams of the success he had since achieved. They were to rejoin him shortly for the trip back to England, and in the interval, he planned to work on his business affairs, which required
attention because the panic of 1837 had swept the country.

Jackson had been a colorful President and in many respects
a good one, but his handling of the nation's finances had finally
resulted in economic disaster. Fortunately for Jackson's political standing in the country, the collapse did not occur while

he was in the White House, but it caught his successor, Martin Van Buren, during the first year of his administration. Even Nicholas Berthoud, an astute businessman, was in trouble. For a time Audubon thought he might have failed but then learned that Berthoud's firm had merely suspended payment. This news relieved him, not only because he and Berthoud were friendly again, but because he kept a large portion of his American earnings with his brother-in-law. Yet even though his deposits with Berthoud were safe, the financial crisis seriously complicated his plans.

In such circumstances, he had to abandon the hope of building up his American subscription list, which meant the hope that *The Birds of America* would ever have a substantial group of purchasers. Ruefully he wrote Lucy that she could not have any idea of the state of affairs in America. When Bachman had written her that they might obtain a hundred additional subscribers, the times had been different. To Dr. Shattuck in Boston, he wrote in similar vein, "My last dates from London are to the twentieth of May, when my beloved wife and son Victor were quite well. My publication was also going on quite well, but alas! The present commercial and monetary revolution has caused me to lose a good number of the subscribers through whose support I did hope to realize a few thousand dollars to comfort and supply with the wants of our later days my beloved wife and my poor self."

Not only were his plans to obtain additional subscribers undermined by the panic of 1837, he also found himself short of the cash he needed right away. As a consequence, he spent his days in New York trying to collect as much gold and silver as possible; and considering the times, he did well. He gathered together more than a thousand pounds. This amount, combined with the money owed him annually by his English subscribers, was enough to ensure the completion of the book. He also had credits in the United States totaling eight thousand dollars.

His trip to Europe was fast, only eighteen days, the company was congenial, and Audubon seasick only once. From Liverpool he took the train to Birmingham, then the coach to London, where he immediately rushed ahead trying to finish both *The*

Birds of America and the *Ornithological Biography*. By the last day of October he had completed thirteen articles for the fourth volume of the *Ornithological Biography* and on December 20 wrote Bachman that four hundred plates had been published and he thought he could complete the work with twenty-five more. Because he wanted his book to contain all the species known at the time, he was constantly examining birds collected by other people as well as by himself. Indeed, he had been carefully reviewing the birds sent back from the Rockies by Townsend and had revised his original estimate of the number of new species downward. He was now convinced that the total was only eight.

Yet he was extremely anxious, since Townsend himself had returned to Philadelphia, to know what additional birds he might have brought and wrote both Dr. Morton at the Academy of Natural Sciences at Philadelphia and his friend Edward Harris to urge Townsend to sell him as quickly as possible any duplicate specimens he might have. He also wanted Townsend to look at the plates of *The Birds of America* at the academy and make a list by plate number of those he had and had not seen. Since Audubon himself had no hope of reaching the Rockies himself before the completion of his book, this seemed the best way to handle the vexing problem. Once again Harris came to his aid. Toward the end of the year, he reported to Audubon that he had examined the collection Townsend had brought back to Philadelphia and it contained some twenty new species. He had purchased a duplicate of each and was sending them to London. This news delighted Audubon; it meant that his book would be completely up-to-date. Weeks later, however, the birds had not arrived, and Audubon was frantic. Townsend's birds had become an obsession with him. What new discoveries had Townsend made in the West? How could Audubon complete his book without having examined what might be a vast reservoir of new information? Yet he had to finish the book and finish it quickly. For years now, his best subscribers had been regularly paying five guineas a piece for each new number, but they were growing weary of what seemed to be an endless expense. If Audubon wanted to keep their subscriptions, he had to complete the book with as few additional plates as possible. This meant putting as many species as he could in each single picture. Without Townsend's birds, therefore, his work had come to a halt.

The book he had begun so joyously at Edinburgh in 1827 was, eleven years later, becoming a millstone around his neck. His remaining subscribers were restless; he himself was worn out by it. All that winter and spring he worked desperately to finish the final volume. He had, of course, the help of many friends. He finally did receive some birds from Townsend; Edward Harris sent him more and so did Bachman and Thomas Brewer, the young ornithologist he had met in Massachusetts. Some were new species that he did not have; some were duplicates of those he had already drawn. These he used for detailed study in connection with the *Ornithological Biography* or gave to MacGillivray to dissect. During this time he worked so hard that he neglected his correspondence, an unusual occurrence with him, and hardly went out. Lucy was not well most of the winter—ever since their first visit to Edinburgh, she had suffered from one ailment after another—and Maria and John were expecting a child. These considerations alone would have kept him at home, but the principal consideration was the book. He had to finish it.

And he did, not in the spring as he had originally hoped, but in the early summer. In June he wrote the news to Dr. Morton at the Academy of Natural Sciences in Philadelphia. "The 'Birds of America' was finished on the sixteenth instant, consisting of 435 plates including 497 species!" he wrote. "An immediate weight from off my shoulders, and a great relief to my ever fidgety and anxious mind respecting this immense undertaking." Yet the end was an anticlimax. After all these years, everyone including Audubon and his subscribers wanted the book completed. The subscribers were tired of paying; Audubon was tired of drawing. Even Havell, now that he had finished his part of the work, was ready to close up his shop and move to America.

As for the subscribers, they had never reached the numbers Audubon once envisioned. When he left Edinburgh in 1827, he had written Lucy that he hoped to obtain two hundred, perhaps four hundred, perhaps even five hundred. These numbers would have made him wealthy, but he never attained them.

Indeed, he fell short of even his lowest goal. Because so many
of the first subscribers dropped out under the burden of the
regular payments and because so many of the new subscribers
purchased some of the back numbers and then failed to keep
up with the new numbers, Audubon himself was never quite
certain how many complete sets were in existence. The record
was too confused, too changing. He was sure, however, that the
total was probably around a hundred and seventy-five. *The
Birds of America* had brought him fame and recognition; it
had given him a living; but it had not made him rich.

In the early summer of 1838, in an effort to finish the *Ornithological Biography* as quickly as possible, he moved to Edinburgh to be near MacGillivray and the printer. Lucy was still
not well, but, as she wrote to a cousin, "the warm weather, with
such good medical aid as I have had ... was of great service to
me, and it was so very disagreeable as well as expensive to us to
be part living in London and part in Edinburgh that the moment it was thought safe for me, we all removed to this beautiful city. I still find myself mending, though obliged to live very
quietly and strictly attend to my physician's orders. Whether I
shall be well enough to undertake the voyage to America this
year or not is still doubtful, even if the work be done in time
and the business closed. But we are fully sensible of the advantage of our living in the United States as soon as we can with
our limited means."

Describing their life in Edinburgh, she continued, "We do
not yet know exactly when the letterpress will be out, but the
printers are working as fast as they can, and all Mr. A.'s time
is fully occupied in correcting the proof sheets. Our sons are
occupying themselves in the most advantageous manner they
can under the present circumstances of not being permanently
settled, and our daughter is quite engaged with her little babe
[John and Maria's child had been born] who grows finely and
takes up nearly all her time; she is indeed a nice little thing,
and we all make quite a pet of her.... I cannot say anything
of my Scotch acquaintance, not having yet made a visit among
them. Indeed as I am at present obliged to retire to bed by
half past eight or nine at the latest, very few persons' habits
and hours would agree with me.... My brothers," she went on,
"have had some pecuniary difficulties to contend with, but they

have happily none of them had the trials we endured for about fifteen years. For the sorrows I have had, I am more than recompensed by the continued and unremitting kindness of my own immediate family, who during these (nearly three years) of illness have watched and ministered to my comfort night and day. When these pains and attacks will cease, we know not, but as I am *better,* I hope at last to be well."

She, too, mused over the anticlimax of having finished *The Birds of America.* "It is strange," she wrote, "how few complete copies of the 'The Birds of America' there will be, every one believing that afterwards it would be cheaper; and already the mistake is beginning to be felt, since the coppers are all put by, in the application of some for a few extra plates which cannot be had even now."

Taking care of the copper plates was one of Audubon's immediate concerns. He could not leave them with Havell, so he decided they should be packed, insured, and sent to America. He was also still worrying about the delivery of various numbers and wrote a long letter of complaint to Havell. "When next we meet," he said, "I will tell you how gross have been the mistakes that have occurred in the packing of prints of my work and in the forwarding of numbers where they were not wanted, such as will make you stare; and all this through the carelessness of the individuals which you have had as attendants in your shop and towards the salary of which I foolishly contributed, though in an indirect manner." He himself had received packages containing, not a complete number, but three or five copies of the same plate; in some instances, the prints of land and water birds had been released before they were supposed to have been. There was also the case of the Earl of Kinnoul, the nobleman whose subscription Audubon had been so pleased to obtain but who had later summoned Audubon to his house and called him a swindler. "Do you not remember," Audubon wrote Havell, "the piece of beef found by Lord Kinnoul among some of the plates that were sent to him, and on account of which we no doubt lost his subscription?" But Audubon was not angry with Havell. Carefully he added, "I write all this not to vex you, but to put you on your guard, to have your eyes open, and to watch what is going on round you even at this late period."

Although he continued to worry about delivering the remaining numbers of *The Birds of America* to the subscribers who had not yet received them, most of his time was devoted to the *Ornithological Biography,* and by September 29 he was able to tell Bachman that the fourth volume was almost ready; only seven more printer's sheets had to be completed. He expected it to be out on December 1. Then he would do a fifth volume, because he had decided the fourth volume could not contain all the information he had accumulated. After that, he planned to publish a *Synopsis* that would list all the birds he knew. When these publications were off the press, he expected to go back to the United States. On October 27, he received the last sheet of the fourth volume; the following May, the fifth volume was published; and on June 30, he wrote Havell that he had finished the *Synopsis.*

He was now free to complete his plans for returning to the United States, where he hoped to remain forever, but he was not yet free to rest. In spite of all his work, he still had not earned the money he needed and sadly faced the fact that the extravagant dreams he had once had in Edinburgh had never been realized. If he were to give Lucy the life she had always desired, if he were to make up once and finally for the horror of those days in Henderson, he had to produce a more profitable work.

He was fifty-four years old when he returned to the United States in the late fall of 1839; and almost immediately after landing he wrote Dr. Morton at the Academy of Natural Sciences, "Having determined to publish 'The Quadrupeds of North America' in our own country, of a handsome folio size ... I hope to be able to present that work to the public at a price which ought to enable me to meet the expenses of such a publication without difficulty. I am also going to publish immediately a new edition of 'The Birds of America,' the figures of which will be reduced from the plates or original drawings of my large work."

Hopefully these books would accomplish for him financially what the first one had failed to do.

CHAPTER XXVIII

1839–1843

WHEN Audubon arrived in the United States, he was not sure where he wanted to live, but he quickly settled on New York and, without further delay, began work on the new edition of his bird book. He had already figured out how he would go about it. The pictures from the original edition would be reduced by the *camera lucida,* an optical device which, by the means of a prism, can project an image on a flat surface so that it can be traced. This meant that the pictures could be copied instead of being redrawn freehand. Audubon intended to make changes in some of them, altering an occasional background or eliminating a figure, but the majority would be reproduced just as they were. As for the actual printing, he had decided to abandon the costly and laborious job of making copper engravings and use instead the relatively new and much cheaper process of lithography, in which the picture is drawn on a flat surface, in those days generally a stone. Parts of the stone are coated with a substance that repels ink; the parts to be printed with a substance to which ink will adhere.

Once again the book was to be issued in numbers, each one comprising five pictures accompanied by the appropriate text from the *Ornithological Biography.* The total numbers in each set were to be a hundred, and the price one dollar a number. This was not inexpensive—a hundred dollars for a book on birds—but nowhere nearly as costly as the original.

In November, while he was supervising the work on the new edition, Audubon also had several other problems on his mind. He still had a few copies of the first book which he was trying to sell—he persuaded John Jacob Astor to buy one along with the five volumes of the *Ornithological Biography* for $1,030; he was also deeply concerned about the health of another of Bachman's daughters, Mary Eliza. Victor and Mary Eliza had become engaged, but Eliza was so ill that Victor had rushed to Charleston to be with her. With his usual concern for members of his family, Audubon was deeply worried about his future daughter-in-law and complained bitterly to Victor for not writing. The whole family had been kept in suspense about Eliza's health, he complained, until they had heard, not from Victor, but from Bachman's sister-in-law. Then he went on to discuss his work and his future plans for his son. He himself was as busy as he had ever been, and John was occupied daily with painting. So what was this report that Victor might spend the winter in Charleston? Did Victor understand that would be utterly impossible? He himself would have to be away selling subscriptions; he therefore needed Victor's help at home.

Although he had been in the United States only a few months, Audubon already had more to do than he could handle by himself. John, as he saw it, was in charge of the art work for the new edition, supervising the reduction of the original pictures and making the necessary changes. He himself would take the responsibility for selling the book; no one could do that better than he after all his experience with the original *Birds of America*. Victor, although he too was an artist, would function as the business manager. Not only had Audubon realized his dream of creating a family business out of his publications, he had become dependent on his sons' assistance.

Early in December, Victor, whom Audubon was supporting, married Eliza, much to Audubon's pleasure; but he himself, as he had said he would be, was off on another canvassing trip, collecting the remaining amounts due him for *The Birds of America* and selling subscriptions to the smaller edition. He left New York for Boston on December 6 and was able to report on the twelfth that he had already obtained thirty-one subscribers. Granted that Boston had always been friendly to him and that he had also revisited Salem, this was an impressive number; and it looked as though his estimates of the possible demand for the new edition might prove correct.

New Year's Day, 1840, found him back in New York. After a canvassing trip of a little less than three weeks, he had obtained ninety-six subscribers, with no less than forty-one from what he called "the beautiful village of New Bedford, Massachusetts," where, as a young man on his way to France, he had waited impatiently while the captain repaired the ship. Compared to the sales of the original *Birds of America*, this was a remarkable record; but it was not solely the result of the smaller size and reduced cost of the new edition. He was now a famous man; he had friends in many important cities; and his first book had created wide comment because of its magnificence. All these factors were working in his favor, and he was reaping the benefit of his previous efforts.

Yet he still was not content and continued giving thought to *The Quadrupeds of North America*. As he planned it, Bachman would prepare the text—Bachman had agreed to do this free— and he would provide the pictures, which would also be lithographed. Of course, the task would be difficult. He admitted that readily to Bachman; but with something like his old flamboyance of spirit, he estimated that he and John could do all the illustrations in two years and that Bachman could complete the text in one more.

He could even afford to laugh at George Ord at this moment, jokingly asking Bachman how many copies Ord would be likely to buy. Life was good. Everything was at last developing as he had hoped it would. In February, he had more than three hundred subscribers to the small bird book; the fifth number was out; and he was on his way to Charleston, canvassing as he went. He stopped in Baltimore and on February 24 reported to Victor that he had already obtained a hundred and one subscribers in that city alone. A week later he had raised the total to a hundred and forty, almost the same number as the total subscription list for *The Birds of America*. His original calculations were proving correct. The small edition, backed by the prestige of the large one, was proving an unqualified success. After all these years, he was at last making money.

Yet he was also having difficulties. The administrative problems in connection with *The Birds of America* had been great; those pertaining to the smaller edition were even greater. Although he no longer checked each print personally and although the monetary value of each number was less, they were being produced much faster, and the list to which they had to be delivered was much larger. Victor was supposed to attend to all the mechanics, but his performance was below the standards Audubon considered acceptable. "I have been disappointed at not hearing from you this afternoon, but hope to do so tomorrow, as I trust you have received my letters to you sending to you the names procured here," he wrote to Victor, who had returned to New York from Charleston. A day later, annoyed and exasperated, he took his son sharply to task. "Again I am sadly disappointed at not hearing from you this afternoon," he wrote, "particularly after having asked of you to return each of my letters by return mail. Here I am with one hundred and ninety-five subscribers crying after me for news about their numbers and have none to deliver them. If this is to continue, I must go home again, for it would prove useless to augment our list without receiving the moneys wanted to support our publication. You must indeed stir yourself." Victor just did not seem to understand what was required of him.

J. B. Chevalier, his printer in Philadelphia, was also causing him problems. As he told Victor, "I have also written this evening to Chevalier to dissuade him from the foolish plan he had in view to deliver odd numbers to our new subscribers, instead of furnishing them with numbers in regular order of *rank and file*." Audubon was enjoying his success, and he was not going to let it slip through his fingers because of his assistants' carelessness. Victor and Chevalier might think that subscribers were easy to obtain and to satisfy; Audubon himself knew better.

To Lucy he wrote in a different vein. In the past few years, he said, he had been amazed at the progress they had made, but his success had never been what it was now. Everything that had happened to him before seemed small in comparison, but he warned her against expecting too much. She wanted five thousand subscribers, but that was too many; it would make the children too rich for their own good. What he would prefer was a total of two thousand.

At the same time, he tried to explain to her that it was not as simple for him to obtain subscribers as she might think. For years, he had been going from town to town, meeting new people, cultivating them, exposing himself to the hurt that came when they were not interested in his work, and trying to gain publicity for himself and his books. He was weary of this life; he was tired of being the center of attention, of always having to make an effort. He was nervous; he was not sleeping well. What he wanted was to stay home with his family.

If Lucy, with her hope of obtaining five thousand subscribers, was pushing him hard, so was Victor. The sudden success of the Audubon family was going to their heads. Audubon had not left Baltimore before he felt compelled to write Victor, promising to do everything he could to help Victor buy a house. In the meantime, he begged him not to invest in any stocks, as Victor wanted to do. They had lost two thousand dollars in Kentucky bank stock, Audubon reminded his son. Was not that enough to teach him a lesson? Caution, caution, he kept advising. They were making money, yes. But all this had cost more than any of them realized, and the victory could be lost more easily than it had been gained.

From Baltimore he made a trip to Annapolis, then dashed to Philadelphia for a few days to see Chevalier, then back to Baltimore, on to Washington and Richmond, and finally arrived in Charleston toward the beginning of May. Maria and John had gone ahead of him for a visit with her parents, and although he had heard that Maria was ill, he was not worried about her. Surely, he said, in the warm climate of Charleston she would mend quickly. When he reached the Bachmans' house, he found that John and Maria had taken a trip to Aiken, South Carolina, for Maria's health, and John had written that she was already much better. But when she returned home a few days later, Audubon was horrified, she was so emaciated and feeble. He prayed to God for her life. In his alarm, he had not exaggerated her condition; Maria had a serious case of tuberculosis. For her to travel back to New York or for John to leave her was clearly out of the question, and Audubon felt compelled to stay in Charleston longer than he had planned in order to be with them and comfort them. On May 31 he wrote to his family, "We must, however, bear up against our misfortunes or else become miserable the remainder of our days, which, with the numberless callings upon us for the relief of the living, must be indisputably attended to. Our beloved Maria *is yet alive,* but, as we have said often, weak and emaciated beyond belief or description. In this state, we are awaiting the Will of God and whatever that may be, must abide by it and align ourselves to it."

On September 15, Maria died. By that time, hopeful that she was improving, Audubon was on a canvassing tour of New England, concentrating largely on towns in Massachusetts. Sometimes he met with success—he sold nineteen subscriptions in Nantucket; sometimes he met with failure—in Portsmouth, New Hampshire, he could not sell one. On the whole, however, the list continued to grow rapidly. But as soon as he received word of Maria's death, he hurried back to New York to be with his family. Under any circumstances, he would have been concerned by the loss of this daughter-in-law he loved so well, but what made the blow even more difficult to bear was the state of Eliza's health. She too was so seriously ill with tuberculosis that she could not remain in the northern climate.

Casting around desperately for advice and help, Audubon wrote to his friend Dr. Morton in Philadelphia, "Our dear son Victor is about to leave us for New Orleans and afterwards the Island of Cuba on account of the health of our beloved daughter, his wife. . . . Trusting to the full extent of the letter in your skill as a physician, I write to you to ask of you to send us ample memorandums of whatever you may think fit to enable Victor to alleviate the sufferings of his wife whilst at sea, as well as whilst on shore. . . . We have heard that you had published a work connected with infections of the lungs, but neither know the title of that work or where it can be procured. If you have a copy of it and think it valuable on such an occasion, please do send it to us forthwith and charge the cost to my account." Dr. Morton replied promptly with a present of his book but added that it would be presumptuous of him to make any suggestions except of the most general kind.

Audubon was so disturbed by the departure of his older son and Eliza that the day after they left he walked alone to the New York harbor to inquire how the ship had fared passing through the Narrows; and all the time they were in New Orleans and later in Cuba, he worried about them. But neither his loving concern nor the book written by Dr. Morton was a cure for tuberculosis. In the spring of 1841, after returning from the months-long trip, Eliza died just as her sister had. In half a year, Audubon had lost both the daughters-in-law he had loved so well. Yet he himself had reminded his family of "the numberless callings upon us for the relief of the living," and to the living he devoted his thought and energy. All the remainder of that year he worked feverishly keeping up with the tasks he had set for himself, checking on deliveries of the small edition of his bird book and trying to finish as many pictures as possible for *The Quadrupeds of North America*.

He had often claimed that he never drew a bird which he had not seen alive, a claim that he did not always live up to, for under the pressure of finishing *The Birds of America*, it was impossible for him to collect personally the necessary specimens. With *The Quadrupeds of North America*, he never made any such pretense. He used skins, stuffed animals, even other people's pictures when he needed them to refresh his memory, but he drew with the same old intensity, often working from daybreak until the time came to go to bed; and by the middle of August had drawn a hundred figures which included thirty-six species.

He was now driven more by the desire to finish the book than by the need for money, because the small edition of the bird book continued to be a success. The total number of subscribers never reached the five thousand mark hoped for by Lucy, or even the two thousand expected by Audubon; but it had passed a thousand, and for the first time since leaving Henderson, Audubon was comfortably off and could satisfy the wishes of his wife and sons. That October, when John was remarried to a woman named Caroline Hall, Audubon could offer his new daughter-in-law the prospect of living in a fashionable house. Tired of the city, he had purchased thirty or forty acres at the edge of the Hudson River, an area now bordered by New York's Amsterdam Avenue and 155th and 158th streets. Here he was building a large, square, three-storied house capable of holding the entire family, the type of house that Lucy had always wanted. The building, which faced the river, was divided by a center hall. On one side was the parlor and dining room, on the other the library, a studio, and the pantry. As in many such houses, the kitchen was in the basement. On the second floor were bedrooms for all the family and a guest room, on the third floor the servants' rooms and more guest rooms.

By April, 1842, the house was finished, and the Audubons had started the long process of moving into it. This took up much of their time for several months; and then, leaving his family assembled under a roof of their own, Audubon started off on a canvassing trip to Washington, Baltimore and Richmond. He had now four plates from *The Quadrupeds of North America* to show to potential subscribers. Unlike the pictures in the original edition of *The Birds of America,* these were lithographed (the work was done by J. T. Bowen of Philadelphia), and of course they were not life-size, but they were large. Like the original book of birds, the pictures were to be issued in numbers of five plates each, at ten dollars a number. Thirty numbers would complete the set, and the text was to be printed and sold separately. On this trip Audubon collected some of the money already due him, sold some subscriptions to *The Quadrupeds* and to the smaller edition of the bird book, then returned home for a few days to make preparations for another journey. This took him through Connecticut, Rhode Island, and Massachusetts and back to New York by August 26. Remaining there only a few weeks, he started off for Canada, where, to his pleasure, the Legislative Council purchased a copy of *The Birds of America* and became subscribers to *The Quadrupeds of North America.* After visiting Quebec, Montreal, and Kingston, he returned home and then went to Boston again.

All during the last half of the year 1842, his movements were almost frenetic, dashing here, dashing there, collecting money, straightening out accounts, selling the few remaining copies of *The Birds of America,* obtaining subscriptions to the smaller edition and to *The Quadrupeds,* working like a man possessed by some demon that kept urging him to go the limits of his strength.

And he had a demon. For years he had wanted to see at least a part of the country west of the Mississippi, but such a trip had always been out of the question. Always he had either lacked the money or lacked the time. Now he had the money, and he was determined to make the time. By pushing himself as he had done, he had launched both his books, realized Lucy's ambition to have a luxurious house of her own, and so organized his business that, with the help of his sons, he could be absent for a while. Therefore on February 26, 1843, he was able to write to Dr. Shattuck, "I send you my adieus ere I depart for my long wished for expedition to the waters of the Yellowstone, and I take this day of rest for the opportunity, because of the many arrangements I have to work out and which fill my every moment." In addition to himself, he had four persons going with him "as companions and laborers in the cause of science. My good friend Edward Harris of Moorestown, New Jersey. One a Mr. John G. Bell, who is a capital hunter, trapper, and preparer of specimens. One Mr. Isaac Sprague of Hingham as a draftsman, &c. One Mr. Lewis Squires of New York as a kind of secretary, &c." Audubon was so excited about the prospect of the trip that for once he put his own plans ahead of his concern for his family. Only as an afterthought did he mention to Dr. Shattuck that "my son Victor was married yesterday to Miss Georgianna Mallory. I believe you are acquainted with her brother."

In the spring, the group reached St. Louis, where Audubon had arranged passage on an American Fur Company steamboat to Fort Union, the company's trading post at the mouth of the Yellowstone; and on April 25 he walked up the gangway with a hundred trappers, all of whom were drunk or hung-over, for they had been out on a last spree before facing another season at their rough and dangerous trade. These men could make high profits from their work, but they also ran the risk of losing everything they owned, including their lives. One trapper, after seven years in the business, reported that he had been robbed five times and all he could show for his work was a debt of six hundred dollars. Even the companies sometimes robbed each other. The American Fur Company had once connived with some Crow Indians to steal the furs and horses of another company, then offered to sell them back to the original owners at a profit. Liquor, too, was a problem. A forty-gallon cask, prop-

erly diluted, made sixteen hundred pints, and each pint was
worth a five-dollar buffalo robe. Such high returns tempted the
traders to violate the law against importing whiskey into the
Indians' territory. (To get around this restriction, the American Fur Company, only a few years before, had built a still
within the forbidden district; the authorities, however, quickly
put an end to this subterfuge.)

Describing their departure from St. Louis, Audubon wrote,
"First the general embarkation, when the men came in pushing and squeezing each other, so as to make the boards they
walked upon fairly tremble. The Indians, poor souls, were
more quiet, and had already seated or squatted themselves on
the highest parts of the steamer, and were tranquil lookers-on.
After about three quarters of an hour, the crew and all the
trappers (these are called *engagés*) were on board, and we at
once pushed off and up the stream, thick and muddy as it was.
The whole of the effects and the baggage of the *engagés* was
arranged in the main cabin, and presently was seen Mr. Sarpy
[the company's representative], book in hand, with the list before him. . . . The men whose names were called filled the fore
part of the cabin, where stood Mr. Sarpy, our captain, and
one of the clerks. As each man was called, and answered to his
name, a blanket containing the apparel for the trip was handed
to him, and he was ordered at once to retire and make room
for the next. The outfit, by the way, was somewhat scanty, and
of indifferent quality. Four men were missing, and some appeared rather reluctant; however, the roll was ended, and one
hundred and one were found. In many instances their bundles
were thrown to them, and they were ordered off as if slaves."

This was the orderly part of the departure, but, Audubon
added, "I forgot to say that as the boat pushed off from the
shore, where stood a crowd of loafers, the men on board had
congregated upon the hurricane deck with their rifles and guns
of various sorts, all loaded, and began to fire what I should
call a very disorganized sort of salute, which lasted for something like an hour, and which has been renewed at intervals,
though in a more desultory manner, at every village we have
passed." Before the day was over, however, the shooting stopped,

and Audubon noted that "we now find them passably good, quiet, and regularly sobered men."

The cabin was so crowded that Audubon preferred sleeping that night on deck, but otherwise the trip was a comfortable one. Occasionally the boat had to stop so the crew could cut more wood for fuel, giving Audubon and his friends chances to go ashore and hunt; and by May 3 they had reached Fort Leavenworth, an important checkpoint on the Missouri. Here the army had an opportunity to search the boats going up the river to see whether they were carrying liquor to the Indians. While two officers came on board to talk to the captain, Audubon and Bell went on land and hunted. Then the *Omega* again started up the Missouri but ran aground on a bar at five o'clock, got off, tried again, and went aground broadside. By six o'clock, all the hands were busily trying to dislodge the boat; and by seven-thirty they had run out a cable, attached it to a snag two hundred yards ahead, and gradually worked the boat around until its bow pointed upstream. All that night, it rained and thundered and lightninged; but at daybreak the captain again had all hands at work, and the boat was finally freed. Navigating the shallow and dangerous waters of the Missouri was like riding on a flatboat, but this time Audubon did not have to plunge into the icy water himself. He could now stand on deck and watch other men do the work; and when, at ten o'clock that morning, they stopped to cut more wood, he went hunting.

A day later they reached the Black Snake Hills near St. Joseph, Missouri, and shortly afterward Audubon wrote in his journal, "The general aspect of the river is materially altered for the worse; it has become much more crooked or tortuous, in some places very wide with sand-banks naked and dried, so that the wind blows the sand quite high. In one place we came to a narrow and swift chute, four miles above the Black Snake Hills, that in time of extreme water must be very difficult of ascent. During these high winds, it is very hard to steer the boat, and also to land her. The settlers on the Missouri side of the river appear to relish the sight of a steamer greatly, for they all come out to look at this one as we pass the different settlements."

Up the river they continued on their clumsy way, stopping at trading posts, passing through the territory occupied by the Fox and Iowa Indians, cutting wood from time to time to keep their boilers going, occasionally spending a few hours ashore hunting. They soon reached Fort Croghan, which was situated up the river from the present city of Omaha, Nebraska. Here they found only a small detachment of soldiers on duty, the rest being camped some four miles away, because the fort had been flooded by four feet of water. Next morning at daylight, the *Omega* was under way again; but it had not moved far when a party of dragoons galloped up to the edge of the river and fired rifle shots across the boat's bow. The *Omega* immediately returned to shore, and one of the soldiers presented a letter from the commanding officer of the fort saying that the cargo was to be examined. Always on the watch for contraband liquor, the soldiers kept spot-checking the boats moving up the river. While the search was being conducted, Audubon visited the commanding officers and then rode back to the *Omega,* which proceeded on its way.

They passed Council Bluffs, where Lewis and Clark had met with chiefs of the Otoe and Missouri Indians and which is located above the present city of the same name; they saw the burial spot of Charles Floyd, a sergeant assigned to the Lewis and Clark expedition; and they met four barges belonging to fur traders. On board they had ten thousand buffalo robes that they were taking to St. Louis. One of them, a partner in the American Fur Company, told Audubon that a clerk of the company had just killed a chief of the Blackfeet and, much to Audubon's disappointment, warned him that it would be un-safe now to travel in their territory.

So far, the Indians had struck Audubon as a rather unfortunate group, many of them poverty-stricken and oppressed, but they had all been friendly. On May 22, however, the passengers on the *Omega* "observed some seven or eight Indians looking at us, and again retiring to the woods, as if to cover themselves; when we came nearly opposite them, however, they all came to the shore, and made signs to induce us to land. The boat did not stop for their pleasure, and after we had fairly passed them they began firing at us, not with blank cartridges, but with well-directed rifle-balls, several of which struck the 'Omega' in different places.

"I was standing at that moment by one of the chimneys," Audubon wrote, "and saw a ball strike the water a few feet beyond our bows; and Michaux, the hunter, heard its passing within a few inches of his head. A Scotchman, who was asleep below, was awakened and greatly frightened by hearing a ball pass through the partition, cutting the lower part of his pantaloons, and deadening itself against a trunk. Fortunately no one was hurt. Those rascals were attached to a war party, and belong to the Santee tribes which range across the country from the Mississippi to the Missouri. I will make no comment on their conduct," Audubon added, "but I have two of the balls that struck our boat; it seems to me a wonder that not one person was injured, standing on deck as we were to the number of a hundred or more."

At the Great Bend of the Missouri, which they approached on May 26, the captain suggested that Audubon and his party walk across the neck of land while the boat followed the sweep of the river. Because the distance overland was so much shorter than the water route, they would be able to camp overnight and rejoin the boat the next day. Audubon accepted the suggestion gladly; it gave him an opportunity to stretch his legs and also do some hunting. After going on board the boat again, they once more saw Indians on the shore. These were Sioux, but instead of firing rifle balls at the boat, they fired a salute. But Audubon noted in his journal, "They are a poor set of beggars after all. The captain gave them supper, sugar and coffee, and about one pound of gunpowder, and the chief coolly asked, 'What is the use of powder, without balls?'"

As the boat kept working up the river, Audubon and his party continued to collect specimens, make notes, and draw pictures. Unlike his trip up the Canadian coast, Audubon was making this journey because he really wished to see the country. He knew, also, that he would never be able to cover the same route again, and took advantage of every moment. But having three competent men to assist him, including Harris, who was a close personal friend, and being able to live in relative comfort on the steamboat, he did not find the journey as strenuous as many of the others he had taken.

He arrived at Fort Union, therefore, in good spirits, ready to make the best possible use of his time. The fort was the property of the American Fur Company, not a fort manned by the Army. It had been constructed by a company employee, Kenneth McKenzie, a relative of the explorer Alexander Mac-Kenzie; and because it dominated the juncture of the Yellow-stone and Missouri rivers, it gave the company a virtual monopoly of all furs gathered in the Yellowstone basin. It was a large establishment—six to eight hundred buffalo were consumed each year by its personnel and guests of the company —and contained within its twenty-foot-high palisades all the facilities needed for trading, living, and defense, including a tinsmith's shop and a blacksmith's shop, a powder magazine, several cannon, a warehouse large enough to hold three thousand packs of buffalo robes, an icehouse, a cooper's shop, dwellings for all the staff, a store where the Indians traded, and a special "reception room." This was at the gate, and when the Indians were unusually numerous or the staff was suspicious of them, they could be let into this room to do their trading without entering the fort itself. By the time Audubon arrived, McKenzie had fallen into disgrace—it had been his idea to build the American Fur Company's still and thus circumvent the regulations controlling liquor—and he had been replaced by Alexander Culbertson, a Pennsylvanian who was married to the daughter of a Blackfoot chief.

Culbertson immediately made Audubon welcome, and the day Audubon's party moved ashore told them that if a wolf made its appearance on the prairie near the fort, he would chase it on horseback and bring it back, dead or alive. Soon they saw a white wolf about a quarter of a mile off. While Audubon and his friends rushed to the palisades to watch, Culbertson mounted his horse and rode out of the fort, clad only in his trousers and shirt and carrying his gun. Suddenly he leaned forward, clapped his knees to his horse, and galloped toward the wolf, which at first paid no attention to him. Then the animal realized its danger and began to run too, but not quickly enough to outpace the horse. It reached the hills, turned into a small ravine, but Culbertson was at its heels. He fired one shot; the wolf fell on its side. Not bothering to dismount, Culbertson galloped up to it, reached down, grabbed it, threw the body across his saddle, and raced back to the fort. When he arrived, the wolf was not quite dead. Its jaws were still moving; and in its last agony, it had slashed one of Culbertson's fingers. Such injuries, Audubon was told, occurred so frequently that no one thought anything about them.

Culbertson's display of horsemanship, marksmanship, and hunting ability set the tone for Audubon's two-month stay at Fort Union; and Culbertson himself proved the perfect host for someone of Audubon's temperament. Finding that Audubon had been given uncomfortable quarters, Culbertson moved him into his own house, a large building that also contained the company's offices and the mess hall. He went hunting with him whenever he could, advised him about hiring hunters and the amounts he should pay for specimens, let him look at his own journals, and gave him accounts of the Indians and animals of the area.

In July he took him on an overnight trip up the Yellowstone River with a wagon to carry their supplies and also a skiff that they could use when they wanted to cross the river. While hunting a wolf, they saw a buffalo and went in pursuit of it. The two nearest hunters were soon close enough to shoot it, but they only halted it instead of killing it. Having no more ammunition, they loaded their rifles with pebbles and fired these in place of bullets. The second buffalo they saw was a bull, and this they killed with less trouble. The third was spotted by Owen McKenzie, one of the company's employees. Audubon was the only one who had any bullets left and would have liked to ride after the bull himself, but his horse was not fast, and he was afraid that he would only lose the meat which the fort really needed. Therefore he gave his gun and bullets to Owen, who approached the bull until they were about seventy yards apart. Then the bull took alarm and began to run. Owen's horse, being already tired, had difficulty keeping up, but Owen finally drew close to the buffalo, fired one shot that slowed the animal down and then another that entered its lungs through its shoulder and brought it to a stand.

Shouting to Owen not to waste any more shots, Audubon and his hunter, Bell, walked on foot toward the wounded animal. The bull did not seem to be exhausted, but it was so stiffened by the shot in its shoulder that it could not turn quickly. Taking advantage of this, the two men moved nearer. Slowly the animal worked itself around to face its pursuers and made a lunge at them. Audubon was now too close for safety, but instead of waiting for Owen, he and Bell began shooting their pistols. This only increased the buffalo's fury, and it began to advance toward Audubon, who was still confident that he could outrun it. Firing a last shot at the bull's head, he turned on his heels; but instead of veering to one side to avoid the buffalo's charge, he simply ran directly in front of it. As he looked back, he saw to his horror that the bull was within three feet of him, its head lowered, its horns pointing at his body. He jumped quickly to one side. Bell grabbed the gun from Owen and fired a shot that entered the buffalo's body directly behind the shoulder blade. The animal tottered; blood spurted from its mouth and nostrils; it fell forward on its massive head, then rolled on its side, dead.

It had been a close call, but Audubon continued to be fascinated by buffaloes and took every opportunity to go out with the hunters. He was, however, astonished at the waste; sometimes only the animals' tongues were brought in, the rest of the meat being left to the wolves. Looking into the future, he wrote about the buffaloes, "Daily we see so many that we hardly notice them more than the cattle in our pastures about our homes. But this cannot last; even now there is a perceptible difference in the size of the herds and before many years the buffalo, like the great auk, will have disappeared; surely this should not be permitted."

In spite of his interest in buffalo hunting, there was one ritual he did not like. Before skinning a freshly killed animal, Culbertson, like most of the other hunters, would break open the skull, take out the still-warm brains and offer them raw to the others as a delicacy. The very sight of this turned his stomach. He was not too fastidious, however, to engage in grave robbing when he wanted an Indian's skull. He and Denig, the second-in-charge at Fort Union, walked off from the fort, he said, "with a bag and instruments to take off the head of a three-years-dead Indian chief, called the White Cow. Mr. Denig got upon my shoulders and into the branches near the coffin [because of the wolves, coffins were sometimes placed in trees rather than buried] which stood about ten feet above ground. The coffin was lowered, or rather tumbled down, and the cover was soon hammered off; to my surprise, the feet were placed on the pillow, instead of the head, which lay at the foot of the coffin—if a long box may be so called. Worms innumerable were all about it; the feet were naked, shrunk, and dried up. The head had still the hair on, but was twisted off in a moment, under jaw and all."

He saw many live Indians, too, including a war party of Assiniboines, who were returning from an attack on the Blackfeet. "They all looked miserably poor," Audubon wrote, "filthy beyond description, and their black faces and foully smelling buffalo robes made them appear to me like so many devils. The leader, who was well known to be a famous rascal, and was painted red, was a tall, well-formed man. The party had only three poor guns, and a few had coarse, common lances; every man had a knife, and the leader was armed with a stick in which were inserted three blades of butcher's-knives." They spent that night at Fort Union, and the chief showed his pleasure over defeating his enemies by borrowing a drum and beating it, while the men at the fort tried to sleep.

Once a hunting party of Crees, who lived on the Saskatchewan River in Canada, arrived, tired and hungry after an unsuccessful trip. They asked for whiskey but, as Audubon pointed out, because of the law they were not permitted to have any. Whereupon they assured Culbertson that the Hudson's Bay Company gave them all the liquor they wanted and hereafter they would trade with the British, not the Americans. Audubon was indignant. "If our Congress will not allow our traders to sell whiskey or rum to the Indians," he demanded, "why should not the British follow the same rule? Surely the British, who are so anxious about the emancipation of the blacks, might as well take care of the souls and bodies of the redskins."

For two months Audubon stayed at Fort Union, enjoying himself to the full, and he said to his family, "My regrets that

I promised you all so faithfully that I would return this fall are beyond description. I am, as years go, an old man, but I do not feel old, and there is so much of interest here that I forget oftentimes that I am not as young as Owen." Yet he was an old man, and his once-great physical powers were fading. On the buffalo hunts he acted only as a spectator, because, as he wrote, "alas! I am now too near seventy to run and load whilst going at full gallop"; and on his first important buffalo hunt, Culbertson, like a younger man dealing with an older one, insisted on calling one of the dead animals "Audubon's" and presented him with the tail, which usually went only to the actual shooter. Even his painting suffered somewhat. One day he wrote sadly in his journal, "I began drawing at five this morning, and worked almost without cessation till after three, when, becoming fatigued for want of practice, I took a short walk, regretting I could no longer draw twelve or fifteen hours without a pause or thought of weariness." The men with him were concerned about him, too. When he considered hunting bighorns, they tried to dissuade him for fear he would become overtired.

It had been a wonderful trip, everything he had hoped it would be, but Lucy had been right in making him promise not to stay at Fort Union during the long, severe winter. So on August 16 he loaded his pictures, specimens, and voluminous notes aboard a forty-foot boat he had had built and, with the rest of his party, started down the river. On October 19 he arrived at St. Louis; and on November 6, wearing a green blanket coat with a fur collar and cuffs, his hair and beard long, he came to the head of the driveway of his new house. Happy and content with his trip but glad to be home, he left his carriage and walked down the steep slope to the piazza, where his family was waiting for him.

CHAPTER XXIX

1844 — 1851

W HEN they had lived in Edinburgh, the family had started calling Lucy "Minnie," the affectionate Scotch word for mother; and when they built their new house on the Hudson River, Audubon named it Minnie's Land. It was a gift to her, a fulfillment of her lifelong dreams and a recompense for the years of hardship and suffering. Yet it was as much his as hers, and now that his great restlessness had been exhausted, he was content to stay there.

He supervised the planting of the fruit orchard; he went seining in the river and once caught a sturgeon weighing more than two hundred pounds; he watched Victor and John in their sailboat (he himself refused to go, he had had enough of sailing on his trips across the Atlantic); he studied the animals he kept in enclosures—elk, deer, foxes, and others that he might be drawing; he played with his grandchildren and sang them French songs from his own childhood. Sometimes he took quiet walks by himself, going to the point on the beach from which he could see down the river, or strolled along the stream that ran through Minnie's Land, a stream that flowed through two pools and dropped over a five-foot waterfall that lay between them. At other times he sat in the house and enjoyed the view of the Palisades, the tall cliffs that lined the other side of the Hudson, and watched the early morning mists that blanketed the river just as they had blanketed Perkiomen Creek at Mill Grove. As the day wore on, the rising sun would pierce the gray cloud, tear it into shreds and drive it upward until the whole beauty of the river lay before him.

To Audubon, all this meant peace. He had funds at last, he had the house that he and Lucy had always wanted, he had his family around him, his children and his grandchildren; but it was not yet time for him to enjoy this life to the full, because on his return from the Missouri he had an accumulation of work to handle. One task was completing the small edition of his bird book, which now included a seventh volume containing the birds he had drawn since the original edition. On April 22, he wrote the final words to precede his acknowledgment to his lithographer and printer: "At the conclusion of this work, and in bidding good-bye to my kind patrons . . ." That job was done, but he still had more pictures to prepare for the book on quadrupeds, notes and specimens to send Bachman, who was busy with the text, and proofs and manuscript to read and correct. He also had to obtain subscriptions for the new book.

By early May he was in New Bedford, Massachusetts, on another canvassing trip, but he was there regretfully; he would have preferred staying at Minnie's Land. Writing to his family in the middle of the month, he said sadly, "At the rate I go on procuring names, I have sixteen more weeks of labor to perform and that will lead me pretty late in autumn! I am sorry for it, as this will make two summers' absence from my dear home and my very little friends." By the middle of June, he figured that he had in all a hundred and sixty-nine subscribers, but he was weary. He was in Boston and planning a trip through New England to Albany. "I then contemplate to go home and sit for a few days," he wrote Victor, "as my feet are swollen and sore by walking on pavement from morn to night every day." On June 16 he wrote again from New Bedford, "Strawberries are *ripe here* and plentiful. I wonder if I will find any left at home. I dare say that Minnie's Land looks very beautiful now, and I will enjoy a few days there dearly." After collecting all the subscriptions he could in Massachusetts, he traveled throughout New York State, going as far west as Buffalo. By August 3 he had obtained a hundred and eighty-five subscriptions and hoped that the total would reach two hundred before his return home. On August 7, on his way back to Utica, he escaped injury in a serious train wreck twelve miles outside the city. The engine went off the track and rather than wait until the damage was repaired, he walked to Utica. But he was no longer the vigorous man who had tramped for hundreds of miles through the frontier and had delightedly outpaced Mr. S. on their way from Trinity to Shippingport, for when he had finished the twelve miles to Utica, he was "tired and greatly hungry." On August 14 he was in Schenectady, New York, and had brought the total subscriptions to one hundred and ninety-six. In September, he canvassed part of Massachusetts and several towns in Connecticut. Then he went back to Minnie's Land to rest.

Although he did more traveling the following year, the book was well launched. He and Lucy at last had money and servants and a house, and he felt himself able to rely more on the work of Victor and John, both of whom he was supporting. Victor, although he too was an artist, now handled most of the business; John, who was the better painter of the two brothers, concentrated his efforts on helping his father with the pictures of the quadrupeds, in the end doing almost half of them. Audubon, however, closely supervised the business he had created. When John Bachman complained that Victor was not sending him the materials he needed for the text—specimens, books, and notes—Audubon tried to straighten out the misunderstanding. When more specimens were required, he arranged to have John make an expedition to Texas; and in 1846 he sent John to England to study some of the arctic mammals—the museums there had specimens that were not available in the United States. Audubon was not yet ready to retire completely, although he was taking more time to enjoy Minnie's Land, his family, and the achievement of the dream he had had so many years before at Niagara Falls. He was famous now, respected, well off; the people he wanted to see came to him, he did not have to go out and seek them. It had all worked out very much as he had hoped it would.

Then one day in 1846, after watching the mists rise from the river, he stepped before his easel to begin painting and found that the morning sun did not drive the mists away. At a distance, objects still stood bright and clear, but he could not remove the blurry fog that veiled his picture. He tried again the next day and the next, but struggle as he did, he could not see clearly enough to paint. The lines were wrong; he could not get the picture into focus; and finally he realized that, as an artist, he was finished. It was useless to struggle further. Reluctantly he turned over all responsibility for painting the animals to John, and from that moment, according to Lucy, "he drooped. Silent, patient sorrow filled his broken heart."

Gradually his interest in the book grew less and less; he slipped away from the world around him; his thoughts turned in upon himself; he began to have difficulty finding the right words to express his ideas, then he had fewer ideas to express; and in May, 1848, Bachman saw him and was horrified by the change. "Alas, my poor friend Audubon!" he wrote. "The outlines of his beautiful face and form are there, but his noble mind is all in ruins. It is indescribably sad." Lucy went for walks with him around Minnie's Land. He liked to have her read to him, and he especially enjoyed having Victor's wife sing a Spanish song, *Buenas Noches,* every night before he went to bed. But he was hardly aware, in 1849, that John had gone on a gold-mining expedition to California, a trip that was both costly and disastrous—the would-be miners were struck by cholera—but from which John returned to Minnie's Land safely.

It was a half-life that he was leading, devoid of dignity and remote from all that he had loved and worked for, a life of instinct rather than feeling and thought. Yet the years dragged on and the broken man continued his childish routine, the walks on which he had to be escorted, the one song repeated every night, the life of a child without the gaiety of childhood, until January, 1851, when he suffered a slight stroke, followed by partial paralysis and great pain. On January 22, his face gaunt and contracted, the large frame of his body an empty shell, he began to sink rapidly; and the end came on January 27, 1851.

"Before he died," Victor wrote Dr. Morton in Philadelphia, "he opened his eyes which had been almost closed for some time, and gave my mother, John, and myself a wistful and clear look—turning his head slightly to look on us. This way his farewell glance fell upon those he has loved so well."

There was no sound in the silent, hushed room. Then Lucy stepped quietly forward. Gently and lovingly, she reclosed the eyes which had seen so much beauty in America and portrayed it so others could see it too.

Epilogue

T HAT spring they came up from the south again and burst
like an opening fan across the continent—Canada geese
and goldeneye ducks, long-legged avocets and wide-winged
whooping cranes—all the great miracle of birdlife that remained
forever captured, motionless yet alive, on the pure white sheets
of the enormous volumes. Some flew over Henderson and lighted
on the roof of the steam mill, whose bulky mass still stood on
the banks of the Ohio. Some paused at Trinity where, driven
by despair, he had written Rozier that he had been "too much
of this world," and at Niagara Falls where, in the arching rainbows of water, he had rediscovered hope. Others flew over Cincinnati and the street he had paced trying to summon his
courage to ask a loan for his fare to Louisville, and over Louisville, where his friends would not offer him a job even as a
steamboat clerk. Some entered the gardens of Philadelphia without discriminating between those that belonged to his friends
and those that belonged to his enemies. For the birds were all
America's; they were not Ord's or Harris's or even Audubon's.
They arched along the Gulf Coast, they flew across Buffalo
Bayou; they circled high above the stockades of Fort Union and
crossed the keys of Florida; they nested on the Magdalen Islands off Cape Breton.

And some passed over the grave near Minnie's Land.

Well, for better or worse, it was all over now. He had been
given Mill Grove and lost it through his own foolishness and
obstinacy and speculation; and after he had lost Mill Grove, he
had lost everything else that Jean Audubon had given him.
Then everything that William Bakewell had given Lucy and
most of the money that the Bakewell children had invested in
his mad and careless ideas and most of what George and John
Keats and his Henderson neighbors had added.

He had repaid the debt, not with money, but by bearing
their scorn.

He had worked at the Cincinnati Museum, but now there was nothing left of that. He had drawn black chalk portraits which were probably worth the twenty-five dollars he had charged for them, but not much more. He had gathered the learned of Edinburgh to hear the truth about rattlesnakes, then diluted the truth with wild tales; he had helped the overtrusting Rafinesque, then deceived him.

But the past was irrevocable. Its threads could not be unraveled and rewoven.

He had not even provided for Lucy's future the way he thought he had. He had given her and the children an opportunity to live comfortably for the rest of their lives. But the boys had never been good at business. John had never tried; and Victor, from the time his father had lectured him on accounting, had not been particularly competent except in his father's eyes, and those eyes were misted by a father's love. The boys built large houses for themselves with the money he had made for them and their mother; they invested funds in new editions of his work, trying to keep the business going. But they lacked his ability and his determination. After Victor died in 1857, John by himself attempted to reproduce the original *Birds of America* in lithographs. Most of the subscribers to the expensive book were in the South, and he published it just before the Civil War. He died in 1862.

Lucy had little of the money left. She rented the house at Minnie's Land. She found a junk dealer who was willing to give her a few dollars for the copper in Havell's magnificent plates. (A handful were rescued by a small boy just before they were pushed into the furnace of a smelter at Ansonia, Connecticut.) After months of dickering, she sold most of the original drawings to the New York Historical Society. She originally asked five thousand dollars, then dropped to four, then to two. She needed two thousand dollars to pay off the mortgage on Minnie's Land. She also asked the society to buy her remaining copies of the *Ornithological Biography*. "I assure you the world is too busy to care for the wants and grievances of an old and lone widow," she wrote. "I find it impossible to keep the rats from the the boxes of the 'Ornithological Biographies.' Therefore I have concluded to sell them for what I can, being in real want. Will not your Historical Society give me something for all I have, say even a dollar a volume rather than have them destroyed." Then she sold Minnie's Land too and went to spend the remainder of her days living with relatives.

The year he died, and for many years after, the hunters continued to line the banks of the Mississippi at New Orleans to shoot the golden plovers by the thousands, reaping the harvest of dead bodies as though it were a harvest of grain. The pigeon hunters were out in force wherever the pigeons lighted, slaughtering them and packing them in barrels for sale and giving the waste to their hogs. Along the coast of Canada, the eggers continued to come back every season almost as soon as the birds and robbed the nests and carried the produce to Halifax and were back again by the second nesting. And out at Fort Union, after shooting a buffalo, they sometimes took only the tongue and left the rest of the carcass for the wolves just as they had done when Audubon was there. As soon as the railroads began to span the country, the slaughter grew even worse.

Across the nation, they chopped the trees and plowed the fields until hundreds of acres, no, thousands of acres, no, millions of acres, blew away in dust when the wind touched them, and the wind touched them often. The steamboats filled the rivers with waste, and so did the factories and the mills that lined them. He had once caught a two-hundred-pound sturgeon at Minnie's Land, but soon no one could do that. A two-hundred-pound sturgeon could not live in the Hudson River.

"I dare say Minnie's Land looks very beautiful now," he had once written from New Bedford, but soon it was encircled by steel-framed, crime-filled buildings, which engulfed the stream and its two ponds and made the edge of the river an unsafe place for a grandfather to sit and dream in the twilight. Minnie's Land was gone too, entirely gone.

But how much can be accomplished by a man in the one lifetime that is given him? Not much. Not even by the best of men, and he had misused so many years, squandered them on aimless and fruitless speculations, wasted them in visions of becoming what he was never intended to become.

Yet he had kept on trying. He had always kept on trying

even when he was forced to beg commissions for black chalk portraits in New Orleans, even when he had despaired of living as he had done at Trinity.

Yes, he had kept on trying. The fine white sheets with the birds of America on them, alive-looking and beautiful, bore testimony to that. In them, he was more fortunate than most men; he at least had something to show for his trying.

Just as he had intended them to be, they were whole pictures—birds and background and sky blended into one—each sheet representing a fleeting instant captured for all time. And they gave visions to other men, enabled them to help a pragmatic people see a bird for what a bird is, to think of golden plovers as something more than a crop that could be harvested free except for the cost of the shot, of beavers as something more than fur for men's hats, of trees as something more than firewood or planks.

There were not many men capable of doing that before his time. There were not many such men after.

But there were some. Just enough to check the ravage before, once and forever, it was too late.

Just enough to give the rest of us one last, irretrievable chance to save what is left.

Acknowledgments

I T would be impossible for me to recognize here all the many
people who, in one way or another, have helped me in the
preparation of this book; but I would be remiss if I did not
mention some of those whose roles were especially specific.
Therefore I would like to thank:

Peter Israel of G. P. Putnam's Sons, who originated the idea
for this book, and William Targ, who helped me nurse it to
completion; Theron Raines, who is not only my agent but a
valued critic; Mr. and Mrs. C. R. Horton, Jr., who gave me
their reactions to the manuscript as general readers; and Mrs.
Walter Pitkin of the Westport Public Library, who translated
for me pertinent portions of Vincent Nolte's book, published in
Hamburg in 1854.

I am also deeply indebted to the many libraries and their
staffs without whose cooperation the research for this book
would have been impossible. The many who have helped me
are listed in the bibliography, but I would like particularly to
thank the following for permission to quote from the manuscripts and other material in their possession: the American
Philosophical Society, the Trustees of the Boston Public Library, the Chicago Historical Society, the Houghton Library of
Harvard University, the Historical Society of Pennsylvania, the
Library Company of Philadelphia, the Massachusetts Historical
Society, the New-York Historical Society, the New York Public
Library, the Cincinnati Historical Society, the Princeton University Library, the Howard-Tilton Memorial Library of Tulane University, and the Yale University Library. The material
they have given me permission to quote is listed in the notes for
each chapter.

I would also like to thank the Yale University Library for
the many facilities it has placed at my disposal, thus greatly
lightening my task, and the staff of the Westport Public Library
for their helpful concern with my problems.

The Club of Odd Volumes, which has published many of the Audubon manuscripts and letters in the possession of Harvard, has graciously given me permission to quote directly from its books; and the Oxford University Press has permitted me to quote from *The Letters of John Keats*. . .

For assistance in securing the illustrations I am indebted to the New-York Historical Society, the American Museum of Natural History, the National Audubon Society, the Museum of the City of New York, and the Princeton University Library.

Bibliography

As every schoolboy knows—to borrow Macaulay's phrase—the compilation of an impressive-looking bibliography requires little more than access to the file catalogues of a few major libraries and the patience to list every newspaper clipping, every document, every pamphlet examined. Most such bibliographies, however, serve little useful purpose and seem hardly worth the typesetter's time. In the following bibliography, I have tried to restrict myself to the major sources of information on which I have drawn.

Libraries

The following libraries most generously gave me access to their collections of letters and other original material pertaining to Audubon and, in some instances, material pertinent to Audubon, but of a local nature and not available elsewhere. It is not practical either to catalogue their collections or attempt to evaluate them individually, but I am grateful for the assistance they have given me and for the courteous cooperation of their staffs.

American Antiquarian Society
American Museum of Natural History
Boston Public Library
Chicago Historical Society
Cincinnati Historical Society
Columbia University
Connecticut Historical Society
Connecticult State Library
Georgia Historical Society
Harvard University—Houghton Library
  (This library has permitted the publication of much of its extensive collection, thus making a large part of it generally available without the need for visiting the library personally.)
Haverford College—Charles Roberts Autograph Collection
Historical Society of Pennsylvania
Howard-Tilton Memorial Library of Tulane University
Indiana Historical Society
Indiana University
Lehigh University

Library Company of Philadelphia
Library of Congress
Louisiana State University
Maryland State Library
Massachusetts Historical Society
National Audubon Society
New-York Historical Society
New York Public Library
Pierpont Morgan Library
Princeton University
University of Cincinnati
University of Virginia
Yale University

Publications

The following publications were searched for the years 1820–1860 for material relating to Audubon.

American Journal of Science and Arts
American Quarterly Review
Blackwood's Edinburgh Magazine
Chamber's Journal
Edinburgh Journal of Natural and Geographical Science
Edinburgh Journal of Science
Edinburgh Literary Journal
Edinburgh Philosophical Journal
Edinburgh Review
Jameson's Philosophical Journal
Journal of the Philadelphia Academy of Natural Science
London and Edinburgh Philosophical Journal
Loudon's Magazine of Natural History
Monthly American Journal of Geology and Natural Science
North American Review
Quarterly Review, Edinburgh

A search was also made of the publications listed in *The Reader's Guide to Current Periodical Literature* and of *The Auk*, published by The American Ornithologists' Union, and *The Cardinal*. The latter publication was formerly issued by the Audubon Society of the Sewickley Valley, Sewickley, Pennsylvania.

The following articles are referred to specifically in the notes or the text.

Audubon, John James, "Four Audubon Letters." *The Cardinal,* Sewickley, Penna. Vol. IV, No. 7, January, 1938, pp. 167-173.

———, "Notes on the Rattlesnake." *Jameson's Philosophical Review,* Edinburgh. Vol. 3, April–October, 1827, pp. 21-31.

Audubon, Victor G., "In Reply to Mr. Waterton's Remarks on Audubon's Biography of Birds." *Loudon's Magazine of Natural History.* July, 1833, p. 369.

Bakewell, Thomas W., "Audubon & Bakewell, Partners." *The Cardinal.* Sewickley, Penna. Vol. IV, No. 2, July, 1935, pp. 34-42. (This contains his autobiographical sketch and a number of his letters.)

Burns, Frank L., "Miss Lawson's Recollections of Ornithologists." *The Auk.* Vol. XXXIV, July, 1917, pp. 275-282.

Coues, Elliott, "William Swainson to John James Audubon." *The Auk.* Vol. XV, 1898, pp. 11-13.

Dallett, Francis James, "Citizen Audubon; A Documentary Discovery." *The Princeton University Library Chronicle,* Princeton, N.J. Vol. XXI, Nos. 1 and 2, Autumn, 1959, and Winter, 1960.

Deane, Ruthven, "William Swainson to John James Audubon (A hitherto unpublished letter)." *The Auk.* Vol. XXII, January, 1905, pp. 31-34.

———, "William Swainson to John James Audubon (Hitherto Unpublished letters)." *The Auk,* Vol. XXII, July, 1905, pp. 248-258.

Dwight, Edward H., "The Autobiographical Writings of John James Audubon." *The Bulletin of the Missouri Historical Society,* St. Louis, Mo. Vol. XIX, No. 1, October, 1962, pp. 26-35.

Perkins, S. E., III, "Episodes in the Life of Audubon in Indiana." *The Wilson Bulletin.* Vol. XLVIII, No. 1, March, 1936, pp. 17-22.

Swainson, William, "Mr. Audubon and His Work, the 'Biography of Birds.'" *Loudon's Magazine of Natural History.* November, 1833, p. 550.

Unsigned. "Audubon's Ornithological Biography." *Blackwood's Edinburgh Review,* Edinburgh. July, 1831, pp. 1-16 and August, 1831, pp. 247-280.

Unsigned. "Ornithological Biography." The *Monthly American Journal of Geology and Natural Science,* Philadelphia. Vol. I, 1831–1832, pp. 136-139.

Unsigned. "Ornithological Biography." *American Quarterly Review.* No. XX, December, 1831, pp. 245-258.

Waterton, Charles, "On the 'Biography of Birds' of J. J. Audubon." *Loudon's Magazine of Natural History.* May, 1833, pp. 215-218.

Waterton, Charles, "The Vulture's Nose" (followed by other comments on Audubon's work). *Loudon's Magazine of Natural History.* May, 1834, pp. 276-283.

Books and Pamphlets

The following list includes the major books and pamphlets consulted.

Audubon, John James, *The Birds of America.* The elephant edition was produced from 1826 to 1838. The first two numbers were engraved by Lizars in Edinburgh, the remainder by Havell in London. The small edition was produced in Philadelphia and New York by J. B. Chevalier and J. J. Audubon in 1840–1844. The lithographs were done by J. T. Bowen and the printing by E. G. Dorsey. Subsequent editions were produced after Audubon's death.

————, *The Birds of America,* with an Introduction and descriptive text by William Vogt. New York: The Macmillan Company, 1937.

————, *Delineations of American Scenery and Character,* with an Introduction by Francis Hobart Herrick. New York: G. A. Baker & Company, 1926.

————, *Journal of John James Audubon Made During His Trip to New Orleans in 1820–1821,* Edited by Howard Corning, Foreword by Ruthven Deane. Boston: The Club of Odd Volumes, 1929.

————, *Journal of John James Audubon Made While Obtaining Subscriptions to His "Birds of America." 1840–1843,* Edited by Howard Corning, Foreword by Francis H. Herrick. Boston: The Club of Odd Volumes, 1929.

————, *Letters of John James Audubon, 1826–1840.* Edited by Howard Corning. Boston: The Club of Odd Volumes, 1930.

————, *Ornithological Biography.* This was published by Adam Black and Adam and Charles Black in Edinburgh in 1831–1839. The first volume was reprinted in the United States at Philadelphia, 1831 and 1835. The second volume was reprinted in Boston, 1835. No other of the original five volumes were reprinted in America.

————, *Scènes de la Nature dans les États-Unis et le Nord de l'Amérique; ouvrage tr. d'Audubon par Eugène Bazin.* Paris: Bertrand, 1857.

————, *A Synopsis of The Birds of America.* Adam and Charles Black, Edinburgh, and Longman, Rees, Brown, Green and Longman, London, 1839.

————, *The Viviparous Quadrupeds of North America.* The pictures were published in New York, 1845–1848, by J. J. Audubon. The text was published by J. J. Audubon and V. G. Audubon, New York, 1846–1854. The book was completed and subsequent editions published after Audubon's death.

Audubon, John Woodhouse, *Audubon's Western Journal: 1849–1850.* Cleveland: The A. H. Clark Company, 1906.

———, *The Drawings of John Woodhouse Audubon, Illustrating His Adventures Through Mexico and California. 1849–1850.* Introduction and notes by Carl Schaefer Dentzel. San Francisco: Book Club of California, 1957.

———, *Illustrated Notes of an Expedition Through Mexico and California.* New York: J. W. Audubon, 1852.

Audubon, Lucy, *The Life of John James Audubon, the Naturalist.* Edited by his widow with an introduction by Jas. Grant Wilson. New York: G. P. Putnam's Sons, 1902.

Audubon, Maria R., *Audubon and His Journals.* New York: Dover Publications, 1960.

* * * * * *

Adams, James Truslow, *The Living Jefferson.* New York and London: Charles Scribner's Sons, 1936.

Allen, Arthur A., *The Book of Bird Life.* New York: D. Van Nostrand Co., 1946.

Arthur, Stanley Clisby, *Audubon, An Intimate Life of the American Woodsman.* New Orleans: Harmanson, 1937.

Ashe, Thomas, *Travels in America.* New York, 1811.

Babcock, Kendric Charles, *The Rise of American Nationality.* New York: Harper & Brothers, 1906.

Bailey, Thomas A., *A Diplomatic History of the American People.* New York: Appleton-Century-Crofts, Inc., 1958.

Bakeless, John, *Daniel Boone.* New York: William Morrow and Company, 1939.

———, *The Eyes of Discovery.* New York: Dover Publications, 1961.

Bakewell, B. G., *The Family Book of Bakewell * Page * Campbell.* Pittsburgh: Wm. G. Johnston & Co., Printers, 1896.

Baldwin, Leland D., *The Keelboat Age on Western Waters.* Pittsburgh: University of Pittsburgh Press, 1941.

Banta, R. E., *The Ohio.* New York: Rinehart & Company, 1949.

Bartram, William, *Travels of William Bartram.* Mark Van Doren, Editor. New York: Dover Publications, no date.

Bartlett, Ruhl J., Editor, *The Record of American Diplomacy.* New York: Alfred A. Knopf, 1954.

Bassett, John Spencer, *A Short History of the United States.* New York: The Macmillan Company, 1917.

Beinecke, Frederick William, *The Birds of America.* New York: 1960. (A pictorial description of the original folios in the library of Frederick William Beinecke.)

Bent, Arthur Cleveland, *Life Histories of North American Birds of Prey.* New York: Dover Publications, 1961.

———, *Life Histories of North American Gallinaceous Birds.* New York: Dover Publications, 1963.

———, *Life Histories of North American Gulls and Terns.* New York: Dodd, Mead, and Company, 1947.

Bemis, Samuel F., *Jay's Treaty.* New Haven: Yale University Press, 1962.

———, *Pinckney's Treaty.* New Haven: Yale University Press, 1960.

Berman, Eleanor Davidson, *Thomas Jefferson Among the Arts.* New York: Philosophical Library, 1947.

Bletrami, J. C., *A Pilgrimage in America.* Chicago: Quadrangle Books, Inc., 1962.

Bonaparte, Charles Lucien. See Wilson, Alexander.

Boorstin, Daniel J., *The Lost World of Thomas Jefferson.* Boston: Beacon Press, 1963.

Brackenridge, Henry Marie, *Views of Louisiana.* Chicago: Quadrangle Books, Inc., 1962.

Bradford, Mary Fluker, *Audubon.* New Orleans: Press of L. Graham & Son Ltd., 1897.

Bragdon, Henry W., and McCutchen, Samuel P., *History of a Free People.* New York: The Macmillan Company, 1960.

Bridenbaugh, Carl and Jessica, *Rebels and Gentlemen.* New York: Oxford University Press, 1962.

Brown, Mark H., *The Plainsmen of the Yellowstone.* New York: G. P. Putnam's Sons, 1961.

Brown, Ralph H., *Mirror for Americans.* New York: American Geographical Society, 1943.

Buchanan, Robert, *The Life and Adventures of John James Audubon, The Naturalist.* London: S. Low Son & Marstton, 1868.

Bush, Raymond. See Kimble, George

Butterworth, Hezekiah, *In the Days of Audubon: A Tale of the "Protector of the Birds."* New York: D. Appleton and Company, 1901.

Cahalane, Victor H., *Mammals of North America.* New York: The Macmillan Company, 1954.

Cantwell, Robert, *Alexander Wilson: Naturalist and Pioneer.* Philadelphia and New York: J. B. Lippincott, 1961.

Cap, Paul Antoine Gratacap, *Audubon, Naturaliste Américain.* Paris: V. Masson et Fils, 1862.

Carter, Hodding, *Lower Mississippi.* New York: Farrar & Rinehart, 1942.

Channing, Edward, *The Jeffersonian System.* New York: Harper & Brothers Publishers, 1906.

Clark, Thomas D., *The Kentucky.* New York: Farrar & Rinehart, 1942.

Commager, Henry Steele. See Morison, Samuel E.

Darling, Louis and Lois, *Bird.* Boston: Houghton Mifflin Company, 1962.

Darby, William, *A Tour from the City of New York to Detroit.* Chicago: Quadrangle Books, Inc., 1962.

Dau, Frederick W., *Florida, Old and New.* New York: G. P. Putnam's Sons, 1934.

DeVoto, Bernard, *Across the Wide Missouri.* Boston: Houghton Mifflin Company, 1947.

———, *The Course of Empire.* Boston: Houghton Mifflin Company, 1952.

———, *The Year of Decision: 1846.* Boston: Houghton Mifflin Company, 1943.

Dick, Everett, *The Dixie Frontier.* New York: Capricorn Books, 1964.

Douglas, Marjory Stoneham, *The Everglades: River of Grass.* New York: Rinehart & Company, Inc., 1947.

Drake, Daniel, M.D., *Anniversary Discourse on the State and Prospects of the Western Museum Society.* Published by the Western Museum Society, Cincinnati, 1820. (In the possession of the Historical Society of Ohio.)

Dunbar, Carl O., *Historical Geology.* New York: John Wiley and Sons, Inc., 1957.

Eaton, Clement, *A History of the Old South.* New York: The Macmillan Company, 1949.

Eifert, Virginia, *River World: Wildlife of the Mississippi.* New York: Dodd, Mead & Company, 1959.

Ellicott, Andrew, *The Journal of Andrew Ellicott.* Chicago: Quadrangle Books, Inc., 1962.

Fisher, Robert Moore, *How to Know and Predict the Weather.* New York: The New American Library, 1953.

Flexner, James Thomas, *Steamboats Come True.* New York: The Viking Press, 1944.

Flint, Richard F. See Longwell, Chester R.

Ford, Alice, Editor, *Audubon's Animals: The Quadrupeds of North America.* Selections from *The Quadrupeds.* New York: The Studio Publications, Inc. in association with Thomas Y. Crowell, 1951.

———, *Audubon's Butterflies, Moths and Other Studies.* New York: Studio Publications, Inc. in association with Thomas Y. Crowell, 1952.

———, Editor, *The Bird Biographies of John James Audubon.* Selections from the *Ornithological Biography.* New York: The Macmillan Company, 1957.

———, *John James Audubon.* Norman, Oklahoma: University of Oklahoma Press, 1964.

Forman, Maurice Buxton, Editor, *The Letters of John Keats*. New York: Oxford University Press, 1948.

Fuess, Claude Moore, *Daniel Webster*. Boston: Little, Brown and Company, 1930.

Fuller, Myron L., *The New Madrid Earthquake*. Washington, D.C.: U. S. Government Printing Office. U. S. Geological Survey Bulletin 494, 1912.

Gardiner, Dorothy, *West of The River*. New York: Thomas Y. Crowell Co., 1963.

Garrett, Mitchel Bennett, *The French Colonial Question: 1789–1791*. Ann Arbor, Michigan: George Wahr, 1918.

Graham, Jack B., *The Geological Story of a River*. Speech Given at the 118th Meeting of the American Association for the Advancement of Science, Philadelphia, Pennsylvania, December 27, 1951.

Grinnell, George Bird, *Audubon Park: The History of the Site of the Hispanic Society of America and Neighboring Institutions*. New York: Printed by Order of the Trustees of the Hispanic Society of New York, 1927.

Griscom, Ludlow, *Birds of America*. Introduction and descriptive captions by Ludlow Griscom. Popular edition. New York: The Macmillan Company, 1950.

Hall, Courtney Robert, *A Scientist in the Early Republic: Samuel Latham Mitchill*. New York: Columbia University Press, 1934.

Hall, Henry Marion, *A Gathering of Shore Birds*. Roland C. Clement, Editor. New York: Devin-Adair Co., 1960.

Hanaburgh, Emory F., *Audubon's "Birds of America"; A Check List of the First Issues of the Plates in the First Folio Edition. 1828–1838*. The Author. Peekskill, New York: The Enterprise Press, 1941.

Hansen, Marcus Lee, *The Atlantic Migration 1607–1860*. New York: Harper & Brothers, 1961.

Harris, Edward, *Up the Missouri with Audubon: the Journal of Edward Harris*, Edited and annotated by John Francis McDermott. Norman, Oklahoma: University of Oklahoma Press, 1951.

Havighurst, Walter, *Upper Mississippi: A Wilderness Saga*. New York: Farrar & Rinehart, 1937.

Herrick, Francis Hobart, *Audubon, The Naturalist*. New York: D. Appleton-Century Company, 1938. Second edition. (The second edition combines two volumes in one. It also includes additional material. The first edition was published in 1917.)

Hickey, Joseph J., *A Guide to Bird Watching*. Garden City, New York: Garden City Books, 1953.

Hofstadter, Richard, *The American Political Tradition*. New York: Vintage Books, 1948.

——, Editor, *Great Issues in American History*. New York: Vintage Books, 1958.

Jaffe, Bernard, *Men of Science in America*. New York: Simon and Schuster, 1958.

James, C. L. R., *The Black Jacobins*. New York: The Dial Press, 1938.

Kimble, George, and Bush, Raymond, *The Weather*. New York: Penguin Books, Inc., 1946.

Koch, Adrienne, *Jefferson and Madison*. New York. 1964. Oxford University Press.

Knopf, Adolph. See Longwell, Chester R.

Kraus, Michael, *The United States to 1865*. Ann Arbor, Michigan: The University of Michigan Press, 1959.

Lincoln, Frederick C., *Migration of Birds*. Washington, D.C.: United States Government Printing Office, 1950.

Longwell, Chester R., Knopf, Adolph, and Flint, Richard F., *Outlines of Physical Geology*. New York: John Wiley and Sons, 1955.

Malone, Dumas, *Jefferson and the Rights of Man*. Vol. 2 of *Jefferson and His Time*. Boston: Little, Brown and Company, 1951.

Marquis, James, *The Life of Andrew Jackson*. New York: Bobbs-Merrill Co., 1938.

Mathews, John Joseph, *The Osages, Children of the Middle Waters*. Norman, Oklahoma: University of Oklahoma Press, 1961.

McCutchen, Samuel P. See Bragdon, Henry W.

Member of the Massachusetts Bar, A, *Clerk's Magazine*. Boston: Lilly & Wait and Carter & Hendee, 1832.

Michaux, F. A., *Travels to the Westward of the Allegany Mountains* (Translated from the French by B. Lambert). London: J. Mawman, 1805.

Mitchell and Hinman, *An Accompaniment to Mitchill's Reference and Distance Map of The United States*. Philadelphia: Mitchell and Hinman, 1835.

Morison, Samuel Eliot, and Commager, Henry Steele, *The Growth of the American Republic*. New York: Oxford University Press, 1950.

Morse, Jedidiah, *Geography Made Easy*. Boston: Thomas & Andrews, 1818.

Murchie, Guy, *Song of the Sky*. Boston: Houghton Mifflin Company, 1954.

Muschamp, Edward A., *Audacious Audubon*. New York: Brentano's, 1929.

Nolte, Vincent, *The Memoirs of Vincent Nolte* (Translated from the German). New York: G. Howard Watt, 1934.

Nye, Russel Blaine, *The Cultural Life of the New Nation*. New York: Harper & Row, 1963.

Ord, George, *Sketch of the Life of Alexander Wilson.* Philadelphia: Harrison Hall, 1828.

Parkman, Francis, *The Discovery of the Great West: La Salle.* New York: Rinehart & Company, Inc., 1956.

Parton, James, *The Life and Times of Aaron Burr.* Boston: Houghton, Osgood, and Co., 1880.

Pearse, James, *A Narrative of the Life of James Pearse.* Chicago: Quadrangle Press, Inc., 1962.

Peattie, Donald Culross, *Audubon's America, The Narratives and Experiences of John James Audubon.* Boston: Houghton Mifflin Company, 1940.

————, *Singing in the Wilderness; A salute to John James Audubon.* New York. G. P. Putnam's Sons, 1935.

Peterson, Roger Tory, *Birds Over America.* New York: Dodd, Mead & Company, 1950.

————, *A Field Guide to the Birds.* Boston: Houghton Mifflin Company, 1947.

Pettingill, Olin Sewall, Jr., *A Laboratory and Field Manual of Ornithology.* Minneapolis, Minn.: Burgess Publishing Company, 1956.

Pierce, Bradford Kinney, *Audubon's Adventures; or Life in the Woods.* New York: Hunt & Eaton; Cincinnati: Cranston & Stowe, 1889.

Potter, Alonzo, *The Principles of Science.* Boston: Thomas H. Webb & Co., 1840.

President's Water Resources Policy Commission, *Ten Rivers in America's Future.* Washington, D.C.: U. S. Government Printing Office, 1950.

Quick, Herbert, and Quick, Edward, *Mississippi Steamboatin'.* New York: Henry Holt and Company, 1926.

Rourke, Constance, *Audubon.* New York: Harcourt, Brace and Company, 1936.

Rozier, Firman, *Rozier's History of the Early Settlement of the Mississippi Valley.* St. Louis: G. A. Pierrot & Son, Printers, 1890.

Russell, Phillips, *Jefferson, Champion of the Free Mind.* New York: Dodd, Mead & Company, 1956.

Saxon, Lyle, *Fabulous New Orleans.* New York: The Century Co., 1930.

————, *Lafitte The Pirate.* New York: The Century Co., 1930.

————, *Old Louisiana,* New York: D. Appleton-Century Co., 1938.

Schlesinger, Arthur M., Jr., *The Age of Jackson.* New York: The New American Library, 1949.

Schurz, Carl, *Life of Henry Clay.* New York: Houghton Mifflin and Company, 1887.

Scott, Walter. *The Journal of Sir Walter Scott.* New York: Harper & Brothers, 1890.

Sitwell, Sacheverell, *Audubon's American Birds from Plates by J. J. Audubon*. London: B. T. Batsford Ltd., 1949.

Select Committee on National Water Resources—U. S. Senate, *Water Resource Activities in the United States*. Washington, D.C.: U. S. Government Printing Office, 1960.

Sinclair, Harold, *The Port of New Orleans*. Garden City, New York. Doubleday, Doran, and Co. Inc., 1942.

Smith, Page, *John Adams*. Garden City, New York: Doubleday and Co., 1962.

Sprunt, Alexander, Jr., *Carolina Low Country Impressions*. New York: Devin-Adair Co., 1964.

St. John, Mrs. Horace, *Life of Audubon, the Naturalist of The New World*. Philadelphia: J. B. Lippincott & Co., 1881.

Stoddard, T. Lothrop, *The French Revolution in San Domingo*. Boston: Houghton Mifflin Company, 1914.

Struthers, Burt, *Philadelphia: Holy Experiment*. Garden City, New York: Doubleday, Doran & Company, Inc., 1945.

Talbot, Lee M., *The International Role of Parks in Preserving Endangered Species*. Washington, D.C.: U. S. Government Printing Office, 1964. *First World Conference on National Parks*, Edited by Alexander B. Adams. pp. 296-303.

Tallant, Robert, *The Romantic New Orleanians*. New York: E. P. Dutton & Co., 1950.

Todd. W. E. Clyde, *Birds of Western Pennsylvania*. Pittsburgh: University of Pittsburgh Press, 1940.

Townsend, Charles Wendell, *In Audubon's Labrador*. Boston: Houghton Mifflin Company, 1918.

Turner, Frederick Jackson, *The Rise of the New West*. New York: Harper & Brothers, 1906.

Tyler, Mrs. Alice Jaynes, *I Who Should Command All*. New York: G. P. Putnam's Sons, 1942.

United States Geological Survey, *Large Rivers of the United States*. Geological Survey Circular 44. Washington, D. C.: U. S. Government Printing Office, 1949.

Unsigned. *John James Audubon*. Paris: Centre Culturel Américan, 1960.

Unsigned. *Kentucky; a Guide to the Bluegrass State*. Compiled and written by the Federal Writers' Project of the Works Progress Administration for the State of Kentucky. New York: Hastings House, 1939.

Unsigned. *New Orleans City Guide*. Compiled and written by the Federal Writers' Project of the Works Progress Administration for the City of New Orleans. Boston: Houghton Mifflin Company, 1938.

Van Every, Dale, *Men of the Western Waters*. Boston: Houghton Mifflin Company, 1956.

Van Vleck, Sarita, *Growing Wings*. Garden City, New York: Doubleday & Co., 1963.

Vestal, Stanley, *The Missouri*. New York: Farrar & Rinehart, 1945.

Ward, Aileen, *John Keats*. New York: The Viking Press, 1963.

West, Jessamyn, *A Mirror for the Sky*. New York: Harcourt, Brace and Company, 1948.

White, Gilbert, *The Natural History of Selbourne*. London: Bickers and Son, 1875.

Wilson, Alexander, *American Ornithology; or The Natural History of The Birds of the United States*. With a continuation by Charles Lucien Bonaparte, Prince of Musignano. The illustrative Notes, and Life of Wilson by Sir William Jardine. 3 Vols. London: Whittaker, Treachers, & Arnot; Edinburgh: Stirling & Kenney, 1832.

————, *Memoir and Remains*. Edited with Memorial, Introduction, Essay, Notes, Illustrations and Glossary by the Rev. Alexander B. Grosart. Paisley: Alex. Gardner, 1876.

————, *Poems, Chiefly in the Scottish Dialect*. London: Longman, Hurst, Rees, Orme, and Brown, 1816. (Also at Edinburgh: Glasgow, Greenock and Paisley.)

Wilson, Alexander, and Bonaparte, Charles Lucien, *American Ornithology; or The Natural History of The Birds of The United States*. Edinburgh: Constable and Co., 1831.

Wright, Louis B., *Culture on the Moving Frontier*. New York: Harper & Brothers, 1961.

Wright, Morris, Editor, *The Mississippi Reader*. Garden City, New York: Doubleday & Co., 1962.

Youmans, William Jay, *Pioneers of American Science*. New York: D. Appleton & Co., 1896.

Zadok, Cramer, *The Navigator*. Pittsburgh: Cramer & Spear, 1802.

Notes

In the matter of notes—which may delight scholars, but which detract from the general reader's attention—I have followed the policy of listing for each chapter the principal sources of material about Audubon during the period covered and those from which I have quoted directly. The notes would have become too cumbersome if I had mentioned separately every one of the hundreds of pages of manuscript that I have studied. I have, however, cited individually those that I have quoted or which have a specific bearing on some aspect of the text. (In the case of Harvard, which has generously given me permission to quote from its manuscript collection, I have either identified the particular manuscript itself or given the appropriate pages in the books issued by the Club of Odd Volumes, which too has kindly let me quote from its publications containing much of Harvard's collection.)

I have also eliminated, for the sake of brevity, the thousand and one other possible references, believing that the reader will take my word for it that each fact mentioned is documented, whether it is a description of Dr. Mitchill or the appearance of the riverfront towns as seen from a keelboat. It seems rather pedantic to point out that I have visited Edinburgh, London, Paris, New Orleans, Houston, New York—to name only a few cities familiar to Audubon—that I have traveled by boat on the Ohio and the lower stretches of the Mississippi, and so have something of a feel for both rivers, or that I have followed Audubon down them with a copy of the then-current *Navigator* on my desk, along with accounts of other journeys taken during the same period. In my opinion, the reader is entitled to assume such attention to detail throughout a book without constantly being reminded of how hard and carefully the writer has worked. The sources of most such collateral information, except direct personal experience, can be discovered by referring to the bibliography.

In many instances, I have made my references to printed source material, which is more generally available than are the original manuscripts and therefore more useful to most readers. This does not mean, however, that I have not checked the originals myself whenever I had the slightest reason to doubt the authenticity of a statement in its printed form and the originals were obtainable. Also I have followed the practice of often citing a late edition of a published work, again for the reason that these are more easily available to those who wish to pursue a particular subject further. Especially when they are printed by offset, there is little cause to doubt their accurate rendition of the text.

The more scholarly may be disappointed that the footnotes contain no comments on the errors that I have discovered in the works of others. Naturally, I have found some, because to do so is inevitable in the research for a book of this sort. To the general reader, however, such questions are of no consequence; and the student is perfectly capable of rooting them out for himself without a commentator urging him on. I also have the faint—although probably futile—hope that future writers will show to me the same courtesy that I have tried to extend to my own predecessors.

Although I have retained some of the misspellings appearing in some of the original material, I have done so without marking them "sic"; in other cases, I have corrected the punctuation, spelling, and inserted words for clarity's sake without resort to such devices as brackets. I have done this to make for easier reading, but only in instances where the changes in no way affected the sense of the original.

Chapter I

No biographer of Audubon can fail to acknowledge his debt to Francis Hobart Herrick, whose investigations in France uncovered many of Jean Audubon's papers and records, many of which he later reproduced in full in his biography. (See especially Vol. I, pp. 24-89, and the Appendix.) These helped immeasurably in clearing up the obscurity surrounding John James Audubon's descent, which was increased by his use of the names Rabin and Fougère and by the supposition that he might be the Lost Dauphin. As to his early use of other names, he was John James Audubon to his wife, his children, and his acquaintances, and so he is called throughout this book. The story of his being the Lost Dauphin is based primarily on his age, his appearance, the Royalist tendencies in the part of

France from which Jean Audubon came, and certain pages in his journal, which, for the curious, are reproduced in Arthur, pp. 373-375. The evidence against this supposition is so massive that I have not introduced the theory into the text. In passing, it should be noted that further confusion about Audubon's birth has developed from a misunderstanding of the word "creole." In both the French and Spanish cultures, the word meant someone of European descent, not someone of mixed blood, either Indian or Negro.

In this chapter, I have drawn heavily on Herrick's documents for the facts concerning Jean Audubon's career and John James's birth, particularly the naval records, the doctor's bill, Jean Audubon's accounting of the slave transaction, and the adoption papers for John James and Rosa. Herrick's work has since been supplemented by Alice Ford, pp. 3-38, who has uncovered additional papers in France.

It is hardly likely that a virile man like Jean Audubon in a place like San Domingo would have brought forth only two children, in which case he left the others behind. But this, it seems to me, does not affect his generosity in bringing to Anne the two he did nor her generosity in accepting them as her own.

Certainly there is considerable question whether Audubon actually studied under David, as he later claimed, particularly as he does not describe his lessons in any detail and gives no dates or places. He made the claim when he was desperately seeking recognition and was especially conscious of his lack of formal training of any sort. Whether he took lessons with David or not seems a matter of small importance, because they could not have lasted any length of time and he did not acquire any significant skill.

For John James's own version of his youthful days and of the stories told him by his father, I have relied on the autobiographical sketch that originally appeared in *Scribner's Magazine* and which was included by Maria Audubon in her *Audubon and His Journals*, Vol. I, pp. 7-15.

Chapter II

Herrick included in his biography, Vol. I, pp. 100-101, one of the letters Jean Audubon wrote in connection with John James Audubon's trip. John James himself described the voyage and his early days at Mill Grove in the autobiographical sketch reprinted in

Maria Audubon's book, Vol. I, pp. 15-20. The description of the phoebes is drawn from the article on pewees (as Audubon called the birds), appearing in his *Ornithological Biography*. "My Style of Drawing Birds," one of the episodes in the same book, tells of his early artistic experiments. The details of William Bakewell's early life can be found in the Bakewell's family genealogy. The research of Alice Ford, pp. 41-52, has helped clarify the chronology of this period. As for Mill Grove itself, it has happily been preserved by the farsighted action of the Commissioners of Montgomery County, Pennsylvania, who purchased the property in 1951 and who operate it as an historic shrine and wildlife sanctuary under its gracious curator, J. d'Arcy Northwood.

Chapter III

Jean Audubon's business dealings with Dacosta over the mine and his instructions concerning John James and Lucy are contained in the copies of his correspondence discovered by Herrick, Vol. I, pp. 113-126. The details of John James's life at Mill Grove and his return to France, as well as his attitude toward Dacosta, are set forth in the autobiographical sketch included in Maria Audubon's book, Vol. I, pp. 21-24. His illness prior to leaving Mill Grove is described by William Bakewell in a letter dated July 19, 1805, in the possession of the Princeton Library. According to his description in the section of pewees in the *Ornithological Biography*, Audubon saw the threads still on the legs of the phoebes in the spring of 1806. They must, therefore, have been on the birds when they returned while he was in France.

Chapter IV

Audubon's letter, dated May 20, 1805, to William Bakewell is in the possession of the Princeton University Library, as is William Bakewell's letter, dated July 19, 1805, commenting on Audubon's English. The description of life at Flatland Ford during Audubon's absence is drawn from two letters also in the Princeton Library, one written by Elizabeth Bakewell and dated September 2, 1805, and another by Lucy Audubon, written on the same day. The partnership agreement between Audubon and Ferninand Rozier, as well as other papers dealing with Jean Audubon's arrangements over the mine, have been reproduced by Herrick in his biography, Vol. I, pp. 132-133, and the Appendix. Dallett discusses Audubon's citizenship in his article, "Citizen Audubon." William Bakewell's description of Audubon's room can be found in Lucy Audubon, pp. 26-27, and Audubon's relationship with Dr. Mitchill is discussed on p. 28. Letters written by Audubon and dated January 10, 1807, April 24, 1807, May 6, 1807, and July 19, 1807, contain Audubon's reports to his father and François Rozier concerning his business affairs. They are in the possession of the Tulane University Library. The autobiographical sketch included in Maria Audubon's book, Vol. I, pp. 24-28, covers this entire period. In it, Audubon says that he took a "mockery of an examination" for the naval service at Rochefort, went on a short cruise, and returned to find that his father had obtained passports for himself and Rozier. It is possible that he confused this with his previous visit to Rochefort. On the other hand, Jean Audubon's ability to handle practical affairs and his long connection with the navy make it probable that he engaged in some maneuver of this sort.

Chapter V

Audubon and Rozier's trip west is described in the journal kept by Rozier and reproduced by Herrick and in Rozier's *History of the Early Settlement of the Mississippi Valley,* p. 298. The discussion of western storekeeping can be found in Ashe's book, pp. 52-53. Thomas Bakewell, in his autobiographical sketch in *The Cardinal,* described his experience working for his uncle.

Chapter VI

Lucy's description of their trip west and her impressions of their life at Louisville appear in a letter dated May 27, 1808, which is in the possession of the Princeton University Library. Mention of the coach tipping over is made by Audubon in the autobiographical sketch included in Maria Audubon's book, but not in Lucy's letter. "Louisville in Kentucky," one of the episodes in the *Ornithological Biography,* contains Audubon's own impressions of the town and of their life there as well as reporting his meeting with Alexander Wilson. The episodes "A Kentucky Barbecue" and "Kentucky Sports" deal with the Fourth of July celebration and shooting at targets; and the episode "A Raccoon Hunt" describes that adventure. Thomas Bakewell's autobiographical sketch in *The Cardinal* discusses Benjamin Bakewell's business affairs. The criticism of Alexander Wilson's work is taken from the unsigned preface to the edition of his poems published in 1816 at London. Audubon described his meeting with Boone in the episode "Daniel Boone." Maria Audubon, when she reprinted it in her book, placed the date as 1815. John Bakeless, who has written the authoritative biography of Boone, believes the meeting took place in 1810. Barking squirrels was a common frontier sport, and both Robert C. Joery, III, Office of Public Affairs, National Rifle Association of America, Washington, D.C., and T. E. Hall, Curator of the Winchester Gun Museum, New Haven, Conn., have verified that it is possible to kill a squirrel without actually hitting it. The drawing of the yellow warbler with Audubon's notation is in the possession of the New-York Historical Society. Audubon's trip to Flatland Ford is referred to in "Four Audubon Letters" appearing in *The Cardinal*. His autobiographical sketch in Maria Audubon's book also covers much of this period.

It is only fair to note that although Lucy complained about the smokiness of Pittsburgh—as did many other travelers, because the condition existed for years—the city has since embarked on a smoke control program that has made it one of the cleanest in the country and a leader in this movement.

Chapter VII

The description of Henderson will be found in Ashe, p. 236. Audubon's autobiographical sketch, reprinted in Maria Audubon's book, covers this period in Henderson. The following episodes in the *Ornithological Biography* describe various aspects of Audubon's life at this time: "Fishing in the Ohio," the trotline; "The Ohio," his trip down the river with Lucy; "Breaking Up the Ice," his journey to Ste. Genevieve. Lucy Audubon, pp. 35-45, reproduces his journal of the same trip. Reference to the shooting of the solitary flycatcher will be found in the article on that bird in the *Ornithological Biography*.

Chapter VIII

Audubon's adventure with the fierce woman is described in the episode "The Prairie" in the *Ornithological Biography*. In the autobiographical sketch appearing in Maria Audubon's book, he dates the event as 1811, although he also says that he purchased a horse for the trip, but in the episode itself, he makes the reader think he was walking. Maria Audubon places the date as 1812 but then quotes a journal dealing with that trip from Ste. Genevieve (Vol. I, pp. 44-46) which makes no mention of the incident. The chronology seems unimportant. What is significant is the picture of frontier life and Audubon's pleasure in a physical challenge. The "carbonated warbler" is discussed under the appropriate article in the *Ornithological Biography*: and the episode "A Wild Horse" in the same book gives Audubon's version of his trip east on Barro. Lucy's description is contained in a letter by her dated January 5, 1812, and in the possession of the Princeton University Library. Thomas Bakewell's business dealings are covered by him in his autobiographical sketch appearing in *The Cardinal*. Audubon's correspondence with Rozier during this period appears in "Four Audubon Letters" in the same publication. The material on the earthquake is drawn from the episode in the *Ornithological Biography* called "The Earthquake." Audubon says he first noticed the disturbance in November. The earthquake took place, however, between December 16, 1811, and March 16, 1812. The event, therefore, probably occurred after his return from Flatland Ford. Nolte's description of their meeting appears on pp. 176-181 of his book. It should be noted that in her letter Lucy said she had not been home for four years. This would invalidate her statement in her biography of Audubon that she went to Flatland Ford while he settled in Henderson. Whether she did or not does not seem to have significant bearing on that brief period of their lives.

Chapter IX

The sale of the horse Barro is mentioned in the episode "A Wild Horse" in the *Ornithological Biography;* and the capture of the broad-winged hawk is described in the article under that title in the same book. Dallett gives the citizenship oath taken by Audubon. Thomas Bakewell, in his autobiographical sketch, discusses his own business affairs, and Herrick, in Vol. I, pp. 243-244, gives the text of two letters written by Audubon describing his. The descriptions of the passenger pigeons, the parakeets, and the unknown bird, which Audubon later named Washington Sea-Eagle, will be found in the appropriate sections of the *Ornithological Biography,* as will the description of the avocets. The incidents concerning the tor-

nado, the skunk, and the wolves are described in the same book
under the titles: "The Hurricane," "The Traveller and the Pole-
Cat," and "The Pitting of Wolves." The autobiographical sketch
reprinted by Maria Audubon again covers much of this period.

Chapter X

In his autobiographical sketch and letters appearing in "Audubon & Bakewell, Partners" in *The Cardinal,* Thomas Bakewell describes the mill, the steamboat, and his business dealings with
Audubon. Audubon gives his version in the autobiographical sketch
reprinted in Maria Audubon's book. The Washington Sea-Eagle is
discussed in the article under that title in the *Ornithological Biography.* The incident of the contract of coon skins is described by
S. E. Perkins. The Yankee workmen appear in Lucy Audubon, pp.
59-60. The muskrats at the mill are mentioned in *The Quadrupeds
of North America.* "The Eccentric Naturalist" is the title of the episode in the *Ornithological Biography* in which Audubon told about
Rafinesque's visit. Rafinesque's own book describes the fish he
attributed to Audubon.

Chapter XI

Audubon's final days in Henderson and his life in Cincinnati
are described in the autobiographical sketch appearing in Maria
Audubon's book and in *Audubon's Journals, 1820–1821,* pp. 47-48.
Thomas Bakewell gives his version of the Henderson difficulties in
"Audubon & Bakewell, Partners." Herrick discusses the steamboat
matter in Vol. I, pp. 257-259, and the settlement of Jean Audubon's
estate in Vol. I, pp. 262-266. John Keats's comments appear in
Forman's *The Letters of John Keats,* pp. 398-399 and 424. The least
bittern and the cliff swallows are described in the appropriate sections of the *Ornithological Biography.* Dr. Drake's speech was
printed in 1820, and a copy is in the possession of the Ohio Historical Society which also supplied information on the organization of
the museum. The letter to Henry Clay appears in *Audubon's
Journals, 1820–1821,* pp. 226-227.

Chapter XII

Audubon's Journals, 1820–1821, contains a detailed description
of his journey from Cincinnati to Natchez, pp. 3-88.

Chapter XIII

Audubon's visit to Natchez, his trip from there to New Orleans, and his first days in that city are covered in *Audubon's Journals, 1820–1821*, pp. 88-125. The two episodes in the *Ornithological Biography*, "Natchez in 1820" and "The Lost Portfolio," also deal with this period.

Chapter XIV

The account of Audubon's adventure painting the naked woman appears in twelve and a half pages of manuscript, which were torn from Audubon's journal and are now in the possession of the American Philosophical Society. He made the entry in May, 1821, several months after the event, in response to Lucy's request for more information. His pathetic letter to Lucy is included in the same pages. Lucy's letter is dated April 1, 1821, and is in the possession of the Princeton University Library. *Audubon's Journals, 1820–1821*, pp. 125-197, covers this period of his life.

Chapter XV

Audubon's Journals, 1820–1821, pp. 197-226, covers the period from his return to New Orleans until Dec. 31, 1821. Maria Audubon, Vol. I, pp. 51-52, describes the Audubons' life in New Orleans until Audubon's departure and gives extracts from his journal. Lucy Audubon does the same in her book, pp. 88-89, and also for the interval between his departure for Natchez and his trip to Trinity in pp. 91-94. Arthur, pp. 252-253, describes Audubon's teaching jobs in Natchez and on pp. 262-263 his quarrel with Mrs. Percy. In the episode "A Long Walk for a Youth" in the *Ornithological Biography*, Audubon tells about his arrival at Trinity and his visit to Cash Creek. His letter to Rozier, dated Oct. 14, 1823, is in the possession of the Yale University Library.

Chapter XVI

In the episode "A Tough Walk for a Youth" in the *Ornithological Biography*, Audubon described the competition between "S." and Victor. Extracts from his journal during his stay at Shippingport are given by Maria Audubon in her book, Vol. I, pp. 54-55, and by Lucy, pp. 96-97. Lucy also reprinted portions of his journal covering the period in Philadelphia, New York, and the trip back to Bayou Sarah, pp. 100-108, 109-110, 113-115. Burns's article, "Miss Lawson's Recollections of Ornithologists," in *The Auk,* contains a contemporary's views of Ord and Audubon at the time of their meeting in Philadelphia. Dwight's "The Autobiographical Writings of John James Audubon," which appeared in *The Bulletin of the Missouri Historical Society,* contains the original version of the introduction to the *Ornithological Biography* before it was edited. In it, Audubon described his reception at Philadelphia. Arthur, pp. 273-274, deals in detail with the meeting between Audubon and Mason. Audubon's letter to Sully, dated Aug. 14, 1824, is in the possession of the Historical Society of Pennsylvania. The episodes in the *Ornithological Biography,* "Niagara" and "Meadville," cover the trip from New York to Pittsburgh.

Chapter XVII

Audubon's arrival at Bayou Sarah, his life there and his preparations for going to England are described in extracts from his journal published by Lucy, pp. 114-120. Arthur, pp. 294-296, discusses the incident involving the itinerant teacher. The episode "A Long Calm at Sea" in the *Ornithological Biography* describes his trip to Europe. Maria Audubon's book, Vol. I, pp. 81-145, contains his journal from the time he left New Orleans until his arrival in Edinburgh. *The Letters of John James Audubon,* Vol. I, pp. 3-13, also covers this period.

Chapter XVIII

Audubon's journal, reproduced in Maria Audubon's book, Vol. I, pp. 145-225, deals with his first visit to Edinburgh. The letter to Lucy, dated Dec. 21, 1826, in which he discusses his future plans is in the possession of the Yale University Library. Scott's account of their meeting is contained in *The Journal of Sir Walter Scott,* Vol. I, pp. 343-345. *The Letters of John James Audubon,* Vol. I, pp. 13-19 deals with this period.

Chapter XIX

Maria Audubon, Vol. I, pp. 225-258, includes Audubon's journal from the time he left Edinburgh through the period in which he made his arrangements with Havell. *The Letters of John James*

Audubon, Vol. I, pp. 19-34, also deals with his trip to London and the change in engravers. A letter from Lizars, dated April 5, 1827, reveals his concern for Audubon. It is in the possession of the New York Public Library.

Chapter XX

Maria Audubon, Vol. I, pp. 258-274, includes Audubon's journal from the time of his departure from London until January 1, 1828. The same period is covered in *The Letters of John James Audubon,* Vol. I, pp. 34-57. The text of his letter to Sully is given by Herrick, Vol. II, pp. 68-71. The letters quoted are to Lucy, Aug. 25, Dec. 5 and 24, 1827, and to Victor, Sept. 21, 1827. They are in the possession of the American Philosophical Society. The text of Audubon's talk on rattlesnakes is taken from his article in *Jameson's Review.*

For a detailed discussion of the picture of the mockingbirds, I am indebted to Neil D. Richmond and Clarence J. McCoy of the Carnegie Museum, Pittsburgh, whose report on this subject follows:

"The painting that shows a rattlesnake in a tree being attacked by mockingbirds was examined. The portion of the rattlesnake that shows could be either the timber rattler or the canebrake rattler. We got out specimens of each and in that side view they can not be distinguished. The flowering vine showing on the painting is yellow jessamine and is native to the southern coastal plain. So the snake is probably a canebrake rattler.

"As to whether or not rattlesnakes climb trees the following is from Klauber, Vol. I, pp. 454-463, in which he discusses instances of rattlesnakes being observed in trees and bushes. 'Nearly every species common enough to be under frequent observation has been observed on some occasion up on a tree or bush.' And he cites one example of a canebrake rattlesnake ten feet above ground in a water oak and another one of a timber rattlesnake ten feet above ground in a tangle of vines. Another observation was that the rattlesnake diet on one study area in Virginia included twelve percent birds and bird eggs.

"Also in line with the painting is the fact that mocking birds nest in fairly low bushes and small trees.

"It is true that ratlesnakes do not climb as frequently nor as well as our other snakes (i.e. blacksnakes).

"The principal criticism we have for that painting is that the

rattlesnake is shown with a round eye pupil and the maxillary teeth
are visible. Normally the maxillary teeth are concealed in the gum.
We hope these comments clarify the status of rattlesnakes in trees
and bushes."

Chapter XXI

Audubon's journal from Jan. 1, 1828, until his return from Paris
is included in Maria Audubon's book, Vol. I, pp. 274-340. Pages
57-70 of Vol. I of *The Letters of John James Audubon* cover the
same period. A letter to Bentley, dated March 16, 1828, gives Audubon's report on his sales at Cambridge. It is in the possession of the
Pierpont Morgan Library. The two letters to Lucy that are quoted
are dated Feb. 2, 1828 and March 17, 1828. The first belongs to the
American Philosophical Society, the second to the New York Public
Library.

Chapter XXII

Maria Audubon, Vol. I, pp. 274-342, includes Audubon's journal
up to his departure from England and, Vol. I, pp. 62-63, an extract
describing his meeting with Lucy. Lucy also gives extracts from his
journals covering parts of this period on pp. 182-184, 197, 202-203.
The same period is covered in *The Letters of John James Audubon,*
Vol. I, pp. 57-102. The episodes in the *Ornithological Biography,*
"Great Egg Harbor" and "The Great Pine Swamp," deal with these
two trips. In the same book, the articles on the pileated woodpecker
and the winter wren also tell of his experiences in the Great Pine
Swamp. The letters quoted are as follows: Harlan to Audubon,
Nov. 19, 1828, New-York Historical Society; Audubon to Lucy,
December 10, 1828, Yale University Library; Audubon to Lucy,
Nov. 17, Dec. 23, 1828, June 18, July 15, and Aug. 8, 1829; to
William Cooper, June 6, 1829; and to Victor, Aug. 25, 1829, all in
the possession of the American Philosophical Society.

Chapter XXIII

Lucy, pp. 203-208, gives extracts of Audubon's journal and of a
letter to his two sons. Herrick, Vol. I, pp. 427-429, 433-435, tells
about his activities in Louisiana. The episode "The Opossum" in
the *Ornithological Biography* describes his shipment of those animals, and the article on the passenger pigeons in the same book tells

about his taking the birds to England. Dallett gives the description of Audubon that appeared on his passport. Audubon's relationship with Swainson is covered by two articles in *The Auk* and one other by Elliott Coues, all three of which reproduce letters between the two men. Audubon's arrangements for returning to the United States are discussed in a letter from him to Harlan, dated Feb. 28, 1831, which is in the possession of the Haverford College Library. The letters quoted are as follows: Audubon to Lucy, June 28, 1830, and Audubon to Harlan, Feb. 2, 1831, the American Philosophical Society; McMurtrie to Audubon, Jan. 18, 1831, the New York Public Library. *Blackwood's* review appeared in the issues of July and August 1831. *The Letters of John James Audubon*, Vol. I, pp. 70-135 also covers this period.

Chapter XXIV

The Letters of John James Audubon, Vol. I, pp. 136-195 deals with this period. The episodes "Spring Garden," "The Live-Oakers," "The Florida Keys," I and II, "The Turtlers," and "The Wreckers of Florida," all in the *Ornithological Biography*, deal with his Florida trips. The two articles mentioned are *"Ornithological Biography"* in the *American Quarterly Review* for Dec., 1831, and *"Ornithological Biography"* in Vol. I of *The Monthly American Journal of Geology and Natural Science*.

Chapter XXV

The Letters of John James Audubon, Vol. I, pp. 195-240, covers the period up to Audubon's return to New York. The letters quoted are as follows: two to Harlan, dated Aug. 14 and 26, 1832, in the possession of the Historical Society of Pennsylvania; to Victor, dated Nov. 11, 1832, the American Philosophical Society; and to Harlan, dated Oct. 17, 1830, the Yale University Library. Maria Audubon's book, Vol. I, pp. 349-445, includes Audubon's Labrador journal. His trips in Maine and Canada are described in the following episodes from the *Ornithological Biography*: "Journey in New Brunswick and Maine," "Labrador," "The Eggers of Labrador," "The Squatters of Labrador," "A Ball in Newfoundland," and "The Bay of Fundy." Ord's letters to Waterton are dated July 20, 1831, and April 23 and 28, 1833. They are in the possession of the American

Philosophical Society. Waterton's article appeared in the May, 1833, issue of *Loudon's Magazine.*

Chapter XXVI

The articles in *Loudon's Magazine* appear in the issues of July and November, 1833, and May, 1834. Lucy Audubon, pp. 376-387, gives extracts of Audubon's journals from the time he returned from Maine until he saw the collection in Philadelphia. Bachman's report was taken from a copy in the possession of the Boston Public Library. *The Letters of John James Audubon,* Vol. I, pp. 240-277, and Vol. II, pp. 3-133, also cover this same period. The letters quoted are Audubon to Rothschild, June 19, 1834, and Audubon to Victor, July 4, 1834, both of which are in the possession of the American Philosophical Society, and Audubon to Bachman, Dec. 3, 1834, Jan. 16, July 20, Dec. 1, 1835, and Sept. 10, 1836, which are in the possession of Harvard University.

Chapter XXVII

Lucy Audubon, pp. 387-415, gives extracts from Audubon's journal for this period, which is also covered by *The Letters of John James Audubon,* Vol. II, pp. 133-222. The letters quoted are: Audubon to Shattuck, July 5, 1837, which is in the possession of the Massachusetts Historical Society; Audubon to Morton, June 25, 1838, and Sept. 9, 1839, the American Philosophical Society; Lucy Audubon to Gifford, Sept. 29, 1838, Princeton University Library; Audubon to Bachman, Oct. 23, 1836, Audubon to Mrs. Bachman, July 2, 1837, and Audubon to Havell, March 13, 1839, Harvard University.

Chapter XXVIII

The Letters of John James Audubon, Vol. II, pp. 222-278, covers the period up to July 30, 1840. *The Journal of John James Audubon, 1840–1843,* pp. 3-65 and 150-156, goes from August 11 to Dec. 18, 1840, and pp. 65-148 from July 12 to Oct. 11, 1842. The New York Historical Society has an excellent collection of material describing Audubon's house. Maria Audubon, Vol. I, pp. 449-532, and Vol. II, pp. 3-195, includes Audubon's journals and other material relating to his trip up the Missouri. The letters quoted are as follows: Audubon to Victor, Feb. 2 and 26, March 1, and May 31, 1840, and Audubon to Morton, Oct. 12, 1840, are in the possession of the American Philosophical Society; Audubon to Shattuck, Feb. 26, 1843, is in the possession of the Massachusetts Historical Society.

Chapter XXIX

Herrick, Vol. I, p. 245, Maria Audubon, Vol. I, pp. 71-77, and Lucy Audubon, pp. 435-443, deal with Audubon's last years. The letters quoted are as follows: Audubon to Dorsey, April 22, 1844, in the possession of the Chicago Historical Society; Audubon to Victor, May 19, 1844, and June 13, 1844, the American Philosophical Society; and Victor to Morton, Feb. 3, 1851, the Library Company of Philadelphia.

Epilogue

The originals of Lucy Audubon's correspondence are in the collection of the New York Historical Society. Although the price eventually paid for Audubon's pictures was considerably less than the amount Lucy wanted, it was still more than anyone else would give her at the time; and by its farsighted action, the society preserved the originals for the enjoyment of future generations. The letter quoted is from Lucy to De Peyster, Nov. 23, 1863.

The Audubon Societies

In 1886, Dr. George Bird Grinnell, who had once taken art lessons from Lucy Audubon and who was then editor of the magazine *Forest and Stream,* first coined the term "Audubon Society." At the time, he was playing an active role in the campaign to prevent the wanton destruction of America's birdlife, and he invited the readers of his magazine to sign pledges to refrain from killing non-game birds or wearing their feathers. By November, 1888, he had obtained more than 48,000 members, most of them schoolchildren. Because he charged no dues for membership, the society was not self-supporting; and the mass of correspondence it entailed became too burdensome for the magazine. He therefore dropped the idea.

The name, however, had caught on. In 1886, an Audubon Society was formed in Pennsylvania but lasted only a few years. In 1896, the Massachusetts Audubon Society was established and continues today an active leader in its field. Since then, numerous other Audubon Societies have been created, some of which have remained independent units and some of which have affiliated with the National Audubon Society, which was incorporated in 1905.

Although the original purpose of these societies was the study and preservation of birdlife, they have since expanded their interests to include practically every aspect of conservation and natural history; and the American public owes them a debt for helping to save at least part of the countryside and wildlife that Audubon himself once knew. They would be the first to admit, however, that they have not done the job alone, for there are many other equally effective organizations, such as the Wilderness Society, the Isaac Walton League, the National Parks Association, the Sierra Club, and the Nature Conservancy—to name only a few—who have, along with many governmental agencies, helped in the struggle to maintain the beauty and magic of the American outdoors.

Index